THE TRIAL AND DEATH OF JESUS

Essays on the Passion Narrative in Mark

Geert Van Oyen and Tom Shepherd (Eds)

THE TRIAL AND DEATH OF JESUS

Essays on the Passion Narrative in Mark

PEETERS
LEUVEN – PARIS – DUDLEY, MA
2006

A CIP record for this book is available from the Library of Congress

ISBN-10 90-429-1834-9
ISBN-13 9789042918344
D. 2006/0602/124

CONTENTS

PREFACE

The theme of Jesus' passion has always been central to Markan exegesis with numerous articles and monographs published regularly. A milestone in the research on the topic was the influential book *The Passion in Mark,* edited by Werner H. Kelber, published in1976. Since that time new elements both of methodology and content have expanded horizons in Markan research.

The studies that follow display this variety. They arose from the annual meetings of the Mark Group of the Society of Biblical Literature in 2003 (Atlanta, Georgia) and 2004 (San Antonio, Texas). In 2003 our topic was the Trial of Jesus in Mark. In 2004 papers were presented on the Meaning of Jesus' Death in Mark. In bringing together revised papers from these meetings it is our hope to provide scholars with these important papers in one location.

The metaphor of prism may best illustrate the two sections of this book. The first section addresses the meaning of Jesus' death by approaching the question using a variety of methodologies. As a double concave prism spreads light in various directions, so these articles provide a "spread" of understandings of how the Gospel of Mark explains the death of Jesus. The second section of the book is more like a double convex prism that focuses light. These studies focus attention on the Jewish trial of Jesus with special emphasis given to the charge of blasphemy.

The first section opens with a reprint of Sharyn Dowd and Elizabeth Struthers Malbon's important article (*JBL* 125, no. 2 [2006]: 271-297) on the narrative context and authorial audience of the death of Jesus in Mark. They challenge the perspective that Mark presents Jesus' death as an atoning sacrifice for sin. In their broad survey of the Gospel (but with special attention to 10:45 and 14:24) they maintain that the death of Jesus is seen as "liberation from both demonic powers and human tyrants."

Next Mark Goodacre presents the concept of "scripturalization" of history in Mark. Goodacre counters John Dominic Crossan's idea of prophecy historicized by illustrating how it is more likely that Mark takes historical accounts and interprets them through the lens of Scripture.

Geert Van Oyen suggests that the real place to find the meaning of Jesus' death in Mark is through the *real* reader. He posits, in an interesting parallel to Sharyn Dowd and Elizabeth Malbon, that the meaning of the death of Jesus is to follow Jesus in discipleship. But this meaning is only known by experience. It is, however, not just an experiential truth, but a *theo*-logical expression dealing with the "mysterious Reality called God" whose answer to the death of Jesus is the open tomb.

Jocelyn McWhirter addresses the question of the use of Old Testament passages in Mark 11-15 and how they came to be part of the narrative. Following Donald Juel she posits messianic exegesis which sought out discrete passages from the Old Testament which helped to explain the crucifixion of the Messiah. McWhirter sees Psalm 89 as the key passage which opened links to others passages.

William Campbell focuses attention on the abandonment of Jesus and demonstrates it as a motif running throughout the Gospel, not merely an experience of the crucified Jesus. Campbell maintains that this motif is a "fundamental christological expression" in Mark.

Stephen Ahearne-Kroll studies Psalms of Lament in the Passion Narrative of Mark. He focuses particularly on Psalm 22 (Psalm 21 LXX) and maintains that understanding this Psalm's role in the Passion Narrative cautions the reader against a triumphalistic reading of the resurrection account. "The crucifixion conditions the meaning of the resurrection as much as the resurrection conditions the crucifixion." For Ahearne-Kroll these Psalms of Lament bring into the story of Jesus a "tradition of endurance, crying out to God in the midst of suffering, and faithful dissent."

The second section of the book begins with a reprint of Adela Collins' cogent article addressing the charge of blasphemy against Jesus in the Jewish trial (*JSNT* 26.4 [2004]: 379-401). Collins argues that the charge was not based on Jesus pronouncing the divine name. Rather, Mark, parallel to Philo, has a broader understanding of blasphemy dealing with a claim to "divine status, authority and power."

Jeffrey Gibson's slightly revised reprint article (*Proceedings of the Midwest Society of Biblical Literature* 24 [2004]: 125-139) argues not from first century historical evidence about the meaning of βλασφημία ("blasphemy") but rather from the narrative structure in Mark. Gibson notes the use of a superfluous σύ in Mark 14:61 and argues from comparisons throughout Mark that the Sanhedrin's view of the Messiah's work stood in sharp contrast to Jesus' view. Gibson then goes on to draw a parallel between the Jewish Sanhedrin in Mark and the Zealot Sanhedrin that tried Zacharias at the time of the Jewish Revolt. In this view Mark writes to warn his readers to not leave the way of the cross to follow the Zealot revolutionaries.

Michael Vines sees parallels between the Passion Narrative of Mark and Jewish stories of martyrs, particularly 4 Maccabees. But Mark subverts the key value of observing *kashruth* in those martyr stories and focuses instead on love, compassion, and justice. Jesus is "God's final envoy" not just another martyr. "Jesus dies a sacrificial death on behalf of others like the Maccabean martyrs, but the kingdom values he champions are very different."

Kelli O'Brien picks up on the martyr story as a parallel to the Jewish trial of Jesus and suggests that the allusions to Scripture in Jesus' trial do not defend him against the charges brought against him. Rather, the basis for the charge of blasphemy is readily admitted. The allusions to Scripture "focus on Jesus' vindication and his adversaries' future punishment."

Tom Shepherd follows a narrative approach in a study of power transactions in the Jewish trial scene. He notes that the scene is one of the Markan sandwich stories which utilizes dramatized irony to illustrate power in powerlessness. Shepherd deduces from his study a narrowing of the semantic domain of the term βλασφημία and evidence on the Markan theology of discipleship.

These studies provide a wealth of interesting approaches to understanding the meaning of Jesus' death in Mark. The articles point toward further questions that can be raised in three main areas:

The theology of Jesus' death – Assuming that Dowd and Malbon are correct in their contention that Jesus' death in Mark is not about forgiveness of sin but rather about liberation, one must address the role played by the abandonment motif Campbell explicates in the Markan theology of the cross. If Jesus' death is ransom from oppression, why the Gospel-wide stress on abandonment? Second, if Vines and O'Brien are correct about parallels between Mark and Jewish martyr stories, what role do these play in understanding Mark 10:45 and 14:24? Do the martyr story parallels point to expiation as Vines contends, or elsewhere?

The role of Scripture – Many of the articles focus on the role of Scripture in explaining the meaning of Jesus' death. What would a conversation between Goodacre's scripturalization, McWhirter's messianic exegesis, and Ahearne-Kroll's study of Psalms of Lament look like? Are there common themes or threads that these studies would point toward for clarifying intertextuality and Gospel composition?

Diachronic and synchronic synergy – Each article utilizes one or more approaches to a study of the text of Mark. Placing them side by side leads naturally to the question of how diachronic research and synchronic study of the Gospels can serve each other. The studies of Collins, Gibson, and Shepherd related to the charge of blasphemy illustrate this well. But could not more be done in linking diachronic and synchronic research in the same study? And finally, from Van Oyen's study, how does an understanding of the real reader's experience interlink diachronic and synchronic study? What other approaches to the text might this suggest?

It has been a privilege for us to bring together and edit these studies. We wish to thank our two student workers, Cherise Hill and Jan Willem Stam, for their work in preparing the indices. It is our hope that this book will help to further the conversation on the meaning of the Gospel of Mark as a whole and particularly on the meaning of Jesus' death in the second Gospel.

Tom SHEPHERD and Geert VAN OYEN

THE SIGNIFICANCE OF JESUS' DEATH IN MARK: NARRATIVE CONTEXT AND AUTHORIAL AUDIENCE

Sharyn Dowd and Elizabeth Struthers Malbon

One of the several New Testament interpretations of the death of Jesus is that Jesus was a sin offering whose death effected the forgiveness of the sins of humankind. But the Gospel of Mark makes no explicit connection between the death of Jesus and the forgiveness of sins. The "ransom saying" in 10:45 is best translated a ransom "in substitution for many,"[1] implying that the problem overcome by Jesus' "giving his life" was captivity or slavery rather than guilt. A first-century Greekspeaking audience would probably have understood that, although the "service" of the Markan Jesus does involve forgiving sins (2:1-12), the narrative taken as a whole suggests that the death of the Markan Jesus performs "for many" the service of liberation *from* bondage to oppression *for* membership in the covenant community that constitutes a "house of prayer for all the nations" (11:17). The "cup saying" in 14:24 alludes to Exod 24:8, where the blood is that of a covenant-sealing sacrifice, not that of a sin or guilt offering. Because Matt 26:28 makes the connection by adding "for the forgiveness of sins" to the cup saying, some scholars believe that Matthew's reading must have been implicit in Mark. Arguments for an emphasis on forgiveness may be found in the work of Adela Yarbro Collins, Rikki E. Watts, and others.[2] However, this question is usually addressed by intertextual arguments somewhat to the neglect of intratextual or narrative analysis. It is the latter that we add to the conversation in the hope of enriching it.

In terms of contextual foci, our look at the narrative context falls in the category of the internal literary context (the interrelations of elements

* Reprint of *JBL* 125 (2006): 271-297.

[1] Robert H. Gundry, *Mark: A Commentary on His Apology for the Cross* (Grand Rapids: Eerdmans, 1993), 590.

[2] Adela Yarbro Collins, "Finding Meaning in the Death of Jesus," *JR* 78 (1998): 175-96; Rikki E. Watts, *Isaiah's New Exodus and Mark* (WUNT 2/88; Tübingen: Mohr Siebeck, 1997), 349-62.

of the text), and our look at the cultural context of the authorial audience includes both the internal historical context (the interrelations of the text with other texts) and the external historical context (the broader societal/cultural situation of the text).[3] Most of the present article comments on the Markan Gospel in sequence, attending to signals of the significance of Jesus' death in narrative context. Because of the importance of dealing explicitly with those readings that do argue for a connection between the Markan Jesus' death and the forgiveness of sins, however, sustained comments on the cultural context of the Markan authorial audience with reference to 10:45 and 14:24 are intercalated at those points. As with Markan intercalations, it is hoped that center and frame will enrich each other in the act of interpretation.

I. Hearing Mark's Story

Mark's Gospel is a story, a sequential narration of events with a beginning, middle, and end designed to be heard in that order.[4] Despite its later liturgical and academic fragmentation, Mark's story works as a whole, and it is the whole Gospel we are regarding as the narrative context of Mark's story of Jesus' death. In addition, Mark's story is

[3] See Elizabeth Struthers Malbon, "Text and Contexts: Interpreting the Disciples in Mark," *Semeia* 62 (1993): 81-102, republished in *In the Company of Jesus: Characters in Mark's Gospel* (Louisville: Westminster John Knox, 2000), 100-130. For the distinction between the "implied audience," used throughout our literary analysis, and the "authorial audience," used when we are commenting on the cultural context, see Peter J. Rabinowitz, "Truth in Fiction: A Reexamination of Audiences," *Critical Inquiry* 4 (1977): 121-42. Different individuals within the Markan audience would have been attuned to hear allusions to different texts, depending on their cultural and religious formation. We will be pointing out references and allusions that would have been heard differently by Jews and Gentiles in the Christian communities that heard Mark read aloud. For a discussion of the internal historical context (the immediate societal/cultural situation of the text, especially its origin or preservation) of the Markan passion narrative, see Adela Yarbro Collins, "The Passion Narrative of Mark," in eadem, *The Beginning of the Gospel: Probings of Mark in Context* (Minneapolis: Fortress, 1992), 92-118; also eadem, "From Noble Death to Crucified Messiah," *NTS* 40 (1994): 481-503.

[4] See David Rhoads, Joanna Dewey, and Donald Michie, *Mark as Story: An Introduction to the Narrative of a Gospel* (2nd ed.; Minneapolis: Fortress, 1999); and Elizabeth Struthers Malbon, "Narrative Criticism: How Does the Story Mean?" in *Mark and Method: New Approaches in Biblical Studies* (ed. Janice Capel Anderson and Stephen D. Moore; Minneapolis: Fortress, 1992), 23-49, republished in *In the Company of Jesus*, 1-40.

designed not for the eye but for the ear.[5] Because the first-century context of this whole Gospel was oral, we will listen for echoes (to use an oral metaphor) of earlier scenes in the story of Jesus' death, or (resorting to a visual metaphor) we will be on the lookout for earlier foreshadowings of the death story in the stories that lead up to it.[6] Martin Kähler's assertion that "one could call the Gospels passion narratives with extended introductions,"[7] while reflecting form-critical presuppositions that we reject, nevertheless suggests that Mark's "extended introduction" prepares the audience to hear the significance of the story of Jesus' death in a particular way.

Kingdom (Mark 1:1–4:34)[8]

Mark's story of "The beginning of the good news of Jesus Christ, the Son of God" (1:1; NRSV, here and throughout unless otherwise indicated) opens at a rapid pace, with "Isaiah" pointing to John the baptizer, who points to Jesus of Nazareth. But as soon as the audience is given reason to share the narrator's (1:1) elevated view of Jesus – through the words of the prophet "Isaiah" (1:2-3), the baptizer John (1:7-8), and even God (1:11: "You are my Son, the Beloved; with you I am well pleased") – the audience is also signaled that being God's son is no easy task. Indeed, the first death omen can be heard by those with sensitive scriptural ears in the words of the voice from heaven, "You are my Son, the Beloved," which echo the words of God to Abraham in Gen 22:2: "Take your son, your only son Isaac, whom

[5] See Joanna Dewey, "Oral Methods of Structuring Narrative in Mark," *Int* 53 (1989): 32-44; also eadem, "From Storytelling to Written Text: The Loss of Early Christian Women's Voices," *BTB* 26 (1996): 71-78; eadem, "The Survival of Mark's Gospel: A Good Story?" *JBL* 123 (2004): 495-507; Christopher Bryan, "Was Mark Written to Be Read Aloud?" Part 2 of *A Preface to Mark: Notes on the Gospel in Its Literary and Cultural Settings* (New York: Oxford University Press, 1993); Elizabeth Struthers Malbon, *Hearing Mark: A Listener's Guide* (Harrisburg, PA: Trinity, 2002).

[6] On Markan echoes and foreshadowings more generally, see Joanna Dewey, "Mark as Interwoven Tapestry: Forecasts and Echoes for a Listening Audience," *CBQ* 53 (1991): 221-36; Elizabeth Struthers Malbon, "Echoes and Foreshadowings in Mark 4-8: Reading and Rereading," *JBL* 112 (1993): 211-30; and Alberto de Mingo Kaminouchi, *'But It Is Not So among You': Echoes of Power in Mark 10.32-45* (JSNTSup 249; London/New York: T&T Clark, 2003), esp. ch. 3, "The Echo Principle," 42-71.

[7] Martin Kähler, *The So-Called Historical Jesus and the Historic Biblical Christ* (German original, 1896; Philadelphia: Fortress, 1964), 80 n. 11.

[8] In this article we follow the outline in Malbon, *Hearing Mark*.

you love…" (LXX: τὸν υἱόν σου τὸν ἀγαπητόν, ὃν ἠγάπησας; Mark: ὁ υἱός μου ὁ ἀγαπητός, ἐν σοὶ εὐδόκησας).[9]

The Genesis narrative interprets God's requirement that Abraham sacrifice his "beloved son" as a "test" (ὁ θεὸς ἐπείραζεν τὸν Αβρααμ [LXX Gen 22:1]) of Abraham's loyalty to God; Abraham is not told to make a sin offering.[10] So the very first hint of jeopardy to the life of the Markan Jesus alludes to the sacrifice of a beloved son made by a father to demonstrate commitment to God. The fact that the voice is "from heaven" transforms the allusion to Genesis 22 into an amazing claim: The God who demanded the sacrifice of Abraham's son but then provided a substitute is now prepared to demonstrate God's own commitment to humankind by allowing God's own son to "give his life a ransom for many" – and for God's son there will be no last-minute reprieve. This allusion to Genesis 22 is important, because other passages that indicate that Jesus' suffering and death are incorporated into the will and purpose of God do not make explicit the cost *to God* as clearly as does this introduction of the theme in the baptism scene. Anyone with ears to hear will remember this threat to the "beloved son" when that son prays in Gethsemane, "Abba, Father,… not what I want, but what you want" (14:36).

Another ominous narrative warning follows closely, in the next verse: "And the Spirit" – that is, the Spirit that just descended upon Jesus like a dove at his baptism – "immediately drove him out (ἐκβάλλει) into the wilderness" (1:12). Not only will the story of Jesus incorporate struggle and suffering (the wilderness is not a place where humans easily survive; the "wild beasts" usually eat them up), but Jesus is thrown into such struggle and suffering not by human antagonists but by the Spirit of God. This testing in the wilderness, whose forty days echo the forty

[9] Pointed out by Sharyn Dowd, *Reading Mark: A Literary and Theological Commentary on the Second Gospel* (Macon, GA: Smyth & Helwys, 2000), 12, following James Swetnam, "On the Identity of Jesus," *Bib* 65 (1984): 412-16. The most obvious allusion is to Ps 2:7, "'You are my son; today I have begotten you.'" Psalm 89:26-27 also mentions the Davidic monarch as God's son, and Ps 44:3 includes "delighted" or "pleased" (cf. Isa 42:1, which, however, in the LXX has no overlapping vocabulary with Mark 1:11), but none of these passages includes "beloved" as Gen 22:2 does. Joel Marcus argues that the "echo of the Aqedah story in Mark 1:11… is very faint if present at all" and that the "best alternative seems to be to see ἀγαπητός as a reflection of Isa. 42:1 that has been interpolated into the text of Ps. 2:7…" (*The Way of the Lord: Christological Exegesis of the Old Testament in the Gospel of Mark* [Louisville: Westminster/John Knox, 1992], 52). As John R. Donahue, S.J., notes of 1:11, "This text contains a 'surplus of meaning'…" (Donahue and Daniel J. Harrington, S.J., *The Gospel of Mark* [SP 2; Collegeville, MN: Liturgical Press, 2002], 65).

[10] The word in LXX Gen 22:2 is ὁλοκάρπωσιν.

years of Israel's testing in the wilderness,[11] is, to be sure, carried out "by Satan," head of the cosmic forces opposed to God, but the experience is framed by the action of agents of God: the Spirit's initiative and the angels' ministering. The πειρασμός of Abraham is echoed by the πειρασμός of Jesus. This whisper of a theme in the beginning of Jesus' ministry will be played *fortissimo* at its end.

Next, as John both echoes and enacts "Isaiah's" prophecy – preparing the way of the Lord Jesus – John's ministry and its results are echoed by Jesus. John's being "handed over," mentioned obliquely in 1:14 ("Now after John was arrested [παραδοθῆαι]..."), is later echoed in Jesus' being "handed over" (παραδιδόναι, 3:19; 9:31; 10:33 *bis*; 14:10, 11, 18, 21, 41, 42, 44; 15:1, 10, 15; cf. 13:9, 11, 12, where the "handing over" of Jesus' followers is predicted; cf. also 4:29, where the [ripe] grain is handed over or yielded up). In fact, John's being handed over is narrated as the introduction to Jesus' initial proclaiming: "The time is fulfilled, and the kingdom of God has come near; repent, and believe in the good news" (1:15), which echoes John's earlier "proclaiming a baptism of repentance for the forgiveness of sins" (1:4). (This, the first mention of sin in Mark's Gospel, suggests that the remedy for sin is repentance and John's baptism.) John foreshadows Jesus, the "more powerful" one; John's proclaiming is not welcomed by the powerful, which leads to his being handed over and killed (6:14-29). Jesus echoes John, proclaiming a challenging message that leads to his own death at the hands of the powerful. And the audience is not halfway through chapter 1!

The second half of ch. 1 and the first half of ch. 2 include intriguing foreshadowings of other important aspects of Mark's Gospel that bear on the story of Jesus' death: Jesus' difficulties with the religious officials (1:22; 2:6-8, 16-17), recognition of Jesus by nonhuman forces (1:24), misunderstanding of Jesus by his own disciples (1:36-37), and Jesus' request for silence about his healing activity (1:34, 43-44). But the next obvious allusion to Jesus' death[12] is presented by the Markan

[11] This parallel reinforces the motif of the new exodus introduced by the quotation from Deutero-Isaiah in Mark 1:3.

[12] The healing of the paralytic (2:1-12) foreshadows the Markan Jesus' "trial" before the Sanhedrin with its reference to blasphemy (2:7; 14:64); the healing of the withered hand (3:1-6) foreshadows the "trial" before Pilate in its function of establishing Jesus' innocence by means of rhetorical questions having to do with "evil" (3:4; 15:14) (so Dowd, *Reading Mark*, 24, following Joanna Dewey, *Markan Public Debate: Literary Technique, Concentric Structure, and Theology in Mark 2:1-3:6* [SBLDS 48; Chico, CA: Scholars Press, 1980], 189).

Jesus in a metaphor he offers in a controversy over the failure of his disciples to fast, as do John's disciples and the disciples of the Pharisees. "Jesus said to them, 'The wedding guests cannot fast while the bridegroom is with them, can they? As long as they have the bridegroom with them, they cannot fast. The days will come when the bridegroom is taken away from them, and then they will fast on that day" (2:19-20). It is difficult to imagine anyone in Mark's first-century audience missing this reference to Jesus' death and the community's remembrance of it with fasting. The passive voice of the verb (ἀπαρθῇ, "is taken away") suggests divine action;[13] the bridegroom does not run away but submits to being taken. The metaphor of the bridegroom and the accompanying metaphors of new cloth/new wineskins occur in the chiastic center of five controversy stories (2:1–3:6). Here at the pivot point of the human controversies, divine agency of the eventual outcome is stressed. Whatever human conflicts occur in the story of Jesus are incorporated into the larger story of God's action, the coming of the reign of God.

At the close of the series of five controversy stories, which, as Joanna Dewey has shown, manifest linear development as well as chiastic structure,[14] human agency comes into focus: "The Pharisees went out and immediately conspired with the Herodians against him, how to destroy him" (3:6). "In order for God to reign, all other powers must abdicate or be defeated, even the powers that claim to represent God. In Mark, not only Rome, but also the Jewish leaders stand to lose when Jesus announces God's reign, so they oppose Jesus."[15] But, as was the case earlier when the divine Spirit threw Jesus out into the wilderness to be tested by the cosmically evil Satan, so here the divine agency of the one who takes away the bridegroom precedes the human agency of the religious and political officials who conspire against him. Furthermore, in this series of five controversy stories, in which Jesus' death is foreshadowed once in the center and again at the end, the Markan Jesus makes it plain that forgiving sins is part of his healing ministry and is apparently not dependent on the cross, the shadow of which hangs over the narrative. Rather, "the Son of Man has [present indicative] authority on earth to forgive sins" (2:10).

[13] "Impersonal third person singular verbs, passive verbs, and sometimes indefinite third person plural verbs were often used in Jewish and Christian literature of the period to refer to the activity of God" (Collins, "Suffering and Healing in the Gospel of Mark," in *Beginning of the Gospel*, 64).

[14] Dewey, *Markan Public Debate*.

[15] Dowd, *Reading Mark*, 24. Dowd continues with this comment, "This is not Christian antisemitism; it is typical of Israelite prophetic rhetoric."

In Mark 3 the audience learns that not only are the religious and political officials implicated in the plot that leads to the Markan Jesus' death, but so is one of Jesus' own disciples. At the very appointing of the "twelve" the narrator concludes the list with "and Judas Iscariot, who betrayed him [or handed him over]" (3:19). At this, Judas' only mention prior to his handing over of Jesus, his epithet is "who betrayed him." Once the process of handing over has begun, Judas' epithet becomes "one of the twelve" (14:10, 43). The hearers of Mark's story are never allowed to forget this ironically fateful and tragically fatal connection. Although the betrayal by Judas, like the plotting of the religious and political officials, is framed by divine agency, it is no less tragic in Mark's plot, and, as a failure of friendship rather than a consequence of deeply felt opposition, it is more pathetic.

Community (Mark 4:35–8:26)

Chapters 4-8 stress the powerful words and deeds of the Markan Jesus – among Jews and Gentiles[16] – and thus offer a brief respite from foreshadowings of his death.[17] Opposition, both demonic and human, is never far from the surface of the story, however (see also 3:20-35); yet the audience has already heard the divine theme of which this is a variation.

The intercalated stories of the mission of Jesus' disciples and the beheading of John in ch. 6 intrude into the narration of Jesus' powerful words and deeds to sound again the tones of (1) going out to preach (and heal), (2) being rejected and handed over, and (3) being killed – for John the baptizer now reaches stage 3; Jesus has entered stage 2 (with the rejection in his πατρίς in 6:1-6, to say nothing of earlier allusions to being handed over); and Jesus' disciples are at stage 1.[18] But eventually those "who, like John and Jesus, insist on relativizing the claims of

[16] See Malbon, "Echoes and Foreshadowings in Mark 4–8."

[17] Although there is a foreshadowing of the "persecution" of the Markan Jesus' followers in the allegorical explanation of what happens to the seed that falls on rocky soil (4:16-17), as Collins points out (*Beginning of the Gospel*, 66). So also Dowd, *Reading Mark*, 50: "The Markan Jesus is not warning the disciples to be good soil; rather, he is warning them (and the overhearing audience) that even as the reign of God takes root and flourishes in some quarters, it will provoke opposition, persecution, and seduction from the forces of evil. It is the nature of the reign of God to provoke opposition; it cannot be otherwise." For an application of the allegorical explanation as central to Mark's Gospel as a whole, see Mary Ann Tolbert, *Sowing the Gospel: Mark's World in Literary-Historical Perspective* (Minneapolis: Fortress, 1989).

[18] See Malbon, "Narrative Criticism," 40-41; eadem, "Echoes and Foreshadowings," 222-23.

human rulers will necessarily find themselves at risk from those rulers who must protect their own right to reign."[19] Thus, Jesus parallels John in death, but as Adela Yarbro Collins points out, it is ironically not John who is raised from the dead (as Herod thinks, 6:16) but Jesus.[20] The fact that John's disciples come and bury John's body is a presumed foreshadowing of what Jesus' disciples might be expected to do when Jesus reaches stage 3; however, this echo is never heard in Mark's Gospel. Rather, the disciples having long since fled the scene, Jesus is buried by one of those who condemned him to death.[21]

Discipleship (Mark 8:22–10:52)

The blindness of the disciples as the Markan Jesus attempts to prepare them for his death is striking. The two-stage healing of the blind man of Bethsaida, unique to Mark's Gospel, works in two stages itself: it concludes 4:35–8:26, in which Jesus journeys to, teaches, heals, and feeds both Jews and Gentiles; and it introduces 8:22–10:52, framing, with the story of the healing of blind Bartimaeus outside Jericho, the section that is structured by three passion predictions given "on the way" to Jerusalem. As the disciples are slow to perceive the depth of Jesus' power ("Who then is this, that even the wind and the sea obey him?" 4:41) and the breadth of his outreach (at 6:45, 53 they fail to go ahead of him to Gentile Bethsaida as requested) in chs. 4-8, so in chs. 8-10 they only "half see" the type of messiah the Markan Jesus understands himself to be. No sooner has Peter correctly confirmed the narrator's (1:1) identification of Jesus as the Messiah (Christ, 8:29), than Peter incorrectly – and dramatically – objects to Jesus' first passion prediction (8:31), which focuses on the suffering the Son of Man (clearly the Markan Jesus as the Christ) "must" undergo.

"Must" (δεῖ) is generally interpreted as a signal of divine agency. The audience has been prepared for this divine agency from early on in the narrative – with the allusion to the binding of Isaac in the voice from heaven at Jesus' baptism and the Spirit's initiative in "throwing" Jesus into the wilderness, but, for the disciples within the narrative, 8:22–10:52 is a direct tutorial. Yet, since the narrative exists for the sake of the audience and not for the sake of its characters, the disciples'

[19] Dowd, *Reading Mark*, 67.
[20] Collins, *Beginning of the Gospel*, 62.
[21] Raymond E. Brown, "The Burial of Jesus (Mark 15:42-47)," *CBQ* 50 (1988): 233-45. We do not intend to imply agreement with Brown's historical conclusions.

tutorial is actually the audience's tutorial. It is a signal of the evangelist's dramatic success that some latter-day commentators have assumed that he must have had a vendetta against the "historical disciples" or those represented by them in the early Christian community. Like the Markan Jesus he portrays, the Markan implied author is trying to teach a challenging lesson and to heal blindness to the unexpected.

The careful structuring of 8:22–10:52 was one of the first observations that led scholarly commentators to a renewed appreciation of the Markan author's literary control over his material. The development of this section clearly involves more than stringing pearls. Each passion prediction (8:31; 9:31; 10:33-34) has been elaborated into a passion prediction unit by the addition of misunderstanding by the disciples and Jesus' discipleship instruction in response. The three resulting passion prediction units offer Mark's most explicit advice on how to understand the meaning or significance of Jesus' death. First and foremost, Jesus' death is not to be understood as beyond the knowledge and purpose of God. At work here is a passion apologetic more than a soteriology of the cross: even Jesus' death does not negate his role as God's Messiah or his proclamation of the in-breaking reign of God.[22] Second, Jesus' suffering and death show what may also happen to any who take up his proclamation; the teacher's life (and death) manifest the pattern for his followers. Third, it is not suffering or death for its own sake that is being advocated for Jesus or for his followers (the Markan Jesus has no martyr complex)[23] but rather the strength to serve others, especially those lowest in the evaluation of conventional society, even if such service may result in suffering or death at the hands of the powerful of that society.

These three points are presented repeatedly – like the Markan Jesus' healing action toward the blind man of Bethsaida. In the first passion prediction unit (8:31–9:1), (1) God's presence in Jesus' death is manifested in Jesus' rebuke of Peter's "setting [his] mind not on divine things but on human things" (8:33);[24] (2) the necessity of followers to

[22] See Morna Hooker, *Not Ashamed of the Gospel: New Testament Interpretations of the Death of Christ* (Grand Rapids: Eerdmans, 1994), 48.

[23] Adela Collins states: "Violent death is not valued in itself. Jesus' death is not to be imitated for the sake of being like Jesus. Rather, such a death may be necessary because of loyalty to Jesus and to the Gospel (8:35) in the face of opposition" (*Beginning of the Gospel*, 67). Collins does not mention how service to the powerless may contribute to opposition.

[24] There is a parallel between the Markan Jesus' human opponents and his demonic ones in relation to power, but the connection is made with Peter, not with the religious authorities. It is natural to associate the demons and unclean spirits with Satan, since

be prepared to endure the fate of their teacher is made explicit in the admonition to "take up their cross and follow me" (8:34); and (3) the primacy not of suffering but of service is heard in the phrase "let them deny themselves" (8:34).[25]

The second passion prediction unit (9:30-50) stresses this third point, the primacy of service: "Whoever wants to be first must be last of all and servant of all" (9:35). Such service is to be rendered to those undervalued in society, for example, powerless children (9:36-37) and "little ones" (9:42). Also stressed in the second passion prediction unit is an implication of the second point (that followers must emulate their teacher): All those who follow Jesus are to "be at peace with one another" (9:50). In response to the report of the disciple John that the disciples have tried to stop an exorcist not in their small group, the Markan Jesus says, "Do not stop him; for no one who does a deed of power in my name will be able soon afterward to speak evil of me. Whoever is not against us is for us" (9:39-40).

The third passion prediction unit (10:32-45) opens with the most detailed passion prediction, a virtual preview of the Markan passion narrative, but it closes with a relatively short yet dramatically powerful discipleship instruction section stressing service and thereby contrasting the community of Jesus' followers with conventional society. In response to

unclean spirits seem to recognize Jesus as "the Holy One of God" who has "come to destroy" them (1:24). But the Markan Jesus associates his most prominent disciple, Peter, with Satan at the point of Peter's failure to understand the centrality of service to the powerless and the inevitability of suffering at the hands of the powerful (8:33). That all-too-human desire of "lording over" is satanic, that is, opposed to the desire of God.

25 Denying oneself (8:34), which is prescribed in the first discipleship instruction, is the opposite of lording it over others (10:42), which is proscribed in the third discipleship instruction. Collins points out that the "notion of 'denying oneself ' calls to mind the dangers of wealth and desires for various things mentioned" in the interpretation of the parable of the Sower (4:19; *Beginning of the Gospel*, 67). But see also Dowd (*Reading Mark*, 89) on interpreting denying oneself as denying the false self imposed by others and being the self that is in line with one's commission from God, as Jesus does in the "trial" before the Sanhedrin. Cf. Joanna Dewey, "'Let Them Renounce Themselves and Take Up Their Cross': A Feminist Reading of Mark 8:34 in Mark's Social and Narrative World," in *A Feminist Companion to Mark* (ed. Amy-Jill Levine; Sheffield: Sheffield Academic Press, 2001), 23-36. Clearly "self denial" has been interpreted in ways dangerous to women, a sad irony given that the early tradition seems to have been intended as a challenge to men who were lording it over (among others) women. As Joanna Dewey notes, "The instruction is addressed to the Twelve, not to women, children, and slaves, those whose social role is already to serve.... The narrator is not presenting universal teaching applicable to all regardless of social status and access to power" ("The Gospel of Mark," in *Searching the Scriptures,* vol. 2, *A Feminist Commentary* [ed. Elisabeth Schüssler Fiorenza; New York: Crossroad, 1994], 494).

the unenlightened request of James and John to have places of honor along the lines of conventional society, and in response to the anger of the other ten at these two, "Jesus called them and said to them, 'You know that among the Gentiles those whom they recognize as their rulers lord it over them, and their great ones are tyrants over them. But it is not so among you; but whoever wishes to become great among you must be your servant, and whoever wishes to be first among you must be slave of all. For the Son of Man came not to be served but to serve, and to give his life a ransom for many" (10:42-45).

Oddly enough – even though the so-called ransom statement is presented as parallel to "came not to be served but to serve," *and* in an immediate context stressing service in contrast to the usual "lording over" in society at large, *and* in a larger context (the three passion prediction units) also stressing service to society's undervalued, even if such service should challenge the authorities and lead to suffering and death – interpreters have often read the statement as if it meant Jesus' death ransomed all people from sin.[26] Wherever the connection between Jesus' death and the forgiveness of sin is coming from – whether other NT texts,[27] or

[26] Two recent exceptions to the ignoring of the narrative contexts of the λύτρον statement are the narrative and feminist commentary on Mark's Gospel by Joanna Dewey in *Searching the Scriptures* (pp. 494-96; see n. 25 above) and the published dissertation of Alberto de Mingo Kaminouchi, *'But It Is Not So among You'* (see n. 6 above). Although Kaminouchi does not deny the possibility of a Markan implication of "ransom" from sin at 10:45 (p. 53), he does not find any reason to argue for this reading from his literary analysis of 10:32-45 in its Markan context. Rather, his "proposal is that λύτρον can be interpreted as liberation from the ideologies and relationships of power in which the world, including its rulers, is entrapped" (p. 154). Kaminouchi provides intriguing illustration of this entrapment in his literary analysis – with "social-scientific sensitivity" (p. 3) – of the portrayal of Herod (6:14-29) and Pilate (15:1-15) as supposedly powerful leaders "unable to do their will" (p. 196) in contrast to the Markan Jesus, who, when approached by James and John "as if he were a royal figure able to grant positions of privilege" (p. 197), is able to do his will because of his freedom from entangling networks of hierarchical power, his freedom to serve (10:32-45). The classic argument against overreading the influence of Isaiah 52-53 and thus importing a theology of vicarious atonement, not only in Mark but in the NT generally, is forcefully presented by Morna D. Hooker, *Jesus and the Servant: The Influence of the Servant Concept of Deutero-Isaiah in the New Testament* (London: SPCK, 1959).

[27] Although the particular term used in Mark 10:45, λύτρον ("ransom"), appears only here and in the Matthean parallel (20:28) in the NT, a term for ransom (ἀντίλυτρον, not λύτρον) appears in 1 Tim 2:6, but not in conjunction with sin. Interpreters are more likely to cite or allude to Gal 1:4; Rom 5:8; or especially 1 Cor 15:3. For example, Collins concludes a detailed study of the pre-Markan and Markan passion narratives with an unlabeled quotation of 1 Cor 15:3, thus making a connection between Jesus' death and sin for which she has not argued explicitly in this article: "For the author of the earliest passion narrative and for Mark, the death of Jesus is admirable, not because he faced it bravely and thus became an example for others, but because it was 'for our

rereadings of the Hebrew Bible,[28] or ancient Greco-Roman culture,[29] or later Christian formulations – it is not coming from the Markan narrative context of this ransom statement. Interpreters are right to focus on 10:45; it is, as Adela Collins notes, the "most explicit statement in the Gospel of Mark about the meaning of the death of Jesus." "This is the clearest such statement in Mark," Collins continues, "but that does not imply that it is actually clear!"[30] Some clarity comes with attention to the statement's narrative context.

In narrative context, what "the many" need – and, in fact, what the Markan Jesus urges his followers to provide – is ransoming from "their great ones who are tyrants over them" and "those whom they recognize as their rulers [who] lord it over them" (10:42).[31] As Ched Myers notes, "The phrase 'as a ransom (*lutron*) for many' appears to be an allusion back to 'slave' [at 10:43-44]. The term referred to the price required to redeem captives or purchase freedom for indentured servants. Jesus promises that the way of 'servanthood' has been transformed by the Human One into the way of liberation."[32] It is true that 10:45 is a crucial statement in a climactic position,[33] but it is an encapsulation of the

sins' and 'according to the Scriptures'" ("From Noble Death," 502). The assumed connection between 1 Cor 15:3 and Mark (see ibid., 488-94) seems to be that Mark's passion story is rich in allusions to Scripture, and Isaiah 53 (which, unlike Mark's Gospel, does mention dying for sins) is part of the general scriptural background of Mark's passion narrative. Morna Hooker argued clearly and strongly against such harmonization years ago: "Although forgiveness is part of the gospel message, it is expressed in the whole ministry of Christ, and it is only later, in the writings of Paul [Rom 4:25, 1 Cor 15:3], in the Epistle to the Hebrews [9:26] and in I Peter [2:24; see also 1 John 1:7], that the association with his sufferings is made" (*Jesus and the Servant*, 153).

28 See Kaminouchi, *'But It Is Not So,'* 142-46.

29 Ibid., 147-51. On the significance of Greco-Roman epigraphical evidence of the word group λύω for interpreting Mark 10:45, see Adela Yarbro Collins, "The Signification of Mark 10:45 among Gentile Christians," *HTR* 90 (1997): 371-82.

30 Collins, *Beginning of the Gospel*, 68; cf. Hooker, *Not Ashamed*, 17: [the evangelists] "attribute [Jesus' death] to the wickedness of men and the will of God, but rarely do they spell out what it achieved."

31 Cf. Exod 6:6: "Say therefore to the Israelites, 'I am the LORD, and I will free you from the burdens of the Egyptians and deliver you from slavery to them. I will redeem [LXX λυτρώσομαι, the verbal form of λύτρον] you with an outstretched arm and with mighty acts of judgment." See the discussion of 10:45 and 14:24 below. See also Kaminouchi, *'But It Is Not So,'* ch. 5, for a careful analysis of Mark 10:32-45.

32 Ched Myers, *Binding the Strong Man: A Political Reading of Mark's Story of Jesus* (Maryknoll, NY: Orbis, 1988), 279.

33 Dowd (*Reading Mark*, 112): "The saying looks both backward and forward in the Markan narrative. All that Jesus has done so far falls into the category of serving. His teaching, preaching, exorcizing, and healing were done not to call attention to himself, but as examples of his service to others. In the upcoming passion narrative Jesus' service will take an additional form: giving his life *lutron antipollon*."

teaching of 8:22–10:52: Service to others, especially those undervalued and "lorded over" by the powerful, is central to the ministry of Jesus (point 3) and thus to his followers (point 2), even if such service provokes a response from the powerful that leads to suffering and/or death.[34] In serving others, God is present, and God remains present in whatever results from such service – life, suffering, even death (point 1).[35]

[34] As Dewey comments on Mark 10:41-45, "The opposite of being powerful is being oppressed, and Mark has taught his audience that persecution is to be expected for following Jesus. Thus one might expect Mark to contrast domination over others with weakness or suffering as the way of God. But Mark contrasts power not with suffering but with service (*diakonia*; see 9:35)" (*Searching the Scriptures*, 2:494). As Hooker notes, "The whole passage [10:45] takes the common form of antithesis, contrasting the rule exercised among the Gentiles and in the flock of Jesus" (*Jesus and the Servant*, 75).

[35] Collins also seeks to interpret 10:45 in its context, but she attends not to the immediate narrative context of the demand for service to those undervalued in society but to the broader Markan context against its rich background of OT texts (*Beginning of the Gospel*, 68-71). "Jesus as the agent of the kingdom of God is plundering the kingdom of Satan [3:23-27]. Just as his exorcisms and healings free people from bondage to demons, so his death ransoms many from the power of Satan" (pp. 70-71). Without attention to the Markan narrative context of human service to the powerless challenging the powerful, Collins's conclusion is somewhat overstated (and, in the hands of other interpreters, can become theologically problematic): "Although Jesus is the agent of God and shares in the power of God, his suffering was *intended* [our emphasis] by the will of God, according to Mark" (p. 70). On the contrary, all we know from Mark's narrative is that Jesus' death, for which humans are accountable (as Collins, of course, recognizes; see p. 65), is not stopped (or removed; see 14:36) by God for whom "all things are possible" (10:27; 14:36). Projecting the "intention" of God back behind the story is a step beyond the one the Markan implied narrator takes in suggesting that Jesus' death does not negate the larger purpose of God; that is, God's purpose can prevail even through Jesus' death at the hands of the powerful. Collins concludes her essay "Suffering and Healing in the Gospel of Mark" with a double proposition: "Thus Mark's solution to the problem of theodicy is a narrative one. [1] All things are possible for God, but God allows evil to be part of the cosmic drama in which every creature has a role to play. [2] The Gospel of Mark and the biblical tradition in which it stands impel us to go further and say that God not only allows what seems to us to be evil but even wills it in order to accomplish a larger purpose – the redemption of all creation" (p. 72). We see only the first proposition in Mark's narrative, and a desire to avoid committing the intentional fallacy theologically on Mark's behalf impels us to go no further. See also the conclusion to Collins's essay entitled "The Passion Narrative of Mark," in which she contrasts a pre-Markan source "narrating it in terms of the traditional type of the suffering just person" and the Markan redaction that presents "an atoning or sacrificial interpretation of Jesus' death" (*Beginning of the Gospel*, 118). We concur with Collins's conclusion in "Finding Meaning in the Death of Jesus" (p. 193): "Many exegetes and theologians find the notion of sacrificial death offensive. Some deal with their distaste for the idea by arguing that it does not actually occur in the New Testament or by minimizing its presence." However, we also note that many exegetes and theologians find the notion of sacrificial death central and essential; some deal with their affirmation of the idea by arguing that it occurs everywhere in the NT or by maximizing its presence. With our reading

Excursus: The Cultural Context of the Markan Authorial Audience with Reference to Mark 10:45

Many attempts have been made to interpret Mark 10:45 as an allusion to the sin-canceling death of the servant of Isa 52:13-53:12.[36] But these arguments (whether or not the scholars making the arguments acknowledge this) depend on one of two presuppositions: (1) The saying goes back to the historical Jesus, who had in mind the Hebrew text; or (2) the author of the Gospel was interpreting the Hebrew text. Presupposition 1 can be neither proved nor disproved, but it speaks to a meaning in the mind of Jesus that would have been unavailable to the Markan audience, who were hearing the Gospel read in Greek. Presupposition 2 is not likely, since many studies have argued Mark's reliance on the LXX, but again not only the author but the audience as well would have to make a connection to the Hebrew text of Isaiah 52-53 for this meaning to be communicated.

This conclusion is reached because neither the verb λυτρόω nor the nouns λύτρον, λύτρα appear in LXX Isa 52:13-53:12. In fact, there is nothing to link Mark 10:45 to this particular passage in LXX Isaiah except two phrases: "ἡ ψυχὴ αὐτοῦ was handed over to death" (LXX Isa 53:12; cf. "to give τὴν ψυχὴν αὐτοῦ," Mark 10:45) and "he bore the sins πολλῶν" (LXX Isa 53:12, cf. "a ransom ἀντὶ πολλῶν," Mark 10:45). Our argument is simple: the former "parallel" simply establishes

compare that of Howard Clark Kee: "In keeping with his view of history as determined by God, and with the blueprint of the divine plan embodied in scripture, it was essential for Mark to show that the suffering and death of Jesus as well as the impending martyrdom of the elect were not to be regarded as occurring outside the divine plan, but that the suffering involved was an essential factor in the fulfillment of that plan. This conviction has not been developed by Mark into a doctrine of atonement, allegedly implied in 10:45 and based on Isa. 53; rather there is throughout Mark the unexplicated assertion that suffering is a necessary pre-condition for the coming of the Age of Deliverance (Mk 8:31; 9:11; 13:7; 14:31 etc.)" ("The Function of Scriptural Quotations and Allusions in Mark 11–16," in *Jesus und Paulus: Festschrift für Werner Georg Kümmel zum 70. Geburtstag* [Göttingen: Vandenhoeck & Ruprecht, 1975], 174). On the broader issue of sacrifice, see Joanna Dewey, "Sacrifice No More," in *Distant Voices Drawing Near: Essays in Honor of Antoinette Clark Wire* (ed. Holly E. Hearon; Collegeville, MN: Liturgical Press, 2004), 159-70.

36 Recently, R. T. France, *The Gospel of Mark* (Grand Rapids: Eerdmans, 2002), 419-21; Watts, *Isaiah's New Exodus and Mark*, 270-84. Joel Marcus argues that "Mark 10:45 and 14:24 imply the atoning value of Jesus' death through allusions to Isaiah 53" without explicit discussion of the forgiveness of sin (*Way of the Lord*, 195). Not forgiveness of sin but apocalyptic transformation is Mark's focus, according to Marcus, who argues that "Mark sets his entire story in the context of Deutero-Isaiah's picture of apocalyptic holy war (1:1-3)" (p. 163).

that both the Isaian servant and the Markan Jesus lost their lives; the latter "parallel" establishes that this was a benefit to "many." But of course the issue is *the nature of that benefit*, which is different in Isaiah and in Mark.[37]

As all parties to the discussion admit, the word group λυτρόω, λύτρον, λύτρα relates to the necessity of setting free those being held captive or enslaved by another. In the biblical tradition, Israel may be God's παῖς ("servant/child"; cf. LXX Isa 42:1), but this is so because of God's election of Israel, not because Israel is enslaved to God on account of sin. When Israel is taken captive because of its sin, Israel is always the captive of an enemy, not of God. And that captivity is a temporary discipline from which, in Deutero-Isaiah, Israel expects liberation from God.

This reading accords with the social contexts of redemption/ransom in Greek and later in Roman culture. Prisoners of war, or the corpses of important military heroes, are always ransomed from the enemy, not from a neutral party who is merely being compensated for a loss, as is the case regarding the redemption/ ransom of a slave. Similarly, those taken captive by pirates have to be ransomed from the criminals who are holding them against their will. Thus, "the many" for whom the Markan Jesus gives his life as a λύτρον are captives of the enemies of God.[38]

[37] Compare Hooker: "Nowhere here [in Isa 53:11-12], apart from the use of the word πολύ, is there any connection, either in thought or in language, with Mark 10.45" (*Jesus and the Servant*, 78).

[38] In "The Signification of Mark 10:45 among Gentile Christians," Collins makes the following points about λύτρον, λύτρα in pagan inscriptions. Our responses follow each point:

1. Some of these inscriptions connect λύτρον with a transaction with the gods. But if the inscriptions contain any references to sin, Collins does not mention them.

2. The ritual usage of λύτρον likely derives from the social practice of slave manumission and prisoner ransom. About slavery, Collins writes, "... the practice implies that human beings, by committing offenses against the gods, make themselves slaves of the gods and must pay a sum or perform a ritual act to free themselves. Thereafter they can resume good relations with the deity" (p. 377). About prisoners of war, "... human beings who have committed offenses are captives of the gods, suffering disease or other punishment, and... they must pay a sum or perform a ritual act to move the gods to free them from this captivity" (p. 378). But in the apocalyptic dualism characteristic of Hellenistic Judaism and Christianity, these enslaving functions have been transferred to the demons. Though pagans would not have known this, Gentile Christians would have been taught monotheism as part of their catechesis (1 Thess 1:9-10).

3. The *Didache* uses λύτρωσιν in conjunction with sins. But the *Didache* has been influenced by Matthew's reading of Mark.

4. The verb λύω appears in the magical papyri in the context of loosing spells. But loosing spells and forgiving sins cannot be regarded as identical actions.

In the Gospel of Mark, the enemies fall into two groups: human beings and spiritual beings. From the humans who wield power, Jesus' death ransoms not "many" but only one: Barabbas. One "son of the father" goes free and the "beloved son" of "Abba" is led away to be crucified. In the apocalyptic dualism characteristic of some strains of Hellenistic Judaism and of the Gospel of Mark, God's reign is opposed by the "unclean spirits" and "demons," of whom the "ruler" is thought to be "Beelzebul" or "Satan" (3:20-30 and passim).[39] In Mark, these powers control individual victims. Jesus expels every demon he encounters. But the ransom saying may have suggested to the audience that for the power of evil to be overcome, a terrible price would have to be paid for the freedom of many.

In the cultural context of the Markan audience, enemies did not let their captives go without payment. In Mark's Gospel, Jesus, God's "beloved son," "gives his life a ransom for many" – but not without questioning his father (14:36; cf. Isaac in Gen 22:7). But the death of the one given in exchange for many is a temporary victory for the forces that oppose God's reign, both cosmic and human. By raising Jesus from the dead, God vindicates him as Messiah and cheats God's enemies, leaving them empty-handed, as they deserve. This understanding of the ransom language continued among Christian theologians from Irenaeus to John of Damascus, including Origen, Athanasius, Basil the Great, Gregory of Nyssa, Cyril of Alexandria, and John Chrysostom. These theologians maintained that God became human in Jesus and became the ransom payment or exchange for humankind. The ransom was understood as paid to Satan, or to Death personified. But in the resurrection, Christ was snatched back, thus cheating the devil.[40] Only with Anselm do we find fully developed the notion that the ransom is paid to God (by God incarnate). This is, in Anselm's view, *Cur Deus Homo*: because humans owed a debt they could not pay but one Jesus as human could pay because as God he had the resources to pay.[41] Even today, Anselm's view is often read back into interpretations of Mark's ransom statement in 10:45.

[39] On "the new designation of the enemy whose defeat must take place before the Rule of God is established" as "the demonic powers" in Mark (with precedents in Daniel, the later parts of Israel's prophetic tradition, and the War Scroll), see Kee, "Function of Scriptural Quotations," 184-85.

[40] Gustaf Aulén, *Christus Victor* (trans. A. G. Hebert; London: SPCK, 1953), 52-71. Aulén points out that the patristic writers did not ignore the role of sin and the need for forgiveness, and, of course, neither did Mark. All we argue is that forgiveness is not connected in Mark with the death of Jesus.

[41] Ibid., 100.

II. Hearing Mark's Story (continued)

In following the presentation of the three passion prediction units in 8:22–10:52, ending with the "ransom" statement, we skipped over three sections of embedded material: the transfiguration and the accompanying Elijah conversation (9:2-13), the immediately following healing story of the so-called epileptic boy (9:14-29), and the linked teachings on marriage and divorce, children, and wealth (10:1-31).[42] These segments are interspersed among the three passion prediction units in the "way" section, 8:22–10:52, with its multiple references to Jesus and his disciples being "on the way" to Jerusalem. Each of the three embedded segments also contributes to the audience's preparation for understanding the Markan Jesus' death.

As Peter's so-called confession at Caesarea Philippi confirms the narrator's application of "Christ" to Jesus (1:1; 8:29), so the transfiguration story, with its voice from heaven echoing the earlier voice at Jesus' baptism, confirms the narrator's application of "Son of God" (1:1; 9:7).[43] Jesus' comment to Peter, James, and John[44] on the way down the mountain sets the limit to the messianic secret: they are "to tell no one about what they had seen, until after the Son of Man had risen from the dead" (9:9). But it is the discussion about Elijah, also narrated during the descent, that reminds the audience of how Jesus' suffering and death as the Son of Man echo the suffering and death of John the baptizer as the embodiment of Elijah. Jesus and John were suggestively linked in this way as early as 1:14, when reference to John's being handed over introduced Jesus' initial proclaiming. The fuller development of the link occurred in ch. 6 with the intertwining

[42] Although Dowd (*Reading Mark*), includes the transfiguration and Elijah statement (9:2-13) as part of the first passion prediction unit, and the teaching segment in ch. 10 as part of the second passion prediction unit, Malbon defines the passion prediction units more narrowly and treats these materials as intervening, along with the so-called confession of Peter (8:27-30); in addition, Malbon treats the framing 8:22-26 and also 8:27-30 with the first passion prediction unit, 9:2-13 with the second passion prediction unit, and 10:1-31 with the third passion prediction unit (see *Hearing Mark*, chapter entitled "Discipleship").

[43] On the textual difficulties with "Son of God" in 1:1, see Adela Yarbro Collins, "Establishing the Text: Mark 1:1," in *Texts and Contexts: Biblical Texts in Their Textual and Situational Contexts: Essays in Honor of Lars Hartman* (ed. Tord Fomberg and David Hellholm; Oslo: Scandinavian University Press, 1995), 111-27.

[44] As Dowd notes, "Jesus selects only Peter, James, and John to accompany him, not because they are his favorites, but because in this Gospel they are singled out as having special difficulty understanding the point he has just made in 8:31–9:1 about the necessity of suffering" (*Reading Mark*, 89).

of Jesus' rejection in his πατρίς, the mission of Jesus' disciples, and the beheading of John. The discussion of Elijah in 9:9-13 is the final reverberation of this echo, which cues the audience how to hear Mark's story of Jesus' death as isolated neither from previous events nor from their own possibilities.

The second of the three segments intervening within the passion prediction units of the "way" section follows immediately: the healing of the boy with a spirit, the so-called epileptic boy (9:14-29). Most of the Markan Jesus' healings are narrated in the first half of the Gospel; the three exceptions occur in the "way" section, and each has a significant symbolic dimension. Two of these three are stories of the healing of blindness (8:22-26 and 10:46-52) that frame the "way" section, where blindness is a metaphor for not perceiving that Jesus' messiahship includes service to the powerless and thus suffering and death at the hands of the powerful. The symbolic aspect of the healing of the boy under the power of the (unclean) spirit, so much under its power that the spirit throws him around, is seen in its foreshadowing of Jesus' death – and resurrection. The Markan Jesus, who had himself been thrown around by the most clean (Holy) Spirit, asks in frustration in response to his disciples' failure to exorcise this particular spirit, "How much longer must I be among you? How much longer must I put up with you?" (9:19). Not much longer, the implied audience answers with a sigh. Then Jesus rebukes the "spirit that keeps this boy from speaking and hearing" (9:25), as the Markan narrator would rebuke the spirit that keeps the implied audience from hearing and speaking. First the boy becomes "like a corpse, so that most of them said, 'He is dead'" (9:26). So later Jesus. Then Jesus takes him by the hand and raises him up (ἀνέστη, 9:27). So later Jesus. What facilitates such movement from death to life? the disciples want to know (9:28). Prayer (9:29). So also for the implied audience (see 11:12-25).

The third intervening segment occurs between the second and third passion prediction units and comprises the linked teachings about marriage and divorce, children, and wealth (10:1-31). This is not a random sample of the teachings of the Markan Jesus but a focused portrayal of teaching that challenges the status quo of first-century society. It is not so surprising that someone who challenges the status quo to this extent is challenged back – even to the point of suffering and death. In brief, what the Markan audience hears as Jesus makes his way to Jerusalem is a teaching about divorce that says men are not to be valued above women, a teaching about children that says adults are not to be valued above children, and a teaching about wealth that says the rich are not to be valued above the poor.[45] Since in the dominant culture of the first century (and even the twenty-first?) all of these formulations run in the opposite direction, the teachings reflected in Mark 10 turn households upside down. It is not surprising that the discipleship instruction of the third and final passion prediction unit that follows this segment contrasts the (Gentile) societal norm of "those whom they recognize as their rulers" (10:42) – rich, married fathers – lording it over others – the poor, women, and children – with the Markan Jesus' norm for himself and his followers: serving rather than being served, and thus ransoming the majority from the tyranny of the elite (10:45).[46]

Are the Markan disciples able to see all this? And, more important for the Markan implied author, is the Markan implied audience able to see? The story of the healing of blind Bartimaeus just outside Jericho, Jesus' final stop "on the way" to Jerusalem, closes the "way" section with hope, for Bartimaeus "immediately... regained his sight and followed him on the way" (10:52).

Suffering (Mark 11:1–16:8)

It is not our present goal to present a full-scale narrative analysis of Mark's passion story; rather we seek to highlight narrative aspects that seem to guide the implied audience to hear (and understand) the story of Jesus' death in a way that suggests its meaning or significance. For example, what the reader/hearer who has just listened attentively to the Markan Jesus' three passion *predictions* notices at the beginning of ch. 11 is that this character Jesus is reliable at predicting the future – at least the near future – since the circumstances he predicts concerning the procurement of a colt for his entry into Jerusalem are fulfilled immediately (11:1-7). Surely the implied audience is meant to understand that the Markan Jesus' predictions of his suffering and death are equally inevitable. It is not just prediction of the future but influence of it through faith in God and through prayer (11:22-24) that is manifest in the following episode of the cursing of the fig tree, which is narratively intercalated and symbolically linked with the clearing (not cleansing) of the temple (11:12-14/15-19/20-25). It is prayer that is the

[45] See Malbon, *Hearing Mark*, 68; see 66-68 for a slightly fuller explication.

[46] The contrast between the elite tyrants and lords and the majority whom they overpower helps make sense of the Markan expression "many" (πολλῶν) at this point rather than "all" used elsewhere (e.g., 13:37, πᾶσιν).

focus of these intertwined stories,[47] and it is prayer that is linked with forgiveness (11:25) in Mark's Gospel, not Jesus' death.[48]

The next series of stories, 11:27–12:40, echoes the series of controversy stories in 2:1-3:6. In the first series, set in Galilee, the opponents of the Markan Jesus were Pharisees and scribes (with Herodians joining them at 3:6); in the second series, set in the Jerusalem temple, the opponents are chief priests, scribes, and elders, Pharisees and Herodians, and Sadducees. Even though he is in his opponents' space, the temple, the Markan Jesus seems even more in charge of the situation: various groups of leaders come to him. Just as the metaphors of the bridegroom taken away and the new cloth/new wineskins were central to the earlier series of controversy stories, so the metaphors of the slain son of the vineyard owner and the stone that the builders rejected are crucial to the second series of controversy stories. All these metaphors cue the implied audience to hear the story of Jesus' death as embedded in a larger story of God's ongoing relationship with the people of God. The echo of Isaiah's allegory of the vineyard (Isa 5:1-7) is hard *not* to hear, and Ps 118:22-23 is quoted explicitly in Mark 12:10-11. Thus, the human opposition from established religious leaders in the second series of controversy stories, like that in the first, is portrayed as within the knowledge and purpose of God in relation to the people of God.[49]

47 See Sharyn Echols Dowd, *Prayer, Power, and the Problem of Suffering: Mark 11:22-25 in the Context of Markan Theology* (SBLDS 105; Atlanta: Scholars Press, 1988).

48 Although the ministry of the Markan Jesus includes many exorcisms and healings, only once is Jesus shown forgiving sins (2:1-12). In fact, most of the Markan Jesus' comments about the forgiveness of sins have to do with people's sins *not* being forgiven. In 3:28-29 we learn that attributing Jesus' powerful acts to Beelzebul will not be forgiven. In 4:10-12 Jesus says (following Isaiah, and ironically?) that the purpose of his teaching in parables is to prevent forgiveness. In 11:25 the disciples are urged to forgive when they pray, *so that* the Father may forgive them. This clause apparently prompted the scribal harmonization with Matthew's threat that appears in some manuscripts as 11:26. Mark makes forgiveness appear to be both limited to "insiders" and conditional upon not committing the "eternal sin" and on forgiving others. Forgiveness in Mark is also linked with repentance and baptism (see 1:4) and with resurrection (see the reference to "and Peter" at 16:7, referred to below).

49 Where Adela Collins sees "ambiguity in [Jesus'] relationship to God" ("Finding Meaning in the Death of Jesus," 192), we see paradox in the overdetermination of the causes of the Markan Jesus' death, with the forces of both demonic and human opponents being neither willed nor blocked by God but somehow surrounded and subverted by God. The Ph.D. dissertation of Ira Brent Driggers, "Disciples at the Mercy of God: The Tension of Markan Theology" (Princeton Theological Seminary, 2004) captures this paradox well: "Stated simply, the Gospel [of Mark] presents the audience with two divergent theological explanations for the Messiah's death. On the one hand, Mark suggests that Jesus' execution stems, through a kind of divine *initiative*, from the logical unfolding of earthly events. This dynamic reflects what I call the 'invasion logic'

In addition, just as the Markan Jesus' threefold prediction of his death is echoed in the slain son and rejected stone metaphors, so his threefold prediction of his resurrection is echoed in the stone's becoming the cornerstone and in his reply to the Sadducee's trick question: God "is God not of the dead, but of the living" (12:27).[50]

The final question asked of the Markan Jesus by a religious leader in the temple is not a trick question. "One of the scribes," who, as the Markan narrator reports, saw that Jesus "answered them well," asks, "Which commandment is the first of all?" (12:28). The Markan Jesus replies with the Shema, "Hear, O Israel..." (12:29-30), central to the Jewish understanding of the active relationship between God and Israel, and the narrator now notes that "Jesus saw that [the scribe] answered wisely" (12:34). The Markan Jesus' direct reply to the scribe is even more complimentary, "You are not far from the kingdom of God" (12:34). In the midst of all these controversies with religious leaders, controversies that play a role in the movement toward Jesus' suffering and death, one thing remains central: "Hear, O Israel: the Lord our God, the Lord is one...." Even Jesus' suffering and death are not beyond the knowledge and purpose of God and God's ongoing relationship with the people of God, which is the larger story that gives meaning to a story that might otherwise seem meaningless – the story of Jesus' death.

of Mark's discourse: God invades the world through Jesus; the threatened religious establishment resolves to stop that invasion; and the disciples, upon Jesus' arrest, abandon Jesus to the cross. On the other hand, Mark's many scriptural allusions, increasing with frequency as Jesus nears the cross, suggest that those same events stem from the long established will of God. This is what I call the 'transcendent logic' of Mark's discourse: the destruction and vindication of Jesus as God's emissary (Isa 5:1-7; Ps 118:22-3), the desertion of Jesus' disciples (Zech 13:7), and the crucifixion itself (Ps 22:1, 7, 18) stem from ancient promises that reach fulfillment in the story. Even Jesus' predictions about the destruction of the temple (13:1-8, 14) and the persecution of his disciples (13:9-13), though existing beyond the narrative, factor into the apocalyptic end times as ordained by God. In the end, then, the Gospel asserts an irresolvable tension I call Mark's 'theologic,' according to which the cross results *both* from the opposition of powerful people to God's eschatological invasion *and, at the same time,* from God himself. Between these two forces hangs Jesus, the 'victim of humanity's lack of imagination' [quoting Nick Cave, introduction to *The Gospel According to Mark* (Edinburgh: Canongate Books, 1998), xi], as well as the mysterious locus of God's faithfulness" (pp. 176-77).

50 Since 3:6 the Pharisees and Herodians have been conspiring to "destroy" (ἀπόλλυμι) Jesus, and he is accused by the false witnesses of threatening to "destroy" (καταλύω) the temple (14:58). At his death, the temple is indeed destroyed symbolically by the tearing of the veil (15:38). It becomes clear, then, that Jesus' human opponents are "blindly" taking precisely the wrong course of action. Like the tenants, the religious leaders think that killing Jesus will leave the vineyard in their unchallenged possession. Instead, the Markan Jesus' death is proleptically linked to the destruction of the very symbol of their power.

Since, after the question of the one scribe, "no one dared to ask him any question" (12:34), the Markan Jesus brings the series of controversy stories to a close with his own question (12:35-37) and critique (12:38-40) of scribes in general. Then the scene of Jesus "walking in the temple" (11:27), where these controversies are engaged, is brought to a close with Jesus' observation of and comment on the gift of the poor widow (12:41-44). Here the NRSV does its contemporary readers a disservice by blunting the force of the final phrase, ὅλον τὸν βίον αὐτῆς, with the translation, "all she had to live on" (12:44). By adding to the first phrase, "but she out of her poverty has put in everything she had," the second, "her whole life," the implied author has moved the story from exemplum to metaphor (although, admittedly, many readers and commentators, frequently led astray by translators, neither see nor hear the transformation).[51] In this, his final scene in the temple, the Markan Jesus sees what lies before him: giving his whole life. Do the disciples see? Does the audience see? The Markan implied author hopes that the implied audience sees more than the disciples do as he moves on with his story.

Chapter 13 marks a narrative shift with a change of scene – not walking in the temple but "sitting [the authoritative position of rabbis while teaching] on the Mount of Olives opposite the temple" (13:3) – and a change of characters, not Jesus and the Twelve but Jesus and the four: Peter, James, John, and Andrew (13:3). Our present concern is not with the eschatological discourse in itself,[52] but with its narrative implications for understanding the significance of the Markan Jesus' death. In this regard, two subsections are most relevant: 13:9-13 and 13:32-37.

In 13:9-13 the Markan Jesus warns the four, and through them the Twelve, and through them the implied audience, that his followers too (like John the baptizer and Jesus himself) will experience rejection by and handing over to religious and political authorities (councils and synagogues/governors and kings). Like Jesus, his followers will face trials,

[51] See Elizabeth Struthers Malbon, "The Poor Widow in Mark and Her Poor Rich Readers," *CBQ* 53 (1991): 589-604, republished in *In the Company of Jesus*, 166-88. See also Dowd, *Reading Mark*, 134, who comments that "in Mark [as opposed to Luke 21:4] the separate phrases are complementary rather than synonymous."

[52] See Dowd, *Reading Mark*, 135-37; Malbon, *Hearing Mark*, 84-88; and eadem, "The Literary Context of Mark 13," in *Biblical and Humane: A Festschrift for John F. Priest* (ed. Linda Bennett Elder, David L. Barr, Elizabeth Struthers Malbon; Atlanta: Scholars Press, 1996), 105-24. Cf. Collins, "Mark 13: An Apocalyptic Discourse," in *The Beginning of the Gospel*, 73-91, who discusses the redaction of pre-Markan sources in Mark 13.

but the Markan Jesus assumes their divine strengthening through the words given to them by the Holy Spirit (13:11). Their future will be as challenging as that of Jesus, "But the one who endures to the end will be saved" (13:13), an echo of the discipleship instruction of the first passion prediction unit: "For those who want to save their life will lose it, and those who lose their life for my sake, and for the sake of the gospel, will save it" (8:35). As the Markan Jesus has three times predicted his own passion, so here he predicts the passion of the community of his followers, which had already been foreshadowed by reference to "trouble or persecution… on account of the word" (4:17) in the interpretation of the parable of the sower.[53] Here, at the chiastic center of the eschatological discourse,[54] the Markan Jesus reaffirms a central teaching of the "way" section (8:22–10:52): Jesus' suffering and death shows what may also happen to any who take up his proclamation. Let anyone with ears to hear hear – and be ready.

Being ready is the thrust of the second subsection of the eschatological discourse that has special relevance for the significance of the story of Jesus' death, and, since 13:32-37 is the final subsection of the eschatological discourse, being ready – "Keep awake" – is its final thrust. Two observations are essential. First, as is often noted, the four times of the night mentioned in the parable of the doorkeeper (13:34-36) are also four significant times in the story of Jesus' passion, and the Markan Jesus, of course, has been "lord [NRSV master] of the house" (13:35). In addition, the Markan Jesus' request of Peter, James, and John at Gethsemane ("keep awake" or watch, γρηγορεῖτε, 14:34), echoes what he says here to Peter, James, John, and Andrew – and "to all": "Keep awake" or watch (γρηγορεῖτε, 13:37). Thus, there is an analogy between Jesus' death and the eschaton; what is needed by Jesus' followers in both cases is readiness, wakefulness, watchfulness.

Second, although the Markan narrator has given the implied audience confidence in the Markan Jesus' ability to predict the future successfully, here the Markan Jesus puts a limit on that very ability. While he can predict the procuring of the colt for his entry into Jerusalem (and later the securing of an upper room for the Passover meal), as well as his

[53] See Dowd, *Reading Mark*, 135, citing John R. Donahue, S.J., *The Gospel in Parable* (Philadelphia: Fortress, 1988), 61. See also Collins, *Beginning of the Gospel*, 66-67.

[54] So Dowd, *Reading Mark*, 135. Dowd also argues that the interpretation of the parable of the sower (4:13-20), with its clear reference to "persecution," is in the chiastic center of the parables discourse (4:1-34), thus making reference to the suffering of his followers central to both of the Markan Jesus' longer speeches (ibid., 39).

own suffering and death and the suffering of his followers, the Markan Jesus states plainly that "only the Father," that is, God, knows about the eschatological "day or hour" (13:32). Central to the ministry of the Markan Jesus has been his proclamation (by word and deed) of the inbreaking reign of God; thus, God provides the frame or background for all that happens. Again a teaching central to the "way" section – and to the entire Gospel – is reaffirmed: the larger story, into which the story of Jesus' suffering and death and that of the suffering of his followers must be fit, is the story of God's relationship with the people of God, the story of God's unfolding purpose.

Mark's passion story proper begins at ch. 14, chs. 11-12 having been a prelude to the passion of Jesus and ch. 13 having been an interlude focused on the passion of the community.[55] Mark 14:1-2 stresses the human agency that leads to the Markan Jesus' death: opposition by religious leaders. But 14:3-9, the story of the woman who anoints Jesus, stresses the divine context in which Jesus' death is to be seen as meaningful. Her anointing is for burial; the Markan Jesus is the anointed one, that is, the Messiah, the Christ, even though he suffers and dies. God's presence with Jesus is not undermined by his death. The coming reign of God that the Markan Jesus announces and makes known in his life does not retreat at his death. Thus the woman's anointing of Jesus beforehand for burial is – and will continue to be – part of the telling of the good news in the whole world (14:8-9).

The human agency of a follower complements the human agency of opponents as Judas' betrayal (14:10-11) enables the plot of the religious leaders (14:1-2) to be carried out, despite the supportive crowds during Passover. The Markan Jesus' preparations for the Passover meal with his disciples (14:12-16) contrast with the preparations of the religious leaders and one of his disciples for his death. Jesus' words at the feast link the two: This Passover bread is "my body"; a Passover cup of wine is "my blood of the covenant, which is poured out for many" (14:22-24). The final phrase, "for many" (ὑπὲρ πολλῶν, 14:24) echoes the final phrase of the Markan Jesus' discipleship instruction in the third and final passion prediction unit, "and to give his life a ransom for many" (ἀντὶ πολλῶν, 10:45). As the majority is in need of ransoming from the tyranny of the elite, so the majority is in need of a renewal of the covenant of God with the people of God. Such freeing, such renewal is possible only because

[55] See Malbon, *Hearing Mark*, 75-88; eadem, *Narrative Space and Mythic Meaning in Mark* (San Francisco: Harper & Row, 1986; Sheffield: Sheffield Academic Press, 1991), 151-52.

the reign of God is breaking in. The Markan Jesus' death is incorporated into that larger story; thus, the Markan Jesus will next drink wine when he drinks it "new in the kingdom of God" (14:25). Jesus' death does not negate his proclamation of the in-breaking reign of God; rather Jesus' proclamation gives meaning to his death.

Excursus: The Cultural Context of the Markan Authorial Audience with Reference to Mark 14:24

The "blood of the covenant" in Mark 14:24 is a reference to Exod 24:8, the only place in the Scripture of Israel where "blood" and "covenant" are connected in a text. The full meaning of διαθήκη (covenant) as relationship of the people to their God would have been available only to those members of the audience familiar with the LXX. They would have understood that those whom God had liberated were in covenant relationship with God, not because their sins had been forgiven, but because God had liberated them. Their sins would have to be forgiven many times, just as Israel's had to be, but that was not accomplished by the "blood of the covenant."[56]

Robert Fowler has shown that the history of interpretation of the Gospel of Mark has been controlled by Matthew's "strong reading" of his source (according to the prevailing source theory).[57] This situation is quite obvious in the interpretation of Jesus' death. The implied author of Matthew corrects the potential misapprehension of the baptism scene that Jesus, like the rest of the crowd, was "baptized by [John] in the river Jordan, confessing [his] sins" (cf. 3:6), by inserting the objection

[56] Again, we hold that the prepositional phrases shared by 10:45 (ἀντὶ πολλῶν) and 14:24 (ὑπὲρ πολλῶν) connect the two metaphors for the purpose of Jesus' death but are not enough to connect them with LXX Isaiah 52-53, where we find "sins of many" but not "for" or "on behalf of " many. Contra Marcus, who sees in 14:24 a reflection of both Zechariah 9-11 and the Hebrew text (not the LXX) of Isa 53:12, the latter also being alluded to, so Marcus argues, in 10:45 (*Way of the Lord*, 187). But with Kee, who affirms with regard to the Markan passion narrative, "There are no sure references to Isa 53 and none of the distinctive language of the Suffering Servant is evident. ... There is no explicit doctrine of atonement... in the Markan passion narrative" ("Function of Scriptural Quotations," 183). See also Hooker, who concludes, "Any exegesis which sees a fundamental connection with Isa. 53 can only arise from reading Mark 14.24 in the light of an already accepted doctrine of the Atonement" (*Jesus and the Servant*, 82-83). More broadly, on the perils and promises of various NT metaphors of atonement, see John T. Carroll and Joel B. Green, *The Death of Jesus in Early Christianity* (Peabody, MA: Hendrickson, 1995), ch. 13, "The Death of Jesus and the Meaning of the Atonement."

[57] Robert M. Fowler, *Let the Reader Understand: Reader-Response Criticism and the Gospel of Mark* (Minneapolis: Fortress, 1991).

of John the baptizer (3:14-15).[58] This prepares for the Matthean Jesus' explanation of his death in the Last Supper scene, "... this is my blood of the covenant, which is poured out for many *for the forgiveness of sins*" (26:28). Jesus is the unblemished (3:14-15) sacrifice for sin (26:28). This addition to Mark makes it unnecessary for the audience to reflect on the meaning of διαθήκη and its connection with blood. They are told that Jesus' blood is poured out for the forgiveness of sins, and that is all they need to know. This framing device overwhelms the ambiguity of the ransom saying (20:28).

It should be noted, however, that even Matthew does not redact the ransom saying to include forgiveness of sins. He does not replace Mark's λύτρον with the LXX's ἁμαρτία, perhaps (but not certainly) because the "ransom saying" was known to have originated with Jesus. Nor does he add to the saying, as he does not hesitate to do in 26:28. The implied author of Matthew seems to know that λύτρον simply has nothing to do with forgiveness of sin and so counts on its meaning being controlled by the frame with which he surrounds it.

We do not deny that the forgiveness of sins was an early and influential interpretation of the meaning of the death of Jesus, nor that Isa 52:13–53:12 was appealed to in support of this interpretation.[59] We argue that the case for this being the interpretation that would have been apparent to Mark's audience has not been made and cannot be made because it relies on unsupportable presuppositions. Further, we argue that the Markan narrative pulls the interpretation of Jesus' death in the direction of liberation from both demonic powers and human tyrants, seeming to regard the forgiveness of sins as part of the good news, but not necessarily connected with the death of Jesus.

[58] Even in John's preaching, Matthew weakens the link between baptism and forgiveness in general (cf. Mark 1:4, "John the baptizer appeared in the wilderness, proclaiming a baptism of repentance for the forgiveness of sins," with Matt 3:1-2, "... John the Baptist appeared in the wilderness of Judea, proclaiming, 'Repent, for the kingdom of heaven has come near'"). Th us, Matthew's parallel with Mark concerning all the others who "were baptized by him in the river Jordan, confessing their sins" (Mark 1:5; Matt 3:5) bears implications not for Jesus' baptism by John but only for the baptisms of the people of Jerusalem and Judea, who had, of course, sins to confess.

[59] Although perhaps not so very early! Hooker concludes her thorough study: "The influence of the Servant Songs upon early Christian thought has, in fact, been greatly overestimated, as the paucity of genuine references has shown. In the light of Christian belief in the atoning death of Christ, commentators have been quick to see the relevance of Isa. 53, not only to the facts of the Passion story, but also to their significance: this connection was well established by the time of Origen, but there is no evidence that it was made during the early years of the Church" (*Jesus and the Servant*, 154-55).

III. Hearing Mark's Story (continued)

The Markan Jesus' death is incorporated into the larger story of the in-breaking reign of God. Thus, at his final meal with his disciples, Jesus proclaims not only that the Passover cup of wine is "my blood of the covenant, which is poured out for many" (14:24) but also that he will next drink wine when he drinks it "new in the kingdom of God" (14:25). Not only does Jesus' death not negate his proclamation of the in-breaking reign of God, but Jesus' proclamation gives meaning to his death.

Yet this larger story is hard to hear, for Mark's implied audience as for the Markan Jesus' explicit audience – his disciples. Although Peter by this time has heard that a disciple must follow his teacher – in both life and death, and Peter voices (even boasts) his intention to do so, the implied audience by this time has heard that the disciples, especially Peter, are often bolder in word than in deed and that what the Markan Jesus predicts will come to pass (14:26-31). Jesus' request to Peter, James, and John to "keep awake" (14:34) at Gethsemane echoes his command "to all" at the close of the eschatological discourse: "Keep awake" (13:37). The implied audience is given little room to feel smug about Peter's failure to "keep awake" and plenty of reason to be concerned for its own wakefulness. Jesus' suffering and death mean that similar suffering and death may be in store for any and all of Jesus' followers. As expected, as predicted, the betrayal of Judas, "one of the twelve" (14:43), enables the opposition of the religious leaders to culminate in Jesus' arrest apart from the Passover crowds. As expected, as predicted, Jesus' followers all desert him and flee (14:50), even an unnamed follower whose desperate running right out of his garment (14:51-52) stands as a striking visual metaphor of abandonment for the implied audience.

The words of the Markan Jesus in response to the high priest's question give the implied audience another reminder of the larger story. The high priest's final question, "Are you the Messiah [Christ], the Son of the Blessed One?" (14:61), echoes the narrator's initial assertion, "The beginning of the good news of Jesus Christ, the Son of God" (1:1). The Markan Jesus' response, "I am" (14:62), first echoes *again* the divine response to Moses from the burning bush (Exod 3:14; cf. Mark 6:50), bringing the implied audience back into a central story of God and God's covenanted people. Then the Markan Jesus' response, "and 'you will see the Son of Man seated at the right hand of the

Power,' and 'coming with the clouds of heaven'" (14:62; cf. Dan 7:13-14; see also Ps 110:1), moves on to a Danielic echo of the eschatological story of the coming reign of God. How is the death of Jesus to be understood? What is its meaning? It can be understood only as part of the ongoing story of God and the people of God, begun long ago, not yet finished.

Is this meaning easy to hear? Of course not – no easier to hear than the implication that Jesus' followers may need to follow his suffering and death as well as his preaching and healing. As expected, as predicted, Peter denies this implication three times (14:66-72). As expected, as predicted, the Markan Jesus is handed "over to the Gentiles," who "mock him, and spit upon him, and flog him, and kill him" (10:33-34 – the third passion prediction, echoed in 15:1-41). This story, of course, is full of ironies: Jesus of Nazareth, recognized by God (the Father) as "my Son" (1:11; 9:7), is to be crucified, while Barabbas (literally "son of the father") is released; Jesus is taunted and crucified as "King of the Jews," while the implied audience hears another truth in that title.

Remember that our present task is not to present a full-scale narrative analysis of Mark's passion story but to highlight narrative aspects that seem to guide the implied audience to hear (and understand) the story of Jesus' death in a way that suggests its meaning or significance. Two details narrated just after the Markan Jesus' death do just that: the splitting of the temple curtain (15:38) and the centurion's statement, "Truly this man was Son of God [NRSV God's Son]!" (15:39).

Turning to the second detail first, we note that, although there are significant differences among contemporary interpreters on how far the irony of the centurion's remark is to be taken, at least two aspects of its irony are generally accepted: the irony that it is Jesus' death that makes plain his status as obedient Son of God, not his wonder-working power, and the irony that the first human character to call Jesus "Son of God," thus confirming the narrator's initial ascription (1:1),[60] is not only a Gentile but one of the Roman soldiers carrying out the crucifixion. What is not universally agreed upon is whether there is an additional irony that the centurion, like Pilate when he calls Jesus "King of the Jews," does not understand the truth of what he is saying. However, the phrase "King of the Jews" itself shows a negative attitude, since the phrase "King of Israel" (although used derogatorily by the chief priests and scribes at 15:32) would be proper in Jewish usage. In addition, the implied

[60] See n. 43 above.

audience is given other indications of the Markan Pilate's negative view of the Markan Jesus – and, in fact, of the Markan Jewish leaders as well. There is no such indication of the centurion's attitude to clarify whether seeing how Jesus dies changes his view as a Roman soldier or whether his acclamation is sarcastic, like the earlier Roman soldiers' mocking with the purple cloak and the crown of thorns (15:16-20). What is clear for the implied audience is the connection between Jesus' death and his role as Son of God. The very aspect of the story of Jesus that might be expected, from both Jewish and Gentile points of view, to discredit him as Messiah or Son of God serves to confirm him as such. The meaning of Jesus' death is first and foremost that it does not cancel the meaning of his life – that the reign of God has begun, that God has come near to the people of God once again. At the Markan Jesus' baptism, the Spirit went into him (1:10, *to pneuma... eis auton*), and "the dying Jesus expels his spirit (15:37, 39, *exepneusen*) with a loud cry";[61] the Holy Spirit will be available to the followers of the Markan Jesus as they too face their arrests and trials (13:11), and possibly their deaths. Jesus' death does not negate the in-breaking reign of God nor God's presence with those who participate in it.

Second, interpreters also find a certain ambiguity in the Markan narrator's statement that "the curtain of the temple was torn in two, from top to bottom" (15:38) at Jesus' death. Since the temple had two significant curtains – one at the entrance of the temple itself, another at the entrance of the Holy of Holies – it is not entirely clear which curtain is intended in Mark's story.[62] It is clear, however, that the "splitting" (ἐσχίσθη, 15:38) of the enormous curtain "from top to bottom" is a divine act, like the "splitting" (σχιζομένους [1:10, the only other Markan use of σχίζω[63]]) of the heavens at the Markan Jesus' baptism. Thus most interpreters concur that "the destruction of the veil is the proleptic destruction of the temple, the cancellation of the cult that had been prophetically enacted by the Markan Jesus in 11:15-16 and explicitly predicted by him in 13:2.... The positive aspect of the tearing of the curtain is the release of the divine presence into the world."[64] What does the Markan Jesus' death mean? It means not the end of God's presence

[61] Dowd, *Reading Mark*, 162.
[62] Dowd (*Reading Mark*, 162) assumes the outer curtain (see David Ulansey, "The Heavenly Veil Torn: Mark's Cosmic Inclusio," *JBL* 110 [1991]: 123-25); Malbon assumes the inner curtain (*Hearing Mark*, 97; and *Narrative Space*, 108-9).
[63] On σχίζω, see Malbon, *Narrative Space*, 187 n. 93.
[64] Dowd, *Reading Mark*, 162.

on earth but its outward expansion. For Mark's Gospel, Jesus' death means the release of the divine presence into the world – into the whole world, to be recognized by Gentiles as well as Jews. The strong yet unstated message of the implied author to the implied audience at this point is soon echoed by the explicit message of the young man at the empty tomb to the three women: "Go, tell" (16:7).

The final signal to the implied audience of the meaningfulness of Jesus' death is his resurrection, narrated only indirectly in the story of the empty tomb. There are significant surprises in the closing of Mark's Gospel even before the final surprise of the women's fear and silence in 16:8. Given the Markan Jesus' teaching his disciples to take up their cross and follow him (8:34), it is surprising that none of the twelve men but only women followers observe the crucifixion of the Markan Jesus (15:40-41). Given that John's disciples buried him (6:29), it is surprising that the Markan Jesus is buried only by Joseph of Arimathea, intriguingly described as "a respected member of the council, who was also himself waiting expectantly for the kingdom of God" (15:43),[65] with three women followers coming the third morning, "[w]hen the sabbath was over" (16:1), with the spices to anoint his body. Given that the Markan Jesus really suffered and really died, the greatest surprise – even after three predictions of his passion *and resurrection* – is his absence from the tomb and his announced presence on the way to Galilee (16:7) – Galilee where his proclamation of the in-breaking reign of God began, Galilee where his fearful and discouraged disciples could be expected to gather. He is going to Galilee to see those who have fled from his death; Peter is mentioned by name. According to Mark's Gospel, it is in the resurrection of Jesus, not in his death, that forgiveness is experienced.

What does the Markan narrative context suggest about the meaning of Jesus' death? That Jesus' death is not the end of the story. That Jesus' death is part of the larger – and ongoing – story of God and the covenanted people of God, who have been ransomed from captivity and set free to follow Jesus in his march toward the reign of God. That the reign of God really is breaking into history – thus the power of evil is

[65] On Joseph of Arimathea as "portrayed as caring nothing for Jesus, but caring a great deal about the requirements of Torah," see Dowd, *Reading Mark*, 164-65 (quotation from 164), following Brown, "Burial." On Joseph of Arimathea as an exceptional religious leader whose portrayal blocks absolute stereotyping, see Malbon, *Hearing Mark*, 98; and eadem, "The Jewish Leaders in the Gospel of Mark: A Literary Study of Marcan Characterization," *JBL* 108 (1989): 259-81, republished in *In the Company of Jesus*, 131-65.

being overthrown. That those who follow Jesus are, like him, called to serve rather than be served, and especially to free the many from the tyranny of the few. That such serving of the powerless will challenge the powerful. That any suffering or death that might result from such service is not the end of the story of God's reign. That fear and cowardice are also not the end of the story and can be forgiven by God – through prayer and mutual forgiveness. Mark's story of Jesus does not link Jesus' death with the forgiveness of sins, but it proclaims perhaps a more powerful message: God is present in the world, even in the face of evil, for God is stronger than evil. God is present in healing those bound by sickness, in serving those whom society neglects or mistreats, in being good news in the whole world. And God remains present in whatever results from such service – both life and death.

SCRIPTURALIZATION IN MARK'S CRUCIFIXION NARRATIVE

Mark Goodacre

The Shame of Crucifixion

One might have thought that it was something of a scholarly cliché to stress the horror, the shame, the degradation, the suffering involved with crucifixion. Yet many of the scholarly reactions to *The Passion of the Christ* (dir. Mel Gibson, 2004), which balked at the scale of suffering endured here by Jesus, provide a timely reminder that many of us still have very little grasp of just how appalling a death crucifixion was. The remarkable thing about Mel Gibson's film was not so much the magnitude of suffering depicted but its restraint in showing many of the true horrors of crucifixion, as Gibson himself realized.[1] Consider, for example, Seneca's mockery of the view that life is worth holding on to at any price:

> Can anyone be found who would prefer wasting away in pain dying limb by limb, or letting out his life drop by drop, rather than expiring once for all? Can any man be found willing to be fastened to the accursed tree, long sickly, already deformed, swelling with ugly weals on shoulders and chest, and drawing the breath of life amid long drawn-out agony? He would have many excuses for dying even before mounting the cross. (Seneca, *Epistle 101 to Lucilius*, Hengel)[2]

But there is a problem with the iconographic focus on Jesus' suffering in *The Passion of the Christ*, for while it gives some hint of the appalling suffering involved in such a death, it masks what for the ancient mind marked the true terror of death by crucifixion. For it was not merely the excruciating physical torture that made crucifixion so unspeakable, but

[1] See further Mark Goodacre, "The Power of *The Passion of the Christ*: Reacting and Overreacting to Gibson's Artistic Vision" in *Jesus and Mel Gibson's The Passion of the Christ: the Film, the Gospels and the Claims of History* (ed. Kathleen E. Corley and Robert L. Webb; London & New York: Continuum, 2004), 28-44 (35-6).

[2] Seneca, *Epistle 101 to Lucilius*; Martin Hengel's translation, *Crucifixion in the Ancient World and the Folly of the Message of the Cross* (ET; London: SCM, 1977), 31-2.

the devastation of shame that this death, above all others, represented.[3] Consider, for example, Cicero's remarks:

> But the executioner, the veiling of the head and the very word "cross" should be far removed not only from the person of a Roman citizen but from his thoughts, his eyes and his ears. For it is not only the actual occurrence of these things or the endurance of them, but liability to them, the expectation, indeed the very mention of them, that is unworthy of a Roman citizen and a free man. (*Pro Rabirio* 16)[4]

It was, as Origen describes it, *mors turpissima crucis*, the utterly vile death of the cross, something the civilized person could not even bear to talk about (Origen, *Commentary on Matthew* 27.22).[5] If we are to have any chance of understanding Mark's crucifixion narrative, it needs to be against this background. Douglas Geyer's recent and evocative phrase *the anomalous frightful* reminds us of this proper context for reading Mark historically:

> Crucifixion is an ideal expression of the anomalous frightful. In accordance with ancient evidence about types of death and the destinies of those killed violently, it is terrifying, ghastly, and laden with uncertainty. It is a violent and abrupt end of mortal life, and it remained this volatile problem for the ancient audience of the Gospels. The tenacity of this problem for early Christianity is not to be underestimated.[6]

Narrating Crucifixion

It is easy to forget that Mark's narrative of the crucifixion is not only the first extant narrative of Jesus' crucifixion, but one of the first narratives of any hero's death by crucifixion. There are, of course, references to crucifixion in many ancient writers, Cicero, Josephus, Plutarch, but it is rare to find a narrative of one man's crucifixion, a fact that is not at all

[3] The honor/shame dynamic is not, however, entirely absent from *The Passion of the Christ*, and is particularly marked in the scourging scene, when Jesus raises himself up before his tormenters' initial series of scourgings, and in the repeated emphasis, carried over from the Gospels, on the mockery of Jesus. The soldiers are publicly shaming Jesus, and delighting in that act of public humiliation.

[4] The translation used here is Martin Hengel's, from *Crucifixion*, 42.

[5] For a helpful study of the honor/shame dynamic in John's crucifixion narrative, see Jerome Neyrey, "Despising the Shame of the Cross: Honor and Shame in the Johannine Passion Narrative," *Semeia* 69 (1996): 113-37. Many of Neyrey's observations concerning the way in which the crucifixion narrative functions in John are relevant for Mark too, and provide a useful insight into the cultural context of the first crucifixion narratives.

[6] Douglas W. Geyer, *Fear, Anomaly and Uncertainty in the Gospel of Mark* (ATLA Monograph Series, 47; Lanham, Md.; London: Scarecrow, 2002), 10.

surprising given the horror of the spectacle.[7] And now Mark, the first, as far as we know, to write a Gospel, has decided to write a narrative in which Jesus' suffering and death is placed in the foreground.[8] In a Gospel where everything points forward to this decisive moment, in which Jesus' very predictions of it are conceived in narrative terms, Mark's only realistic option is to provide some kind of narrative account of the crucifixion.[9] It is the climactic moment of the story, the goal of Mark's theology of Christ crucified. To stop short of narrating the event that is at the heart of Mark's Gospel was clearly not a possibility.

But how would such an author, the first to construct a written narrative of Jesus' crucifixion, go about his task? How does one make the well known instrument of ultimate shame the occasion of the highest glory? On the whole, the very idea of any victim of crucifixion being the kind of hero who would warrant a literary narrative telling the story of his misery would have been unthinkable, far less that such a narrative would be the climax of the story of Israel's Messiah.

No doubt there were precedents for what Mark was now attempting. Paul frequently points to the shame, the scandal, the foolishness of the cross and makes it the heart of his gospel, the event around which all history pivots. But in Paul's letters, and perhaps his preaching too, the very mention of crucifixion would have conjured up terrifying images to the ancient mind. There is no need for a narrative of Jesus' death. Martin Hengel's intriguing suggestion that Paul must have presented a vivid narrative of Jesus' crucifixion[10] is less likely than the alternative explanation that Paul's own flogged and persecuted body was the occasion of the "public portrayal" of Christ's crucifixion before the Galatians (Gal 3:1).

[7] The authoritative work on the topic remains Martin Hengel, *Crucifixion*, though this should be supplemented with Joe Zias, "Crucifixion in Antiquity: The Evidence," n.p. [cited 4 June 2006]. Online: http://www.centuryone.org/crucifixion2.html, also available on Joe Zias's homepage, http://www.joezias.com/CrucifixionAntiquity.html. The closest one gets to the narration of a hero's death by crucifixion is Herodotus, *The Histories* 7.194.1-4, which narrates the crucifixion and subsequent freeing of Sandoces. See also the story of the Widow of Ephesus in Petronius, *The Satyricon* 110.6-113.4. On the horror of the spectacle see M. Tullius Cicero, *Speech before Roman Citizens on Behalf of Gaius Rabirius, Defendant Against the Charge of Treason* V[16].

[8] I am assuming Marcan Priority here; for a defense see my *Case Against Q: Studies in Markan Priority and the Synoptic Problem* (Harrisburg, Pa.: Trinity Press International, 2002), Chapter 2 (pp. 19-45).

[9] This is particularly clear in the third Passion prediction, 10:34, which has a seven point narrative sequence: (1) going to Jerusalem, (2) handing over to the religious authorities, (3) condemning to death, (4) handing over to the Gentiles, (5) mockery, (6) death, (7) resurrection.

[10] Martin Hengel and Anna Maria Schwemer, *Paul Between Damascus and Antioch: The Unknown Years* (ET, London: SCM 1997), 17.

In an attempt to probe for an answer to this fascinating question about the origin of Mark's crucifixion narrative, it is worth bearing in mind how the claim that the Messiah had been crucified would have sounded to many an ancient hearers – preposterous. The point of crucifixion was to terrorize the population; it was an example; it was not an honorable death like a death on the battlefield.[11] One of Mark's tasks, therefore, will be to demonstrate that, against every instinct of an ancient reader, this crucifixion was neither at best a tragic accident, a horrific mistake, nor at worst, the demonstration of the fate of one deserving of the *summum supplicium*, the most terrible of retaliatory tortures. So how could one deal with the anomalous frightful? How might one anticipate the very charges that the earliest critics of Christianity like Celsus in fact went on to make?[12]

Mark uses several strategies to deal with these problems. This, his biggest challenge, is his invitation to produce a raw but nevertheless brilliant literary work. One strategy is to show that this death, though violent, was not accidental by having Jesus himself prophesy these events. Three times Jesus will tell his disciples what will happen to him in detail, all of which is explicitly fulfilled in the Passion Narrative. While everyone else, the disciples, the Jewish leaders, the Romans, either misunderstands or mocks him (only the women of Mark 14–15 seem to understand that there is no contradiction between Jesus' Messianic identity and his suffering), Jesus himself knows that his mission is "the way" of the cross. It is a point that could but will not be developed here, but it is intriguing that Mark does not simply have Jesus predict his passion and then fulfill it. The fulfillment of Jesus' own prophecies happen in the most darkly ironic context, as if Mark knows that the only way of writing a compelling narrative is to combine the fulfillment motif with the nasty, stark reality of pre-crucifixion mockery. Thus, as Peter is in the very act of denying Jesus outside, and so fulfilling one of Jesus' predictions, the soldiers inside are spitting at Jesus, beating him and taunting him to "Prophesy!" (Mark 14:65). The shame of Jesus' public humiliation is trumped by the dramatic irony which confirms him as a prophet.[13]

[11] Contrast, for example, the death of Spartacus as reported by Florus (*Epitome* 2.8), an honorable death on the battlefield: "Spartacus himself fell, as became a general, fighting most bravely in the front rank."

[12] See Origen, *Contra Celsum* 6.34.

[13] Among several useful discussions of dramatic irony in Mark's Passion Narrative, see Donald H. Juel, *The Gospel of Mark* (Interpreting Biblical Texts; Nashville: Abingdon, 1999); Jerry Camery-Hoggatt, *Irony in Mark's Gospel: Text and Subtext* (Cambridge: Cambridge University Press, 1992); see too Tom Shepherd, "The Irony of Power in the Trial of Jesus and the Denial by Peter: Mark 14:53-72" (see further in this book).

Use of the Scriptures

But the primary strategy used by Mark to deal with the sensational nature of the claims being made in the narrative he is developing is the use of the Scriptures. The Scriptures are the obvious place to go for an author like Mark immersed in early Christianity's obsession with demonstrating promise and fulfillment. Any approach to Mark's passion story that fails to take seriously its extensive use of scriptural quotation, allusion and precedent is unlikely to be able to explain what is going on here. So, why the Scriptures? Why the obsession with the Greek Bible?[14]

It is a tribute to Gospel scholarship of recent times that it has so stressed the role played by the Old Testament in the formation of the New. Monograph after monograph appears on the topic, conferences are held which center on this topic alone, and it is now rightly perceived to be quite impossible to understand the New Testament without intimate knowledge of the Old. And yet in spite of the sheer volume of studies on this all important topic, it is surprising to see how often the function of the Old Testament in the New is simply taken for granted, as if it is self evident to any intelligent reader. But one of the elements that requires an explanation is the variation in the usage of the Scriptures at different points in the Gospel narratives. Why, for example, are references to the Old Testament so thick on the ground in the Passion Narratives but so scant when it comes to the neighboring resurrection stories, a problem that is sharply focused given the fact that both passion and resurrection were, from the earliest times, held to have happened *according to the Scriptures* (1 Cor 15:3)?

In order to probe for an answer, it is worth bearing in mind what the Scriptures signified for first century Jews as well as the earliest Gentile Christian converts, and what it meant to say that Jesus died for our sins *according to the Scriptures*. The Scriptures were the perfect expression of the will of God. If you wanted to understand the mind of God, you went to the Scriptures. And this is one of the driving forces in the formation of the Passion Narrative. It is only when one combines the realization of the sheer horror of crucifixion with the fact that the Scriptures encapsulated God's will that one remembers that there is no more powerful way of explaining that this horrific event was in God's perfect plan, that it was his own divine will, than to narrate the very story of

[14] In Mark's case the term "Greek Bible" is the most appropriate one in this context since it seems most likely that Mark is familiar with Greek rather than Hebrew versions of the Jewish Scriptures.

crucifixion using the language of Scripture. And it is Mark's genius that he mounts this powerful argument for frightful death as God's will by narrating it in scriptural terms, by using their vocabulary, their imagery, their very fabric to tell his surprising story.

In Mark's Passion Narrative, Jesus himself prays that what God wants will come to pass, "Not my will, but yours" (14:36, 39), and shortly afterwards it becomes clear that God's will does indeed involve Jesus' shame and abandonment. In contrast to key moments earlier in the Gospel (1:11 and 9:7), neither Jesus nor the reader hears God's voice. In answer to this prayer, there is silence. Now God's will is established by what already stands written in the Scriptures. Jesus knows this and says, as his fate is sealed at his arrest, "But let the Scriptures be fulfilled" (14:49). The Scriptures are the answer to Jesus' prayer in Gethsemane. This is God's will, that Jesus is to be humiliated; its announcement is in the Scriptures that Mark is going to bring forward at point after point in his narrative of the crucifixion.

This reference in Mark 14:49 represents the last explicit mention of "the Scriptures" in Mark's Gospel. Every allusion that follows is precisely that, an allusion. There are no formula citations here and no other direct comment on "the Scriptures." Jesus' chilling pronouncement at his arrest, "Let the Scriptures be fulfilled," echoes throughout the narrative, so that now, on the only two occasions when Jesus speaks more than two words, it is to speak, like the narrator, utilizing scriptural language, first to answer the High Priest with the quotation from Daniel 7:13-14 (Mark 14:62) and second, on the cross, in the quotation of Psalm 22:1 (15:34).

In the Crucifixion Narrative, the scriptural allusions are, in other words, embedded in the account. It is not as if one could take away the scriptural elements and still have a coherent narrative. They are fundamental to it, not tagged on extras acting as commentary on a narrative that would make sense without them. But if it is the case that Mark's primary reason for relying so heavily here on the Scriptures is to make clear that the frightful business of crucifixion was, on this extraordinary occasion, in God's will, its victim vindicated by a narrative that celebrated this as an event that the Scriptures themselves predicted, then we run up against a tough historical question, and a question that is already starkly posed in much recent literature on Jesus and the Gospels. Given the extensive use of the Scriptures here, in the Passion Narrative, could it be that the Scriptures themselves provided the very *sources* for the details of the story? Could it be, to use the catchy phrase coined by John Dominic Crossan, that we are looking here at *prophecy historicized*?

Prophecy Historicized or History Scripturalized?

In the *Birth of Christianity*, Crossan explains the concept like this:

> The individual units, general sequences, and overall frames of the passion-resurrection stories are so linked to prophetic fulfillment that the removal of such fulfillment leaves nothing but the barest facts, almost as in Josephus, Tacitus or the Apostles' Creed.[15]

For Crossan, and in this he is followed by a good number of scholars, especially those in the Jesus seminar, the *prophecy historicized* model is plausible because the alternative, that the Passion Narratives are *history remembered* is weak.[16] Such a view, for Crossan typified in the work of Raymond Brown, is simply inadequate to the task.[17] It is just not plausible, for Crossan, that memory could so have imbued the text with these scriptural resonances.

The severity of the contrast Crossan sets up between his own view and that of Raymond Brown, between prophecy historicized and history remembered, is unnecessary. The reader is presented with a choice: is it history or is it prophecy? Did it happen or is it fictional? The contrast between the two views presented is simply too stark. Given these sole alternatives, *history remembered* or *prophecy historicized* and given the undisputed level of scriptural allusion in the Passion Narratives, few critical scholars would be able to resist Crossan's conclusion. But the choice offered by Crossan is not a necessary one. Only the most ardent fundamentalists would go for the view that the Passion Narratives were simply made up of *history remembered*, and the term is in fact not one that is used by Raymond Brown, whose work Crossan is caricaturing.[18]

15 John Dominic Crossan, *The Birth of Christianity: Discovering What Happened in the Years Immediately After the Execution of Jesus* (Edinburgh: T & T Clark, 1998), 521.

16 See, for example, Daryl D. Schmidt's endorsement of the thesis in "Septuagintal Influence in the Passion Narratives," *Forum* New Series 1.1 (Spring 1998): 95-118, especially p. 107. Cf. Marcus Borg's use of Crossan's terms in N.T. Wright and Marcus Borg, *The Meaning of Jesus: Two Visions* (London: SPCK, 1999), 84-5. The Jesus Seminar overall finds the thesis persuasive. The proposition "Detailed information about the crucifixion of Jesus is derived from prophecy historicized" receives a "red" rating, "The Jesus Seminar: Voting Records: The Passion Narrative," *Forum* New Series 1.1 (Spring 1998): 227-33 (230).

17 Raymond E. Brown, *The Death of the Messiah: From Gethsemane to the Grave: A Commentary on the Passion Narratives in the Four Gospels* (2 vols.; ABRL; New York: Doubleday, 1994).

18 Although Brown does indeed see the "basic incidents" of the Passion Narrative as derived from "early Christian memory" (*Death of the Messiah*, 1:16), he also sees the whole process, from eye-witness and "ear witness" through to the evangelists, as involving embellishment from the Christian imagination (for example *Death of the Messiah*, 1:14).

There is a plausible answer to Crossan, and it is not the *history remembered* view of Crossan's caricature of Brown. Rather, it involves introducing a helpful, if rather cumbersome term from recent Hebrew Bible scholarship, *scripturalization*. This term is adopted and developed by Judith H. Newman in her recent monograph *Praying by the Book: The Scripturalization of Prayer in Second Temple Judaism.*[19] Newman's essential thesis is that in the Second Temple Period, Jewish prayers increasingly used scriptural models, precedents and language. Increasing devotion to developing Jewish Scriptures, in a liturgical context in which such Scriptures were getting used more and more, led inexorably to the intermingling of those Scriptures with Jewish prayers. Jews were "praying by the book"; they were scripturalizing their prayers.

What is so interesting about this model in our context is that it makes such good sense of Mark's Passion Narrative. For here the multiple echoes of Biblical themes and the varied allusions to scriptural precedent can be explained on the basis of intimate interaction between the tradition and the scriptural reflection. The traditions generated scriptural reflection, which in turn influenced the way the traditions were recast.

The point might best be illustrated in engagement with Crossan. Right at the end of the Crucifixion Narrative, in Mark 15:40-41, there is a note about named women watching the crucifixion from a distance.[20] This is how Crossan works with this material and the related mention of the women in 15:47–16:8:

> Their existence and names in 15.40-41 are pre-Markan tradition, but their criticism in 15.47–16.8 is Markan redaction. In other words, the inclusion of women observing the burial and visiting the tomb is no earlier than Mark, but the inclusion of women watching the crucifixion

[19] Judith H. Newman, *Praying by the Book: The Scripturalization of Prayer in Second Temple Judaism* (Atlanta: Scholars Press, 1999). The term is borrowed from her teacher James L. Kugel, "Topics in the History of the Spirituality of the Psalms" in *Jewish Spirituality from the Bible Through the Middle Ages* (New York: Crossroad, 1986), 113-44, where he uses it with reference to the increasing perception of the Psalms as Scripture. Newman takes the term in a different direction. It is her usage of the term that I am working with in this paper.

[20] Gerd Theissen argues for the historicity of this detail by pointing out that the names given appear to presume the readers' knowledge of their identity, *The Gospels in Context: Social and Political History in the Synoptic Tradition* (ET, Edinburgh: T & T Clark, 1992), 177-8. But while that may have been the case for the traditions on which Mark is basing his account, it is not convincing that Mark himself knows the identity of these women, not least given the (deliberate?) vagueness in the three mentions of 15:40, 15:47 and 16:1. For a recent examination of the material on these women, see Susan Miller, *Women in Mark's Gospel* (JSNTSup, 259; London & New York: T & T Clark International, 2004), 153-192.

> is received tradition. But is the latter historical fact? My best answer is yes, because the male disciples had fled; if the women had not been watching, we would not know even the brute fact of crucifixion (as distinct, for example, from Jesus being summarily speared or beheaded in prison).[21]

The example is an interesting one because of the wording of the verse in question,

> Ἦσαν δὲ καὶ γυναῖκες *ἀπὸ μακρόθεν* θεωροῦσαι
> And there were also women watching *from a distance* (Mark 15:40; cf. Matt 27:55 // Luke 23:49)

The note that they were watching ἀπὸ μακρόθεν echoes the wording of Psalm 38:11 LXX, "My friends and companions stand aloof from my affliction, and my relatives stand afar off," ἀπὸ μακρόθεν.[22] It is one of those details that virtually every commentator on the passage mentions – critical texts list it as an Old Testament parallel and even Raymond Brown thinks he may hear an echo.[23] It is unlikely, and, indeed, it is rarely argued, that Mark has invented this verse on the basis of Psalm 38:11, which does not refer solely to women, let alone to those particular named women. Rather, the traditional element gets retold in the light of the scriptural passage that was thought to be fulfilled. In other words, in this verse we see the exact opposite of the process of prophecy historicized. A verse that Crossan takes to be historical has, it seems, been expressed using the terminology of the Scriptures. Or, we might say, the tradition was scripturalized.

[21] Crossan, *Birth of Christianity*: 559. See also John Dominic Crossan, *Who Killed Jesus?: Exposing the Roots of Anti-Semitism in the Gospel Story of the Death of Jesus* (San Francisco: HarperSanFrancisco, 1995), 181-5 for reflections on the role played by the women in the story. In *The Historical Jesus: The Life of a Mediterranean Jewish Peasant* (San Francisco: HarperSanFrancisco, 1991), 415, Crossan suggests that the first version of Mark originally ended just before these verses, at 15:39, the Centurion's Confession.

[22] Contrast John 19:25-27 where the Beloved Disciple and Jesus' mother are close enough to hold a conversation with Jesus. Joel Marcus, "The Role of Scripture in the Gospel Passion Narratives," in *The Death of Jesus in Early Christianity* (ed. John T. Carroll and Joel B. Green; Peabody: Hendrickson, 1995), 205-33 speculates that the Johannine account "may be more accurate historically than the Synoptics" in view of the fact that "Romans often allowed friends of crucified criminals to stand by them until they died" (p. 212). But on this point contrast Brown, *Death of the Messiah*, 2:1029 and 2:1194, "it would be unusual for the Romans to permit family and sympathizers such proximity."

[23] Brown, *Death of the Messiah*, 2:1158. Kathleen E. Corley, "Women and the Crucifixion and Burial of Jesus," *Forum* New Series 1.1 (Spring 1998): 181-226, notes that "Luke reinforces this connection with Psalm 38:11 by the addition of οἱ γνωστοί (friends) (Luke 23:49), p. 212, n. 211. Her full discussion of the passage, with some useful bibliography, is on pp. 209-17.

There is a still more fundamental problem with the logic of Crossan's case here. He remarks that "the male disciples had fled" and so could not have provided anyone with details of the crucifixion.[24] But this raises the question: how do we know that the male disciples had fled? What is the source of information for this key background assumption in Crossan's case? The detail is found in Mark 14:50, "Everyone deserted him and fled," where it follows directly from Jesus' announcement in 14:49, "Let the Scriptures be fulfilled." And the Scripture in view here is clearly Zechariah 13:7, "Strike the shepherd and the sheep will be scattered," quoted by Jesus in Mark 14:27, where Jesus predicts the falling away of the disciples. But if this key foundational detail is itself so explicitly scriptural, Crossan's model demands that we see this too as prophecy historicized. And if this detail is prophecy historicized, how – to use Crossan's logic – can we trust it as history? If we cannot trust the historicity of this element, there is no obligation to accept the absence of the disciples as a foundational premise for the whole. In other words, without the knowledge that there was no one present at the crucifixion, we do not require the thesis of the inevitability of the prophecy historicized model.

A Liturgical Context?

The term scripturalization, and the process it describes, raises a key question about the origin of Mark's crucifixion narrative. In what context does scripturalization happen? For Judith Newman's *Praying by the Book*, the context is clear – it is worship, in which communal prayers are molded in the very context where the Scriptures are being read. It is worth asking whether something similar might be claimed for Mark and his predecessors. The answer is that there is both external and internal evidence to suggest that early Christian worship may have provided the context for the development of Mark's Passion Narrative.

The external evidence is well known but surprisingly rarely applied in this context. 1 Corinthians 11 features Paul's narrative of the Lord's Supper, discussed in the context of the celebration of the Eucharist in Corinth. So, as early as our evidence takes us, we have liturgy as the context in which the retelling of the story appears.

[24] See the quotation above, Crossan, *Birth of Christianity*, 559.

Significantly, Paul appears to be referring to a connected story. "In the night that he was handed over..." (1 Cor 11:23), Paul says, as if the Eucharist tradition is familiar as part of a larger narrative known to the Corinthians. What we have, in other words, is a liturgical context for the earliest known narration of the events in Jesus' Passion, in Corinth in the early 50s. It is hardly a stretch to think that Mark's community, only a few years later (in the 60s?), might also have been recounting traditions about the Passion in the context of their worship.[25] And there is some further evidence, albeit circumstantial, that this was exactly what was going on.

In order to explore the point, it will be useful to do so by engaging again with Crossan. One of his favourite examples of the prophecy historicized model is the darkness coming over the earth at noon, Mark 15:33. He writes:

> To explain those accounts as "history remembered" means that Jesus' companions observed the darkness, recorded it in memory, passed it on in tradition, and recalled it when writing their accounts of the crucifixion. It happened in history, and that is why it is mentioned in gospel.[26]

The explanation of prophecy historicized, on the other hand, involves reading the Gospel accounts alongside Amos 8:9-10, which speaks of the day of the Lord when God promises to "make the sun go down at noon and darken the earth in broad daylight." "I will make it like the mourning for an only son," He says, "and the end of it like a bitter day." Crossan explains:

> By "prophecy historicized" I mean that no such *historical* three-hour-long midnight at noon accompanied the death of Jesus, but that learned Christians searching their Scriptures found this ancient description of future divine punishment, maybe facilitated by its mention of 'an only son' in the second-to-last line, and so created that *fictional* story about darkness at noon to assert that Jesus died in fulfillment of prophecy.[27]

[25] I use the term "Mark's community" of the community from which the Gospel emerged rather than to which it was written. Richard Bauckham (et al.)'s useful corrective to the scholarly fixation with Gospel communities in *The Gospels for all Christians: Rethinking the Gospel Audiences* (ed. Richard Bauckham; Grand Rapids: Eerdmans/Edinburgh: T. & T. Clark, 1997), deals primarily with the issue of the "Gospel audiences" of its subtitle, and has relatively little to say about the communities in which the Gospels were written.

[26] Crossan, *Who Killed Jesus?*, 2.

[27] *Ibid.*, 4.

Although touted by Crossan as a key example, it actually demonstrates quite effectively the limitations of his model. All that Amos 8:9 is able to explain is, at best, one element in the story – the darkness at midday. But this time reference is one of many in the Passion Narrative and they all have one thing in common: they happen at three hour intervals. The darkness that comes over the earth at 12 lasts three hours until 3 p.m., when Jesus dies (15:33-34). Before the darkness begins, Jesus has already been on the cross for three hours, since 9 a.m. (15:25). Before that, Jesus was brought before Pilate at dawn, πρωΐ (15:1). Nor does the pattern stop there. There appears to be something like a twenty-four hour framework, broken up neatly into three hour segments. Thus, if we imagine the Last Supper taking place at 6 p.m. (14:17, "When it was evening..."), Jesus and the disciples would then go to Gethsemane at 9 p.m., Jesus would be arrested at midnight, and Peter denies Jesus during the Jewish trial at 3 a.m., cockcrow (14:72).

Nor is it simply that these stories fit nicely into this schedule. Individual units themselves seem to be patterned in such a way that they reflect this kind of structure. Jesus in Gethsemane asks his disciples to watch with him and is distressed that they could not stay awake for "one hour" (14:37), and then twice again he comes to them (14:40-41). And then, similarly, Peter denies Jesus three times at cockcrow, the Roman watch at 3 a.m. (14:54, 66-72).

Explanations for this marked three-hour structure that so dominates the Passion Narrative have not, on the whole, been forthcoming. The difficulty is, of course, that life is not quite as neat and tidy as this – events do not happen in even three hour units. That the pattern is intentional and in some way significant seems to be confirmed by a saying of Jesus located just before the beginning of Mark's Passion Narrative:

> Therefore keep watch because you do not know when the owner of the house will return – whether in the evening, or at midnight, or when the cock crows, or at dawn. If he comes suddenly, do not let him find you sleeping. What I say to you, I say to everyone: "Watch!" (Mark 13:35-37)

The text itself appears to be drawing attention to the three hour pattern, alerting the bright reader to what is to come. And though an explanation has been put forward separately by three different scholars, a Canadian (Philip Carrington) in the 1950s, an Englishman (Michael Goulder) in the 1970s, and a Frenchman (Étienne Trocmé) in the 1980s, it is still hardly known at all in mainstream scholarship.[28] These three scholars claim that the liturgy is the only thing that would make sense of this. What is happening, they suggest, is that the early Christians were holding their own annual celebration of the events of the Passion at the Jewish Passover, remembered as roughly the time of Jesus' death. While other Jews were celebrating Passover, Christian Jews held a twenty-four hour vigil in which they retold and relived the events surrounding Jesus' arrest and death, from sunset on 14/15 Nisan, and for twenty-four hours. Perhaps Mark's account of the Passion, with its heavy referencing of Scripture, its regular time notes, was itself influenced by such a liturgical memory of the Passion.

It is straightforward to see why the theory of a liturgical origin of the Passion Narrative has not proved popular. In both Carrington's and Goulder's cases, it was bolted on to thoroughgoing but less plausible cases for lectionary origins of one or more Gospels. In a far ranging, over-ambitious thesis like this, strong elements that make up a part of the less compelling whole are easily lost.[29] But the advantages of seeing the footprints of the liturgy in Mark's Passion Narrative are several. It explains several of the famous anomalies in the account, the rushed timetable, the night-time trial, crucifixion on a festival, and so on. And, more importantly for our purposes, it provides us with a plausible context for the creation of the first Passion Narrative, with its marked scripturalizing tendency, and so – ultimately – it sheds light on the genesis of the Gospels themselves.[30]

[28] Philip Carrington, *The Primitive Christian Calendar: A Study in the Making of the Marcan Gospel* (Cambridge: Cambridge University Press, 1952); Michael Goulder, *Midrash and Lection in Matthew* (London: SPCK, 1974) and *The Evangelists' Calendar* (London: SPCK, 1978); Étienne Trocmé, *The Passion as Liturgy: A Study in the Origin of the Passion Narratives in the Four Gospels* (London: SCM, 1983). However for recent, relatively sympathetic comments see D. Moody Smith, "When did the Gospels become Scripture?," *JBL* 119 (2000): 3-20 (see especially pp. 5-6).

[29] See further my examination of the lectionary theories, which concludes that the case for a liturgical origin of the Passion Narrative has been unfairly overlooked, Mark Goodacre, *Goulder and the Gospels: An Examination of a New Paradigm* (JSNTSup, 133; Sheffield: Sheffield Academic Press, 1996), Part 3 (pp. 294-362).

[30] I am planning to develop this thesis at greater length in a book provisionally entitled *When Prophecy Became Passion: The Death of Jesus and the Birth of the Gospels*.

Summary

So, to summarize our discussion. (1) Scholars still seldom appreciate just what an extraordinary undertaking it is to have tried to write a narrative about a hero who was crucified. (2) Mark overcomes the problem with this *anomalous frightful* by grounding his story in God's will as revealed in the Scriptures. (3) The process concerned is one of *scripturalization*, the retelling of traditional materials in the light of the Scriptures, a view more plausible than the one now common, *prophecy historicized*. (4) The context for the scripturalizing work was one in which Mark was in continuity with Christians going back at least to 50s Corinth, and no doubt to 30s Jerusalem, and it was the liturgy, something that has left its own mark on the text and which may have explanatory power; it deserves further exploration.

Concluding Thoughts: Scripturalizing Abandonment

We began by reflecting on the shame, the horror, the humiliation of death by crucifixion. The task that faced Mark was daunting, in this first attempt to produce a written narrative of Jesus' death. It is a mark of his success in constructing the narrative that he is able to draw together what might at first appear to be two very contrasting forces, the need to write a compelling and plausible narrative suitable to *bios*, and so to be realistic about crucifixion, and the desire to scripturalize, to depict the ghastly death as God's will. One of the key ways in which Mark achieves this is by the use of the theme of desertion, loneliness, abandonment. The theme enables Mark to underline the shame of crucifixion and thus to render his narrative plausible, but at the same time to express it by using the language of the Scriptures that Mark sees as being fulfilled.

Jesus' abandonment is stressed from the moment that he declares, in 14:49, "Let the Scriptures be fulfilled" (presumably Zechariah 13:7, prophesied by Jesus in Mark 14:27). Now, in 14:50-52, all forsake Jesus and flee, first the general statement (14:50, "All forsook him and fled") and then the specific example (14:51-52, "And he left the linen cloth and fled from them naked"). Likewise, perhaps the closest scriptural quotation of all, and certainly the one most stressed by Mark, is Jesus' cry of dereliction (15:34) – once again abandonment and desertion are juxtaposed with the Scriptures, as Jesus utters a cry that is, of course, straight from the opening verse of Psalm 22. The hideous, lonely death of this wretched crucified man is scripturalized so as to make clear that the crucified Messiah is indeed in God's will.

Among other things this is a warning against one of the clichés of historical Jesus scholarship. In these verses, where Jesus is, of necessity, largely silent, the Scriptures speak all the more loudly. They provide Mark with the means of telling a plausible story (a crucified victim might be depicted uttering a few choice words but extensive conversations are quite out of the question if one wishes to keep one's narrative plausible) at the same time as making it theologically robust. It acts as a useful reminder that discussions about the cry of Jesus from the cross as being an "embarrassment," as being the more likely historically because of that, are quite out of place.[31] Mark is not in the least "embarrassed" by this cry. It is an ideal means of expressing plausibly the horror of the cross at the same time as reaffirming, by quoting the Psalms, that it is in God's will.

It is this utterly abject, lonely, shameful death, characterized by an eerie silence, which provides the invitation to Mark to scripturalize the tradition, and thus to construct the first narrative of Jesus' crucifixion by subverting the readers' expectations, to say that here, where you would least expect it, honor, glory and vindication are found.

[31] Cf. John P. Meier's comments on the difficulties with this criterion in this context, *A Marginal Jew: Rethinking the Historical Jesus Volume 1: The Roots of the Problem and the Person* (ABRL; New York: Doubleday, 1991), 1:170-1. For a useful expression of the contrasting view, cf. Joel Marcus, "The Role of Scripture," 213: "It is difficult... to imagine that the church would have placed Ps 22:1 on the lips of the dying Jesus if the verse had not originally belonged there, since Jesus' use of this psalm verse created major difficulties...The church probably would not have created such problems for itself; rather, the cry of dereliction was simply too securely rooted in the tradition about Jesus' death to be dislodged."

THE MEANING OF THE DEATH OF JESUS IN THE GOSPEL OF MARK A REAL READER PERSPECTIVE

Geert VAN OYEN

The real reader and the construction of meaning

The interpretation of the death of Jesus is complicated, even if from the outset one deliberately leaves out both the issue of the meaning Jesus himself could have given to his own death and the many examples of later dogmatically influenced *eis*egesis. It seems that the ideas about Jesus' self-consciousness and the perspective of dogmatic reflection are both presuppositions that often determine exegetical research about Jesus' death.[1] The survey of S. McKnight (2001), though focused on the historical Jesus and thus not exclusively on Mark, offers enough material to illustrate the diversity of scholarly opinions about Jesus' death.[2]

> At the end of the article, McKnight mentions two important points to be considered when discussing how Jesus understood his own death. First, concerning the *historical* reliability of the Jesus' sayings it is

[1] In the interpretation of Mark 10:45 the so-called Tübingen school is clearly influenced by the interest the group gives to the relevance of historical reliability; see Werner Zager, "Wie kam es im Urchristentum zur Deutung des Todes Jesu als Sühnegeschehen? Eine Auseinandersetzung mit Peter Stuhlmachers Entwurf einer 'Biblischen Theologie des Neuen Testaments,'" *ZNW* 87 (1996): 165-186. See also Günter Röhser review of T. Knöppler, *Sühne im Neuen Testament. Studien zum urchristlichen Verständnis der Heilsbedeutung des Todes Jesu* (WMANT 89; Neukirchen-Vluyn: Neukirchener, 2001) on website (http://www.znt-online.de/roehser.html [cited 31 May 2006]). There are hundreds of articles and books on the theme of Jesus' death from a systematic perspective. A small selection should contain Wolfgang Pfüller, "Der Tod Jesu – Manifestation der göttlichen Heilsmacht, nicht Grund des menschlichen Heils," *Münchener theologische Zeitschrift* 53 (2002): 236-250; Ralf Stolina, "Zur Heilsbedeutung des Todes Jesu," *Neue Zeitschrift für Systematische Theologie und Religionsphilosophie* 44 (2002): 89-106; Harald Schöndorf, "Warum mußte Jesus leiden? Eine neue Konzeption der Soteriologie," *Zeitschrift für katholische Theologie* 124 (2002): 440-467; see further http://www.theologie-systematisch.de/christologie/11passion.htm. and http://stauros.webhotel.be/ [cited 31 May 2006].

[2] Scott McKnight, "Jesus and his Death: Some Recent Scholarship," *CR:BS* 9 (2001): 185-228; see also Idem, *Jesus and His Death. Historiography, the Historical Jesus and Atonement Theory* (Baltimore MD: Baylor University Press, 2005).

important to realise that method determines the outcome. He summarizes scholarly opinion as follows: "there is a near-consensus that Jesus knew he was going to die, that he knew it would be at the hands of those who opposed what he was saying and doing, and that he predicted such a death – in various images, to his chosen few, but with enough polyvalence that specifics are hard to determine with probability" (216-217). Second, on the scale of what scholars would *theologically* ascribe to the historical Jesus, five perceptions can be distinguished: (1) unintended and shocking death, (2) heroic and exemplary death, (3) death of a martyr (prophet, righteous sufferer, atoning sacrifice for the people), (4) self-conscious assumption of the eschatological woes, for some as "the first," and for others in a "vicarious role," (5) Jesus' intentional self-claim that involves his death as having atoning significance for his people or for the world. Although these issues are not always directly inspired by Markan exegesis, something quite similar could be said about theological interpretations of Mark.

The starting point for exegetical approaches to the Gospel of Mark should be the Markan text itself. But scholars are aware that discovering the meaning of a text is a dialogical event and involves the whole process of how people reach understanding. The general rule that interpretation is not an objective and neutral enterprise undertaken in a vacuum, is especially true with regard to central themes such as the meaning of Jesus' death (in Mark). One inevitably brings in one's personal history and pre-understanding.

To make one position in this paper clear from the beginning: the meaning of Jesus' death in Mark is multiple because the answer to that question also depends on the personal situation of the real reader. Before I start my exposition with what is probably a rather well known diagram I want to stress that this position does not mean that subjectivism would be the right scientific attitude. On the contrary, my approach is a claim for reading the text of Mark as a narrative, i.e. a story which permanently and critically confronts the reader with his/her own point of view. It is my conviction that this critical function of the gospel is possible because of the multiple meaning of Jesus' death that is offered to the reader by the openness Mark himself created within the story.

The diagram I propose as representing the literary theory for my reading process is found in B. van Iersel's commentary on Mark.[3] It rightly corrects the well-known one-dimensional scheme of S. Chatman (from author towards reader) in a twofold way: the starting point of interpretation is not on the side of the author but on the side of the reader, and the *real* reader (and not only the implied reader) becomes an active participant in the process.

[3] Bas van Iersel, *Mark. A Reader-response Commentary* (JSNT SS 164; Sheffield: Sheffield Academic Press, 1998).

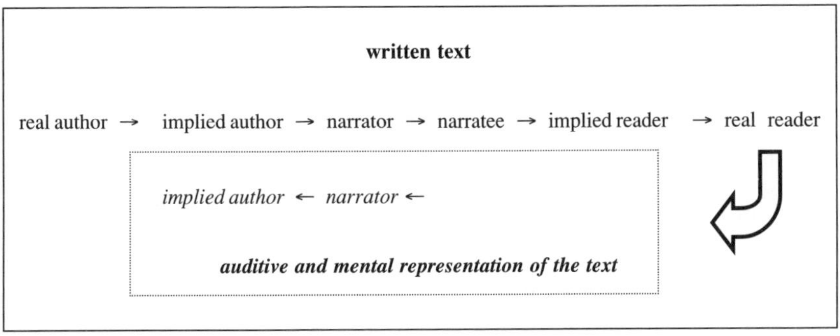

This scheme could be seen in combination with the insight of scholars who are more concerned with the semantics of a text. They make a distinction between three levels of communication: level 1 is the communication between characters in the text (actorial communication); level 2 contains all communication between the implied author and the implied reader (narrative communication); level 3 is the dialogue where the real reader dialogues with the text (enunciative communication).[4] It is on this third level that real readers "make" different final interpretations of the same text. But although it is accepted nowadays that the reader has gained the place s/he deserves in exegesis, this reader is mostly the implied reader. R.M. Fowler and E. Struthers Malbon, each in their own way, have rigorously applied these insights from narrative criticism in their exegesis of Mark.[5]

A. Yarbro Collins added the dimension of the real "original" readers who read the text and she elaborated how they would have understood the titles for Jesus according to their own background (Jewish or Greco-Roman).[6] What she has demonstrated is particularly interesting and should in fact be applied again and again for every different and new reader situation. The same is true for the "commentary" on Mark by Peter

[4] For a short description (with reference to G. Philips, *Semeia* 26 [1983]: 23-56), see Patrick Chatelion Counet, "Paroimiai (John 16:25): A Post-Hermeneutical Model," *Philosophical Hermeneutics and Biblical Exegesis* (ed. P. Pokorný and J. Roskovec; Wissenschaftliche Untersuchungen zum Neuen Testament 153; Tübingen, 2002), 252-269, note especially p. 263.

[5] Robert M. Fowler, *Let the Reader Understand*, Minneapolis: Fortress; for Malbon, see below.

[6] Adela Yarbro Collins, "Mark and His Readers: The Son of God among Jews," *Harvard Theological Review* 92 (19990: 393-408; "Mark and His Readers: The Son of God among Greeks and Romans," *HTR* 93 (2000): 85-100.

G. Bolt[7], who analysed the suppliant stories in Mark. Studies like the ones of Yarbro Collins or Bolt confirm that the meaning of a text is created by real readers and their contexts and that this is not only a hypothetical or theoretical possibility, but real practice. They show that there are more meanings possible in one text. I quote from Ruth A. Reese:[8]

> It is no use pretending, fortunately, that all readers read the same way, for they do not. And it is these differences among readers that provide such a variety of interpretations, not only in biblical studies but in all of the disciplines. Different readers bring new backgrounds and perceptions to their reading, and these influence the way they read, the way they view the text, and the method they use to think about it when they consider how they read. Modern literary theory portrays new understandings of readers and the role they have in interpreting and understanding – namely reading – a text.

The role of the *real* reader has been underestimated in critical exegesis, in historical criticism by the claim of objectivity as in narrative criticism by the priority of the implied reader. Of course, most if not all authors rightly warn that one has to understand the text in its original context in order to better understand it today. But there is something like a hermeneutical circle: when we try to understand a text in its original context we always do it from our present perspective. So I think every interpretation always has to reckon with the present situation of the interpreter.

> What then should we do if we want to explain and understand a narrative text, and – let us make it more concrete – the text about the death of Jesus in Mark's Gospel? First, some preliminary questions should be answered. Or better: they should at least be brought to the attention of the exegete, because the answers are not always clear. Where do you stand theologically? How do you think about the historical Jesus research? In what sense is it determining your insight in the evaluation and judgment about Jesus' sayings about his death? How do you see

[7] Peter G. Bolt, *Jesus' Defeat of Death. Persuading Mark's Early Readers* (SNTS MS 125; Cambridge: Cambridge University Press, 2003).The flesh-and-blood reader of the first century is the one who is confronted with the text. The interesting thing is that the whole perspective of death in Mark 14-16 is seen against the background of the antecedents on the death in Mark 1-13 (the author analyses thirteen passages of suppliants). Bolt takes as his paradigm the book of Mary Ann Beavis (1989). Other attempts to situate Mark in its original context are made by Whitney T. Shiner, *Proclaiming the Gospel. First-Century Performance of Mark* (Harrisburg – London – New York: Trinity Press International, 2003); Brian J. Incigneri, *The Gospels to the Romans. The Setting and Rhetoric of Mark's Gospel* (Biblical Interpretation Series 65; Leiden – Boston: Brill, 2003).

[8] Ruth Anne Reese, *Writing Jude. The Reader, the Text, and the Author in Constructs of Power and Desire* (Biblical Interpretation Series 51; Leiden – Boston – Köln: Brill, 2000), 45.

> the relationship between the Hebrew Bible and the New Testament? Are you satisfied with a literary or a historical answer? Or is theological language a necessity? Do you think the problem of Jesus' death is relevant for people today? And if so, for believers only or as well for non-Christians and how do these interact? Are you standing in a certain reading tradition and what is your relationship towards that tradition (critical, positive, negative)? Do you have pastoral responsibility? In which socio-political or economic context do you live? The word "meaning" is affected by the responses to all these and more questions. I am convinced that these questions often play a role before one starts thinking about Jesus' death. Becoming aware of one's own personal point of view on all these issues is the first step scholars should take. My second point is that I would propose we not act as though these contexts do not exist. Rather, I believe it is useful to clarify them and to bring them in in the theological debate. Just as we need historical criticism in order to purge our pre-critical understanding of the past, we need "theological criticism" in order to understand better our pre-understanding about the sources of (for instance Christian) religion.

Much theological meaning of the death of Jesus in Mark is created by a limited analysis of only one or a couple of verses of the Gospel, especially 10:45 and/or 14:24.[9] My purpose is to describe how meaning originates when a reader listens to the whole story. I am aware that this is *my* reading and that other readings are possible, but I am convinced that the meaning of Jesus' death is construed while reading the whole text, and not so much by a tradition-historical or redaction-critical analysis of a couple of verses. It is obvious that I will be talking about the narrative meaning: there is no meaning to the death of Jesus in Mark that comes to us from outside the narrative.[10] The meaning is something we create in dialogue with the text. Here are some elements of my pre-understanding:

[9] So rightly McKnight, *Jesus and his Death*, 201-204, p. 201: "One cannot settle into thinking that we need only look at Mark 10.45 and then the last supper traditions,... discern which words – if any – are authentic, interpret and move on"; Christoph Niemand, "Zur Heilsbedeutung des Todes Jesu. Historisch-rekonstruktive und bibeltheologische Thesen und ihr biographischer Ort," *Leben – Erleben – Begreifen. Zur Verbindung von Person und Theologie. Festgabe S.J. Singer* (ed. F. Gmainer-Pranzl; Linzer Philosophisch-Theologische Beiträge 5; Frankfurt/Main: Peter Lang, 2001) 59-75, p. 73: "*Markus* kennt die Heilstod-Rede in kerygmatischer Form (Mark 10,45 und 14,24), löst sie aber vor allem in eine narrative Struktur auf (Weg zum Kreuz, Schweigegebote bei Wundern, Unverständnis der Jünger, offener Evangelien-Schluss)." For a similar remark about the Gospel of Luke, see Susan R. Garrett, "The Meaning of Jesus' Death in Luke," *Word &World* 12 (1992): 11-16, p. 11.

[10] See also Michael L. Cook, *Christology as a Narrative Quest* (Zaccheus Studies: Theology; Collegeville: Liturgical Press, 1997), especially 67-108: "A Biblical Image: 'The Beloved Son' in the Gospel of Mark." A very good synthesis of the implications of narrative exegesis for Christology can be found in Adolphe Gesché, "Pour une identité narrative de Jésus," *Revue théologique de Louvain* 30 (1999): 153-179, 336-356.

(1) I do not think the *meaning* of the death of Jesus can ever be or become a system or a fact based on objective events (see also the end of this article).[11] For this reason I prefer those interpretations of Jesus' death that create the possibility of a continuing dialogue between the reader and the text. (2) Mark's gospel narrative consists of a mixture of theology and history which can be explained by the origin of it: there is no resurrection experience without the historical Jesus, and there would be no gospel story about Jesus if there had not been "paschal imagination" (Sandra M. Schneiders). Therefore the appropriate way for reading the gospel is to look for the narrative truth (Camille Focant).[12] This option, like all options, has its limitations, but is, on the other hand, an enrichment, since we all know that meaning is not only based on historical reconstruction or study of literary intertextuality.

The story of Jesus and God and the other characters

A narrative consists of the exposition of relations between characters. In her 1999 article on "reflected Christology" Elizabeth Struthers Malbon offers a map of all Markan transcendental and human characters and their relationship to Jesus.[13] She rightly makes a distinction between the unique way Jesus as a character considers himself in relation to God and

[11] Niemand, *Zur Heilsbedeutung des Todes Jesu*, 75: "Sinn macht das alles nur *als glaubendes Nach-denken des Weges Jesu.* Wird es einfach als Faktum und System hingestellt, das in sich stehen und wahr sein soll, dann wird daraus leicht die zynisch-brutale Veranstaltung eines blutrünstigen Gottes, der Menschenopfer / Kinderopfer verlangt, um irgendeine verletzte Ordnung oder Ehre wieder hergestellt zu sehen."

[12] For an application of this approach to the passion narrative, see Camille Focant, "Vérité historique et vérité narrative. Le récit de la Passion en Marc," *Bible et histoire. Écriture, interprétation et action dans le temps* (ed. M. Hermans and P. Sauvage; Connaître et croire 6; Namur [Belgium]: Presses Universitaires de Namur, 2000), 83-104, p. 102: "En effet, la vérité évangélique va bien au-delà d'une description de faits sur le mode de la chronique, puisque les Évangiles entendent développer pour le lecteur le sens symbolique de ces faits, celui par lequel dans ces faits singuliers se déploie une portée universelle. Ce faisant, la vérité évangélique se propose au lecteur qui reste libre d'adhérer à cette proposition de sens ou de la récuser. Et il convient d'observer que le jugement de vérité historique n'est qu'un des éléments, et peut-être pas le plus important, entrant en ligne de compte pour la réponse que le lecteur apportera à la proposition évangélique."

[13] Elizabeth Struthers Malbon, "'Reflected Christology': An Aspect of Narrative 'Christology' in the Gospel of Mark," *Perspectives in Religious Studies* 26 (1999): 127-145. Compare Idem, "The Christology of Mark's Gospel: Narrative Christology and the Markan Jesus," *Who Do You Say I Am? Essays in Christology. In Honor of Jack Dean Kingsbury* (ed. M.A. Powell and D.R. Bauer; Louisville KY: Westminster John Knox Press, 1999), 33-48.

the description of this relationship by the narrator whose focus is on Jesus as the Son of God. Jesus for instance diverts attention away from himself to God and gives a new meaning to traditional understandings. The narrator has a different point of view because he is also interested in how other characters think about Jesus, although he shares the idea that Jesus' relationship with God is essential to the gospel. The process of how God and Jesus interact in Mark is very important for the orientation of the reader who is looking for the meaning of the death of Jesus.[14] The death of Jesus is the culmination of a conflict. This conflict is a two-level phenomenon in Mark: it takes place at a transcendental level and it develops in the world of human characters.[15] The deepest theological level is the transcendental one (though in the story it is in the background): this means that Jesus can first of all be considered as the main focal point of the conflict between God and Satan. This conflict does not start with the passion story. The whole ministry of Jesus – not only his passion and death but also his words and deeds – is to be placed in the context of this conflict. The narrator has created the story in such a way that from the beginning the reader is biased since he knows whose side Jesus is on: Jesus and God are on the same side.[16]

The role of the prologue in this regard is fundamental. The first verse, the title of the book, makes clear that the central theme of the Gospel is Jesus in relationship to God. It has been pointed out several times that the prologue is meant to convince the reader by the use of four arguments that Jesus is Christ and Son of God: the Scripture announces his coming (vv. 2-3), John the Baptist says Jesus is stronger (vv. 4-8), the baptism with the voice form heaven (vv. 9-11), and the victory of Jesus in the desert over Satan (vv. 12-13).[17] From a reader perspective it is

[14] Paul Danove, "A Rhetorical Analysis of the Characterization of God in Mark," *Novum Testamentum* 53 (2001): 12-30; repr. in Idem, *Rhetoric of Characterization of God, Jesus and Jesus' Disciples in the Gospel of Mark* (JSNT SS 290; New York: Clark/Continuum, 2005), 53-95, contains a profound analysis of the role God plays as a character in the story and focuses on the relationship with Jesus and its effect on the broader characterization of the other characters as well.

[15] One should read again James M. Robinson, *The Problem of History in Mark* (Studies in Biblical Theology 21; London: SCM – Naperville IL: Allenson, 1957, [4]1971), 21-32 (on Mark 1:1-13); Elizabeth Struthers Malbon, "'Reflected Christology,'" 130.

[16] It is striking that in Mark the word "God" is used predominantly by Jesus. Out of the 46 instances the narrator uses it in 1:1, 14; 2:12; 15:43, the demons in 1:24; 3:11; 5:7, the opponents in 2:7, and the centurion in 15:39.

[17] In the words of Danove, "Characterization of God," 26: "The direct or indirect insinuation of Jesus into every aspect of the characterization of God in 1:1-15 engenders an indelible bond between the characters, God and Jesus, that precludes any understanding of either character without immediate reference to the other."

also clear how the dynamics of the text direct the readers in the process of understanding. While from the beginning the reader is aware of the true position of Jesus with regard to God (and Satan), the characters in the Gospel on the contrary have to discover who Jesus is. This additional information for the reader, vis-à-vis the characters in the Gospel, is questioned through the behaviour of the other characters in such a manner that the audience itself becomes uncertain about the identity of Jesus as Son of God. The audience becomes rather confused by the ambiguous role of the disciples, and is thus led to recognize that it probably does not understand any more or any better than the disciples or, at least, it questions itself about the proper understanding of what it means to confess Jesus as Son of God. The opinion of the readers about Jesus is indeed mainly created by the round character of the disciples who are constantly torn between enthusiastic following and fearful distance.[18]

The mixture of positive and negative elements in the role of the disciples has been interpreted since W. Wrede (1901) as part of the messianic secret.[19] This secrecy motif could be formulated in a positive way in that, of all the characters, only God unambiguously calls Jesus his "Son" (1:11; 9:7). All other instances where Jesus is called Son (of God) are problematic because of Jesus' commandment to be silent to the demons (3:11 and 5:7), his unexpected answer about the Son of Man (in the trial scene 14:61-62) or the ambiguous saying by the centurion (15:39). Jesus as a character also knows he is the Son, but he does everything to "deflect" it when other characters (in the line of the narrator!) recognize him as such. He acts as if he wants to express the idea that all honour and merit for the title do not belong to him but rather to God. This kind of reaction of Jesus shows the story is oriented toward a new understanding or a new significance of God. It is not unfair to say about the gospel of Mark that the real issue of the story is not so much the problem of understanding how Jesus has become Son of God, but how one can believe in a God and understand a God who accepts Jesus as his Son. From a reader response critical point of view the secret about Jesus is an invitation to discover how God acts through

[18] Could it be possible to say that the readers through this learning process get involved in better understanding the deflective Christology of Jesus (his reactions in response to what others are saying about him)?

[19] On the link between Christology and discipleship in the framework of the messianic secret, see now Christopher M. Tuckett, "The Disciples and the Messianic Secret in Mark," *Fair Play: Diversity and Conflicts in Early Christianity. Essays in Honour of Heikki Räisänen* (ed. I. Dunderberg, et al.; Leiden – Boston – Köln: Brill 2002), 131-150.

Jesus and in Jesus. A *new* understanding of God implies that the image of God enacted by Jesus is a confrontation and a challenge to the reader. In the story several elements orient the reader towards a rethinking of God's way of acting in the world. We have already mentioned the tension between the narrator's emphasis on Jesus as Son of God and at the same time on the deflection of Jesus when he is recognized as such. Another element is the attitude of the enemies and the other characters who are afraid it might be true that God is acting in Jesus. Their role and function is sometimes underestimated, but as opponents they reveal the opposite view of how Jesus is thinking and thus, by contrast, they are of great help for the reader in understanding who Jesus then might be. More specifically, as they reveal their own portrayal and interpretation of God through their discussions with Jesus and their actions against him, they make clear to the reader that the God of Jesus differs from theirs: "Characters, through their reaction to Jesus, establish relationships opposing him; and these negative relationships ultimately accrue to God by way of Jesus' positive alignment with God."[20]

Briefly, constantly the reader is challenged about how the idea that Jesus acts as Son of God can be in harmony with Jesus' refusal to be recognized, the disciples' misunderstanding of Jesus and the negative reactions of other characters. What kind of God is it and what is Jesus' position in relation to the transcendental level if on the earthly level Jesus and the people around him act as they do? The story on the human level is meant to direct the reader's attention towards the transcendental level where the conflict has to be resolved by the audience as well, because "the central character, Jesus, continually draws the disciples, the fallible followers, [I would add the enemies] and the implied audience into the broader story of God."[21] The defeat of Jesus on the human level is obvious: the enemies are the winners of the conflict when Jesus is crucified. But what happens in the transcendental world?

God and the passion of Jesus

It is obvious that the conflict that leads to Jesus' death does not start at the beginning of the passion story but is already present during the

[20] Danove, "Characterization of God," 24.

[21] Malbon, "'Reflected Christology,'" 136.

ministry of Jesus. Thus the search for the meaning of Jesus' death cannot be limited to the passion story and isolated from the rest of the gospel. If one were to conclude that God is present at the moment of Jesus' death, He must be identical to the God who is present during his lifetime. It is said by many authors that at the cross Jesus' identity is revealed. At that moment the reader is told who Jesus is, since for the first time his true identity is understood by nobody else but a Roman soldier. Mark 15:39 is therefore said to be the "climax of Mark's Christology."[22] But what does that mean? What more do we in fact know about him and about God at the moment of his death? Surely, Morna Hooker correctly summarizes the majority opinion of biblical scholars when she writes that "in dying he is recognized as Messiah and acknowledged as God's Son."[23] But I wonder if in general too much emphasis has been laid on this single moment of recognition by the Roman centurion (even if one disregards the possibility of irony in this verse). This overemphasis has at least two consequences: (1) too often the death is disconnected from the life of Jesus and (2) full attention is given to the significance Jesus would have given to his death, while the significance of the death of Jesus for the understanding *of God* is neglected. The question "What kind of Messiah?" has had far more attention than the question "What kind of God?" is present at the cross. For the readers, however, – note that they are the only witnesses of the centurion's words since the disciples are not present! – the moment of Jesus' death is not an isolated event. They are not only already informed about the transcendental struggle concerning Jesus (God versus Satan), but they are also told about the possibility, even certainty, that Jesus will be crucified (cf. below). Jesus' death is no surprise for the readers. For them the real issue under discussion when Jesus is dying at the cross is *God*: the question of whether one can believe if and how God can be present in Jesus' death. As we will see, in the story Jesus himself gives signals that the presence of God is not a rock solid. The reader becomes part of this uncertainty and thus through Jesus will be challenged about what faith in God is all about. The narrative climax

[22] Michael Bird, "The Crucifixion of Jesus as the Fulfillment of Mark 9:1," *Trinity Journal NS* 24 (2003): 23-36, p. 29; for many other references, see Geert Van Oyen, "Irony as Propaganda in Mark 15:39," *Persuasion and Dissuasion in Early Christianity, Ancient Judaism, and Hellenism* (ed. P. van der Horst, et al.; Contributions to Biblical Exegesis and Theology, 33; Leuven – Paris – Dudley MA: Peeters, 2003), 125-141.

[23] Morna D. Hooker, *Not Ashamed of the Gospel. New Testament Interpretations of the Death of Christ*, (Carlisle: The Paternoster Press, 1994), 65.

on the transcendental level at 15:39 is about God. I could not find a better summary than in Christopher Tuckett's *Christology*:[24]

> The narrative seems to be emphasising starkly that God is to be seen in this figure of powerlessness, weakness and death. This too is what Mark's narrative has been leading up to as a climax. It is the moment when Jesus' true identity is seen in its clearest light and hence shows what it means to be "Son of God." But it also shows something about the God who lies behind the whole story, who defines and accepts Jesus as his Son, and who reveals himself – on the cross. The very first line of Mark's Gospel defines the terms of the story that is to come: Jesus *is* Son of God. But what sonship means, *and* what "God" means, is determined by the story itself. It is thus very much the case that Mark offers a *narrative* Christology. The story is vital and indispensable for his message. It is almost as if Mark is aware that christological terms can be multivalent. Hence he writes his story to show what he regards as the true significance of words that can be spoken. Jesus is the Christ, the Son of God. But the nature and kingship, sonship and of divinity, are all given a stark new meaning by Mark's story, especially by his account of Jesus' death on the cross. Mark's Jesus is perhaps closest to the "crucified God" of some modern theologians.

If the story of Jesus' life and death cannot be separated from the rethinking of God, then it is very important to see what is new about God in the life of Jesus in order to better understand what could be revealed about God at the moment of Jesus' death. It would take too much time to analyse in detail the story line of Jesus' ministry before his death, but I am suggesting here that the terminology readers use to describe and interpret Jesus' message and deeds in the story with reference to God, will influence the way they will try to understand the meaning of his death. My reading is that Jesus reveals the God of Israel as a liberator (for instance 2:1-3:6; 6:34-44; 8:1-9), that the character God through Jesus has other ideas about faith than the existing "orthodox" religious authorities have (8:14-16; 11), that He forgives sins of those who are not forgiven by the authorities (2:1-12), that He heals and touches women (5:24-34; 7:24-30), children (5:34-43), Jews and non-Jews (7:31-37), takes away fear, crosses boundaries that separate people geographically, historically or religiously. The portrayal of God manifested in Jesus is one of a God who is present with those who are denying themselves and taking up their cross (8:34), losing their lives for Jesus' sake (8:35), serving and being the slave of all (10:43-44). The Markan Jesus uses the

[24] Christopher M. Tuckett, *Christology and the New Testament. Jesus and His Earliest Followers* (Louisville KY: Westminster/John Knox, 2001), 116.

expression βασιλεία τοῦ θεοῦ (1:15; 4:11; 4:26, 30; 9:1, 47; 10:14-25; 12:34; 14:23) for the reality that is being realized when people act and live according to this belief. In his life Jesus consciously opts for the marginalized groups in society (2:17; "little ones" 9:42). This βασιλεία τοῦ θεοῦ announced and proclaimed by Jesus as the main message of the gospel (1:14-15) is proclaimed with authority (1:22, and especially the discussion in 11:27-33) and therefore threatens the position of the authorities. It is not surprising that the evangelist has interwoven between these actions and words about the kingdom several elements that make the whole narrative stream towards the death of Jesus.[25] The death of Jesus is thus integrated into the story that precedes it.

Several examples of this phenomenon can be given. Because they are well known I mention some of them briefly. Jesus, for instance, corrects the disciples when they consider him as the Christ only on the basis of his miracles and without taking into account the passion (8:14-21, 27-33). The fate of John the Baptist serves as a witness to Jesus (1:14; 6:14-29).[26] In some passages, like in 2:18-22 the passion theme and the kingdom of God interface with each other.[27] The evangelist has added remarks on the plans of the authorities to destroy Jesus (3:6; 11:18; 12:13; compare 2:6, 16, 24; 3:22; 7:1-3; 8:11; 10:2). Judas is said to be the one "who betrayed him" (3:14). The impression for the reader is that from the beginning Jesus' death has coloured Mark's characterization of Jesus as if this death could not be avoided or as if his mission was to be killed. The main elements of this "necessity" are of course given in the two sayings in which Jesus himself expresses the purpose of his death (10:45 and 14:24), the three specific passion predictions, the fulfilment of OT quotations (e.g., 15:24, 29, 34 and Ps 22),[28] the linking

[25] On the anticipation of the passion motif, see McKnight, "Jesus and His Death," 201-202. For a redaction critical approach of these passages see Lorenz Oberlinner, *Todeserwartung und Todesgewissheit Jesu. Zum Problem einer historischen Begründung* (Stuttgarter Biblische Beiträge 10; Stuttgart: Katholisches Bibelwerk, 1980). For emphasis on the section Mark 8:27-10:45, see also Ernest Best, *Mark: The Gospel as Story* (Studies of the New Testament and its World; Edinburgh: T&T Clark, 1983, ^{2}1988), 66-68, and many others.

[26] Extensively documented in Hooker, *Not Ashamed of the Gospel*, 48-51.

[27] See M. Bird, *The Crucifixion of Jesus as the Fulfillment of Mark 9:1*; the author also mentions in this regard 14:22-25; 14:62; 15:1-40. I do not agree that "Mark's kingdom theology directs us *unequivocally* to the cross as the central symbol of its arrival" (35; italics mine).

[28] Howard C. Kee, "The Function of Scriptural Quotations and Allusions in Mark 11–16," *Jesus und Paulus. Festschrift für Werner Georg Kümmel zum 70. Geburtstag* (ed. E.E. Ellis and E. Grässer; Göttingen: Vandenhoeck & Ruprecht, 1975), 165-188.

of the disciples' suffering with Jesus' suffering. Now the way we interpret all this is decisive for the way we interpret Jesus' death in Mark. One could for instance say that God is responsible for the death of Jesus, or that he wanted it, and that all men are sinners and are saved by Jesus' death, or that the kingdom of God is coming through his death. All these formulae are of course interpretations of the text. My reading and interpretation is that the story does not tell us that soteriology is implemented as an automatism by Jesus' death. It is a story "to be continued..." by those who are called disciples in the story, by anyone who has ears and wants to listen (4:9), by readers who read the text till the end. Jesus' death is saving, but not because God wanted it, nor because Jesus himself says that he is giving his life as a ransom for many, nor because Mark or Jesus tell us that the OT is fulfilled, nor because Jesus would have been innocent (see e.g. in 14:5-65; 14:66-72; 15:1-15[29]). All these elements might possibly be discovered in the text but they are not the ultimate answer of the story. Real understanding of Jesus' death – according to the story – necessitates the meeting of one permanent requirement: to follow Jesus.

In the three passion predictions Mark shows that Jesus went freely to Jerusalem and knew what would happen. And what happened – he says – is not against the will of God. But he also emphasizes that this divine perspective never excludes Jesus' own responsibility which is illustrated by his own actions: e.g., the cleansing of the temple, the discussions with the disciples and his enemies, the last meal. Jesus as an individual acts on the human level as God's agent. The so-called "divine" δεῖ (only once in the passion predictions) tightens the link between Jesus and God (8:31). It is meant as a warning to the readers that they should not too easily accept "as normal" the fact that Jesus will be crucified, since anything that happens to Jesus has consequences for the way of thinking about God! There has been a lot of writing about the divine δεῖ in 8:31. It is of course a redactional and theological interpretation of the evangelist, but the term "divine" can be misleading and is theologically dubiously understood when God is seen as having planned what would happen in the future and when a kind of inevitable fate is meant. There is no need to interpret the role of God from such a magical conception with the transcendental level controlling the human level. The verse is better considered as the "translation" on the transcendental level of what was already decided by Jesus' opponents (3:6)

[29] For all those interpretations names of authors could be added. And more interpretations could be given depending on the authors' preference of the pericopes or sayings.

and was not going to be avoided by Jesus. If Jesus was going to Jerusalem he would be confronted with the plans of the enemies and he would be challenged to remain faithful to what he was doing.[30] Jesus is never a kind of robot in the plan of God. If there really are characters who deliberately want to eliminate Jesus it is his enemies and not God.[31] The three passion predictions do not explain why Jesus died and thus do not contain the meaning of the death.[32] The concern of the narrator is rather that the reader should understand that the protagonist in everything he did and in everything that would happen to him was supported by the divine Father. That was the belief of Jesus. And the fact that these sayings are inserted within the story of Jesus' life, is clearly meant to say that Jesus' ministry itself is at the basis of his death, and not a kind of plan God would have had in mind. There is altogether at least a double effect on the reader. First, Jesus' death does not come as a surprise since he knew what would happen; he is conscious about what would happen and whatever he does will be his personal choice. Second, and more shocking, is that God will not be absent at that very moment since he has not been absent in the rest of Jesus' life.

I want to repeat again that I am not interested here in the reliability of this interpretation on the historical Jesus level. Or let me be more specific. I do not think that all that is said above provides us with a better understanding of how Jesus thought. It is a construction of the early Christians to be dated after the passion event and the resurrection experience. The development of this interpretation started after Jesus' death. Maybe there is a connection with the way Jesus thought about all this but it is almost impossible and theologically irrelevant to reconstruct it in a very precise manner.[33]

30 See Van Iersel, *Mark. A Reader-response Commentary*, (at 8:31).

31 For a balanced view on the historical responsibility for Jesus' death, see Gerd Theissen and Annette Merz, *Der historische Jesus. Ein Lehrbuch* (Göttingen: Vandenhoeck & Ruprecht, 1996, [3]2001), §15 ("Die Passion"). Leander E. Keck, *Who Is Jesus? History in Perfect Tense* (Studies on Personalities of the New Testament; Edinburgh: T&T Clark, 2001), 126: "Whatever the exegetical and historical problems may be, the trial narratives not only exonerate Pilate and indict the Jerusalem priesthood, they also show that Jesus was put to death deliberately by persons in power, religious as well imperial."

32 Hooker, *Not Ashamed of the Gospel*, 56-57: "Mark emphasizes the necessity for suffering – both Jesus' own and that of his disciples, but he says almost nothing about its meaning. It is necessary for Jesus to die; it is written that he must suffer. But *why*?"

33 Oberlinner, *Todeserwartung und Todesgewissheit*, 166: "Es muss zumindest offen bleiben, mit welchem Grad von Gewissheit Jesus den Tod auf sich zukommen sah. Eine selbstverständliche Hinordnung des Wirkens und damit verknüpft der Erwartungen Jesu auf seine Hinrichtung steht zu stark unter dem Einfluss der rückblickenden Orientierung am Kreuz." For an "update" of Oberlinners position, see Idem, "Der Weg Jesu zum Leiden," *Jesus von Nazaret – Spuren und Konturen* (ed. L. Schenke, et al.; Stuttgart: Kohlhammer, 2004), 275-318. Strongly Paula Fredriksen, "What Does

The meaning of Jesus' death

By turning our attention to God as a character in the story it seems that Jesus' death cannot be disconnected from the way Jesus reveals God. The death of Jesus is a *theo*-logically orientated item. Many answers have been given to give the death a meaning so that it would be understandable and/or acceptable. We have already mentioned the interpretation of the divine δεῖ. Most of these answers are based on the elaboration of a single theme that one has discovered in one verse or a couple of verses in the gospel. Morna Hooker has enumerated some of these "solutions" in the Chapter on Mark of *New Testament Interpretations of the Death of Christ* (1994): "The death of Jesus is the beginning of something new: it is the ransom which creates a new people, the means of establishing a new covenant, the event which signifies the destruction of the temple and the beginning of a new form of worship."[34] While she recognizes all of them in Mark's gospel, other authors opt for one of those alternatives. The common aspect of all those answers is that they are on a rational, ideological or – if one prefers – theological level, not on the practical level. I wonder if for the story-teller "Mark" things might not be different.

First of all, when reading the Gospel as a whole a different theme pops up. It is mentioned in the next sentence of Hooker's text quoted above and it concludes the section on Mark: "But those who belong to his new community are those who are prepared to follow Jesus in the way of discipleship, who are not ashamed of him and of his call to take up the cross. The death and resurrection of Jesus do not absolve the disciple from the need to obey that call but reaffirm it. His death is not a substitute, but an exemplar. The true disciples of Jesus will still be found, trudging along the road that leads to a cross, following their crucified and risen Lord."[35] I agree with this conclusion and I even think

Jesus Have to Do with Christ?," *Christology: Memory, Inquiry, Practice* (ed. A.M. Clifford and A.J. Godzieba; Maryknoll NY: Orbis Books, 2003), 3-17, p. 12: "Whatever the criteria of legitimacy churches use to validate their christologies – and different churches will judge by different criteria – what the historical Jesus 'would have thought' cannot be one of them. Intentionalist fundamentalism is both silly history and bad theology."

[34] Hooker, *Not Ashamed of the Gospel*, 67. Compare Best, *The Gospel as Story*, 71: "Looking back we see that the death of Jesus has not only a place in the purpose of God but it is set in relation to all people who may benefit from it. Jesus bears their judgement; he ransoms them from sin; he brings them into God's community as those who have previously been left out."

[35] Hooker, *Not Ashamed of the Gospel*, 67.

that it has been mentioned in many studies.[36] The idea is not new. In Mark discipleship and Christology are linked together. What I am arguing is that for a real reader who reads the story of Mark this theme comes in the *first* place. It is part of the "Golgotha hermeneutic" as Leander E. Keck calls it. The paradox of serving in order to be the greatest should be on the top of the list of possible interpretations. It says that the one who lives according to the gospel and who follows Jesus will have to reckon with the extreme event of being killed because of the commitment to the gospel. The gospel is full of paradoxes illustrating that the kingdom of God is entered or experienced by living a way of life. It is summarized in 12:28-34 where the commandment of loving God and one's neighbour are united since "there is no other commandment than these" (v. 31). "This is much more important than all whole burnt offerings and sacrifices" (v. 33). And after Jesus had answered the scribe "You are not far from the kingdom of God," the evangelist adds: "After that no one dared to ask him anything" (v. 34).

I know (or presume) that a reading of Mark that emphasizes that the meaning of Jesus' death is in the first place known by experience will raise all kind of questions among theologians and exegetes who are mostly looking for explanation and understanding which fit in a theological framework. They will object: "Where is the theology here? Where is the soteriology?" Mostly these questions mean: What do you do with the atonement theology in Mark 10:45 and 14:24? I limit myself here to 10:45. The question is first of all if Mark 10:45 is really about the (soteriological) meaning of Jesus' death alone in the sense of atonement offering.[37] In the classical formulation it sounds for instance like this: "By laying down his life for a humankind enslaved to sin, Jesus fulfilled the saying about the Servant in Is 53:10-11. Jesus had paid the universal debt: he had given his life to redeem all others. But this is metaphor, not crude commerce. The death of Jesus, in the Father's purpose and in the Son's acceptance, was a gesture of sheer love. Any suggestion that the death of the Son was, in

[36] Many authors mentioned the indissoluble link between following Jesus on the road to the cross and the way of true understanding of Jesus' death. See for instance Oberlinner, *Todeserwartung und Todesgewissheit*, 168-172. Worth reading is the section in Keck, *Who Is Jesus?*, 140-150 ("A Golgotha Hermeneutic"). The idea is also mentioned in many books about spirituality or pastoral theology.

[37] For this idea, see Johan S. Vos, "De plaatsvervangende zoendood van Jezus in de synoptische evangeliën. Een bijdrage over het debat over de verzoening," *Gereformeerd Theologisch Tijdschrift* 98 (1998): 141-157 [unfortunately in Dutch]. The meaning of 10:45 depends on how one sees the relationship with Isa 53 or other texts and how one interprets this instance of intertextuality.

any sense at all, literal payment of a debt, the placating of an offended God, is blasphemy. God is ever motivated by love, not 'justice.'"[38] I agree on the metaphoric character of the verse, but does the context allow for such an interpretation alone? The pericope 10:32-45 is about following Jesus on his way to the passion. The theme of discipleship that was manifested in Mark 1–8 (for instance in the triple occurrence of a summary followed by a pericope about disciples: 1:14-15, 16-20; 3:7-12, 13-19; 6:6b, 7-13) is repeated in 8:30–10:52 in the threefold passion summary followed by sections about non-understanding of disciples and catechesis by Jesus. Each time the context of Jesus' catechesis is about the service of the disciple. See especially Mark 8:34-35, 38: "The paradigmatic role of the cross is manifest in the first saying [8:34], where it is used as a vivid symbol of the self-denial that following Jesus requires.... The first saying also assumes that this self-denial was the defining moral characteristic that took Jesus to the cross. The saying does not call on would-be disciples to follow Jesus to *his* cross in order to die with him."[39] Mark 10:45 concludes the section on following Jesus in Mark 8–10 and thus (1) the narrow soteriological meaning focusing exclusively on Jesus' death has to be broadened into a larger one about his life[40] and (2) the verse summons the disciples to take their responsibility to live according to Jesus' gospel with a possible death as its very last consequence.[41] By following Jesus and

[38] Wilfrid J. Harrington, *Mark Realistic Theologian. The Jesus of Mark* (Dublin: Columba Press, 1996, rev. ed. 2002), 117. For a survey of all possible interpretations, see McKnight, *Jesus and His Death*, 188-201. A short but comprehensible presentation of the "substitutionary atonement" and some alternatives (esp. René Girard) can be found in S. Mark Heim, "Why Does Jesus' Death Matter? Christ Crucified," *Christian Century* March 7, 2001, 12-17.

[39] Keck, *Who Is Jesus?*, 147; further on he writes: "To be a follower, then, entails more than appropriating his ideas and heeding his words; it requires also his way of being in the world – a way in which the primary opponent to be overcome is not an external enemy, as in messianism, but a power internal to the self."

[40] See especially Karl Kertelge, "Der dienende Menschensohn (Mark 10,45)," *Jesus und der Menschensohn. Für Anton Vögtle* (ed. R. Pesch et al.; Freiburg: Herder, 1975), 225-239.

[41] Because of the importance of the ransom saying in this debate I quote again from Keck, *Who Is Jesus?*, 147-148: "Jesus' death as a ransom (Mark 10:45) does not free his followers from struggling with the same drive toward self-preservation above all that he too had contended with, but it does assure them that they will indeed 'find' exactly what they 'lost' – life. In other words, the 'ransomed' ones cannot expect a better cost-benefit ratio than can the 'ransomer,' whether or not they are put to death for following him." On the saying see also Alberto de Mingo Kaminouchi, *'But it is Not So Among You.' Echoes of Power in Mark 10.32-45* (JSNT SS 249; London: T&T Clark, 2003); Otto Schwankl, *Machtwille und Dienstbereitschaft. Zur Jüngerbelehrung in Mark 10,35-45, Forschungen zum Neuen Testament und seiner Umwelt. Festschrift A. Fuchs* (ed. C. Niemand; Linzer Philosophisch-Theologische Beiträge 7; Frankfurt: Peter Lang, 2002, 235-257.

becoming a servant of all, the disciples save their lives. Jesus is going ahead of them on this road. The reader who is searching for the meaning of the death of Jesus receives a question in return: "Why would you follow Jesus on the way to Jerusalem?"

Although I called this interpretation a "practical" one, I would like to emphasize that in my view it *is* theological. Theology and praxis do not exclude each other. Through the Markan story of Jesus' life and death God himself is at stake. The death of Jesus like the death of any "innocent" person cannot be explained. The question *why* is not answered on the level of human understanding. In this regard we should mention also the texts in which Jesus himself struggles with the idea that self-denial would be in accordance with the will of God. Mark 14:36 and 15:34 are very important verses because in their own way they refer to God as the only one who eventually can "interpret" Jesus' death. In a certain sense these verses are a necessary complement to what we have said already about the "divine" δεῖ. The "must" of God's action is never an absolute certainty, not even for Jesus. In Jesus' death is manifested for the reader the deepest crisis about faith in God and at the same time a person who gives himself away. It is the moment in which the future of God himself is put on the agenda, the God in whom Jesus believed and for whom he lived.[42] There is for the reader only one possibility to really understand what the death of Jesus is about, i.e., the experience of being as remote from God as Jesus is at the moment of his death.[43] Other interpretations run the risk of ascribing to God power or insights which make Jesus less human.

[42] Oberlinner, *Todeserwartung und Todesgewissheit*, 166-167: "Damit geht es in Jesu Tod um viel mehr als nur um seine Hinrichtung; es geht um das 'Recht' Gottes. Eine Formulierung, die den Tod als nur Jesus betreffendes Ereignis und Geschick betrachtet, nur *seine* Gegenwart und Zukunft hier betroffen wähnt und die Frage seines Erfolges bzw. Scheiterns hier beantwortet sieht, kann in der Tat Jesus auswechseln. Jesus hat aber mit seinem Leben die Gegenwart und Zukunft Gottes ins Spiel gebracht, – kann dies bei seinem Tod einfach ausgeblendet werden? Wurzel und tragende Basis für die *Heils*funktion dieses Todes konnte deshalb auch einzig die 'Antwort' Gottes sein.... Konnte überhaupt jemand Jesu Tod 'deuten' ausser Gott?"

[43] In the narrative this is well illustrated by the narrative function of God's characterization. See Danove, *Rhetorical Analysis*, 28-29: "Whereas the narrative rhetoric previously [before Chapter 14] employed the apprehension of God's remoteness to encourage and confirm for the reader a profound identification of Jesus with God, it now [14:1–15:41] employs the apprehension of God's remoteness from both Jesus and the reader to encourage a more profound identification of the reader with Jesus. This deepened identification aligns the reader with Jesus in the only three explicit references to God's agency in 14:1–15:41: God will strike the shepherd [Jesus] (πατάσσω, 14:27 [cf. Zech 13:7]); God does not will to take this cup from Jesus (παραφέρω, 14:36), and God abandons Jesus (ἐγκαταλείπω, 15:43 [cf. Ps 22:1])."

Epilogue

Does God answer? It is the answer to that question which will be decisive for the disciple-readers in making their mind up about following Jesus. Before the death of Jesus the disciples were not able to follow him and the story does not tell us what happened to them after Jesus' death. The only answer given "by God" in the story is an open tomb with its interpretation by the young man, dressed in a white robe: "You are looking for Jesus of Nazareth, who was crucified. He has been raised: he is not here" (16:6). Compared to the passion story the empty tomb story is very short, quasi written as an appendix to the larger story. However, it reminds the reader that each of the three passion predictions had a similar appendix after a longer description of the passion: "and after three days he will rise again" (8:31; 9:31; 10:34). If the evangelist sees Jesus' death as (1) the last consequence of his faith in God and (2) the moment in which only God himself can continue the story, then Jesus' life and death can only turn out to be positive when God has indeed transformed the dead Jesus (not the death of Jesus!) into new life.[44] For the writer of the gospel of Mark, the short formula "he has been raised" – in Greek only one word: ἠγέρθη (16:6) – was brilliant enough to shine its light upon every word that he was going to write about Jesus' life and death and about discipleship. That was Mark's belief. But the evangelist was aware that this victorious light could never take away the shadow of Jesus' death and that therefore for him belief in the God of Israel would never be the same as it was before. From this moment on people could start to search for the meaning of Jesus' death in multiple ways. Mark's main answer is that the meaning could best be found in following Jesus (read 8:35). And since God and nobody else was able to continue the story after Jesus' death, all other human answers are a matter of never ending dynamic belief, *fides quaerens intellectum*. "Easter requires Christian theology to keep pondering the meaning of the cross for its understanding of both Jesus and the God he trusted. In

[44] Niemand, *Zur Heilsbedeutung des Todes Jesu*, 63-70: "Der Osterglaube als Voraussetzung und Ort der urchristlichen Rede von Jesu Heilstod"; Keck, *Who Is Jesus?*, 128-131 ("Resurrection and the silent Abba"); Oberlinner, *Der Weg Jesu zum Leiden*, 318: "Mit Jesu Tod schien die Sache gegen ihn, gegen seinen Anspruch und seine Botschaft von der Gottesherrschaft entschieden. Die Frage, ob mit dem Tod Fluch oder Segen zu verknüpfen sei, konnten die Jünger erst auf der Grundlage einer neuen Erfahrung entscheiden. Sie hat sich niedergeschlagen in dem Bekenntnis: Gott hat ihm auferweckt."

short, if God validated and vindicated precisely the Jesus who was executed on Golgotha, then he remains the fractured prism through which one sees into that mysterious Reality called 'God.'"[45]

[45] Keck, *Who Is Jesus,* 130; cf. 140: "Jesus' death, isolated from neither the life that preceded it nor from his resurrection that followed it, continues to be the prism through which Christian Gentiles must understand both God and themselves."

MESSIANIC EXEGESIS IN MARK'S PASSION NARRATIVE

Jocelyn McWhirter

How does the Second Evangelist interpret Israel's Scriptures with reference to Jesus? Why does Mark's Jesus describe himself as "the stone that the builders rejected," quoting Ps 118:22-23?[1] Why does he cry out the opening complaint of Ps 22 as he dies on the cross? I would like to demonstrate the possibility that a process of "messianic exegesis" lies behind these and other christological citations in Mark 11-15 – a process that allows Mark to interpret them as prophecies about the Messiah. My theory is that this process begins with Ps 89, a passage easily accepted as messianic prophecy. Then, on the basis of shared vocabulary with Ps 89 – words like "scorn (הרפה; ὄνειδος, ὀνειδισμός)," "reject (מאס; ἀποδοκιμάζω, ἐξουδενόω)," "enemies (איבים; ἐχθροί)," and "right hand (ימין; δεξιῶν)" – christological significance is imparted to Pss 22; 69; 118; and 110. Messianic exegesis of these four psalms allows for messianic exegesis of Zech 9:9; 13:7 and Dan 7:13. This explains why Mark uses all of these Scriptures to describe the death and exaltation of Jesus. For Mark, Jesus is the scorned Messiah of Ps 89 who comes to Jerusalem on a donkey (Zech 9:9; Ps 118:25-26), is rejected there (Ps 118:22-23), and dies abandoned by his followers (Zech 13:7), tormented by his enemies (Pss 22:18; 69:32), and forsaken by God (Ps 22:1). Soon, this same Messiah will be seen sitting at God's right hand (Ps 110:1) and coming with the clouds (Dan 7:13).

In making this claim, I offer an alternative to the conclusions of Charles H. Dodd and Barnabas Lindars that the New Testament authors mined the biblical tradition not so much for messianic prophecies as for theological concepts and patterns developed in various portions of

[1] For the sake of convenience, I refer to this anonymous author using the traditional name. Unless otherwise noted, all English quotations are taken from the NRSV. Hebrew and Greek quotations come from *Biblia Hebraica Stuttgartensia* (ed. Karl Ellinger and Wilhelm Rudolph; Stuttgart: Deutsche Bibelgesellschaft, 1967), *Septuaginta* (ed. Alfred Rahlfs; Stuttgart: Deutsche Bibelgesellschaft, 1979), and *Novum Testamentum Graece* (Nestle-Aland, 27th ed.).

Scripture.[2] Therefore, when they cite a particular verse, they intend to evoke its larger literary and theological context. These theories have paved the way for many subsequent studies on various aspects of Scripture citation both in Mark's Gospel as well as in the Passion Narratives.[3]

[2] C. H. Dodd, *According to the Scriptures: The Substructure of New Testament Theology* (London: Nisbet, 1952), 126-127; Barnabas Lindars, *New Testament Apologetic: The Doctrinal Significance of the Old Testament Quotations* (Philadelphia: Westminster, 1961); "The Place of the Old Testament in the Formation of New Testament Theology: Prolegomena," *NTS* 23 (1977): 59-66. This general approach to the use of Israel's Scriptures in the New Testament has been followed by Herbert Braun ("Das Alte Testament im Neuen Testament," *ZTK* 59 [1962]: 16-31), Roland E. Murphy ("The Relationship between the Testaments," *CBQ* 26 [1964]): 349-59), and Peder Borgen ("The Place of the Old Testament in the Formation of New Testament Theology: Response," *NTS* 23 [1977]: 67-75). Martin C. Albl concludes that, whereas the NT writers often sought to develop a pattern from Scripture, at other times they used *testimonia* as prophetic proof texts (*"And Scripture Cannot Be Broken" : The Form and Function of the Early Christian* Testimonia *Collections*, NovTSup 96 [Leiden: Brill, 1999], 288, 290).

[3] Such studies include the following: William Manson, *Jesus the Messiah: The Synoptic Tradition of the Revelation of God in Christ: With Special Reference to Form-Criticism* (Philadelphia: Westminster, 1956); F. F. Bruce, "The Book of Zechariah and the Passion Narrative," *BJRL* 43 (1961): 336-53; John Bowman, *The Gospel of Mark: The New Christian Jewish Passover Haggadah* (StPB 8; Leiden: Brill, 1965); Norman Perrin, "Mark XIV.62: The End Product of a Christian Pesher Tradition?" *NTS* 12 (1965-66): 150-55; Ellen Flesseman-van Leer, "Die Interpretation der Passionsgeschichte vom Alten Testament aus," in *Zur Bedeutung des Todes Jesu* (ed. Fritz Viering; Exegetische Beiträge; Gütersloh: Mohn, 1967), 79-96; Matthew Black, "The Christological Use of the Old Testament in the New Testament," *NTS* 18 (1971): 1-14; Lothar Ruppert, *Jesus als der leidende Gerechte? Der Weg Jesu im Lichte eines alt- und zwischentestamentlichen Motivs* (SBS 59; Stuttgart: Katholisches Bibelwerk, 1972); Hartmut Gese, "Psalm 22 und das Neue Testament: Der älteste Bericht vom Tode Jesu und die Entstehung des Herrenmahles," in *Vom Sinai zum Zion: Alttestamentliche Beiträge zur biblischen Theologie* (BevT 64; Munich: Chr. Kaiser, 1974), 180-201; John H. Reumann, "Psalm 22 at the Cross," *Int* 28 (1974), 39-58; Howard Clark Kee, "The Function of Scriptural Quotations and Allusions in Mark 11-16," in *Jesus und Paulus* (ed. E. Earle Ellis and Erich Gräßer; Göttingen: Vandenhoeck & Ruprecht, 1975), 165-88; Rudolf Pesch, *Das Markusevangelium* (2 vols., 4th ed., HTKNT 2; Freiburg: Herder, 1991), 79; Rikki Watts, *Isaiah's New Exodus in Mark* (WUNT 88; Tübingen: Mohr Siebeck, 1977; repr., Grand Rapids: Baker, 2000); Dieter Lührmann, "Biographie des Gerechten als Evangelium: Vorstellungen zu einem Markus-Kommentar," *WD* 14 (1977): 25-50; Julius Oswald, "Die Beziehungen zwischen Psalm 22 und den vormarkinischen Passionsbericht," *ZKT* 101 (1979): 53-66; Fritz Stolz, "Psalm 22: Alttestamentliches Reden vom Menschen und neutestamentliches Reden von Jesus," *ZTK* 77 (1980): 129-48; Hans-Jörg Steichele, *Der leidende Sohn Gottes: Eine Untersuchung einiger alttestmentlicher Motive in der Christologie des Markusevangeliums* (Biblische Untersuchungen 14; Regensburg: Pustet, 1980); U. P. McCaffrey, "Psalm Quotations in the Passion Narratives of the Gospels," *NeoT* 14 (1981): 73-89; Douglas J. Moo, *The Old Testament in the Gospel Passion Narratives* (Sheffield: Almond, 1983); Robert D. Rowe, "Is Daniel's 'Son of Man' Messianic?," in *Christ the Lord* (ed. Harold H. Rowdon; Leicester: Inter-Varsity, 1982), 71-96; Frank J. Matera, *The Kingship of Jesus: Composition and Theology in Mark 15* (SBLDS 66; Chico, Calif.:

They stand behind recent proposals that Mark portrays the dying Jesus as the "Suffering Servant" of Isaiah 42-53, the "Shepherd-King" of Zechariah 9-14, and the "Righteous Sufferer" of the Psalms' individual laments.[4]

Donald Juel argued strenuously against this trend.[5] In his book *Messianic Exegesis*, he contends that the first Christians searched the Scriptures not for theological concepts and patterns but for discrete passages that would help them to explicate Jesus' messianic identity.[6] The process

Scholars Press, 1982), 131, 134; Seyoon Kim, "Jesus – The Son of God, the Stone, the Son of Man, and the Servant: The Role of Zechariah in the Self-Identification of Jesus," in *Tradition and Interpretation in the New Testament* (ed. Gerald F. Hawthorne and Otto Betz; Grand Rapids: Eerdmans, 1987), 134-48; Richard J. Dillon, "The Psalms of the Suffering Just in the Accounts of Jesus' Passion," *Worship* 61 (1984): 430-40; Wolfgang Roth, *Hebrew Gospel: Cracking the Code of Mark* (Oak Park, Ill.: Meyer-Stone, 1988), 69-60; Gérard Rossé, *The Cry of Jesus on the Cross: A Biblical and Theological Study* (trans. Stephen Wentworth Arndt; Mahwah, N. J.: Paulist, 1987), 52-59; Dale Miller and Patricia Miller, *The Gospel of Mark as Midrash on Earlier Jewish and New Testament Literature* (Studies in the Bible and Early Christianity 21; Lewiston, N. Y.: Edwin Mellen, 1990); Joel Marcus, *The Way of the Lord: Christological Exegesis of the Old Testament in the Gospel of Mark* (Louisville: Westminster/John Knox, 1992); Raymond E. Brown, *The Death of the Messiah: A Commentary on the Passion Narratives in the Four Gospels* (2 vols., ABRL; New York: Doubleday, 1994), 2:1445-67; Willard M. Swartley, *Israel's Scripture Traditions and the Synoptic Gospels: Story Shaping Story* (Peabody, Mass.: Hendrickson, 1994); Iain Duguid, "Messianic Themes in Zechariah 9-14," in *The Lord's Anointed: Interpretation of Old Testament Texts* (ed. Philip E. Satterthwaite, Richard S. Hess, and Gordon J. Wenham; Carlisle: Paternoster, 1995); John R. Donahue and Daniel J. Harrington, *The Gospel of Mark* (Sacra Pagina 2; Collegeville, Minn.: Liturgical Press, 2002); Richard T. France, *The Gospel of Mark* (NIGTC; Grand Rapids: Eerdmans, 2002), 575-576. Alfred Suhl (*Die Funktion der alttestamentlichen Zitate und Anspielungen im Markusevangelium* [Gütersloh: Mohn, 1965]) and Hugh Anderson ("The Old Testament in Mark's Gospel," in *The Use of the Old Testament in the New and Other Essays* [ed. James M. Efrid; Durham: Duke University Press, 1972], 280-309) dissent from the prevailing view. Both argue that Mark uses the Scriptures to demonstrate that Jesus' God is Israel's God.

4 Watts, *Isaiah's New Exodus*, 309, 365; Moo, *Old Testament in Passion Narratives*, 80-172, 215-217, 287-300, 360; Marcus, *Way of the Lord*, 154-163, 174-195.

5 See especially his comments in *Messianic Exegesis: Christological Interpretation of the Old Testament in Early Christianity* (Philadelphia: Fortress, 1988), 19-22, and his review of Marcus, *Way of the Lord*, *JBL* 114 (1995): 147-150.

6 Juel, *Messianic Exegesis*, 11-13. A similar point is made by Martin Dibelius (*From Tradition to Gospel* [trans. Bertram Lee Woolf; London: Ivor Nicholson & Watson, 1934], 184), Martin Hengel (*The Atonement: The Origins of the Doctrine in the New Testament* [trans. John Bowden; Philadelphia: Fortress, 1981], 41), and Adele Yarbro Collins ("The Appropriation of the Psalms of Individual Lament by Mark," in *The Scriptures and the Gospels* [ed. Christopher M. Tuckett, BETL 131; Leuven: Leuven University Press, 1997], 231). Willem S. Vorster and Thomas R. Hatina agree that the literary function of Mark's biblical citations is to portray Jesus, whether as the Messiah (Vorster, "The Function of the Use of the Old Testament in Mark," *NeoT* 14 [1981]:

began with two seemingly contradictory beliefs. On the one hand, they were convinced that Jesus was the Messiah whose coming is foretold in prophecies like Gen 49:8-12; Num 24:17; Ps 2; Isa 11; Jer 33:14-16.[7] On the other hand, a crucified messiah did not seem to fulfill these prophecies, which predict defeat for Israel's oppressors and the restoration of David's dynasty.[8]

Juel suggests that in order to resolve this contradiction, the first believers relied on creative exegesis of messianic prophecies. This exegesis proceeded according to conventional methods of argumentation. Like other first-century Jewish exegetes, the earliest Christians assumed that since all Scripture is God's word, it contains one unified theological message. Therefore, they felt free to interpret one passage by means of a second if both passages share identical words or phrases.[9] For Juel, this explains why passages such as Gen 22 and Isa 53, not acknowledged as messianic prophecies by Jews, are nevertheless used in the New Testament to describe the life and death of Jesus. They share vocabulary with accepted messianic prophecies, namely 2 Sam 7:10-16 and Ps 89.[10]

According to Juel, Mark's Passion Narrative probably reflects a process of messianic exegesis. Juel observes that Mark portrays Jesus first and foremost as a crucified Messiah. A concern with Jesus' messianic identity, evident in prominent passages like Mark 1:1 and 8:29, dominates Mark's account of Jesus' trial and execution with its charges

65) or as an eschatological king (Hatina, *In Search of a Context: The Function of Scripture in Mark's Narrative* [JSNTSup 232; Sheffield: Sheffield Academic Press, 2002]). Harvey D. Lange takes both sides: Jesus' cry from the cross testifies to his own typological understanding of Ps 22, which then leads to christological interpretation of the entire psalm by the first believers ("The Relationship between Psalm 22 and the Passion Narrative," *CTM* 43 [1972]: 610-21).

[7] Juel, *Messianic Exegesis*, 11, n. 16, 141.

[8] Ibid., 25-26. Here Juel builds on the ideas of Nils A. Dahl ("The Crucified Messiah," and "The Crucified Messiah and the Endangered Promises," in *Jesus the Christ: The Historical Origins of Christian Doctrine* [ed. Donald Juel; Minneapolis: Fortress, 1990], 36-37, 39-40, 73-74).

[9] Juel, *Messianic Exegesis*, 38-46. Austin M. Farrer also views Mark's citations as the result of an exegetical process that uses Scripture to interpret Scripture (*A Study in St. Mark* [Philadelphia: Westminster, 1951]). He insists that Mark uses a slightly different method, however: the Prophets and Writings are always used to interpret Torah, and the governing principle is theological. For example, he argues that Mark conflates Isa 40:3 with Exod 23:20 because Mark views Isa 40, a prophecy about a second Exodus, as a commentary on the book of Exodus (p. 55; see also pp. 259-64, 282-84). Juel's proposal that the connection requires not only shared theological themes but also shared vocabulary is more consistent with Jewish exegetical practice (see *Messianic Exegesis*, 31-45).

[10] Juel, *Messianic Exegesis*, 82-88, 131-133.

(14:62-64; 15:2, 25) and royal imagery (15:9, 12, 16-20, 32).[11] If the need to understand a crucified messiah led Mark to engage in messianic exegesis, then the results would be especially evident in the ten clear christological citations of Mark 11-15. These include Zech 9:9 in Mark 11:1-7; Ps 118:25-26 in Mark 11:9-10; Ps 118:22-23 in Mark 12:10-11; Ps 110:1 in Mark 12:36; Zech 13:7 in Mark 14:27; Dan 7:13 and Ps 110:1 in Mark 14:62; Ps 22:18 in Mark 15:24; Ps 22:1 in Mark 15:34; Ps 69:32 in Mark 15:36. Interestingly, of the seven texts evoked in these ten citations, four are psalms: Pss 118; 110; 22; and 69. This is probably why Juel surmises that, for Mark, the exegetical process begins with the psalms.

> If there is a pre-Markan passion tradition that can be isolated, the psalms surely form the basis of the tradition. It is unlikely that Jesus' story was ever told as a recitation of facts. And from the outset, psalms were employed to tell the story not of a paradigmatic righteous one or a prophetic martyr, but of the King of the Jews, "the Christ, the Son of the Blessed," whose resurrection proved that he was indeed the Christ, the Stone, rejected by the builders, which became the head of the corner.[12]

In particular, Juel focuses on Mark's use of Pss 22 and 69 to describe Jesus' crucifixion. He shows how these laments can be understood as messianic prophecies because they share vocabulary with Ps 89.

The Crucified Messiah: Messianic Exegesis of Ps 22 and Ps 69 in Light of Ps 89

Psalm 89 is a song about David, whom God has "anointed (משחתיו; ἔχρισα)" with holy oil (v. 20).[13] The psalm begins by affirming God's faithfulness to David (vv. 1-37), until v. 38 introduces a complaint:

> But now you have spurned and rejected him;
> you are full of wrath against your anointed (משחתיו; ἔχρισα).

[11] Ibid., 93-98. See also his "The Origin of Mark's Christology," in *The Messiah: Developments in Earliest Judaism and Christianity* (ed. James H. Charlesworth; Minneapolis: Fortress, 1992), 449-60. Herein lies a major difference between Juel and Marcus, who insists that Mark's Christology must be viewed in terms of apocalyptic eschatology (*Way of the Lord*, 22-23, 41, 59, 83, 114, 132-34, 158-59, 165, 177-79, 190-93).

[12] Juel, *Messianic Exegesis*, 113.

[13] Unless otherwise noted, all chapter and verse numbers correspond with the reckoning used in English Bibles.

The following verses lament the demise of David's dynasty, describing the many ways in which God has failed David (vv. 39-45) and begging God to remember God's promises (vv. 46-51).

In his discussion of Ps 89, Juel initially speculates that Jesus' first followers imparted christological significance to this lament for two reasons. One is that it contains the term "anointed." In fact, the term appears three times: in vv. 20, 38, and again in v. 52. The other is that it clearly refers to the promises made to David in 2 Sam 7:10-16 (cf. Ps 89:1-4, 19-37) – promises that formed the basis for much messianic expectation.[14] In order to demonstrate how easily Ps 89 can be interpreted as a messianic psalm, Juel gives some examples from rabbinic tradition. He quotes midrash from (among others) *Genesis Rabbah* on Gen 49:8 and the Targum on Ps 89:51-52, in which the exegetes assume messianic interpretation of Ps 89.[15] Juel then points out that the New Testament writers made the same assumption, often using Ps 89 to describe Jesus the Messiah. He notes christological references to Ps 89 in six separate sources: Luke-Acts, Revelation, Colossians, Hebrews, John, and 1 Peter.[16]

Although Mark never explicitly quotes Ps 89, Juel is confident that it lies behind his citations of Pss 22 and 69. It makes sense, Juel argues, that Ps 89 could play such an important role behind the scenes without taking center stage. After all, it does not offer much in the way of useful verses for Mark to cite. It provides very little detail that might describe the actual experience of Jesus. It does, however, constitute a reasonable starting point for understanding a crucified messiah. Juel explains, "Psalm 89 provides a link between humiliation and messiahship. It offers a specific way of speaking about Jesus' vindication as a testimony to God's fidelity to his word: in delivering Jesus from Sheol (89:48), God keeps his word to David about an everlasting dynasty."[17] Although Ps 89 cannot extensively illustrate Jesus' torments, it does enable messianic interpretation of passages that can.[18]

Such passages include Pss 22 and 69, which more effectively describe the pain, humiliation, and spiritual agony associated with Jesus' crucifixion. That Pss 22 and 69 refer to the same individual can be argued on

[14] Juel, *Messianic Exegesis*, 104.
[15] Ibid., 105-7.
[16] Ibid., 107-8. Juel cites Luke 1:51, 69; Acts 2:30; Rev 1:5; Col 1:15; Heb 1:6; John 12:34; Heb 11:26; 1 Pet 4:14.
[17] Ibid., 109.
[18] Ibid.

the basis of several shared words or phrases. Most significant is the fact that both are attributed to "David."[19] Moreover, their descriptions of David's sufferings and petitions are remarkably similar. In each psalm, David describes himself as "lowly (עני; πτωχός)" (Pss 22:24; 69:29). He locates part of his physical discomfort in his "throat (כח; גרון; λάρυξ)" (Pss 22:15; Ps 69:3). He "cries (קרא; κράζω)" (Pss 22:2; 69:3) for God's "salvation (ישועה; σωτερία)" (Pss 22:1; 69:13, 29) and entreats God to "rescue (הציל, פדה; ῥύομαι)" his "soul (נפש; ψυχή)" (Pss 22:20; 69:14, 18). "Save me (הושיעני; σῶσόν με)," he begs (Pss 22:21; 69:1, 14). In Ps 69, he pleads, "Answer me (ענני; εἰσακουσόν μου), O LORD" (v. 16), "Answer me (ענני; ἐπακουσόν με)" (vv. 13, 17, 18); in Ps 22:24 he reports, "[The LORD] heard (ענני עוות; εἰσηκουσέν με) when I cried to him."

Not only can the suffering individuals of Pss 22 and 69 be identified with each other, they can also be understood as the spurned and rejected Messiah of Ps 89. For one thing, Pss 22 and 69 can be read as David's own cries of agony in the midst of his humiliation as described in Ps 89:38-51.[20] Moreover, they describe that humiliation in terms similar to those used in Ps 89.[21] In Ps 22, David complains that he is "despised (בזוי; ἐξουδένημα)" by the people (v. 6), that "there is no one to help (אין עוזר; οὐκ ἔστιν ὁ βοηθῶν)" (v. 11), and that God lays him "in the dust of death (מות; θάνατου)" (v. 15). In Ps 69, David describes his "enemies (איבי; οἱ ἐχθροί μου)" (vv. 4, 18) and his "shame (בשתי; αἰσχύνην)" (v. 19). He pleads with God, "Do not hide (על־תסתר; μὴ ἀποστρέψῃς) yourself" (v. 17), and relies on God's "steadfast love (חסדך; τοῦ ἐλέους σου)" (v. 13). Both psalms eventually affirm that God does not "despise (בזה; ἐξουδένωσεν)" those who are needy and afflicted (Ps 22:24; 69:33).

All of these conditions exist in Ps 89:38-51, which laments that God has "rejected (תמאס; ἐξουδένωσας)" the anointed one (v. 38), "exalted the right hand of his foes (אויביו; τῶν ἐχθρῶν αὐτῶν)" (v. 42), "made all his enemies (אויביו; τοὺς ἐχθρούς αὐτούς) rejoice" (v. 42), "turned back the edge (תשיב צור; ἀπεστρέψας τὴν βοήθειαν) of his sword" (v. 43), and "covered him with shame (בושה; αἰσχύνην)" (v. 45).[22] The psalmist then asks God a series of questions: "Will you hide (תסתר;

[19] Ibid., 110.

[20] Ibid. Swartley also surmises that the attribution of Ps 22 to David lends a messianic flavor to Mark's citations (*Scripture Traditions*, 210).

[21] Juel, *Messianic Exegesis*, 110-11.

[22] The terms for "rejected" and "one to help" are shared only in Greek.

ἀποστρέψεις) yourself forever?" (v. 46). "Who can live and never see death (מות; θάνατον)?" (v. 48). "Where is your steadfast love (חסדיך; τὰ ἐλέη σου)?" (v. 49).

According to Juel, the most important term that links both Pss 22 and 69 to Ps 89 is the noun "scorn."[23] In Ps 22:6, David is "scorned by others (חרפת אדם; ὄνειδος ἀνθρώπου)"; in Ps 69:7, 9-10, 19-20, he has received "insults (חרפה; ὀνειδισμός)"; in Ps 89, the petitioner declares that God's anointed one "has become thc scorn (היה חרפה; ἐγενήθη ὄνειδος) of his neighbors" (Ps 89:41).

Juel contends that because of these similarities, first-century exegetes could argue that the sufferers of Ps 22 and 69 can be identified with the Messiah of Ps 89.[24] All three psalms refer to a Davidic king defeated by his enemies. He is scorned, shamed, rejected, and dying, and there is no one to help. God seems hidden, and God's steadfast love is not at all apparent. It would have been very easy for Christian interpreters to recognize this suffering Messiah as Jesus.

Does such an exegetical tradition lie behind Mark's citations of Pss 22 and 69? If so, it has left a small but significant trace. In Mark 9:12, Jesus uses a prominent term from the Greek version of Pss 22:6, 24; 69:33; and 89:38 to illustrate how his death accords with Scripture: "How then is it written about the Son of Man, that he is to go through many sufferings and be treated with contempt (ἐξουδενηθῇ)?"[25] In addition, the description of Jesus' sufferings in Mark 15:32 echoes Pss 22:6; 69:7, 9-10, 19-20; and 89:41: "Those who were crucified with him also taunted (ὠνείδιζον) him." These telling references, along with three clear allusions to Pss 22 and 69 in Mark 15, seem to reflect Mark's belief that Jesus is the despised and scorned Messiah of Pss 89, 22, and 69. His clothes were divided by his tormentors (Ps 22:18 in Mark 15:24), he accuses God of having abandoned him (Ps 22:1 in Mark 15:34), and he is given a drink of sour wine (Ps 69:21 in Mark 15:36).[26] For Mark, Pss 22 and 69 prophesy the death of the Messiah, who "goes as it is written of him" (Mark 14:21).[27]

[23] Juel, *Messianic Exegesis*, 110-11.

[24] Ibid., 90, 116-17.

[25] Pesch agrees that this term alludes to these four verses (*Markusevangelium*, 2:79). Collins, however, would limit the reference to Ps 22:6. She excludes Ps 22:24; 69:33 on account of their location in the psalms' thanksgiving sections, and 89:39 because the Lord's "anointed" is not speaking ("Appropriation of Psalms," 234-35). These objections would have carried no weight with an ancient interpreter, however, since all four verses can be taken to refer to the Messiah.

[26] A less prominent allusion to Ps 22:3 can be detected in Mark 15:30-31.

[27] Juel, *Messianic Exegesis*, 93-98, 102-103, 111-17; *Mark*, ACNT, (Minneapolis: Fortress, 1990), 219.

I aim to strengthen Juel's case by extending its method to the seven clear christological citations in Mark 11-14: Zech 9:9 in Mark 11:1-7; Ps 118:25-26 in Mark 11:9-10; Ps 118:22-23 in Mark 12:10-11; Ps 110:1 in Mark 12:36; Zech 13:7 in Mark 14:27; Dan 7:13 and Ps 110:1 in Mark 14:62. This list does not include all citations in these chapters. Some (such as Isa 56:7 and Jer 7:11 in Mark 11:17) do not bear directly on Jesus' messianic identity. Also excluded are less prominent allusions, such as references to Zech 14:4's Mount of Olives in Mark 11:1; 13:3, along with reported echoes of Isa 53 in Mark 10:45; 14:24, 61; 15:27. The case must first be demonstrated with regard to more widely-recognized citations.[28] I should also emphasize that I am not attempting a comprehensive historical reconstruction. The limited scope of this project does not allow for any definite attribution of messianic exegesis in Mark, whether to the evangelist, to an early Christian exegetical tradition, or to Jesus himself.[29] Although I assume that the exegetes in question relied on written texts, I refrain from deciding whether they worked in Hebrew or in Greek.[30] I seek only to reconstruct a logical process capable of explaining how the first believers, working either in Hebrew or in Greek, might have interpreted Ps 118; Zech 9:9; 13:7; Ps 110; and Dan 7:13 as prophecies about Jesus the Christ.

The Messiah's Rejection and Vindication: Messianic Exegesis of Ps 118, Zech 9:9, and Zech 13:7 in Light of Ps 89

Psalm 118 seems to have served Mark as an important catalyst for understanding the Messiah's coming to Jerusalem, his rejection, and his vindication. Mark is not alone in his regard for Ps 118. Like Ps 89, it accounts for a substantial number of New Testament citations with messianic significance. Thirteen references stem from five sources: Mark,

[28] There is general agreement concerning the most prominent citations among those authorities who tend to be conservative in identifying them. These include Lindars (*New Testament Apologetic*), Brown (*Death of the Messiah*, 2:1445-1467), and Marcus (*Way of the Lord*).

[29] Among scholars who have taken on such reconstructions, with varying results, are Lindars (*New Testament Apologetic*), Bowman (*Passover Haggadah*), Matera (*Kingship of Jesus*), Moo (*Old Testament in Passion Narratives*), Marcus (*Way of the Lord*), and Albl (*Scripture Cannot Be Broken*).

[30] For the most part, verbal parallels exist in both languages. I note each exception. Of course, this issue becomes even more complicated when considering Dan 7:13, which was preserved in Aramaic and Greek but not in Hebrew.

Q, Luke-Acts, John, and 1 Peter.[31] Significantly, three separate gospel traditions presume a christological interpretation of Ps 118:26, "Blessed is the one who comes in the name of the LORD" (Mark 11:9; Matt 23:39/Luke 13:35; John 12:13). Unless Paul wrote Col 1:15, these traditions predate any obvious mention of Ps 89 in extant Christian literature.[32]

This is not to say, however, that messianic interpretation of Ps 118 necessarily predates attention to Ps 89. Indeed, it is unthinkable that Ps 89, with a verse that reads, "You are full of wrath against your anointed" (v. 38), could have long eluded the first followers of the crucified Messiah. Moreover, messianic interpretation of Ps 89 – with its references to David, the Lord's "anointed," and its appeal to the divine promises in 2 Sam 7:8-16 – is more straightforward than messianic interpretation of Ps 118, which is not even ostensibly a royal psalm. Anyone looking for christological meaning in Ps 118 needs a creative method.

Such a method seems to have been employed in the Aramaic Targum, which interprets Ps 118 as a song about David. According to Craig Evans, this interpretation is probably based on the similarity between two Hebrew words: "stone (אבן)" and "son (בן)." This similarity enables a wordplay that allows exegetes to read Ps 118:22 as a reference to "the son that the builders rejected" – a reading given in the Targum. The exegete's conclusion is that Ps 118:22 refers to David, the "son" of Jesse, initially overlooked by Israel but eventually proclaimed king.[33]

Several commentators speculate that this tradition lies behind Christian interpretation of Ps 118.[34] Others propose a different source for Mark's understanding of this psalm. Frank Matera suggests that its original *Sitz im Leben* – a cultic celebration of a royal victory – laid the foundation for a tradition of messianic exegesis.[35] Seyoon Kim and Jane Schaberg find significance in a link between Ps 118:22 and Dan 2:34, 44, Schaberg arguing that the psalm was interpreted in light of Daniel's

[31] Matt 11:3; 21:9, 42; 23:39; Mark 8:31; 11:9; 12:10-11; Luke 13:35; 19:39; 20:17; John 12:13; Acts 4:11; 1 Pet 2:4, 7. While all three references in Luke depend either on Mark or Q, we shall see that the quotation of Ps 118:22-23 in Acts 4:11 may not be a straightforward adaptation.

[32] The less obvious allusion to Ps 89:38 in Mark 9:12 is excepted.

[33] Craig A. Evans, *Mark 8:27-16:20* (WBC 34B; Nashville: Thomas Nelson, 2001), 229.

[34] Black, "Christological Use," 11-14; Kim, "Son of God, Stone, Son of Man, Servant," 135-38; Robert H. Gundry, *Mark: A Commentary on His Apology for the Cross* [Grand Rapids: Eerdmans, 1993], 689-90; Evans, *Mark 8:27-16:20*, 228-30.

[35] Matera, *Kingship of Jesus*, 83.

vision of a communal representative, reminiscent of Jesus, who is symbolized by a "stone."[36] According to Joel Marcus, Mark interprets Ps 118 as an eschatological passage about the temple, perfect for Jesus' polemic against that institution.[37]

More obviously important to Mark than the Aramaic Targum, the cultic setting of Ps 118, the stone of Daniel 2, or even apocalyptic eschatology, however, is the conviction that Jesus is the crucified Messiah. Perhaps this conviction led to christological interpretation of Ps 118 in light of an accepted messianic prophecy. The exegetical process could easily have started with Ps 89. Psalm 118 can in fact be read as a thanksgiving for God's answer to the lament in Ps 89. According to Ps 89:38-51, the Lord apparently is not keeping the promise of steadfast love to David detailed in vv. 1-37. Instead, God has enabled the triumph of David's enemies. In Ps 118, on the other hand, the Lord has helped the psalmist to defeat his enemies (vv. 5-18), and so the psalmist affirms God's steadfast love (vv. 1-4, 29).

The notion that Ps 118 thanks God for vindicating the rejected Messiah of Ps 89 is enforced by several shared words. For example, both psalms refer specifically to their protagonists' "enemies." In Ps 89:22-23, God swears, "The enemy (אויב; ἐχθρὸς) shall not outwit him," and, "I will crush his foes (צריו; τοὺς ἐχθροὺς αὐτοῦ) before him." According to Ps 89:42, God seems to have forgotten this oath. "You have exalted the right hand of his foes (צריו; τῶν ἐχθρῶν αὐτοῦ)," laments the psalmist; "you have made all his enemies (אויביו; τοὺς ἐχθροὺς αὐτοῦ) rejoice." According to Ps 118:7, however, God comes to the psalmist's aid. He declares, "I shall look in triumph on those who hate me (בשנאי; τοὺς ἐχθρούς μου)."[38]

Two other common words appear in a verse from Ps 118 that affirms an answer to one of the complaints in Ps 89:

> Who can live (יחיה; ζήσεται) and never see death (מות; θάνατον)?
> Who can escape the power of Sheol? (Ps 89:48)
>
> I shall not die (אמות; αποθανοῦμαι), but I shall live (אחיה; ζήσομαι),
> and recount the deeds of the LORD. (Ps 118:17)

Within the context of Ps 89, v. 48 seems to express the speaker's fear that he will perish before the Lord finally remembers the promise to David and vindicates the rejected Messiah. Interpreted together with Ps 118:17, however, it can be understood as the lament of the Messiah himself. In Ps

[36] Kim, "Son of God, Stone, Son of Man, Servant," 142; Jane Schaberg, "Daniel 7,12 and the New Testament Passion-Resurrection Predictions," *NTS* 31 (1985): 212-17.

[37] Marcus, *Way of the Lord*, 114-116.

[38] The shared vocabulary occurs only in Greek.

89:48, he contemplates his apparent mortality; in Ps 118:17, he affirms that he will be saved from death.

A fourth common word is "steadfast love." The Lord's "steadfast love" is celebrated in Ps 89:1-2, 14, and promised to David in Ps 89:24, 28, 33, but hidden in Ps 89:49:

> Lord, where is your steadfast love (חסדיך; τὰ ἐλέη σου) of old,
> which by your faithfulness you swore to David?

Psalm 118 answers this complaint by reaffirming the constancy of the Lord's "steadfast love." It begins and ends with this refrain:

> O give thanks to the LORD, for he is good;
> his steadfast love (חסדו; τὸ ἔλεος αὐτοῦ) endures forever!
> (vv. 1, 29)

The beginning refrain is followed by vv. 2-4, which enjoin Israel, Israel's priests, and everyone who fears the Lord to repeat, "His steadfast love (חסדו; τὸ ἔλεος αὐτου) endures forever!" God has displayed steadfast love to David after all.

Psalms 89 and 118 also make the same affirmations about the Lord's power. According to Ps 89:10, he scatters his enemies with his "mighty (עזך; τῆς δυνάμενως) arm." Verse 13 echoes this theme:

> You have a mighty (גבורה; μετὰ δυναστείας) arm;
> strong (תעז; κραταιωθήτω) is your hand, high (תרום; ὑψωθήτω) your right hand (ימינך; δεξιά σου).

According to v. 26, David will declare, "You are my God, and the Rock of my salvation (ישועתי; τῆς σωτηρίας μου)!" God is similarly praised in Ps 118:14-16, 21:

> The LORD is my strength (עזי; ἰσχύς μου) and my might;
> he has become my salvation (לישועה; μοι εἰς σωτηρίαν).
> There are glad songs of victory
> in the tents of the righteous;
> "The right hand (ימין; δεξιά κυρίου) of the LORD does valiantly;
> the right hand (ימין; δεξιά κυρίου) of the LORD is exalted (רוממה; ὕψωσέν με);
> the right hand (ימין; δεξιά κυρίου) of the LORD does valiantly (עשה; δύναμιν)."
>
> I thank you that you have answered me,
> and have become my salvation (לישועה; μοι εἰς σωτηρίαν).[39]

[39] In the LXX, the Psalm's penultimate verse also ends with this expression. Christian attention to Ps 118:15-16, 17 may be indicated by allusions in Luke 1:51 (also reminiscent of Ps 89:2, 11); Acts 5:31; 1 Cor 6:9. It is perhaps not insignificant that the Hebrew for "salvation" in Pss 89:26; 118:14, 21 is ישועה.

Psalm 118 affirms that God's strength and exalted right hand have rescued the Messiah from his enemies.

Finally, both psalms praise the Lord using the same words. "Happy are the people who know the festal shout," declares Ps 89:15. "They exult in your name all day long and extol (ירומו; ὑψωθήσονται) your righteousness" (v. 16). Psalm 89 ends with a doxology: "Blessed be the LORD (ברוך יהוה; εὐλογητὸς κύριος) forever" (v. 52). A similar blessing is reiterated in Ps 118:26:

> Blessed (ברוך; εὐλογημένος) is the one who comes in the name of the LORD (יהוה; κυρίου).
> We bless you (ברכנוכם; εὐλογήκαμεν) from the house of the LORD (יהוה; κυρίου).

The celebration continues with an echo of Ps 89:15-16:

> You are my God, and I will give thanks to you;
> You are my God, and I will extol you (ארוממך; ὑψώσω σε).
> (v. 28)

When the Lord's strong right hand rescues the Messiah of Ps 89:38-51 from death, God's mighty acts and steadfast love are praised as in Ps 89:1-37, 52 and Ps 118.

Interestingly, Ps 118 can also be read in concert with Pss 22 and 69 as prophecies about the rejected and vindicated Messiah. Since all three psalms are spoken by one who suffers and then praises God for deliverance, it is not difficult to imagine that they might refer to the same person. Five verbal links establish the connections. The first involves the way the speaker is treated by his enemies. "All the nations surrounded me (סבבוני; ἐκυκλωσάν με)," recalls Ps 118:10-12, while the protagonist of Ps 22:16 declares, "Dogs are all around (סבבוני; ἐκυκλωσάν με)." Second, each psalm includes a similar petition to the Lord. "Save now (הושיעה נא; σῶσόν δή)," cry the worshippers of Ps 118:25, and the sufferers in Ps 22:21 and Ps 69:1 echo, "Save me (הושיעני; σῶσόν με)." Third, all three parties use similar terms – terms that also appear in Ps 89:48 – to express confidence that God will rescue. "I shall not die, but I shall live (אחיה; ζήσομαι)," declares Ps 118:17, while Ps 22:29 affirms, "I shall live (ζῇ) for him" and Ps 69:32 reiterates, "You who seek God, let your hearts revive (ויחי; ζήσεται)."[40] Fourth, the complaint of Ps 22:11, "There is no one to help (אין עוזר; οὐκ ἔστιν ὁ βοηθῶν)" is answered in Ps 118:6-7, "The LORD is on my side (יהוה לי עזרי; κύριος ἐμοὶ βοηθός)."[41]

[40] The MT of Ps 22:29 is corrupt.

[41] As we have seen, the complaint of Ps 22:1 is echoed in Greek at Ps 89:43.

Finally, each psalmist proclaims that the Lord has heard him. Psalm 118:21 reads, "I thank you because you answered me (עניתני; ἐπήκουσάς μου)"; Ps 22:24, "[The LORD] heard me (ענות עני; εἰσηκουσέν με) when I cried to him"; Ps 69:33, "The LORD hears (שמע; εἰσήκουσεν) the needy." Like Pss 22 and 69, Ps 118 describes a messiah surrounded by enemies, confident that the Lord will save him from death, and thankful that God hears his prayer.

Perhaps most importantly, Psalms 89 and 118 both concern one who has been "rejected." Psalm 89:38 identifies this figure as the Lord's anointed:

> But now you have spurned and rejected (תמאס; ἐξουδένωσας) him;
> You are full of wrath against your anointed.

In Ps 118:22, however, the circumstances are somewhat different:

> The stone that the builders rejected (מאסו; ἀπεδοκίμασαν)
> has become the chief cornerstone.

If the "rejected" stone of Ps 118:22 can be identified with the "rejected" Messiah of Ps 89:38, then Ps 118:22 provides a way to speak about his vindication.[42] As we shall see, this concept, as expressed in this verse, constitutes the essence of Mark's Christology.

It would seem that messianic interpretation of Ps 118:22 in light of Ps 89:38 in order to describe the death and resurrection of Jesus is not just a possibility. Evidence that early Christians did indeed make this exegetical move can be found in Acts 4:10-11. Here Peter explains to the council that "Jesus Christ of Nazareth, whom you crucified,... God raised from the dead." In order to illustrate this point, he quotes Ps 118:22:

> [Jesus is]
> 'the stone that was rejected by you, the builders;
> it has become the cornerstone.'

The quotation has been modified from the LXX in three ways. First, it conforms to its new grammatical setting in which "Jesus" is the subject and "stone" is the predicate. Second, having identified the "stone" as Jesus, Peter then identifies the "builders" with the council. Finally, he substitutes the verb ἐξουδένωσας, found in Ps 89:38 (and also in Ps 22:6, 24; 69:33), for ἀπεδοκίμασαν.[43] This substitution can be taken as

[42] The verb is the same only in Hebrew.

[43] See also Pesch, *Markusevangelium*, 2:79. Lindars attributes the substitution to influence from Isa 53:3, "He was despised and rejected (נבזה וחדל; τὸ εἶδος αὐτοῦ ἄτιμον ἐκλεῖπον) by others" (*New Testament Apologetic*, 170). I find this option less likely, since Mark does not adopt Isaiah's Greek vocabulary.

evidence that these verses were conflated on the basis of similar vocabulary to show that the rejected Messiah of Ps 89 is the vindicated Messiah of Ps 118.

If this exegetical process is reflected in Acts, then it is not strange to think that it might also be reflected in Mark. More direct evidence that Mark uses shared vocabulary to interpret Ps 118 in light of Ps 89 comes from his apparent theological reflection on three key words that link Ps 118:22-23, 25-26 to Ps 89 on the one hand and Pss 22 and 69 on the other. Mark associates all three words with Jesus' death. The first of these is the verb "reject," which establishes a connection between Ps 118:22 and Ps 89:38 in Hebrew. The Greek term used in Ps 118:22 finds its way into Jesus' first passion prediction in Mark 8:31: "Then he began to teach them that the Son of Man must undergo great suffering, and be rejected (ἀποδοκιμασθῆναι) by the elders, the chief priests, and the scribes, and be killed, and after three days rise again."[44] A few verses later, Jesus uses the verb "save," found in Pss 118:25; 22:21; 69:1 (together with its cognate noun in Pss 89:26; 118:14, 21), and the noun "life," found in Pss 22:20; 69:14, 18 (together with its cognate verb in Pss 89:48; 118:17): "Those who want to save (σῶσαι) their life (τὴν ψυχὴν) will lose it, and those who lose their life (τὴν ψυχὴν) for my sake, and for the sake of the gospel, will save (σώσει) it" (Mark 8:35). The noun "life" also appears in one of Mark's few reflections on the theological significance of Jesus' death: "The Son of Man came not to be served but to serve, and to give his life (τὴν ψυχὴν) a ransom for many" (Mark 10:45). Finally, Jesus dies to an ironic echo of Mark 8:35: "He saved (ἔσωσεν) others; he cannot save (σῶσαι) himself" (Mark 15:31). "Save (σῶσον) yourself, and come down from the cross!" (Mark 15:30). For Mark, the council "rejects" Jesus when they condemn him, and Jesus "saves" his "life" when he gives it. Psalm 118, interpreted in light of Pss 89; 22; and 69, constitutes a logical source for these ideas.

At the very least, it is clear that Mark interprets Ps 118 as a messianic prophecy. He places Ps 118:25-26 in the mouths of the crowds who welcome Jesus to Jerusalem:

> Hosanna!
> Blessed is the one who comes in the name of the Lord!
> (Mark 11:9)[45]

[44] See also Moo, *Old Testament in Passion Narratives*, 97; Cilliers Breytenbach, "Das Markusevangelium, Psalm 110,1 und 118,22f. Folgetext und Prätext," in *The Scriptures in the Gospels* (ed. Tuckett), 214-16.

[45] "Hosanna (ὡσαννά)" is a Greek transliteration of the Hebrew phrase הושיעה נא.

The christological importance of this passage for Mark is indicated both by its placement and by the emphasis accorded to it. This scene introduces Mark's account of Jesus' last days in Jerusalem in much the same way that the stories of Jesus' baptism (1:9-11) and transfiguration (9:2-8) introduce his Galilean ministry and journey to Jerusalem respectively. Each of these three pivotal scenes contains a declaration that Jesus is the Messiah. In Mark 1:11 and 9:5, the proclamations come from God and seem to depend on Ps 2:7; in Mark 11:9-10 the people acclaim Jesus by reciting Ps 118:25-26. In effect, Mark quotes Ps 118:25-26 to finish off this prominent series of messianic declarations.

Mark further emphasizes the citation by making the triumphal entry narrative itself reminiscent of Ps 118. Psalm 118:26-27 describes a festal procession with branches, accompanied by blessings from the house of the Lord. In Mark 11:8 the people welcome Jesus with branches, and in Mark 11:11 Jesus' first act upon entering Jerusalem is to go into the temple. Mark seems to have evoked the celebration described in Ps 118:26 – a celebration that involves the cry of "Hosanna," one "who comes in the name of the LORD," branches, and a procession to the temple – in order to show how the Messiah comes to Jerusalem.

The next clear christological citation in Mark 11-15 reflects on what will happen to him there. It expresses Mark's christology in a nutshell:

> The stone that the builders rejected
> has become the cornerstone;
> this was the LORD's doing,
> and it was amazing in our eyes. (Ps 118:22-23 in Mark 12:10-11)

This verse succinctly summarizes the career of Mark's Messiah, who is condemned by his own religious leaders to suffering and death (Mark 8:31; 9:12, 31; 10:33-34; 14:43-15:39), whom God raises up and exalts to God's right hand (Mark 8:31; 9:31; 10:34; 14:62; 16:1-8), and who will come again in glory (Mark 8:38; 13:26-27; 14:62).

Besides its obvious significance for Mark's understanding of Jesus, another indication of this citation's importance is its location at the end of the parable of the tenants (Mark 12:1-12). Just as the parable of the sower (Mark 4:1-20) explains much of the conflict in the Gospel's first ten chapters, the parable of the tenants clarifies the events of Mark 11-16.[46] It portrays the antagonism between Jesus and the council as a struggle for sovereignty over the temple. Because he is God's own Son,

[46] Mary Ann Tolbert, *Sowing the Gospel: Mark's World in Literary-Historical Perspective* (Minneapolis: Fortress, 1989), 121-24.

Jesus is destined to win the struggle. The council, in contrast, are merely tenants who can be replaced. They may think they have gained the upper hand when they have Jesus executed, but this will only lead to their ultimate destruction (Mark 12:9). All this, warns Jesus, is foretold in Ps 118:25-26 (Mark 12:10-11).

The importance of Ps 118 in the development of Mark's Christology should not be underestimated. Messianic interpretation of this psalm is crucial for Mark's understanding of Jesus' final days. It builds on the notion that Jesus is the "rejected" Messiah of Ps 89:38 by portraying the council as agents of rejection (Ps 118:22), by affirming that God will vindicate him (Ps 118:22-23), and by identifying him as "the one who comes in the name of the Lord" to Jerusalem (Ps 118:26).

In addition, it permits messianic exegesis of two prophecies from Zechariah that further explicate Jesus' fate. One of these prophecies, Zech 9:9, is used by Mark to set the scene that evokes the acclamation from Ps 118:25-26:

> Rejoice greatly, O daughter Zion!
> Shout aloud, O daughter Jerusalem!
> Lo, your king comes to you;
> triumphant and victorious is he,
> humble and riding on a donkey,
> on a colt, the foal of a donkey (πῶλον νέον).

Anyone familiar with Zech 9:9 cannot help recognizing its fulfillment when the Messiah, Jesus, enters Jerusalem seated on a "donkey (πῶλον)" on which no one has ever ridden as described in Mark 11:2, 4, 5, 7.[47] In addition, anyone familiar with Ps 118:25-26 can easily spot the shared words that apparently prompted Mark to conflate it with Zech 9:9 in this scene. One is the verb "come." Psalm 118:26 is about "one who comes (הבא; ὁ ἐρχόμενος)," and Zech 9:9 announces, "Lo, your king comes (יבוה; ἔρχεται)."[48] The coming king of Zech 9:9 can be easily identified with the Messiah who comes in Ps 118:26. Moreover, for readers of the LXX, this Messiah who comes can be understood as a messiah who saves. In Ps 118:25, the people petition the Lord, "Save us (σῶσον δή)!" In Zech 9:9, the king is "saving (σῴζων)" when he

[47] This includes Matthew, who explicitly quotes the prophecy and demonstrates its exact fulfillment (21:1-7).

[48] See also Deborah Krause, "The One Who Comes Unbinding the Blessing of Judah: Mark 11:1-10 As a Midrash on Genesis 49:11, Zechariah 9:9, and Psalm 118:25-26," in *Early Christian Interpretation of the Scriptures of Israel: Investigations and Proposals* (ed. Craig A. Evans and James A. Sanders; JSNTSup 148; Sheffield: Sheffield Academic Press, 1997), 145.

comes. (This parallel may have served as an additional incentive for Mark's reflections on this verb.) Finally, both scenes take place in Jerusalem. The procession in Ps 118:27 winds up at the altar, and in Zech 9:9 the king's destination is Jerusalem. This similarity does not involve shared vocabulary. Nevertheless, it is hard to miss.

One or all of these connections can account for Mark's use of Zech 9:9 together with Ps 118:25-26 to describe Jesus' entry into Jerusalem – a conflation that constitutes one of the clearest indications that Mark uses Scripture to interpret Scripture by means of shared vocabulary. More concrete evidence that Mark uses the word "come" to link Zech 9:9 and Ps 118:25-26 can be found in Mark 11:10. Using a technique found elsewhere in the New Testament (e.g. Gal 3:10-14; 1 Cor 15:24-28; Heb 2:5-9), this verse reiterates words from the conflated passages. "Blessed is the coming kingdom (εὐλογημένη ἡ ἐρχομένη βασιλεία) of our ancestor David!" shout the crowds. Their acclamation echoes the prophecy of Zech 9:9, "Lo, your king (βασιλεύς) comes (ἔρχεται) to you," together with the benediction of Ps 118:26, "Blessed is the one who comes (εὐλογημένος ὁ ἐρχόμενος) in the name of the Lord!" Mark gives the conflation messianic significance by adding the reference to David. For Mark, the savior Jesus who comes to Jerusalem on a donkey, and who immediately enters the temple, is the Messiah prophesied in Ps 118:25-26.

Mark's Messiah is not only rejected by the authorities; he is also abandoned by his own disciples. Mark shows that this unexpected event fulfills a messianic prophecy by including a quotation of Zech 13:7:

> Jesus said to them, "You will all become deserters; for it is written,
> 'I will strike the shepherd,
> and the sheep will be scattered.'" (Mark 14:27)

It comes as no surprise that Mark should portray the Messiah as a shepherd. "Shepherd" was a popular designation for David (1 Sam 16:11; 17:34-37; 2 Sam 7:8-11) and his descendants (Jer 3:15; 23:1-4; Ezek 34:1-10, 23-24). Passages like 2 Sam 7:8-11 and Ezek 34:23-24 lead the author of the Psalms of Solomon to envision the Messiah "faithfully and righteously shepherding the Lord's flock" (*Ps. Sol.* 17:40).[49] The first Christians could also have identified the Messiah as a shepherd on these grounds, thus concluding that Zech 13:7 – a prophecy about a stricken shepherd and scattered sheep – has messianic significance.

[49] Trans. Robert B. Wright, "Psalms of Solomon," *OTP* 2:668.

Could they have done so based on similar vocabulary with passages like Ps 89 and Ps 118 that seem to have shaped Mark's Christology? One possibility involves a link with Ps 118 by way of Isa 40:1-11. The connection between Isa 40:1-11 and Ps 118 is based on the words "come" and "Lord." The Messiah of Ps 118:26 "who comes (הבא; ὁ ἐρχόμενος) in the name of the LORD (יהוה; κυρίου)" can be identified with the "Lord GOD (אדני יהוה; κύριος)" who "comes (יבוא; ἔρχεται) with might" in Isa 40:10.

That Mark makes this connection between Ps 118:26 and Isa 40:10 may account for the citation of Isa 40:3 in Mark 1:2-3. It may also account, at least in part, for its conflation with Mal 3:1, a verse which goes on to anticipate – in the words of Ps 118:26 – that "the Lord (האדון; κύριος) whom you seek will suddenly come (יבוא; ἥξει) to his temple," as well as to declare, "Indeed, he is coming (בא; ἔρχεται)."[50] To a greater extent, the conflation is based on shared vocabulary between Isa 40:3 and Mal 3:1, including the verb "prepare (פנה; ἑτοιμάσατε, ἐπιβλέψεται)" and the noun "way (דרך; ὁδός)."[51] Like the conflation of Ps 118:25-26 and Zech 9:9, it clearly indicates the importance to Mark's exegetical enterprise of interpreting one passage in light of another by means of shared vocabulary.[52] In addition, it may help to explain the substantial role played by the verb "come" in Mark's citations of Scripture. For Mark, Jesus is the coming Messiah whose messenger prepares his way (Mal 3:1 and Isa 40:3, 10 in Mark 1:2-3) and who comes to Jerusalem on a donkey (Zech 9:9 in Mark 11:1-7) – the blessed one who comes in the name of the Lord (Ps 118:26 in Mark 11:9).[53]

The Messiah, the Lord who comes with might in Isa 40:10, is "like a shepherd (כרעה; ὡς ποιμήν)" who tends his flock in Isa 40:11. This is

[50] The Hebrew version of Mal 3:1 does not use the same term for "Lord" found in Ps 118:26.

[51] Isaiah 40:3 and Mal 3:1 do not use the same Greek verb for "prepare." Marcus (*Way of the Lord*, 16), Gundry (*Apology for the Cross*, 35), and France (*Gospel of Mark*, 63) agree that Mark conflates these verses on the basis of shared vocabulary.

[52] Mark even extends this exegetical process to a third verse. Like Mal 3:1, Exod 23:20 reads, "I am going to send an angel (הנני שלח מלאכי; ἰδοὺ ἐγὼ ἐξαποστέλλω τὸν ἄγγελόν μου) in front of you, to guard you on your way (בדרך; ἐν τῇ ὁδῷ)." See also Marcus, *Way of the Lord*, 13, and Gundry, *Apology for the Cross*, 35.

[53] Others who note the possible messianic significance of Mark's designation of Jesus as the one who "comes" include Vincent Taylor (*The Gospel According to St. Mark* [London: Macmillan, 1952], 457), Lindars (*New Testament Apologetic*, 172), Matera (*Kingship of Jesus*, 74), and Christopher S. Mann (*Mark* [AB 27; Garden City: Doubleday, 1986], 437). Taylor suspects that the verb's christological significance is derived from Ps 118:26 and Dan 7:13.

all that is needed to justify christological interpretation of Zech 13:7. Here, the "shepherd (הרעה; ποιμήν)" will ultimately lose his sheep. It is important for Mark to make this connection in light of what actually happened to Jesus. This Messiah's followers were not loyal sheep. They did not stick to the protocol for the subjects of the coming king. Instead, they abandoned him when he was arrested and crucified. Mark realizes that this accords with messianic prophecy. They are the scattered sheep foretold in Zech 13:7.

The Exalted Lord and Coming Son of Man: Messianic Exegesis of Ps 110 and Dan 7:13 in Light of Ps 89

Out of all the passages he cites in his Passion Narrative, Mark imparts the clearest christological significance to Ps 110:1. Both citations are attributed to Jesus. First, while teaching in the temple, Jesus addresses the scribes' assertion that "the Messiah" is David's son. In support of his opinion that the Messiah is David's Lord, Jesus quotes Ps 110:1:

> The Lord said to my Lord (τῷ κυρίῳ μου),
> "Sit at my right hand (Κάθου ἐκ δεξιῶν μου)
> until I put your enemies under your feet." (Mark 12:36)

His argument is based on the premise, presumably shared with his opponents, that Ps 110:1 concerns the Messiah.[54] Jesus cites this verse a second time during his trial before the council. The high priest asks, "Are you the Messiah?" Jesus replies, "I am; and 'you will see the Son of Man (τόν υἱὸν τοῦ ἀνθρώπου) seated at the right hand (ἐκ

[54] The point of this argument, although important for Mark's Christology, is difficult to discern and therefore a matter of some debate. It does not pertain directly to this thesis, however. The following works discuss it more thoroughly: Evald Loevestam, "Die Davidssohnfrage" (*SEÅ* 27 (1962): 81; Black, "Christological Use," 6; David M. Hay, *Glory at the Right Hand: Psalm 110 in Early Christianity* (SBLMS 18; Nashville: Abingdon, 1973), 106-7, 111; Kee, "Function of Scriptural Quotations," 178; Matera, *Kingship of Jesus*, 87; Bruce D. Chilton, "Jesus *ben David*: Reflections on the *Davidssohnfrage*," *JSNT* 14 (1982): 101-5; Gerhard Dautzenberg, "Psalm 110 im Neuen Testament," in *Liturgie und Dichtung: Historische Präsentation* (ed. Hansjakob Becker and Reiner Kaczynski; vol. 1 in *Liturgie und Dichtung: Ein interdisziplinäres Kompendium*, ed. H. Becker and R. Kaczynski; 2 vols.; Sankt Ottilien: EOS, 1981), 150-1; Marinus de Jonge, "Jesus, Son of David and Son of God," in *Intertextuality in Biblical Writings* (ed. Sipke Draisma; Kampen: Kok, 1989), 98; Marcus, *Way of the Lord*, 39, 137-50; Breytenbach, "Markusevangelium, Psalm 110,1 und 118,22f.," 203-5.

δεξιῶν καθήμενον) of the Power,' and 'coming with the clouds of heaven (ἐρχόμενον μετὰ τῶν νεφελῶν τοῦ οὐρανοῦ)'" (Mark 14:62).

Christological interpretation of Ps 110:1 is not without precedent among pre-Markan Christians, and continues into some of the later gospels and epistles. Paul uses Ps 110:1 in 1 Cor 15:25 to demonstrate that Christ "must reign until [God] has put all his enemies under his feet," and again in Rom 8:34 to describe how, now that Christ is raised, he intercedes for believers "at the right hand of God." Ephesians 1:20 reflects this exegetical tradition, while the quotation of Ps 110:1 in Mark 12:36 is repeated in Matt 22:44; Luke 20:42-43 and echoed in Acts 2:33-35. The argument of Hebrews also relies heavily on christological interpretation of Ps 110, citing v. 1 in Heb 1:3, 13 and v. 4 in Heb 5:6; 7:17, 21. In each of these passages, Ps 110 is used to prove a point. The consistent premise is that Ps 110 concerns the Messiah.

This premise seems perfectly reasonable, since Ps 110 can easily be understood as a messianic prophecy. Not only is it a "Psalm of David," it is also a royal psalm. In *Midr. Ps.* 18§29 (on Ps 18:35), R. Yudan assumes that Ps 110:1 is about the Messiah. A rationale for this assumption is given in *Gen. Rab.* 85:9: the king of Ps 110:2 wields a "scepter (מטה)" like the "staff (מטה)" of Judah in Gen 38:18.[55] Further rationale could have come by way of comparison with Ps 2, a song about the Lord's "anointed." Like the king of Ps 110, his reign is established in Zion (Ps 2:6; cf. Ps 110:2), he confounds his enemies with a scepter (Ps 2:9; cf. Ps 110:2), he is identified in a direct address from the Lord (Ps 2:7; cf. Ps 110:4), he becomes an instrument of God's wrath (Ps 110:5; cf. Ps 2:5, 11), and he defeats the nations who oppose him (Ps 110:5-6; cf. Ps 2:1-3, 8-9).[56] The author of Hebrews apparently shares this understanding. Hebrews 5:5-6 quotes Ps 2:7 and Ps 110:4 in tandem to confirm Christ's divine appointment, seemingly because in both verses God declares, "You are (אתה; σὺ εἶ)."[57]

What, then, led Mark to interpret Ps 110 as a messianic prophecy? Perhaps it was the psalm's royal characteristics and its similarity to Ps 2. Perhaps it was reliance on a previous tradition, such as those reflected in rabbinic literature and in the New Testament. More integral to Mark's

[55] Both Hay (*Glory at the Right Hand*, 21-33) and Juel (*Messianic Exegesis*, 137-39) survey early Jewish interpretation of Ps 110. Messianic interpretation is not consistent, but it is practiced here and there.

[56] The term "scepter" appears in extant Greek versions of both psalms but is missing from the MT of Ps 110:2.

[57] Juel, *Messianic Exegesis*, 135-86.

apparent understanding of Jesus, however, is the compelling fact that the king of Ps 110 can be identified with the "rejected" Messiah of Ps 89. In fact, Ps 110 – like Ps 118 – can be read as confirmation of the declarations in Ps 89:1-18, as the Lord's fulfillment of the promises in Ps 89:19-37, and as the Lord's answer to the petitions in Ps 89:38-51. For example, in Ps 89:19 God declares, "I have set the crown on one who is mighty (δυνατόν)." Psalm 110:2-3 makes similar affirmations about the king: he has a "mighty (δυνάμεως)" scepter, and exercises dominion in the day of his "might (δυνάμεως)."[58] Both psalms also refer to God's right hand. Psalm 89:13 extols God's "mighty arm": "Strong is your hand (ידך; ἡ χείρ σου), high your right hand (ימינך; ἐκ δεξιῶν μου)." According to Ps 89:21, this hand will attend the Lord's anointed: "My hand (ידי; χείρ μου) shall always remain with him." In Ps 110:1, God keeps this promise:

> The LORD says to my lord,
> "Sit at my right hand (לימיני; ἐκ δεξιῶν μου)."

Psalm 110 describes the fulfillment of God's covenant with David as articulated in Ps 89. Twice the Lord reiterates, "I have sworn (נשבעתי; ὤμοσα)" (Ps 89:3, 35). God's commitment to the king is echoed in Ps 110:4: "The LORD has sworn (נשבע; ὤμοσεν) and will not change his mind." In Ps 89:20, the people are reminded that God raised up David to be their king: "I have exalted (הרימותי; ὕψωσα) one chosen among the people." God then recalls the promise to David: "In my name his horn shall be exalted (תרום; ὑψωθήσεται)" (v. 24). Psalm 110:7 affirms that the king will indeed be exalted: "He will lift up (ירים; ὑψώσει) his head." Another promise involves the Messiah's enemies. As we have seen, Ps 89:22-23 contains God's assurances that the Messiah will defeat his "enemy (אויב; ἐχθρὸς)," followed by a complaint in v. 42 that those "enemies" have in fact defeated him. In Ps 110, the situation is reversed. The Lord has made the king's "enemies (איביך; τῶν ἐχθρῶν σου)" his footstool, and he is told, "Rule in the midst of your foes (איביך; τῶν ἐχθρῶν σου)" (Ps 110:1-2).

Three of these joint affirmations find parallels in Pss 69 and 118. The first concerns the Messiah's triumph over his "enemies." As we have seen, Ps 69:4, 18 shares the concern of Ps 89:42 over the enemies' victories. Psalms 118:7 and 110:1, however, maintain that the enemies will

[58] These parallels exist only in extant Greek versions. The MT of Ps 110:2-3 does not contain any word that can be translated by the Greek "δυνατός" or one of its cognates.

ultimately suffer defeat. The second affirmation concerns God's "right hand," described as "high" in Ps 89:13, as "valiant" in Ps 118:15, and as the privileged position of the king in Ps 110:1. The third deals with the king's "exalted" status, mentioned in Pss 89:20, 24; 118:15; and 110:7.

There is also one word that links Ps 110 to Ps 118 alone. That word is "nations." In Ps 118:10, the speaker testifies:

> All the nations (גוים; ἔθνη) surrounded me;
> In the name of the LORD I cut them off!

According to Ps 110:5-6, the Lord, who is at the king's right hand, "will execute judgment among the nations (בגוים; ἐν τοῖς ἔθνεσιν)."

Psalm 89 depicts a mighty Messiah whom God has exalted, to whom God has sworn, and who will always be attended by God's hand. Despite these assurances, God allows his enemies (the nations) to triumph, as confirmed in Ps 69. In Ps 110, as in Ps 118, however, God affirms the oath, defeats his enemies (the nations), lifts him up, restores his might, and places him at God's right hand. Thus the rejected Messiah of Pss 89 and 69 becomes, not only the vindicated stone of Ps 118, but also the exalted king of Ps 110.

Accordingly, Mark uses Ps 110:1 to stress the Messiah's exalted status in the face of his impending doom.[59] First comes the quotation in Mark 12:36, which continues the series of implicit messianic identity markers that punctuate Jesus' arrival in Jerusalem. He is the king who comes on a donkey (Zech 9:9 in Mark 11:7), the "beloved son" (Mark 12:6), and the rejected and vindicated stone (Ps 118:22-23 in Mark 12:10-11). Now he proves that the Messiah is David's Lord (Ps 110:1 in Mark 12:36).

Jesus has not yet explicitly declared that he is the Messiah, however. He has hinted with increasing frequency – sometimes blatantly (Mark 11:1-10), sometimes coyly (Mark 12:6-11) – but he is still keeping the "messianic secret" (Mark 1:15, 34, 44; 3:11-12; 5:43; 7:36; 8:30; 9:9, 30). This is because he is not immediately going to usher in David's kingdom as expected (Mark 11:10; cf. 8:31-33; 10:42-45). Instead, he is arrested by the religious leaders who assemble to try him before the high priest. When Jesus cites Ps 110:1 at his trial, the

[59] See also Hay, *Glory at the Right Hand*, 64-65; Martin Hengel, "Psalm 110 und die Erhöhung des Auferstandenen zur Rechten Gottes," in *Anfänge der Christologie* (ed. Cilliers Breytenbach and Henning Paulsen; Göttingen: Vandenhoeck & Ruprecht, 1991), 68.

emphasis shifts from the Messiah's identity as David's Lord (as in Mark 12:10) to Jesus' status as the Messiah, the Son of Man, who sits at God's right hand. The "messianic secret," kept since Mark 1:25, is now revealed.[60]

In this citation, the Gospel's most audacious christological claim coheres with its sharpest irony. The irony is that Jesus' revealing the messianic secret is what prompts the council to condemn him to death (Mark 14:63-64) – a fate that confounds messianic expectations. The audacious claim is that those who accuse the Messiah of blasphemy and petition Pilate to have him crucified will eventually see him seated at God's right hand, in fulfillment of Ps 110:1. Jesus' previous prognostications will come to pass. God will vindicate the rejected Messiah (Mark 12:10). In losing his life, Jesus will save it (Mark 8:35).

Jesus' confession in Mark 14:62 alludes not only to Ps 110:1 but also to Dan 7:13, part of a vision in which "with the clouds of heaven there came one like a son of man (μετὰ τῶν νεφελῶν τοῦ οὐρανοῦ ὡς υἱὸς ἀνθρώπου ἐρχόμενος ἦν)."[61] Here, as in Mark 1:2-3 and 11:1-10, Mark conflates two passages and applies them to Jesus. In the previous instances, Isa 40:3 was joined with Mal 3:1 and Zech 9:9 with Ps 118:25-26 on the basis of similar vocabulary. Could this also be the case with Ps 110:1 and Dan 7:13?[62] Clearly, both Ps 110 and Dan 7:9-14 describe similar scenes of God's enthronement and beneficence towards a human figure.[63] Still, no distinctive vocabulary serves to establish a verbal link.

Perhaps a third verse could act as a catalyst. In *Midr. Ps.* 2§9 (on Ps 2:7), this technique is used to interpret Ps 110:1 and Dan 7:13 in light of Ps 2:7. The exegete argues that the "lord" of Ps 110:1 is the "son" of Ps 2:7, since both are addressed by the Lord. He then connects the "son (בן)" of Ps 2:7 with the "son (בר)" of Dan 7:13. This "son" is identified as Israel.

60 See also Matera, *Kingship of Jesus*, 73; Dautzenberg, "Psalm 110," 151.

61 The English text is quoted from the RSV. The Greek of Mark 14:62 conforms most closely to the version of Dan 7:13 preserved in B and A. Verbal parallels between Dan 7:13 and passages from any other book of Israel's Scripture are extant only in Greek, as the MT of Dan 2:4b-7:28 appears only in Aramaic. Probable allusions to Dan 7:13 in Mark 8:38; 13:26 are not considered here.

62 Kim stresses the connection between Ps 118:22 and Dan 7:13 as mediated by Dan 2:34, 44 ("Son of God, Stone, Son of Man, Servant," 142). The conflation in Mark 14:62, however, makes it much more likely that Dan 7:13 was introduced because of Ps 110.

63 Juel, *Messianic Exegesis*, 167; Hengel, "Psalm 110," 58; Evans, *Mark 8:27-16:20*, 451. Juel attributes this idea to Dahl.

Mark seems to accord some significance to Ps 2:7, judging by the probable allusions in Mark 1:11 and 9:7. Maybe he too uses Ps 2:7 to forge a connection between Ps 110:1 and Dan 7:13, giving it messianic significance. This is the opinion of C. S. Mann, who notes that in Mark 14:62 Jesus cites Ps 110:1 and Dan 7:13 in response to a question that reiterates important terms from Ps 2:2, 7 (LXX): "Are you the Messiah (ὁ χριστός), the Son (υἱός) of the Blessed One?" (Mark 14:61).[64]

Other verses that might enable messianic interpretation of Dan 7:13 in light of Ps 110:1 include Ps 80:17 and Ps 8:4-6. The possible connection with Ps 80:17 was first proposed by Dodd.[65] The verse reads:

> But let thy hand be upon the man of thy right hand (ימינך; δεξιάς σου), the son of man (בן־אדם; υἱὸν ἀνθρώπου) whom thou has made strong forthyself.[66]

According to Ps 80:17, the one at God's right hand is the son of man. Therefore, the "son of man" described in Dan 7:13 can be identified with the Messiah seated at God's "right hand" in Ps 110:1.

A similar connection can be made using Ps 8:4-6. These verses from a psalm of David reflect on the lordly status of the "son of man (בן־אדם; υἱὸς ἀνθρώπου)." God has given him dominion over creation and "put all things under his feet (תחת־רגליו; ὑποκάτω τῶν ποδῶν αὐτοῦ)." He can thus be associated both with the king of Ps 110:1, whom God seats at God's right hand "until I make your enemies your footstool (הדם לרגליך; ὑποπόδιον τῶν ποδῶν σου)," and with the "son of man" in Dan 7:13.[67]

There is no direct evidence for messianic exegesis of Dan 7:13 in light of Ps 110:1 by way of Ps 2, Ps 80, or Ps 8. Indeed, Ps 80:17 is never cited in the New Testament. As we have seen, however, there is a clear indication that the first Christians interpreted Ps 110:1 in light of Ps 2:7. There is also ample evidence – some of it in Mark – that the first

64 Mann, *Mark*, 625; Gundry, *Apology for the Cross*, 912.

65 *According to the Scriptures*, 101-2. See also Oscar J. F. Seitz, "The Future Coming of the Son of Man: Three Midrashic Formulations in the Gospel of Mark," *SE VI* (1973): 482-86; Hay, *Glory at the Right Hand*, 26, n. 32; Charles F.D. Moule, *The Origin of Christology* (Cambridge: Cambridge University Press, 1977), 24-26; Juel, *Messianic Exegesis*, 167-68; Gundry, *Apology for the Cross*, 912.

66 The English text is quoted from the RSV. A direct connection between Ps 80:17 and Dan 7:13 can be made only in Greek. In the MT of Dan 7:13, the phrase "like a son of man" is rendered כבר אנש.

67 Again, the connection with Dan 7:13 can be made only in Greek. See also Hay, *Glory at the Right Hand*, 109; Michael D. Goulder, "Psalm 8 and the Son of Man," *NTS* 48 (2002): 26-28.

believers interpreted Ps 8 as a prophecy about their Messiah, Jesus, and that they did so in light of Ps 110:1. First Corinthians 15:25-27 attests to the antiquity of this tradition. Here Paul cites both passages to wrap up his argument that "Christ has been raised from the dead" (1 Cor 15:20), that he will be joined at his coming by "those who belong to Christ (v. 23)," and that, at the end, "he hands over the kingdom to God the Father, after he has destroyed every ruler and every authority and power" (v. 25). Paul alludes first to Ps 110:1: "He must reign until he has put all his enemies under his feet." To further demonstrate his point, Paul then quotes Ps 8:6: "God has put all things in subjection under his feet." He is apparently impressed by the verbal similarities. So are the authors of Ephesians and Hebrews, who both cite Ps 110:1 in tandem with Ps 8:4-6 in order to support arguments about the Messiah (Eph 1:20, 22; Heb 1:13; 2:5-9).[68]

That Mark was no stranger to this exegetical tradition is perhaps indicated by the allusion to Ps 110:1 in Mark 12:36. Here Mark faithfully quotes the LXX except for one phrase: he substitutes ὑποκάτω – possibly imported from Ps 8:6 – for ὑποπόδιον.[69] We cannot give too much weight to this, since some of the best manuscripts (including א and A) read ὑποπόδιον. Still, internal evidence favors the possibility that Mark originally wrote ὑποκάτω (as attested in B and D). No other New Testament citation of Ps 110:1 substitutes this word. The only exception is that in Matt 22:44, best explained as an exact rendering of Mark 12:36.[70] Of course, Mark could have used ὑποπόδιον, and Matthew could have changed it to ὑποκάτω. Since this would have involved a deviation from both the LXX of Ps 110:1 and Mark's exact quotation of it, this possibility is not very likely. Nevertheless, it cannot be ruled out.[71]

[68] For a brief discussion about the importance of the connection between Ps 110:1 and Ps 8:6 to the development of New Testament Christology, see Martinus C. de Boer, *The Defeat of Death: Apocalyptic Eschatology in 1 Corinthians 15 and Romans 5* (JSNTSup 22; Sheffield: Sheffield Academic Press, 1988), 117-18.

[69] Helmer Ringgren, "The Use of the Psalms in the Gospels," in *The Living Text* (ed. Dennis E. Groh and Robert Jewett; Lanham, Md.: University Press of America, 1985), 39; *Hengel*, "Psalm 110," 54-55; Morna D. Hooker, *The Gospel According to St. Mark* (BNTC; London: Black, 1991), 293; Marcus, *Way of the Lord*, 130-32; Breytenbach, "Markusevangelium, Psalm 110,1 und 118,22f.," 213; Albl, "*Scripture Cannot Be Broken*," 222, 227.

[70] Luke corrects the misquote in Mark 12:36 at Luke 20:43; Acts 2:36.

[71] Bruce Metzger rates this a "C" decision (*A Textual Commentary on the Greek New Testament* [Stuttgart: United Bible Societies, 1971], 111).

More evidence that messianic exegesis of Dan 7:13 involves the phrase "son of man" lies in fact that Mark's Jesus often refers to himself as "the Son of Man."[72] This phrase appears fourteen times in Mark's Gospel, three of them in probable allusions to Dan 7:13 (Mark 8:38; 13:26; 14:62). Clearly, "Son of Man" is significant for Mark – perhaps because it enables messianic exegesis of Dan 7:13 by way of Ps 8:6 or Ps 80:17 and Ps 110:1 in light of Ps 89.

This method for interpreting Dan 7:13 may also explain why Jesus uses the self-designation when speaking of his suffering (Mark 8:31; 9:12; 9:31; 10:33, 45; 14:41). Most commentators agree that these assertions seem incongruous when applied to Daniel's triumphant "son of man."[73] If an underlying tradition of messianic exegesis links Dan 7:13 to Pss 89; 22; 69; and 118, however, then a suffering Son of Man does not seem so inconsistent. For Mark, the Son of Man who sits at God's right hand and who will come with the clouds (Mark 14:62; cf. Ps 110:1; Dan 7:13) is the Messiah of these four psalms. This enables Mark's Jesus to speak also of a rejected Son of Man (Mark 8:31; cf. Ps 118:22) who is treated with contempt (Mark 9:12; cf. Pss 22:6, 24; 69:33; 89:38).

It may be, as suggested by the preponderance of evidence, that Mark conflates Ps 110:1 and Dan 7:13 because he interprets them, together with Ps 8:4-6, as messianic prophecies. On the other hand, perhaps the catalyst is Ps 80:17 or Ps 2:7. A fourth possibility is that both Ps 110 and Dan 7:13 were associated with Ps 118 – Ps 110 on the basis of words like "nations," "enemies," "right hand," and "exalt," and Dan 7:13 using the verb "come." We have observed that Mark has apparently reflected on this word, since it appears in several of the passages he cites. The idea that Mark interprets these passages together on the basis of this verb is supported by the fact that they neatly combine to describe the coming of Mark's Messiah, Jesus. As we have seen, Jesus first comes (Mark 1:7, 9) for baptism by John, who prepares his way as in Isa 40:3 and Mal 3:1, prophecies about the "Lord" who "comes." Next, Jesus comes to Jerusalem (Mark 11:15) as foretold in Zech 9:9, which describes a "king" who "comes," as well as Ps 118:26, a benediction for "one who comes in the name of the LORD." In Jerusalem (Mark 11-15) he is rejected by the council (Ps 118:22), abandoned by his followers (Zech 13:17), abused by his enemies (Pss 22:18; 69:32),

[72] Juel, *Messianic Exegesis*, 165-67.
[73] See e.g. ibid., 157, 161.

and forsaken by God (Ps 22:1). Even as Mark tells the story of Jesus' sufferings, however, he looks forward to his resurrection and parousia. The rejected Messiah will be vindicated (Ps 118:23) and exalted to God's right hand (Ps 110:1). Finally, he will "come" again (Mark 8:38; 13:26; 14:62), this time with the clouds of heaven (Dan 7:13).[74]

"As It Is Written of Him"

Mark offers no conclusive proof that he interprets these passages as messianic prophecies in light of Ps 89. He does not display the mechanism – nor does he need to, if his audience already attributes christological significance to the texts he cites. On the whole, however, there is sufficient evidence to suggest that some tradition of messianic exegesis lies behind Mark's Passion Narrative. First, Mark certainly possessed the ability and the inclination to engage in this type of exegetical enterprise. He had access to Israel's Scriptures, they informed his Christology, and, as demonstrated by the citations in Mark 1:2-3 and 11:1-10, he employed the technique of interpreting passages together on the basis of shared vocabulary.

Second, the passages cited in Mark 11–15 do in fact share significant words, both among themselves and with Ps 89. Among the most frequently shared are "scorn," "enemies," "save," "live," and "right hand." Messianic interpretation of these passages together yields the portrait of a Messiah oppressed by his opponents and ultimately rescued by God. This makes them easily applicable to Jesus.

Third, Mark seems to have reflected on some of the shared vocabulary. Words like "come," "Son of Man," "reject," "life," and "save" appear at important junctures in his narrative. "The Son of Man must undergo great suffering, and be rejected by the elders," teaches Mark's Jesus (Mark 8:31). "Those who want to save their life will lose it, and those who lose their life for my sake, and for the sake of the gospel, will save it" (Mark 8:35). "For the Son of Man came not to be served but to serve, and to give his life a ransom for many" (Mark 10:45). By enabling messianic exegesis of the passages Mark cites, these words have apparently illuminated Mark's understanding of Jesus' passion.

[74] Mann also points out the possibility that the Gospels describe Jesus as "the one who comes" under the influence of Ps 118:26 together with Dan 7:13 (*Mark*, 437).

Fourth, some of the connections possibly used by Mark are actually used by other ancient exegetes in order to facilitate messianic exegesis. Acts 4:11 seems to reflect a tradition of interpreting Ps 118:22 as a prophecy about the Messiah in light of Ps 89:38 on the basis of the word "reject." In 1 Cor 15:25-27; Eph 1:20, 22; and Heb 1:13; 2:5-9, Ps 8:4-6 is quoted in tandem with Ps 110:1. Each psalm is understood to refer to the Messiah, at whose feet the Lord will subject his enemies. It would have been quite easy for Mark to make these exegetical moves.

Of course, Mark's tradition of messianic exegesis did not necessarily depend on Ps 89. The same results can be achieved by starting with Ps 110:1, whose christological interpretation predates Mark (cf. 1 Cor 15:23). Genesis 49:10-11, a prophecy (possibly echoed in Mark 11:2, 4-5) about a ruler from Judah, contains the word "come" and therefore would serve as an equally good foundation.[75] In my opinion, however, the best case can be made for Ps 89. Its reference to God's "anointed" who has been "rejected," along with its strong connections to Pss 22; 69; 110; and 118, make it an essential aid for understanding the apparent contradiction of a crucified Messiah. To arrive at this understanding seems to be the burden of Mark's Gospel. The connections from the lament in Ps 89 to the descriptions of suffering in Pss 22 and 69 and the affirmations of Pss 118 and 110, and from there to the prophecies in Zech 9:9; 13:7 and Dan 7:13, offer some indication of a process by which that contradiction might have been resolved.

[75] The following scholars have proposed that Mark 11:1-10 conflates Ps 118:25-26 and Gen 49:10 on the basis of the word "come": William L. Lane (*The Gospel of Mark* [NICT; Grand Rapids: Eerdmans, 1974], 395-396); Juel, *Mark*, 153; Krause, "The One Who Comes," 145.

“WHY DID YOU ABANDON ME?” ABANDONMENT CHRISTOLOGY IN MARK’S GOSPEL[1]

William Sanger CAMPBELL

The meaning and significance of the cry of abandonment in Mark 15:34 (par. Matt 27:46) have been controversial and emotional issues in Markan studies over the years. Indeed, Jesus’ outburst has been a source of considerable embarrassment for many who, as Raymond E. Brown notes, refuse to accept “the surface import that would have Jesus expressing the sentiment of being forsaken by God.”[2] Others accept Jesus’ lament as a pivotal statement of Mark’s vision of atonement. William L. Lane, for example, argues that “[t]he cry of dereliction expressed the unfathomable pain of real abandonment by the Father. The sinless Son of God died the sinner’s death and experienced the bitterness of desolation. This was the cost of providing ‘a ransom for the many’ (Ch. 10:45).”[3] What has not been sufficiently explored, however, is the connection of Mark 15:34 to the motif of abandonment that extends throughout the Second Gospel. Jesus’ cry from the cross is not an isolated narrative event, but the culmination of one of the governing story lines in Mark’s drama. It completes Mark’s pattern of abandonment, a pattern that belongs to the fabric of the narrative and to the core of the Gospel’s Christology. This essay examines Jesus’ abandonment (or rejection) by every character who at one time either is or should be supportive of him, specifically neighbors and family, disciples, the crowd that follows him

[1] I wish to thank members of the Mark Group, the faculty of Columbia Theological Seminary, and participants in Columbia’s Lifelong Learning program who offered helpful observations on earlier versions of the essay. I am indebted in particular to Brian K. Blount, Stanley P. Saunders, Christine Roy Yoder, Robert H. Gundry, and Shawn J. Kelley whose generous and constructive criticisms and suggestions have informed and strengthened the essay in valuable ways.

[2] Raymond E. Brown, *The Death of the Messiah: From Gethsemane to the Grave: A Commentary on the Passion Narratives in the Four Gospels* (2 vols.; ABRL; New York: Doubleday, 1994), 2:1047; see also 2:1047-51 for Brown’s extended summary and counterarguments.

[3] William L. Lane, *The Gospel according to Mark* (Grand Rapids: Eerdmans, 1974), 573.

throughout his ministry, even the bandits executed with him.[4] The analysis establishes abandonment by putative friends and supporters as perhaps the most striking and prominent feature of Mark's characterization of Jesus, encompassing not only passages that explicitly narrate abandonment but also passages that anticipate or accentuate the overt scenes of rejection. I then argue that Jesus' abandonment by God, represented in the cry from Ps 22, is an integral part of – indeed the inevitable conclusion to – the narrative's abandonment motif. Finally, I conclude that Jesus' cry of abandonment, read in the context of the Gospel's overarching theme of abandonment, represents in Mark a fundamental christological expression.

Isolation and Abandonment

Jesus' isolation is a vital component in Mark's depiction of his deteriorating circumstances, a trajectory that is foreshadowed as early as 1:14 with the arrest of John the Baptist and the series of controversies with Jewish leaders that commences only a few verses later (2:6). Indeed, the Gospel is framed with passages that lift up Jesus' isolation, setting the tone for the narrative that unfolds within its borders. Mark's introduction of Jesus underscores his initial isolation in two scenes. First, only Jesus is mentioned as seeing the skies split and the Spirit dove descend, and the voice from the heavens addresses him alone (1:10-11). In contrast, Matthew's and Luke's versions of this scene soften the sense of Jesus' isolation (Matt 3:16-17; Luke 3:21-22). Both are vague as to who might have shared the visionary experience, and in Matthew the voice addresses a broader audience ("This is my beloved Son in whom I have taken delight"; οὗτός ἐστιν ὁ υἱός μου ὁ ἀγαπητός, ἐν ᾧ εὐδόκησα).[5] The experience (spending forty days alone) and location (in the wilderness) in Mark's subsequent temptation scene (1:12-13) further dramatizes Jesus' solitude. Completing the frame, the Gospel concludes with

[4] One scholar who has given attention to abandonment by Jesus' "closest circle" in Mark's Gospel and its implications for understanding Jesus' citation of the Ps 22 lament is Mary Ann Tolbert, *Sowing the Gospel: Mark's World in Literary-Historical Perspective* (Minneapolis: Fortress Press, 1989), 284-88. Though her analysis is not as extensive nor as developed and her conclusions differ in several significant ways, my interpretation corresponds with her earlier insights at a number of points (see also Wilfrid Harrington's brief treatment of the issue in *Mark* [New Testament Message 4; Wilmington: Glazier, 1979], 237).

[5] Except where noted, translations are my own.

the account of Mary Magdalene, James's mother Mary, and Salome who, when they arrive at Jesus' tomb to anoint his body, encounter instead a young man in white garb who informs them of Jesus' resurrection and instructs them to deliver to the other disciples the message to meet Jesus in Galilee. The reaction of the women is quite the reverse, however. Fearful, they abandon the directive, keeping the angel's information to themselves (16:1-8). Again, Mark's account is decidedly different than the burial anointing stories in Matt 28:8-10 and Luke 24:1-11, which report that the women (two Marys in Matthew and, in Luke, a number of women, among them Mary Magdalene, James's mother Mary, and Joanna) fulfill the instructions of the messenger and, in Matt 28:10, of the risen Jesus himself. Mark's Gospel, then, emphasizes that Jesus begins and ends alone.[6] Within this framework, the motif of abandonment by supporters drives the accelerating sense of Jesus' separation from others as the story develops.

Neighbors and Family

The first explicit rejection of Jesus by supporters in Mark's Gospel occurs at what is seemingly the height of his ministry. The narrative recounts that, while enjoying a remarkable and widespread reputation as a preacher and healer, Jesus decides to visit his hometown (πατρίδα αὐτοῦ), Nazareth in Galilee (6:1-6).[7] His neighbors and friends take offense after hearing him preach in the synagogue, a setting that recalls the hardening of opposition among Jewish religious leaders after their synagogue encounter with Jesus in 3:1-6.[8] The reaction of the

[6] Although text-critical analysis has persuaded an overwhelming majority of scholars that Mark's Gospel originally ended at 16:8, challenges to the consensus continue to be advanced. Most of those who reject 16:8 as Mark's intended ending argue for a lost ending, conceding that text-critical evidence disqualifies alternative endings in the manuscript tradition; see, for example, Robert H. Gundry, *Mark: A Commentary on His Apology for the Cross* (Grand Rapids: Eerdmans, 1993), 1012. Such vigorous defenses of a lost ending as Gundry's (*Mark*, 1009-21) and more recently N. Clayton Croy's (*Mutilation of Mark's Gospel* [Nashville: Abingdon, 2003]), however, have not overcome the weight of evidence supporting the consensus view.

[7] Mark 6:1-6 does not name Jesus' hometown, as Luke 4:16 does (ἦλθεν εἰς Ναζαρά, οὗ ἦν τεθραμμένος; "he came into Nazareth where he had been raised"; see also 2:39, 51). Nonetheless, Mark 1:9 ("In those days, Jesus came from Nazareth of Galilee"), references to "Jesus of Nazareth" (Ἰησοῦς [ὁ] Ναζαρηνός) sprinkled throughout the narrative (1:24; 10:47; 14:67; 16:6), and consistent gospel tradition leave little doubt that Nazareth is the location designated by πατρίδα αὐτοῦ.

[8] Robert A. Guelich, *Mark 1–8:26* (WBC 34A; Dallas: Word, 1989), 308.

Nazarenes elicits from Jesus the well-known response of 6:4: "A prophet is not without honor except in his hometown, and among his relatives, and in his house."[9] As Joel Marcus points out, rebuff and renunciation of prophets by their compatriots is a common feature of biblical prophecy, and a theme "extensively developed in the New Testament."[10] Nonetheless, the effect of the community's rejection on Jesus and his ministry is devastating: "he was *not able* to do any powerful deeds there" (6:5).[11]

Only Mark among the evangelists includes "among his relatives" (τοῖς συγγενεῦσιν) in the proverbial saying (cf. Matt 13:57; Luke 4:24; John 4:44), and this allusion to Jesus' family connects his rejection at Nazareth to an earlier episode in the Gospel.[12] In 3:20-35, Mark discloses tension between Jesus and his family over his preaching,

[9] Joel Marcus (*Mark 1–8* [AB 27; New York: Doubleday, 2000], 376) notes that the saying is "widely attested in Greco-Roman literature; see, for example; Plutarch *De Exilio* 604D: 'You would find that the most sensible and wisest people are little cared for in their own hometowns.'"

[10] Marcus, *Mark 1–8*, 376.

[11] Emphasis added, though the double-negative grammatical construction suggests as much (καὶ οὐκ ἐδύνατο ἐκεῖ ποιῆσαι οὐδεμίαν δύναμιν; see H.W. Smyth, *Greek Grammar* [rev. Gordon M. Messing; Harvard: Harvard University Press, 1984], §2761; W.W. Goodwin, *Greek Grammar* [rev. C.B. Gulick; Boston: Ginn, 1930], §1622). Mark regularly employs double-negative constructions to emphasize or reinforce negation (3:27; 5:37; 7:12; 9:8; 12:14, 34; 14:25, 60, 61; 15:4, 5; 16:8). The exceptive clause (v. 5b), therefore, qualifies the extent of the claim in 6:5a, but not its force, contra Guelich's (*Mark 1–8:26*, 311-12; see also Gundry, *Mark*, 292-93) argument that the exception softens Mark's statement to, in effect, an equivalent of the parallel in Matt 13:58, "And he did not do many powerful deeds there because of their unbelief" (καὶ οὐκ ἐποίησεν ἐκεῖ δυνάμις πολλὰς διὰ τὴν ἀπιστίαν αὐτῶν). Mark is insistent that Jesus is, for the most part, unable to perform mighty deeds in his hometown in the wake of his neighbors' rejection of him. Vincent Taylor's (*The Gospel according to Mark* [London: Macmillan, 1952], 301) restraint, therefore, is wise, "All that we can say is that 5b modifies the rigour of 5a by stating an exception."

[12] Marcus (*Mark 1–8*, 376) suggests that Mark may have added the family reference to the proverb. C.E.B. Cranfield (*The Gospel according to St. Mark* [CGTC; Cambridge: Cambridge University Press, 1959], 143) notes another family allusion that connects the two passages, viz., in Mark only 3:31-32 and 6:3 mention Jesus' mother. In the view of a growing number of scholars, however, based on its similarity to the description of Jesus in 6:3 as "the son of Mary and brother of James and Joses and Judas and Simon," Mary the mother of the younger James and Joses in 15:40 (cf. 15:47; 16:1) also refers to Jesus' mother (e.g., Gundry, *Mark*, 977; Kathleen E. Corley, "Slaves, Servants and Prostitutes: Gender and Social Class in Mark," in *A Feminist Companion to Mark* [ed. Amy-Jill Levine with Marianne Blickenstaff; Sheffield: Sheffield Academic Press, 2001; repr., Cleveland: Pilgrim, 2004], 202). If this identification is correct, it of course modifies Cranfield's insight. At the same time, as Corley ("Slaves, Servants and Prostitutes," 202) argues, Mary's "desertion of the tomb would contribute… to the theme of the failure of Jesus' family."

describing how they attempt to prevent him forcibly from continuing his work because of their assessment that he is mentally unstable (3:21). Οἱ παρ' αὐτοῦ ("those with him"; 3:21) can designate envoys or followers, but is also used of those "intimately connected with someone," including family.[13] Some scholars have identified οἱ παρ' αὐτοῦ as the disciples and the action taken as calming the overly excited crowd, a translation that insulates Jesus' family from the allegation that they, too, rejected him.[14] Marcus rightly objects, however, that οἱ παρ' αὐτοῦ in this instance "are distinguished from the disciples mentioned in the previous verse."[15] Furthermore, the intercalation structure necessitates understanding the phrase in relation to 3:31, which explicitly associates it with Jesus' family (καὶ ἔρχεται ἡ μήτηρ αὐτοῦ καὶ οἱ ἀδελφοὶ αὐτοῦ).[16] Additionally, some translators render ἔλεγον in 3:21 as indefinite (so NRSV, "people were saying, 'He has gone out of his mind'"), which takes the accusation out of his family's mouth. As C.E.B. Cranfield argues, however, "a plural verb can hardly be understood as indefinite when the immediate context contains an obvious plural subject."[17] Friction between Jesus and his family is not unique to Mark. John 7:5 also recalls a tradition of familial disaffection, reporting that Jesus' siblings "did not believe in him" (RSV).[18]

[13] BDAG, 756. In classical Greek writings, οἱ παρ' αὐτοῦ commonly referred to envoys. Koine, however, also used the expression for those closely connected with someone, in particular relatives (e.g., Prov 31:21; 1 Macc 11:73; 12:27; 13:52; Josephus, *Ant.* 1.193; BDAG, 756; Cranfield, *Mark*, 133; Guelich, *Mark 1–8:26*, 172; Taylor, *Mark*, 236).

[14] Henry Wansbrough, "Mark 3:21 – Was Jesus Out of His Mind?" *NTS* 18 (1971-72): 233-35; David Wenham, "The Meaning of Mark 3:21," *NTS* 21 (1974-75): 295-300; John Painter, "When Is a House Not Home? Disciples and Family in Mark 3.13-35," *NTS* 45 (1999): 501-9; see also Guelich, *Mark 1–8:26*, 172.

[15] Marcus, *Mark 1–8*, 270.

[16] James R. Edwards ("Markan Sandwiches: The Significance of Interpolations in Markan Narratives," *NovT* 31 [1989]: 209-10) demonstrates that, although "less obviously a sandwich" than other passages in Mark, 3:20-35 does in fact exhibit Markan intercalation form; see also Guelich, *Mark 1–8:26*, 168-69. As Edwards ("Markan Sandwiches," 197) explains, framing episodes in Mark's intercalation style "require one another to complete their narrative."

[17] Cranfield, *Mark*, 134. Following Ernst Best, Marcus (*Mark 1–8*, 270-71) adds that "if this were the meaning, the clauses in 3:21 would be in the reverse order ('and they were saying, "He's gone out of his mind"; and his relatives... went out to seize him'")."

[18] Matthew and Luke do not contain the material in Mark 3:21, and locate the rest of the pericope in other narrative contexts that diminish the sense of familial disagreement (see Matt 12:22-50; Luke 8:19-21; 11:14–12:10).

As a number of commentators note, κρατέω ("seize") employed in 3:21 to describe the effort of Jesus' family to halt his public ministry, is the same term used of opponents who desire to arrest him later in the narrative (12:12; 14:1, 44, 46), a parallel that foreshadows future events and links the behavior of Jesus' family with that of his enemies.[19] The intercalated episode in Mark 3 links as well the attitude of Jesus' relatives with the view of his scribal adversaries that he is satan-possessed.[20] Their reaction is not unimaginable since, as Mark further illustrates in the narrative of the Gerasene demoniac (5:1-20), insanity was commonly identified with demon possession in the first century.[21] The feelings of Jesus' family toward him and his ministry and the actions motivated by those feelings occasion the estrangement with which the passage closes (3:31-35), the distance between the sides made abundantly clear through the repetition of "mother and brothers and sisters" (ἡ μήτηρ καὶ οἱ ἀδελφοί; vv. 31, 32, 33, 34, 35)[22] and of their location with respect to Jesus: while he gathers with his new family inside, his family of origin waits outside (ἔξω; vv. 31 and 32).[23]

[19] E.g., Taylor, *Mark*, 559; Marcus, *Mark 1–8*, 279; Edwards, "Markan Sandwiches," 210.

[20] So also Guelich (*Mark 1–8:26*, 183).

[21] George Aichele, "Jesus' Uncanny 'Family Scene,'" *JSNT* 74 (1999): 32; Peter G. Bolt, *Jesus' Defeat of Death: Persuading Mark's Early Readers* [SNTSMS; Cambridge: Cambridge University Press, 2003], 147-48). In addition, Marcus (*Mark 1–8*, 271) notes that persons denounced as possessed by demons were often those "at variance with their nuclear families."

[22] The weight of external evidence favors the exclusion of καὶ αἱ ἀδελφαί σου ("and your sisters") from v. 32 (א B C K L W Δ Θ etc.). The phrase is missing as well from the Synoptic parallels (Matt 12:46-50; Luke 8:19-21). Cranfield (*Mark*, 144) speculates that its addition here reflects assimilation to 3:35 or 6:3. Bruce M. Metzger (*A Textual Commentary on the Greek New Testament* [New York: United Bible Societies, 1975], 82) also argues for expansion, disagreeing with the majority of UBS editorial committee members, who support the inclusion of καὶ αἱ ἀδελφαί σου on the ground that it represents the more difficult reading. Metzger adds that, historically, "it is extremely unlikely that Jesus' sisters would have joined in publicly seeking to check him in his ministry." Οἱ ἀδελφοί, however, does not necessarily exclude sisters; indeed, in the absence of contextual directives, it should be translated "brothers and sisters" (BDAG, 18), making αἱ ἀδελφαί unnecessary (its addition in v. 35 being for emphasis).

[23] E. Elizabeth Johnson, "'Who Is My Mother?': Family Values in the Gospel of Mark," in *Blessed One: Protestant Perspectives on Mary* (ed. Beverly Roberts Gaventa and Cynthia L. Rigby; Louisville: Westminster John Knox, 2002), 35; Raymond E. Brown et al., eds., *Mary in the New Testament* (Philadelphia: Fortress Press, 1978), 53. Johnson ("Who Is My Mother," 38; see also 33-37) argues for mutual rejection, that "Jesus' rejection of his mother and brothers in 3:31-35 results in their reciprocal rejection of him in 6:1-6a."

Disciples

Judas

The disciples, Jesus' closest friends, abandon him next. First, Judas resolves to betray him to the Jewish authorities (14:10-11). The narrative does not provide a motive for Judas's decision. Matthew 26:15 specifies greed as the reason, but in Mark the promise of reward is made only after Judas offers to cooperate.[24] Neither does Mark allege that it is Satan's influence that prompts Judas's disloyalty, as do Luke and John (Luke 22:3; John 13:2, 27).[25] Judas's intimate association with Jesus is made plain: he is "one of the twelve" (εἷς τῶν δώδεκα; 14:10; cf. 3:14, 19; 14:20, 43) specially chosen by Jesus in 3:14-19. Readers, who have been expecting treachery since Judas first entered the story in 3:19 as the member of the twelve "who also handed him over" (ὃς καὶ παρέδωκεν αὐτόν), have no difficulty identifying which unnamed dinner partner is meant when Jesus predicts his betrayal at the Last Supper (14:18-21). Mark does not include Judas's remarks to the authorities in the narrative of their meeting in 14:10-11, but ἀκούσαντες in v. 11 taken with the purpose clause in v. 10 (ἵνα αὐτὸν παραδοῖ αὐτοῖς) and 3:19 supports the interpretation that he offered to hand Jesus over to them.[26] As good as his word, after celebrating Passover dinner with Jesus and the others in his entourage, Judas leads a sword and club wielding mob of the chief priests' henchmen to Gethsemane where Jesus has gone with Peter, James, and John to pray privately. Irony drips off the page as the conspirator points Jesus out with a kiss that signals the "affection and respect that a disciple has for his rabbi" (14:43-45).[27]

24 Eduard Schweizer, *The Good News according to Mark* (trans. Donald H. Madvig; Atlanta; Westminster John Knox, 1970), 293.

25 See Luke Timothy Johnson, *The Gospel of Luke* (SP 3; Collegeville, Minn.: Liturgical, 1991), 332, 335; Joseph A. Fitzmyer, *The Gospel according to Luke X-XXIV* (AB 28A; Garden City, N.Y.: Doubleday, 1985), 1374. I find no basis in Mark's narrative for the speculation of Craig A. Evans (*Mark 8:27–16:20* [WBC 34B; Nashville: Thomas Nelson, 2001], 366) that, in frustration, "Judas has given up on Jesus, who continues to speak of his death."

26 Judas's value to the Jewish authorities apparently rests in his ability to provide them with information as to the time and place to arrest Jesus quietly, avoiding the possibility of a riot about which they are quite anxious (12:12; 14:2); Lane, *Mark*, 495-96; see also Morna D. Hooker, *The Gospel according to Saint Mark* (BNTC; London: Black, 1991; repr., Peabody, Mass.: Hendrickson, 1999), 331; Evans, *Mark 8:27–16:20*, 365-66.

27 Evans, *Mark 8:27–16:20*, 423; see also Lane, *Mark*, 525. Both cite examples from Jewish literature for the custom of kiss greetings between rabbis and colleagues or disciples.

Other Disciples

More surprising at first glance than Judas's conduct is that of the other disciples who, as soon as Jesus' captors have their prisoner in hand, abandon him by running away (14:48-50). The initial reaction to the arrest recorded in 14:47, namely, that someone attacks the high priest's servant, cutting off the slave's ear with a sword, seems more in keeping with the relationship between Jesus and his friends (though it is not clear in Mark that the sword-wielding bystander is one of the disciples).[28] The incongruity of the disciples' behavior with their original response to Jesus' invitation to join his public ministry amplifies the impact of their rejection. In 1:16-18, Simon (Peter) and his brother Andrew instantly abandon their fishing gear and careers to follow Jesus (εὐθὺς ἀφέντες τὰ δίκτυα ἠκολούθησαν αὐτῷ), and the second pair of siblings approached by Jesus, James and John, go so far as to quit their own father, leaving unfinished tasks for him and hired servants to complete in order to join Jesus without delay (1:19-20).[29] Indeed, Mark 3:13 characterizes Jesus' efforts at recruiting disciples as a complete success.[30]

On the other hand, the narrative at least twice alludes to the cowardice that overcomes the disciples and the forsaking of Jesus that it occasions. In the more overt adumbration in 14:27, Jesus warns the disciples during their walk to the Mount of Olives after Passover dinner that, when trouble arises, all of them will fall away (σκανδαλίζω), that is, desert him.[31] This sense for σκανδαλίζω is confirmed by the prophecy that Jesus cites to support his claim, "I will strike the shepherd, and the

[28] Gundry, *Mark*, 859-60; Hooker, *Mark*, 351.

[29] In the Synoptic tradition, Simon receives the name "Peter" from Jesus at his nomination to the twelve (Mark 3:16; Luke 6:14; cf. Matt 10:2). The repetition of εὐθύς and ἀφέντες link the call of James and John, and their sense of urgency in responding, to the call and response of Peter and Andrew. Marcus (*Mark 1–8*, 182) details the parallel structure that connects the two call narratives: each opens with a participle mentioning Jesus' movement, followed by εἶδεν ("he saw"); then another participle identifies whom Jesus sees (in both cases brothers) and their occupation (both related to fishing); lastly, Jesus summons the brothers and at once they abandon their current pursuits to follow him; see as well Jack Dean Kingsbury, *Conflict in Mark: Jesus, Authorities, Disciples* (Minneapolis: Fortress Press, 1989), 90. Luke 5:10 also joins the two sets of brothers, describing them as partners (κοινωνοί) in the fishing business.

[30] The emphatic use of αὐτός (προσκαλεῖται οὓς ἤθελεν αὐτός, ἀπῆλθον πρὸς αὐτόν) in 3:13 stresses that the selection of disciples was at Jesus' initiative and prerogative.

[31] The root meaning of σκανδαλίζω, "to scandalize," is evoked in several ways in Mark, including "cause to sin" (9:42-50) and, in passive voice, "be repelled by/take offense at" (6:3) and "fall away" (4:17; 14:27, 29; BDAG, 926; Evans, *Mark 8:27–16:20*, 400; Marcus, *Mark 1–8*, 309).

sheep will be scattered" (πατάξω τὸν ποιμένα, καὶ τὰ πρόβατα διασκορπισθήσονται).[32] The reaction of the sheep would resonate with those familiar with, perhaps even responsible for tending, farm animals. The same term is used of Jesus' reception from his Nazarean neighbors in 6:3, associating the prediction about the disciples with the "'deep religious offence' at the preaching of Jesus which 'causes the denial and rejection'" of him by childhood friends and neighbors in 6:1-6.[33] Even earlier Mark employs σκανδαλίζω with reference to "rocky ground" believers in Jesus' explanation of the sower parable (4:16-17; cf. 4:5-6). These are individuals who instantly (εὐθύς) and joyfully accept the word but, because their faith is not sufficiently rooted, just as quickly wilt (εὐθύς σκανδαλίζονται) at the first sign of opposition (θλίψσεως καὶ διωγμοῦ) – a description that well describes the disciples' performance in the Gospel.

A second, though less transparent, allusion to the disciples' faintheartedness occurs in 13:9-13. In the midst of the apocalyptic discourse, Jesus alerts the disciples that they too will be arrested, beaten, and tried with false testimony. As part of that persecution, he forewarns that they will be despised and rejected by those closest to them, including their families, a warning that mirrors the treatment Jesus receives from his own family and closest associates.[34]

Moreover, the inability of Peter, James, and John to stay awake in Gethsemane as Jesus anguishes over upcoming events indicates that the fervor of his companions is flagging (14:32-42), a shift in attitude made more noticeable by the fact that these three disciples are the ones singled out as impatient to follow Jesus at the beginning of his public ministry and "boasted of their ability to share his suffering (10.35-40; 14.29ff.)."[35] Indeed, the Gethsemane narrative underscores their apathy by chronicling that three times the triumvirate of friends fails to comply

[32] Zech 13:7 (LXX), πατάξατε τοὺς ποιμένας καὶ ἐκσπάσατε τὰ πρόβατα ("strike the shepherds and draw out the sheep"). Mark has likened Jesus and those who follow him to shepherd and sheep previously in 6:34. For a summary of the use and understanding of shepherd/sheep imagery in Greek and Roman culture, see Bolt, *Jesus' Defeat of Death*, 192-94, and for its Old Testament usage, see Marcus, *Mark 1-8*, 406; Gundry, *Mark*, 340.

[33] Guelich, *Mark 1–8:26*, 306, note d, citing Gustav Stählin ("σκανδαλίζω," *TDNT* 7:350).

[34] Discipleship and Christology (including the abandonment motif) are not unrelated themes in Mark. In addition to Jesus' warning in Mark 13, see other indications that those who follow Jesus will be subject to a similar fate; e.g., 8:34-38; 10:28-31, 35-39; 13:9-13.

[35] Hooker, *Mark*, 348.

with Jesus' comparatively painless request at the precise moment when his distress becomes most severe (14:33) and so the need for deference to his wishes is most pronounced.[36]

Peter

Mark considers Peter's abandonment separately from the other disciples, a not unexpected move given the attention he receives elsewhere in the Gospel.[37] On the contrary, what is startling is the omission of any mention of Peter during the arrest scene in Gethsemane. When Jesus predicts a few verses earlier the desertion of all the disciples (πάντες σκανδαλισθήσεσθε; 14:27), Peter boldly counters that, even if the others leave, he will not (εἰ καὶ πάντες σκανδαλισθήσονται, ἀλλ' οὐκ ἐγώ; 14:29). At a minimum, therefore, readers might expect him to make an appearance when Judas and posse arrive to take Jesus into custody. John's Gospel satisfies this expectation in naming Peter as the one who cuts off the ear of the high priest's slave (18:10). This is not the case in Mark, however. In fact, Peter next surfaces following from a *very* safe distance (ἀπὸ μακρόθεν; 14:54) as Jesus is being led to the high priest's home for questioning in what Brown characterizes as a "half-hearted attempt to fulfill the boast that he would not be like the other disciples."[38]

After the account of Jesus' trial before the Jewish council, the narrative returns to Peter's actions, recalling his repeated and progressively

[36] As also Robert C. Tannehill ("The Disciples in Mark: The Function of a Narrative Role," *JR* 57 [1977]: 403). 'Εκθαμβέω has the sense of being in an "intense emotional state" (BDAG, 303). Its combination with ἀδημονέω ("be troubled;" ἤρξατο ἐκθαμβεῖσθαι καὶ ἀδημονεῖν) in 14:33 – the only instance of ἐκθαμβέω used of Jesus in the NT (Evans, *Mark 8:27-16:20*, 409) – intensifies the depth of Jesus' distress (i.e., "he was overwhelmingly distraught"). Thus, Cranfield (*Mark*, 431) argues that the compound verbs describe Jesus as "in the grip of a shuddering horror in the face of the dreadful prospect before him."

[37] See 1:16–18, 29-31, 36; 3:16; 5:37; 8:27-33; 9:2-13; 10:23-31; 11:21; 13:3-4; 16:7.

[38] Brown, *Death of the Messiah*, 1:602. Mark consistently uses the adverbial ἀπὸ μακρόθεν to express spatial distance (see also 5:6; 8:3; 11:13; 15:40), and all but two of the nine other NT occurrences of μακρόθεν include ἀπό (one of the exceptions being the parallel passage to 14:54 in Luke 22:54). BDAG, 612, argues that the addition of the preposition was prompted by the loss of "separative force" that the suffix –θεν sustained. Nonetheless, ἀπὸ μακρόθεν retains a pleonastic quality that magnifies the sense of spatial separation (BDF §104; Max Zerwick and Mary Grosvenor, *A Grammatical Analysis of the Greek New Testament* [4th ed.; Rome: Pontifical Biblical Institute, 1993], 158 and 163).

defensive and comprehensive denials of Jesus (14:66-72). Peter begins by disavowing (ἀρνέομαι) association with Jesus, first privately to the high priest's maidservant (14:67-68), then publicly to the bystanders in the high priest's courtyard (14:69-70a).[39] In frustration over their refusal to accept his word (fraudulent though it is), Peter then disowns Jesus entirely, forswearing before all who have assembled any knowledge of his leader and friend (14:70b-71). The compound infinitives (ἀναθεματίζειν καὶ ὀμνύναι) bring out the force of Peter's denial. He puts himself under curse and takes an oath – in other words, he swears to God on his life that he does not know who Jesus is.[40] The juxtaposition of Peter's disclaimer and Jesus' acknowledgment of his identity as he stands alone before the Jewish leadership (14:55-65) heightens the narrative impact of the apostle's abandonment.[41] Indeed, Mark presents Peter's betrayal as even more repugnant and hurtful than the flight of the other disciples. The narrative summons a smidgen of humor in their retreat, inserting an amusing note about a young disciple who runs out of his clothes to get away from the mob as a comment on how foolish their flight appears (14:51-52).[42] No such anecdote accompanies the account of Peter's failure to acknowledge Jesus to a gaggle of servants and bystanders despite his assurances of undying – or perhaps better said, *to the death* – loyalty (14:31).[43] As in the case of the other disciples, however, Jesus has prophesied Peter's denial beforehand (14:30), employing the same term (ἀπαρνέομαι) used by Peter in pledging unswerving loyalty in 14:31 and from the same root (ἀρνέομαι) used of Peter's denials in 14:68 and 70.[44]

Women at the Tomb

The last disciples to desert Jesus are the women who go to the tomb to anoint him, namely, Mary Magdalene, Mary (James's mother), and

[39] The imperfect ἠρνεῖτο in v. 70 indicates that Peter repeatedly disclaims any involvement with Jesus (Cranfield, *Mark*, 447).

[40] BDAG, 63, 705; see also Taylor, *Mark*, 575.

[41] So also Edwards, "Markan Sandwiches," 212-13.

[42] Although interpreting the passage differently, Howard M. Jackson ("Why the Youth Shed His Cloak and Fled Naked: The Meaning and Purpose of Mark 14:51-52," *JBL* 116 [1997]: 286) likewise reads the account of the naked young man in connection with the disciples' desertion of Jesus. For a list of various interpretations of this enigmatic passage, see Evans, *Mark 8:27–16:20*, 428-29.

[43] Note the use of the imperfect ἐλάλει in 14:31, i.e., "he went on maintaining" that he would never deny Jesus (Zerwick and Grosvenor, *Grammatical Analysis*, 156).

[44] See BDAG, 97, 132-33.

Salome (16:1-8). They belong to the group of women introduced explicitly into the narrative at Jesus' death (15:40-41).[45] Although the women are said to have steadfastly followed and supported Jesus in Galilee and during his fateful pilgrimage to Jerusalem (15:41), at his crucifixion they retreat to a distance (ἀπὸ μακρόθεν) reminiscent of that maintained by Peter at Jesus' arrest.[46] Unlike their colleagues, however, the women marginally maintain their connection with Jesus until his execution and burial (15:47), and their fidelity includes the willingness to anoint his body even after the decomposition process is already quite advanced (16:1-2). The women's failure, therefore, is not of the same caliber as the other disciples.[47] Their loyalty to Jesus to his grave highlights all the more their total withdrawal only moments later. Instead of obeying the instructions of the angelophany to report to Peter and the other disciples that Jesus is risen and would meet them in Galilee as he advised prior to his arrest (16:6-7; cf. 14:28), the Gospel closes with the women fleeing in fear from the tomb and remaining silent about what they see and hear there (16:8).[48]

Crowd

Another constituency to abandon Jesus is the crowd that throughout his public ministry seems to follow him constantly.[49] Readers may be

[45] Winsome Munro ("Women Disciples in Mark?" *CBQ* 44 [1982]: 241) clarifies that women disciples in Mark are not limited to these scenes, but are a regular part of Jesus' company.

[46] See also Munro, "Women Disciples," 235; Elizabeth Struthers Malbon, "Fallible Followers: Women and Men in the Gospel of Mark," *Semeia* 28 (1983): 43.

[47] Malbon ("Fallible Followers," 45) argues that "minimal emphasis is placed on [the women's] fallibility as followers in comparison with the crowd and especially the disciples." Victoria Phillips offers an even more forceful defense of the women in "The Failure of the Women Who Followed Jesus in the Gospel of Mark," in *A Feminist Companion to Mark* (ed. Amy-Jill Levine with Marianne Blickenstaff; Sheffield: Sheffield Academic Press, 2001; repr., Cleveland: Pilgrim, 2004), 222-34. Her suggestive interpretation is that the women are abandoned by Jesus, discovering at the tomb that he has gone ahead to Galilee and that he had previously instructed some of his disciples to meet him there, but not them (pp. 230-31).

[48] See the prior discussion of the Gospel's frame of isolation. The irony of the women's silence when instructed to speak in contrast to the disregard by many characters of Jesus' commands to keep silent has been noticed by a number of scholars (e.g., Hooker, *Mark*, 387; but cf. Malbon, "Fallible Followers," 45).

[49] Variously designated as ὄχλος, πλῆθος, and πολύς; occasionally modified with intensifying adjectives, e.g., πολύς (or its superlative form, πλεῖστος; 3:7, 8; 4:1; 5:21, 24; 6:34; 8:1; 9:14; 12:37) and ἱκανός (4:1; 10:46).

tempted to consider the crowd less closely associated with Jesus than his family or disciples, but he calls its members "my mother and my brothers and sisters" (3:34-35). Nonetheless, when Jesus stands falsely accused before Pilate, this previously receptive and sympathetic audience reverses its stance and demands his execution (15:6-15).

The crowd's about face is stunning given its role in Jesus' career prior to his arrest. The impression one gets from Mark's Gospel is that Jesus draws huge, sometimes unmanageable, throngs wherever he goes. Mark describes Jesus' home at Capernaum, for example, as overflowing with people such that on one occasion a paralyzed person must be lowered through the roof to reach him (2:1-12), and on another the crush prevents Jesus and his disciples from eating (3:20; cf. 6:31). More than once in the narrative, the mass of spectators surrounding him becomes dangerously large, requiring the implementation of crowd control measures (3:7-10; 4:1). Although typically the exact size of the crowd is not announced, the two feeding stories in Mark specify the attendance, and the numbers – five thousand (6:44) and four thousand (8:9) respectively – are substantial. In addition, a multitude often accompanies Jesus while he is traveling (e.g., 10:46). In truth, Jesus' only respite from the crowd comes when he takes the initiative to send them away (8:10) or withdraws.[50]

To be sure, Mark portrays the opportunity to enjoy a good argument or to see Jesus perform wonders as the appeal for some individuals and groups. When he descends from the mountain after the transfiguration, for example, Jesus discovers a large crowd assembled to listen to the dispute between his disciples and the scribes (9:14-17), and moments later they scramble to watch him heal a boy suffering from epilepsy (9:25). Indeed, in Mark's narrative healing and teaching are both central to Jesus' ministry and reputation. As 1:39 reports, he travels through Galilee preaching and casting out demons (καὶ ἦλθεν κηρύσσων εἰς τὰς συναγωγὰς αὐτῶν εἰς ὅλην τὴν Γαλιλαίαν καὶ τὰ δαιμόνια ἐκβάλλων).[51] On one hand, therefore, the cure of a leper is said to be responsible for Jesus' early popularity (1:45), and many are attracted to him because they have heard about his

[50] Jesus disengages from the crowd for several reasons, including (a) prayer (1:35; 6:45-47); (b) spending time with his disciples (3:13; 4:10, 34, 36; 6:1, 31-32; 7:17; 8:27; 9:2, 28, 30-31; 10:32; 13:3; 14:17-42); (c) and healing people in private (5:37-43; 7:33; 8:23). At times, κατ' ἰδίαν ("privately; by oneself") expressly signals such moments in the narrative (BDAG, 467).

[51] Accordingly, Guelich (*Mark 1–8:26*, 308) cautions against making a sharp distinction between Jesus' teaching and miracles.

deeds (ἀκούσαντες ὅσα ἐποίει; 3:7-8).[52] In fact, oftentimes those who come to Jesus are bringing someone to be cured or are themselves seeking healing.[53] On the other hand, Mark narrates a number of instances in which crowds are drawn to Jesus because of his preaching. In 4:1, for example, the crowd gathered to hear him teach grows so large that he is compelled to speak from a boat on the lake.[54]

Whether interested in his healing or teaching ministries, the reaction of the crowd to Jesus prior to his arrest is uniformly positive in Mark. One reason for the concern of the Jewish leaders about Jesus is people's approving response to him (11:18, 32). Indeed, crowd support creates major difficulties for Jesus' opponents. Twice the narrative reports that fear of the crowd's reaction thwarts the plans of the Jewish leaders to seize and kill him (12:12; 14:2). Yet a sense that the crowd's attitude toward Jesus is about to change emerges in the arrest scene when the underlings sent by the Jewish authorities with Judas to arrest Jesus are designated as ὄχλος (14:43). A few verses later, the crowd wholly rejects Jesus by cooperating with the Jewish leadership in insisting that Pilate crucify him (15:5-15).[55]

Bandits Crucified with Jesus

In the case of the two bandits executed alongside Jesus, waning support is replaced by unmet expectations (15:27, 32b). The bandits are not friends or disciples of Jesus whose companionship and support has sustained him during his ministry. Indeed, they enter the narrative only after their crucifixion. Attention to them introduces and surrounds the accounts of others who witness and react to Jesus' execution, namely, the passersby and Jewish leaders, two groups who relentlessly berate and lampoon him.[56]

[52] Mark 3:7-8 illustrates how widespread Jesus' reputation as a healer has become, listing Galilee, Judea, Jerusalem, Idumea, Transjordan, Tyre and Sidon as among the locales represented by the horde of people (πολὺ πλῆθος) accompanying him.

[53] For examples of the former, see 1:30, 32; 2:3; 5:22-23; 6:54-56; 7:25-30, 32; 8:22; 9:17; for the latter, see 1:40; 3:10; 5:25-28; 10:46-52.

[54] The superlative adjective (ὄχλος πλεῖστος) in 4:1 indicates that the gathering was quite large. For additional examples of crowds gathering to hear Jesus teach, see 2:2, 13, 15; 6:2, 31, 33-34; 10:1; 11:18; 12:37.

[55] Evans (*Mark 8:27–16:20*, 482) goes so far as to call the crowd's involvement a "plebiscite."

[56] The passersby (οἱ παραπορευόμενοι) are not part of the crowd that has been following Jesus; rather, they represent ordinary Jews who only know what they have heard about him, viz., the false accusation that he had threatened to destroy their sacred place (15:29; see 14:57-59).

The difference in circumstances between the crucified prisoners and these groups could not be more acute, and readers may reasonably anticipate that the contrast will carry over to the prisoners' attitude toward Jesus. In other words, convicts who share the same fate as Jesus might be counted on to empathize with him, a tendency exploited in Luke's shaping of the tradition into the story of the penitent thief (23:39-43).[57] Although Mark's narrative is silent about it, readers could plausibly imagine the treatment of the other condemned prisoners prior to execution to be similar to that endured by Jesus. The flogging of criminals before and on their way to execution was routine in that period, as was the parading of condemned offenders to the site of execution while carrying the crossbeam upon which they were to be fastened.[58] Again, Luke's account fills a bit of the narrative gap by stipulating that the two criminals (κακοῦργοι) are led to their execution with Jesus (23:32).

In addition to their common fate, the narrative endorses in other ways the expectation that those crucified with Jesus will be supportive of him. First, the location of their crosses, "one on his right and one on his left," brings to mind Jesus' earlier conversation with James and John, who request that they be allowed to sit on his right and left once he was glorified (10:35-37). Second, the same term that Jesus applies to himself at his arrest (λῃστής) is used to identify the convicts crucified with him.[59] Given all of this, the prisoners' unsympathetic and unsupportive response, corresponding exactly with the reaction of the Jewish passersby and leaders ("those who were crucified with him also kept berating him" [15:32b]) is jolting, and drives home the totality of Jesus' isolation at his death.

Cry of Abandonment

The context for understanding the cry of abandonment from Ps 22 in Mark 15:34, therefore, transcends the narrative of Jesus' crucifixion in which it is situated. This claim does not diminish the role that the psalm performs in the depiction of the brutal, desolate, and agonizing death

[57] Matthew 27:44, like Mark, has both bandits mock (ὀνειδίζω) Jesus repeatedly. John says nothing about their demeanor, simply noting that they are crucified on either side of him (19:18).

[58] For discussion and examples of this practice, see William Sanger Campbell, "Engagement, Disengagement and Obstruction: Jesus' Defense Strategies in Mark's Trial and Execution Scenes (14.53-64; 15.1-9)," *JSNT* 26 (2004): 291-300.

[59] Jesus employs the term with irony in 14:48, "As against a bandit (λῃστής), you came out with swords and clubs to apprehend me?"

that Jesus experiences. The sense of loss inherent in the cry itself is deepened by narrating it in Jesus' own language, a technique that "gives the impression of words coming genuinely from Jesus' heart."[60] Mark further escalates the tragic and chilling tenor of the crucifixion scene (15:24-39) by interspersing verses from Ps 22 in reverse order from their original context.[61] As a result, the psalm as employed in Mark descends toward defeat and abandonment instead of ascending toward deliverance and thanksgiving, a decline capped by Jesus' outcry in 15:34. In addition, describing Jesus' two lone utterances during his execution, the cry from Ps 22 and his dying gasp in 15:37, as φωνὴ μεγάλη (lit. "a loud voice") makes palpable the severity of his suffering; that is, Jesus' death wails demand tremendous exertion and are blurted out in overwhelming physical, psychological, and spiritual torment and exhaustion.

In the Gospel taken as a whole, however, the cry represents the culmination of the motif of abandonment that is featured throughout the narrative. Thus far the story has involved the inevitable fragility of human relationships; that is to say, every human character who at one time either was or should have been supportive of Jesus has deserted, disclaimed, or dismissed him. As Wilfrid Harrington writes, "It would have seemed that... Jesus' isolation could go no further."[62] Nonetheless, despite the disturbing and even embarrassing effect of Jesus' words on readers, Mark's Gospel does not flinch from its pattern of abandonment.[63]

[60] Brown, *Death of the Messiah*, 2:1046. The technique employed several times in Mark of narrating discourse material in Aramaic followed by its Greek translation (5:41; 7:34; 14:36; and the cry of abandonment in 15:34) emphasizes as well as personalizes what is said.

[61] Vernon K. Robbins, "The Reversed Contextualization of Psalm 22 in the Markan Crucifixion: A Socio-Rhetorical Analysis," in *The Four Gospels 1992: Festschrift Frans Neirynck* (ed. F. Van Segbroeck et al.; Leuven: Leuven University Press, 1992), 2:1179-80; see also Daniel Guichard, "La reprise du psaume 22 dans le récit de la mort de Jésus: Mark 15:21-41," *FoiVie* 87 (1988): 59-65; Campbell, "Engagement, Disengagement and Obstruction," 299.

[62] Harrington, *Mark*, 237.

[63] While retaining the substance of Mark's account, Matthew's Gospel subtly mitigates the effect of the cry of abandonment, first by describing Jesus as more actively involved in his death (he "gave up [ἀφῆκεν] his spirit" [27:50]), and then by alluding to his resurrection immediately thereafter (27:53). A number of Matthean commentators consider the mention of Jesus' resurrection at this point odd, and argue that the evangelist or an early corrector added it later to solve the problem created by notice of the resurrection of other humans in vv. 52-53 (e.g., Eduard Schweizer, *The Good News according to Matthew* [trans. David E. Green; Atlanta: Westminster John Knox, 1975], 515-16; Daniel J. Harrington, *The Gospel of Matthew* [SP 1; Collegeville: Liturgical Press, 1991], 400-401).

As with the rejection of Jesus by human characters, earlier passages anticipate or accentuate God's abandonment. First, the lack of response by God to Jesus' petition in Gethsemane forebodes God's disappearance at his crucifixion.[64] Jesus' prayer in Mark 14:36 is direct, hopeful, and expectant, "Abba, Father, all things are possible to you; remove this cup from me" (πάντα δυνατά σοι· παρένεγκε τὸ ποτήριον τοῦτο ἀπ' ἐμοῦ).[65] As Brown argues, the Markan petition radiates a "familial confidence that God would not make the Son go through the 'hour,'" a conviction captured in the address of God as "Abba Father" for the only time in the Gospels.[66] God's silence both in word and deed to Jesus' request is an ominous harbinger that God will not intervene in the events that are about to transpire.

Second, the impression that the cry of abandonment produces becomes even more powerful read in light of passages that lift up Jesus' singular relationship to God. In the only two scenes in the Gospel in which God has a speaking part, God's words confirm the special bond shared with Jesus.[67] First, at Jesus' baptism, God announces to him, "You are my beloved Son. I am delighted with you" (1:11). Later, God acknowledges Jesus' sonship publicly at the transfiguration episode in

64 The following discussion of Jesus' Gethsemane prayer is taken from Campbell, "Engagement, Disengagement and Obstruction," 287-88.

65 Matthew's and Luke's requests convey a more conditional tone: "*if it is possible*, let this cup pass from me" (εἰ δυνατόν ἐστιν, παρελθάτω ἀπ' ἐμοῦ τὸ ποτήριον τοῦτο; Matt 26:39); "*if you are willing*, remove this cup from me" (εἰ βούλει παρένεγκε τοῦτο τὸ ποτήριον ἀπ' ἐμοῦ; Luke 22:42; emphases added).

66 Brown, *Death of the Messiah*, 2:1046; Hooker, *Mark*, 348. The hopeful expectation of Mark's prayer is not diminished by its ending ("yet not what I will, but what you will") nor by the more provisional indirect address that precedes it in 14:35, "[Jesus] prayed that, if it were possible, the hour might pass from him." As Sharyn Dowd (*Prayer, Power, and the Power of Suffering: Mark 11:22-25 in the Context of Markan Theology* [SBLDS, 105; Atlanta: Scholars Press, 1988], 156) argues, "[t]he issue of possibility changes from a condition in 14:35b to a statement of fact in 14:36.... The condition imposed in 35b is met. Everything is possible for God." Brown (*Death of the Messiah*, 1:176 n. 22) adds, "The supposition of the prayer is that what God wills is going to come about; and, of course, Jesus wills that. His hopeful prayer is that it does not include the cup."

67 In neither instance is the "voice from heaven" (φωνὴ ... ἐκ τῶν οὐρανῶν) explicitly identified as God's, leading to speculation that Mark is employing the rabbinic concept of בַּת קוֹל ("daughter of a voice"), a mediated, and so inferior, form of divine communication – an echo of God's voice (Cranfield, *Mark*, 54; Guelich, *Mark 1–8:26*, 33; Hooker, *Mark*, 47; Marcus, *Mark 1–8*, 160-61). The interpretation that God's voice is mediated does not diminish the effect of 1:11 and 9:7 on Mark's abandonment motif; however, the recognition of Jesus as God's Son at key moments in the Gospel by the narrator (1:1), demons (3:11; 5:7), the centurion at the cross (15:39), and Jesus himself (13:32; 14:36, 61-62) suggests that God is the speaker in these passages (see Guelich, *Mark 1–8:26*, 33; Schweizer, *Mark*, 40-41).

Mark 9, declaring to Peter, James, and John who ascend the mountain with Jesus, "This is my beloved Son, listen to him" (9:7). These words reverberate in the background as Jesus' lament over God's absence pierces the moments before his death and when, immediately after he succumbs, the centurion's declaration reminds readers of Jesus' distinctive relationship to God (15:39).[68] The allusions to Jesus as God's child sharpen the awareness of divine loss that saturates the atmosphere of Mark's death scene. That loss is poignantly conveyed by the formality of Jesus' dying words, not identified in Mark as a psalm quotation and so presented as Jesus' own.[69] In what is arguably the most personal moment of his life, Jesus calls to "God" – the language of divine address "common to all human beings" – instead of to his "Father."[70]

Conclusion

Tracing the motif of abandonment in Mark's Gospel reveals a pattern that encompasses substantially more of the narrative than the plaintive cry from Ps 22 on which many commentators and other readers focus. Indeed, except that it befalls Jesus, God's Son and Christ, God's absence would not have been unprecedented for Mark's first-century readers to whom the withdrawal of divinity from human affairs was not an alien concept. For example, the major hellenistic philosophies considered it, as Helmut Koester argues, "disgraceful for the truly wise man to be dependent upon divine intervention in his personal affairs," and adherents of popular religions were frequently disappointed by the indifference of the gods to their appeals.[71] In addition, of course, the psalmist's words witness to Jewish tradition intimately familiar with the possibility of God's disregard in times of need.

[68] Mark's Gospel is framed by pronouncements of Jesus divine sonship (1:1; 15:39; the text-critical uncertainty of υἱοῦ θεοῦ in 1:1 is much discussed in the literature; e.g., see the summary of variants by Croy, *Mutilation*, 114-17, and "Where the Gospel Begins: A Non-Theological Interpretation of Mark 1:1," *NovT* 43 [2001]: 106-10).

[69] Brown, *Death of the Messiah*, 2:1046. The impression that the words belong to Jesus is reinforced by first citing the passage in Aramaic.

[70] Brown, *Death of the Messiah*, 2:1046.

[71] Helmut Koester, *Introduction to the New Testament: Volume 1: History, Culture, and Religion of the Hellenistic Age* (Berlin: de Gruyter, 1982), 146; Paul Veyne, "The Roman Empire," in *A History of Private Life: From Pagan Rome to Byzantium* (ed. Paul Veyne; trans. Arthur Goldhammer; vol. 1 of *A History of Private Life*, ed. Philippe Ariès and Georges Duby; Cambridge: Belknap, 1987), 210.

It *is* God's Son and Messiah, however, who exclaims godforsakenness in Mark's account, an experience that has collided with the expectations of generations of Gospel readers. Willing to concede that Jesus is wrongfully executed in the most inhumane way imaginable, many readers nonetheless presume God's presence in that suffering. Indeed, without the conviction that at the very least God remains with Jesus throughout his ordeal, the challenge for readers to reconcile Jesus' suffering with the image most have of a merciful and loving God is complicated appreciably. But Mark's narrative is resolute in testifying to the totality of the Christ's abandonment.

On one level, the prayerful outburst of 15:34 does in fact crystallize Mark's powerful and penetrating presentation of Jesus' human condition and the role of his family and community in his messianic identity and destiny. Beyond the unjust condemnation and cruel execution that Jesus endures at the hands of his more influential opponents – a sufficient tragedy in itself – his humiliation is compounded by dying without the comfort of family, friends, supporters, or colleagues, all of whom have in their own way abandoned him as well. One aspect of Mark's Christology finding expression in the words of Ps 22, then, is the desertion of allies that reaches its bleakest point in Jesus' cry.

Mark's pattern of abandonment by those most intimately associated with Jesus, however, is incomplete without God's participation. Indeed, divine presence would largely empty the abandonment by these human characters of its significance. The cry, therefore, also voices a more profound dimension of the Gospel's christological vision; namely, that human defections anticipate, accompany, illumine, and mirror God's absence in Jesus' messianic suffering. Mark's abandonment Christology provides the Gospel's response to Jesus' desperate question: God forsakes him because that is the fate of the Messiah and an essential element in the paradox of the messianic experience – the crucified Christ is also the abandoned Christ. The narrative's final scene focuses on the other pole in the christological paradox. The crucified Christ becomes the resurrected Christ and, in that event, Jesus' deep and abiding bond with God is confirmed. In other words, inevitable as God's abandonment of Jesus is in Mark's Gospel, separation from God does not mean loss of God.

CHALLENGING THE DIVINE: LXX PSALM 21 IN THE PASSION NARRATIVE OF THE GOSPEL OF MARK

Stephen P. AHEARNE-KROLL

In the Gospel of Mark, Jesus the Messiah dies a horribly painful and shameful death at the hands of the soldiers who serve Pontius Pilate, only after he suffers through the abandonment of his disciples, a trial before the Jewish authorities where he is mocked and beaten, and a second trial before Pilate where he is rejected by his people and mocked and beaten by Pilate's soldiers. Yet Mark tells the story of these terrible events of the end of Jesus' days with copious references to his Scriptures. Jesus goes "as it is written of him," even though he goes in such a horrific way. Upon close examination of one subset of the Scripture passages evoked, namely, the psalms of individual lament (hereafter, PssLam), the reader begins to question what it might mean for Jesus the Messiah to die "as it is written of him."[1]

The Septuagint form of Psalm 22 (LXX Psalm 21[2]) is the most prominent of these PssLam used in Mark's Passion Narrative, and it offers a rich resource for reflection on the question of Jesus' suffering and death as presented in Mark. I will explore the ways that David's response to suffering presented in the psalm might inform the story of Jesus' suffering and death.

I. Issues of Methodology

Although I recognize and appreciate that the text of Mark as we know it has a pre-history that includes the adoption and adaptation of stories and

[1] I use the term "evoke" and its cognates to avoid using the term "allude" and its cognates. As I explain below, I use the term "allusion" in concert with Ziva Ben-Porat's usage of it, which she defines as a process of recognition of a marker, the text to which the marker refers, and the reconsideration of the meaning of the marker in light of the text to which it refers. See "The Poetics of Literary Allusion," *PTL: A Journal for Descriptive Poetics and Theory of Literature* 1 (1976): 105-128. Biblical scholars usually use "allusion" to refer to the phenomenon of referring to another text outside of the text under study. I am in agreement with Ben-Porat that allusion is a more complex literary process than a simple reference to an outside text.

[2] Hereafter, I will refer to this psalm by its LXX numbering.

traditions received by the author, I wish to examine the Gospel as a narrative in its final form. In this respect, I will read the narrative of Mark in light of Paul Ricoeur's narrative theory, namely, that narratives are configurations of human time, and, that through the process of reading, human time and experience are re-figured or transformed because the narrative attempts to render aporias of human experience productive.[3] In the case of the Gospel of Mark, I will read the narrative as one that addresses the aporia of the suffering and death of Jesus the Messiah. In particular, my task will be to read Mark through the lens of Psalm 21 as evoked in Mark's Passion Narrative and then raise some questions for further research that might allow for the reevaluation of one's understanding of the relationship between Jesus and God in Mark and the relationship between Jesus' suffering and death, on the one hand, and his resurrection on the other.

Psalm 21 is evoked clearly in two places in Mark 15 – a virtual quote from Ps 21:19 woven into the narrative context of Mark 15:24 and a direct quote from Ps 21:2 in Mark 15:34.[4] A third evocation is that of Ps 21:8-9 in Mark 15:29-30, which comes between these two in narrative order and is primarily based upon the content of the psalm rather than extensive lexical similarity. Although there are other biblical texts that are most likely evoked in Mark 15:29-30, the fact that Ps 21:19 is evoked in such a prominent way four short verses earlier guides the reader to Psalm 21 as the primary referent.[5] Mark evokes Psalm 21 three

[3] Ricoeur describes aporias as doubts, questions, or gaps in understanding of human experience. For his most thorough explanation of his narrative theory, see *Time and Narrative* (trans. Kathleen McLaughlin and David Pellauer; 3 vols.; Chicago: University of Chicago Press, 1984-88), especially 1:1-87.

[4] The second of these two evocations, Ps 21:2 in 15:34, is first presented in transliterated Aramaic and then translated into Greek, which matches quite closely to the Greek of Ps 21:2a.

[5] In particular, it can be argued that Lam 2:15, Ps 109:25 (MT) and Wis 2:17 are all evoked along with Ps 21:8-9. See Vincent Taylor, *The Gospel According to St. Mark* (2d ed.; Grand Rapids: Baker Books, 1981), 591; Eduard Schweizer, *The Good News According to Mark* (trans. Donald H. Madvig; Atlanta: John Knox, 1970), 348-49; and Francis J. Moloney, *The Gospel of Mark: A Commentary* (Peabody: Hendrickson, 2002), 322. At least one ancient reader, namely the author of the Gospel of Matthew, seems to have interpreted Mark's mocking on the crucifixion as a reference to Psalm 21. Although Matthew does not quote Ps 21:9 directly in 27:43, there is much lexical similarity between the verses and two synonyms. Matt 27:43 reads, *πέποιθεν* ἐπὶ *τὸν θεόν*, ῥυσάσθω νῦν εἰ θέλει αὐτόν: εἶπεν γὰρ ὅτι Θεοῦ εἰμι υἱός. Ps 21:9 reads, *Ἤλπισεν ἐπὶ κύριον*, ῥυσάσθω αὐτόν· σωσάτω αὐτόν, ὅτι θέλει αὐτόν. (The exact matches are underlined and the synonyms are in italics in each verse.) Matthew uses a technique commonly used among New Testament authors in that he changes the syntax of a biblical reference to match the narrative context of his own work without obscuring the reference.

times, and this raises the question of how one ought to deal with the psalm. Should one read only the phrases associated with the evocations in Mark, the entire verse or verses of each evocation, or the entire psalm?

I will read the entirety of Psalm 21, although I will focus on specific areas of the psalm when discussing in detail the places where it is evoked in Mark 15. I do this for two reasons. First, a word or phrase gains particular meaning when it is placed in a context, in this case, the context of the verse or section of Psalm 21. Second, since there is no way to prove that the author of the alluding text meant only to refer to the word or phrase found in the alluding text, then there is no good reason not to read the entire evoked text.[6] Not doing so risks superficiality of interpretation and perhaps oversight of something crucial for understanding the alluding text. Allusion adds depth to a text, and to shortchange that depth is to rob the alluding text of its potential richness. In addition, as we will see below, this impulse is supported by the methodological principles of Ziva Ben-Porat, whose work on literary allusion will provide the main theoretical tools that will focus and nuance Ricoeur's general narrative theory by foregrounding the evocation of Psalm 21 in Mark's Passion Narrative.

The poetics of allusion has garnered a considerable amount of attention in literary theory over the past thirty years.[7] All agree that an allusion, in general, is a literary device used to join a text with a referent outside that text. That outside referent can be another literary text or a cultural referent such as a current event, a person, a song, or other commonly known cultural element of a current or past time. According to Ben-Porat, indirectness or tacitness is the common base of all allusions, although subsequent critics have moved away from this as a necessary element of an allusion.[8] She goes on to distinguish the term "marker" from allusion to indicate that the signal in the text should not be confused with the more complex process of allusion.[9] Identification of the marker begins a four-stage process; the culmination of at least the third

[6] I borrow the terms "alluding text" and "evoked text" from Ben-Porat, "The Poetics of Literary Allusion." In short, "alluding text" refers to the text that contains the marker, and "evoked text" is the text referred to by the marker in the alluding text.

[7] For a good review of scholarship, see Udo J. Hebel, "Towards a Descriptive Poetics of *Allusion*," in *Intertextuality* (ed. Heinrich F. Plett; Berlin: Walter de Gruyter, 1991), 135-164.

[8] See Carmella Perri, "On Alluding," *Poetics* 7 (1978): 289-307; Hebel, "Descriptive Poetics of Allusion;" and Benjamin D. Sommer, *A Prophet Reads Scripture: Allusion in Isaiah 40-66* (Stanford: Stanford University Press, 1998), 10-17.

[9] For Ben-Porat, the terms "sign" and "marker" seem to be synonymous.

stage characterizes an allusion. The four stages are (1) recognition of the marker, (2) identification of the evoked text, (3) modification of the interpretation of the marker in the alluding text, and (4) activation of the evoked text as a whole to form connections between it and the alluding text that are not based on the markers and marked items themselves.[10]

In the process of examining a text closely, steps (1) and (2) happen almost simultaneously or alternate back and forth. This happens because, if a marker signals something in the mind of a reader, there is an instantaneous impulse to try to recall its origin. A marker that signals an evoked text may be simple or complex. As Benjamin D. Sommer points out, "The sign may be a poetic line or sentence or phrase, or it may consist of a motif, a rhythmic pattern, an idea, or even the form of the work or its title."[11] As a result, the process for identifying a marker is not uniform and oftentimes quite complex. Although particular words or phrases make the evocation of a previous text more certain, one must be open to other elements or complexes of elements in a given text that may act as markers to an outside text. An exhaustive list of the categories of elements to be examined cannot be created before one actually begins the analysis, but Sommer's list of elements just cited is a good basic list. An interpreter must be alert to any and all narrative, grammatical, linguistic and rhetorical elements in a given text.

Stages (3) and (4) from Ben-Porat's process of allusion determine whether a marker acts as an allusion or not. According to Ben-Porat, unless the text to which the marker refers is identified, then the marker simply signals a vague recollection in the mind of the reader of something outside the text. This would be categorized as an echo rather than an allusion.[12] Once the evoked text is identified, stage (3) entails some modification of the interpretation of the marker in the alluding text. In other words, in most instances a reader is able to understand the marker without recourse to the evoked text, but once the evoked text is identified there is a modification of the understanding of the marker in light of the evoked text.[13]

[10] Ben-Porat, "The Poetics of Literary Allusion," 110-111.

[11] Sommer, *A Prophet Reads Scripture*, 11. See also, Perri, "On Alluding," 305, and James K. Chandler, "Romantic Allusiveness," *Critical Inquiry* 8 (3, 1982): 480-81. Robert Alter notes that the evoked text may be short (a line or section) or much longer (a whole work or even a corpus) (*The Pleasures of Reading in an Ideological Age* [New York: Norton, 1989], 123).

[12] Richard B. Hays is most famous for using the term "echo" in biblical scholarship. He makes little distinction between "echo" and "allusion," except "in general... *allusion* is used of obvious intertextual references, *echo* of subtler ones" (*Echoes of Scripture in the Letters of Paul* [New Haven: Yale University Press, 1989], 29).

[13] Ben-Porat, "The Poetics of Literary Allusion," 110-111.

Once the marker is re-read in light of the evoked text, the reader may wish to stop there in his or her investigation, but that is not necessary. "Most literary allusions possess the potential for the fourth stage," namely the activation of the evoked text as a whole.[14] This allows the reader to draw a more complex, in-depth and wide-ranging correspondence between the alluding and evoked texts than exists at the location of the marker.[15] The process of doing so need not include the marker or the marked elements of the two texts, but it can include other elements that can now be identified as intersections between the texts, unseen before the identification of the evoked text.[16] The thinking behind this fourth step is, I believe, that once an author evokes an earlier text, the reader cannot help but read the alluding text in light of it. For our purposes, the only criterion that can be relied upon when determining to what extent the two texts intersect is whether the connections between the texts affect the reading of the alluding text.

Some thoughts are in order regarding who "the reader" is in this study. One of the major difficulties in dealing with the Gospel of Mark is that we know almost nothing specific about the circumstances of its creation. Although there is consensus that Mark was written within a few years of 70 CE, we can only make educated guesses at who the author was, where it was written, to whom it was written, or the makeup of its original audience. With regard to Mark's original audience, or at least the readers/hearers he had in mind when he wrote the Gospel, we can know some specifics.

[14] Ben-Porat, "The Poetics of Literary Allusion," 111. See also the discussion by Perri, which culminates in her working definition of allusion. The last part of the definition states, "the property(ies) evoked modifies the alluding text, and possibly activates further, larger inter- and intra-textual patterns of properties with consequent further modification of the alluding text" ("On Alluding," 289-95).

[15] Perri argues that allusion is distinguished from other ways of referring to outside texts by its complexity of reference. It denotes and specifies all in one sign; it denotes a concept, object, or person while specifying a set of properties associated with the referent ("On Alluding," 292). I would argue that the properties associated with the referent are not fully realized without a complete reading of both the context of the sign and that of the referent.

[16] Ben-Porat, "The Poetics of Literary Allusion." See the examples she uses to demonstrate the process on pages 113-116. Most subsequent scholars of literary allusion still rely on Ben-Porat's basic four-stage process in developing their own version of the process of allusion, and these critics do not stray very far from her basic process. See Beth LaNeel Tanner who relies heavily on Ben-Porat for her methodology for reading the psalms intertextually (*The Book of Psalms Through the Lens of Intertextuality* [Studies in Biblical Literature, 26; New York: Peter Lang, 2001], 70-72). See also Sommer's, *A Prophet Reads Scripture*, 10-13; and Hebel who modifies Ben-Porat's process, but keeps the basic core of it intact ("Towards a Descriptive Poetics of *Allusion*," 135-164).

Following Ernest Best's careful analysis,[17] we can say that Mark's readers/hearers knew Greek, were believers in Jesus, had some basic knowledge of Jewish tradition from a literary perspective (even if Mark got some of the details wrong; cf. Mark 1:2; 2:26; 10:19), and did not know Aramaic (cf. Aramaic words or phrases translated into Greek in Mark 5:41; 7:11, 34; 14:36; 15:22, 34), some specific customs of the Pharisees (cf. Mark 7:3-4) or Sadduceean lack of belief in the resurrection (cf. 12:18). Given these last three qualities, and the Gospel's special interest in Gentiles (cf. 7:24-30; 11:17; 13:10; 14:9; 15:39) Best argues that the majority of Mark's original intended audience were Gentile.[18] Donald Juel argues that the implied audience probably was envisioned as part of Israel because (1) they had extensive knowledge of Jewish Scripture; (2) they had inside knowledge of the Jewish community (cf. the distinction between the use of the terms "Jew" and "Israel" in 14:61 and the way Jews speak of Jesus' claims about his status as compared to the way the Romans speak in 15:31); and (3) the "readers are addressed throughout the Gospel as having an investment in Israel's tradition and Scripture."[19] In addition to Juel's argument, one need not conclude that Mark's audience is Gentile if one envisions diaspora Jews far removed from the everyday workings of Palestinian Judaism and with more knowledge of the local Gentile world than the Palestinian Jewish world. Whether Jew or Gentile, the intended audience would have some detailed knowledge of Jewish Scripture, either obtained through a Jewish upbringing and synagogue education or passed on through the course of communal life as a believer in Jesus as a Jewish messiah.[20]

Whatever the details of the Mark's intended audience, ultimately, I am the reader. But I hope to read both Psalm 21 and Mark's Passion Narrative as much as possible through the imaginative lens of an ancient believer of Jesus as Messiah who was fluent in Greek, and, therefore, who received the psalm in its Greek version as a Greek document in the

[17] Ernest Best, "Mark's Readers: A Profile," in *The Four Gospels* (ed. F. Van Segbroeck, et al.; Leuven: Peeters, 1992), 2:839-858.

[18] Best, "Mark's Readers," 850.

[19] Donald Juel, *A Master of Surprise: Mark Interpreted* (Minneapolis: Fortress, 1994), 133-139. The quotation is from page 138.

[20] Juel argues very persuasively that Mark's audience "has a knowledge of the Scriptures." His argument points to (1) the eleven quotations introduced by formulas; (2) the extensive use of allusions to biblical passages not marked with a formula, especially in the Passion Narrative; (3) the employment of scriptural interpretation used by Jesus in arguing with characters in the Gospel (cf. 7:1-13; 12:18-27 and 12:35-37). See *A Master of Surprise*, 133-36.

voice of David (more on this below), and who had recourse to the Greek text in his or her attempts to understand how Mark uses this psalm in telling the story of Jesus.

I do not wish to claim that I am describing a reading that an actual person in the ancient world performed either on Psalm 21 or on Mark's Passion Narrative. I am simply trying to follow the lead of the texts (and implicitly the authors of the texts) in trying to understand their literary dynamics. The author of Mark most likely evoked the Greek version of the Jewish Scriptures for the sake of his earliest addressees, so I must respect this reality and read the Greek version as well. Any literary analysis of an ancient text should strive for historical accuracy, but in the end, the questions that drive that analysis are those of a modern critic.[21]

II. David and the PssLam

As the Psalms moved away from their original setting and the Psalter was compiled and redacted, David became an increasingly important figure with regard to the Psalms. As early as the Book of Chronicles, the Chronicler "presupposes an established corpus of psalmody associated with David."[22] The practice of adding Davidic superscripts to psalms in the Hebrew *Vorlage* continued on into the Old Greek and then further into subsequent transmissions of the original Greek translation.[23] By the

[21] See *1 Clem* 16:3-14, where the author quotes from a Isa 53:1-12 in his attempts to understand and explain the humility of Jesus to the point that he would suffer and die on the cross. Just after this passage, the author of *1 Clement* appeals also to LXX Ps 21:7-9 to make the same point. Later in 35:7-12 he offers a long quotation from LXX Ps 49:16-23. See also *Barn.* 2:5 and 3:1-6, where he quotes from Isa 1:1-13 and Isa 58:4-10, respectively, and 11:6-7, where he quotes Ps 1:3-6 and then discusses it for the rest of the next verse. These are just a few examples where the authors of *1 Clement* and *Barnabas* appeal to large sections of Scripture to make points about Christ or to exhort the audiences to a certain understanding of God's actions in Christ. Use of these texts goes beyond atomistic use of verses from unrelated texts to prove something about Jesus. It is the result of long reflection on whole sections of Scripture in relation to the story of Jesus, similar to what I am doing in this study.

[22] Margaret Daly-Denton, *David in the Fourth Gospel: The Johannine Reception of the Psalms* (Leiden: Brill, 2000), 73. See 1 Chr 16:7 where David commands the Asaph and his kindred to sing praises to God. What follows are excerpts from Pss 105, 96 and 106. Later in 1 Chronicles 23 and 25, David assigns specific groups to sacred worship duties; the singing of psalms is among the duties given to the sons of Asaph, Heman, and Jeduthun.

[23] Albert Pietersma has convincingly argued that not all of the Davidic superscriptions go back to the Old Greek and has suggested several changes to Rahlfs' *Psalmi cum Odis*. See "David in the Greek Psalms," *VT* 30 (1980): 225-226 for a list of suggested changes to Rahlfs' text.

time of the Dead Sea Scrolls, David had become viewed as a prolific composer of psalms.[24]

Margaret Daly-Denton has recently completed a study on the influence of the character of David on the Fourth Gospel through its appropriation of the Psalms. She argues that the presumed Davidic authorship of the Psalms makes it "*inconceivable* that some of the psalm references in the Gospel would not have carried for the original readers resonances of David and his story. This is especially true of references to 'laments of the individual' such as Psalm (21) 22 or Psalm (68) 69 which could easily be envisaged as actual utterances of David."[25] These insights hold equally well for the present study, namely, the high likelihood that David would be evoked when a particular psalm is referred to in Mark

[24] The famous passage from 11QPs[a] XXVII, 2-11 reads:

And David, son of Jesse, was wise, and a light like the light of the sun, /and/ learned, and discerning, and perfect in all his paths before God and men. And YHWH gave him a discerning and enlightened spirit. And he wrote psalms: three thousand six hundred; and songs to be sung before the altar over the perpetual offering of every day, for all the days of the year: three hundred and sixty-four; and for the Sabbath offerings: fifty-two songs; and for the offering of the first days of the months, and for all the days of the festivals, and for the <Day> of Atonement: thirty songs. And all the songs which he spoke were four hundred and forty-six. And songs to perform over the possessed: four. The total was four thousand and fifty. All these he spoke through (the spirit of) prophecy which had been given to him from before the Most High.

The translation is from F. G. Martinez and E. J. C. Tigchelaar, eds. *The Dead Sea Scrolls Study Edition* (Leiden, Grand Rapids: Brill and Eerdmans, 1997): 1179. 11QPs[a] has been paleographically dated to the first half of the first century CE by James H. Charlesworth and James A. Sanders in "More Psalms of David," in *OTP* 2:611-24. See Margaret Daly-Denton, *David in the Fourth Gospel,* 70 for a brief discussion of this text.

In addition, two passages from Josephus and Philo clearly indicate their assent to the tradition of David as psalmist. Josephus says,

David, being now free from wars and dangers, and enjoying profound peace from this time on, composed songs and hymns to God (ᾠδὰς εἰς τὸν θεὸν καὶ ὕμνους) in varied meters – some he made in trimeters, and others in pentameters. He also made musical instruments and instructed the Levites how to use them in praising God on the so-called Sabbath day (*Ant.* VII, 305).

Philo says,

One after taking a sheer draught of this bright joy [of the worship and service of the Only Wise], a member indeed of Moses' fellowship, not found among the indifferent, spake aloud in hymns of praise, and addressing his own mind cried, "Delight in the Lord" (Ps 36:4), moved by the utterance to an ecstasy of the love that is heavenly and Divine.... while his whole mind is snatched up in a holy frenzy by a Divine possession, and he finds his gladness in God alone (*Plant.* IX, 39).

These two passages from Josephus and Philo corroborate the clear assertion in 11QPs[a] that David was thought to be the author of thousands of psalms. See Mark 12:36 || Matt 22:43 || Luke 20:42; Acts 1:16; 2:25, 31, 34; Rom 4:6-8 for the view that David was author of the Psalms.

[25] Margaret Daly-Denton, *David in the Fourth Gospel*, 110-111. Italics are mine.

because of David's assumed authorship and the tradition of linking certain psalms with events in David's life. Also, her point about the PssLam being envisaged as "actual utterances of David" is very important and raises interesting questions with regard to the words of some of these psalms being put into Jesus' mouth in Mark's Passion Narrative.[26] I will rely on both of these insights as I read Psalm 21 in tandem with the Passion Narrative.

III. Psalm 21: An Appeal to God from Beginning to End

Due to limitations of space, I am not able to perform as thorough a treatment of Psalm 21 as it deserves. However, there are several key points that I would like to make here that distinguish my reading of the psalm from most other readings and that affect my reading of Mark's Passion Narrative, as a result.

New Testament scholars generally follow Psalms scholars, who usually read the Hebrew Psalm 22 (MT) as a PsLam that has two major sections. The first is the lament section, which runs from verse 1 through verse 22. The second is the praise section, which runs from verse 23 through the end of the psalm. The relation between these two sections is usually solved by appeal to its original liturgical setting in which the psalmist or supplicant supposedly received an oracle from God through the liturgical presider. At the end of verse 22, the divine oracle would be pronounced, and what follows for the rest of the psalm was the psalmist's response to God's saving action.[27]

[26] There are five PssLam evoked simply in Mark's Passion Narrative (Psalms 21, 40, 41, 42 and 68) in at least six places. Three of these six evocations are used in Jesus' direct speech (Mark 14:18; 14:34 and 15:34). The other three evocations are used to describe actions in reference to Jesus (15:24; 15:29-32 and 15:36).

[27] See Joachim Begrich, "Das priesterliche Heilsorakel," *ZAW* 52 (1934): 81-92 for the first full expression of this theory. Because Begrich was Hermann Gunkel's student, his argument closely follows Gunkel's form-critical work. Sigmund Mowinckel argues in favor of this liturgical setting for the Psalms, going as far as detailed reconstruction of the liturgy in Ancient Israel (*The Psalms in Israel's Worship* [trans. D. R. Ap-Thomas; 2 vols.; Nashville: Abingdon Press, 1962], 29-31). Many subsequent Psalms scholars adopt this basic way of dealing with the relationship between the lament and praise/thanksgiving sections of the PssLam. See the treatments of Psalm 22 (MT) in Hans-Joachim Kraus, *Psalms 1-59* (trans. H. C. Oswald; Minneapolis: Augsburg, 1988); Peter C. Craigie, *Psalms 1-50* (WBC 19; Waco: Word Books, 1983); and Erhard S. Gerstenberger, *Psalms; Part 1: With an Introduction to Cultic Poetry* (FOTL 14; Grand Rapids: Eerdmans, 1988).

However plausible the reconstructed liturgical setting is for the PssLam in general, and Psalm 22 (MT), in particular, there is little, if any, direct evidence for the divine oracle's existence within the Ancient Israelite liturgy to which the PssLam supposedly witness. Hermann Gunkel, the father of modern form criticism on the Psalms, admits, "In our texts [i.e., the PssLam], *the oracle is almost always lacking*. Only Ps 62:12ff concludes a similar poem with a revelation which the poet had just received."[28] And it is not even clear to me that Psalm 62 should be included in the list of PssLam. Yet many scholars, including New Testament scholars, support the distinction of significance between the lament and the praise section of Psalm 22 (MT), arguing that the second part of the psalm does not follow logically from the lament portion without a recognition of deliverance from suffering. This underlying way of reading the psalm fundamentally affects New Testament scholarship because these scholars read the psalm as ending on a triumphal or even eschatological note, one that shows the vindication of the psalmist. It is not a leap to read the evocation of this psalm in Mark as an indication of Jesus' death as lamentable and his resurrection as vindication for his "innocent" or "righteous death" according to the supposed pattern of Psalm 22 (MT).[29] This reading of Psalm 22 (MT) so colors the reading

[28] *Introduction to the Psalms: The Genres of the Religious Lyric of Israel* (completed by Joachim Begrich; trans., James D. Nogalski; Macon: Macon University Press, 1998), 125. Italics mine. In Chapter 2 of my forthcoming monograph, I argue for a revision of Gunkel's standard list of PssLam, and Psalm 62 does not make my list (*The Suffering of David and the Suffering of Jesus* [SNTSMS; Cambridge: Cambridge University Press, forthcoming]). If one excludes this psalm from the list of PssLam, then there is no evidence of a Heilsorakel in the Psalter as we have it.

[29] Joel Marcus follows Harmut Gese in saying that "not only the psalm's description of innocent suffering but also its promise of vindication are essential background for understanding the Gospel accounts of the crucifixion of Jesus." Marcus goes on to argue that, based on the trajectory of interpretation of Psalm 22 in "later Judaism," and based on the parallels in imagery between Mark 15 and all parts of the psalm, the entirety of the psalm should be considered in interpreting Jesus' death in Mark. In particular, the movement from innocent suffering to eschatological vindication in Psalm 22 should govern how we understand Jesus' death. See *The Way of the Lord: Christological Exegesis of the Old Testament in the Gospel of Mark* (Louisville: Westminster John Knox, 1992), 180-182. Frank J. Matera says, "In the psalm, the scope of thanksgiving is such that it lends itself to a messianic and eschatological interpretation.... Not only does it describe the suffering of the just one, it also portrays his victory in language that is susceptible to messianic and eschatological interpretation." (*The Kingship of Jesus: Composition and Theology in Mark 15* [SBLDS 66; Chico: Scholars Press, 1982], 135). Raymond E. Brown also assumes an eschatological thrust to the psalm as well as a depiction of "the just one." He also says that the use of Psalm 22 would have caused Christians "to highlight the reversal in an abandoned death and subsequent victory" (*The Death of the Messiah: From Gethsemane to the Grave* [2 vols.; New York:

of Mark's Gospel for most scholars that the details of Mark's story that are ambiguous regarding the relationship between Jesus' suffering/death and his resurrection or that contradict an understanding of the resurrection as vindication for his death are usually passed over.

In the wake of the lack of evidence for such an understanding of the psalm, it is better to make sense of the psalm without appeal to unverifiable, exterior events, if at all possible. Because I am interested in the way that this psalm affects the story of Jesus' death in the Gospel of Mark, I will focus my attention on the Greek version of the psalm, namely, LXX Psalm 21 (hereafter, Psalm 21).[30] One can make sense of Psalm 21 as a rhetorical whole if one considers the praise section as *promised* praise rather than *actual* praise or praise *in anticipation* of expected salvation.[31] In other words, David finishes his lament and then says, "If you answer me, I will tell of your name to my brothers,"

Doubleday, 1994], 2:1459, 1462). John R. Donahue and Daniel J. Harrington say, "Psalm 22 is the prayer of a righteous person who has suffered greatly but has been vindicated, all the while retaining and being sustained by trust in God's power and care." (*The Gospel of Mark* [SP 2; Collegeville, Minn.: Liturgical Press, 2002], 445). Moloney says, "The use of Ps 22, the lament par excellence of the righteous sufferer which has dominated the Markan passion account... reaches its climax and high point in these final words of Jesus in the Gospel." (*The Gospel of Mark*, 326). Whitney Shiner, in an otherwise carefully argued and insightfully nuanced study of the death scene in Mark, says without argumentation about Jesus' cry in the words of Psalm 22, "It is unlikely that the listeners would not sense a second meaning as well, pointing beyond the literal sense of the cry to the vindication promised by the psalm." ("The Ambiguous Pronouncement of the Centurion and the Shrouding of Meaning in Mark," *JSNT* 78 (2000): 17). Craig A. Evans says, "Some wonder if Jesus has the whole psalm [22] in mind, especially the concluding part that relates vindication and restoration." (*Mark 8:27-16:20* [WBC 34B; Nashville: Thomas Nelson, 2001], 507).

[30] I do this because the vast majority of direct quotations of Scripture found in Mark correspond most closely to the LXX, and the Gospel was written in Greek, presumably the primary language of Mark's audience. See Howard Clark Kee, "The Function of Scriptural Quotations in Mark 11-16," in *Jesus und Paulus: Festschrift für Werner Georg Kümmel zum 70. Geburtstag* (ed. E. Earle Ellis and Erich Gräßer; Göttingen: Vandenhoeck & Ruprecht, 1975), 172.

[31] Claus Westermann argues for an overall pattern to the PssLam that includes a vow of praise because he believes that there is always the understanding that God has heard the petition of the psalmist. In response to the confidence that God has heard the petition, the psalmist promises to praise God, and eventually there is actual praise. The actual praise does not always show up in the PssLam, but there is the understanding that it will happen at some point. See *Praise and Lament in the Psalms* (trans. Keith R. Crim and Richard N. Soulen; Atlanta: John Knox,1981), 75-78. Westermann imposes a certain pattern on all the PssLam that always ends in actual praise for God's mercy in response to petition. According to Westermann, lament has no meaning without ending in salvation and praise of God. So, his understanding of the vow of praise is always in anticipation of expected salvation and never as a way of convincing God to act.

etc.[32] A more detailed look at Psalm 21 is in order to substantiate this reading.

As I mentioned earlier, the psalm falls into two major sections – the lament section (vv. 2-22) and the praise section (vv. 23-32). The lament section is dominated by David crying out to God for help in the midst of some kind of suffering at the hands of some unspecified enemy. Interspersed within the lament section, David reflects on his past experience of God – both national and individual – in order to try to make sense of God's lack of response to his suffering and in order to try to convince God to act on his behalf. For example, verses 4-6 recall God's interaction with Israel, the most important feature of which is the cause and effect relationship between the ancestors' hope in God and their salvation. David's hope is present, but his salvation is absent in his current situation. In verses 10-12, David's thoughts become much more personal. He describes the intimate relationship that he has shared with God right from the beginning of his life, so much so that he describes God as a midwife who drew him from his mother's womb (v. 10-11). This gives the clear indication that David is wondering why God is not answering in the present, given the fact that he and God have been so close for so long. The rest of the lament section uses vivid descriptions of abandonment (vv. 2-3), mocking (vv. 7-8), and suffering (vv. 13-19), amidst intermittent cries to God for help. The section ends with a series of four imperative constructions directed towards God: "do not delay [my help]" (μὴ μακρύνῃς), "be attentive" (πρόσχες), "deliver" (ῥῦσαι), and "save" (σῶσον). Clearly, this first major section of the psalm is meant to get God's attention and persuade God to act on David's behalf by using all of the techniques just described.

32 Westermann argues that the vow of praise is part of the cry to God, not as something that is used to bargain with God, but as something that is owed to God. "I know then that the matter is not finished when I have pled and God has heard, but that something else must still come.... It is totally false to belittle this as a bargain, as a *do ut des*. On the contrary, it is only through the promise that I bind to my petition that the petition gains its weight and value." (*Praise and Lament in the Psalms*, 78).
In contrast, Tony W. Cartledge argues that many psalms that have been understood with the reception of Heilsorakel as the element that holds the praise/thanksgiving section together with the lament section should actually be understood differently. Instead, he argues that the praise/thanksgiving section is vowed and not actual praise/thanksgiving ("Conditional Vows in the Psalms of Lament: A New Approach to an Old Problem," in *The Listening Heart: Essays in Wisdom and the Psalms in Honor of Roland E. Murphy* [ed. Kenneth G. Hoglund; JSOTSS 58; Sheffield: JSOT Press, 1987], 77-94). Although I adopt his basic point, his argument is based on the MT version of these psalms. In order to make the case for Psalm 21, one must argue on the basis of the LXX version, which has different syntax than MT Psalm 22.

Before we deal with the question of how the praise section is related to the lament section, I should point to one crucial difference between the Hebrew and Greek versions of this psalm. In the Hebrew, verse 22 ends with the word **עניתני**, whose form and significance are disputed by commentators. When viewed in morphological terms, the form is a second person singular Qal perfect with a first person singular object suffix of **ענה**, which should be translated as "you answered me." Verse 22 translated would read, "Save me from the mouth of the lion; from the horns of the bulls you answered me." But because this is poetry, one could argue that the last word should be understood as leading into the next verse with the connotation of "you answered me, so I will tell of your name to my brothers," and so forth. According to E. S. Gerstenberger, in its present context, the parallelism within this verse and the parallelism with the previous verse suggests that there has been a corruption in the text and that it should be taken as a noun **עניתי** ("my poor one" or "my poor life") in parallel with the noun **יחידתי** ("my precious one" or "my precious life") from verse 21b. So, as we can see, there is a great deal of uncertainty around this word, which can lead to multiple understandings of the literary transition to verse 23.

Luckily for us, the Greek is not so convoluted or disputed. For some unknown reason, verse 22 of the Greek differs from the Hebrew. Instead of the Hebrew, "Save me from the mouth of the lion; from the horns of the bulls you answered me,"[33] the Greek reads, "Save me from the mouth of the lion and from the horns of the unicorns [save] my lowliness."[34] This change in the text eliminates any possible indication in the text that David has heard an oracle proclaiming his deliverance or that he has had some experience in the moment that would lead him to believe God has heard him and will deliver him at some unspecified time.

But how should we understand the sudden change in tone that happens beginning in verse 23? The goal here is to make sense of the psalm as a literary unity, without recourse to unverifiable, exterior elements or events, so that we can understand its overall rhetorical purpose. Two important features of the psalm allow us to understand it as a literary whole: the function of the lament section and the future tense of the main verbs in verses 23 and 26-32. As we saw above, the main function of the lament section was to appeal to God in various ways (crying out

[33] הושיעני מפי אריה ומקרני רמים עניתני

[34] σῶσόν με ἐκ στόματος λέοντος / καὶ ἀπὸ κεράτων μονοκερώτων τὴν ταπείνωσίν μου.

to God, reflecting on the past action of God and the past relationship between God and David, and vivid description of suffering, abandonment and mocking) in order to persuade God to act on David's behalf. The overall rhetorical purpose of the psalm, then, should be consistent throughout, namely to persuade God to act.

Starting in verse 23, the main verbs of all the sentences, except verses 24-25, are in the future tense, indicating not actual praise in the present, but future praise. Without any indication in the psalm of an experience of salvation or a belief in anticipated salvation, we can understand the future tense of the verbs as praise promised to God, if God acts to save David. In other words, David is promising his praise (vv. 23, 26), describing what that praise will be (vv. 24-25) and the future results of that praise (vv. 27-32) *if* God acts to deliver him from his enemies. The persuasive effect of this vowed praise lies in the fact that God is "the praise of Israel" (v. 4), and might be persuaded by David's promise of praise. If David is saved, then God will get what is due, namely the praise of Israel and the praise of all the nations, which in some ways is the ideal for the God of Israel who claims dominion over all the world. If one reads the second half of the psalm this way, then the lament and praise sections hang together quite well in that they both function rhetorically as attempts to persuade God to act on David's behalf in the midst of his suffering.

Not only does this reading of the psalm treat its Greek version as a Greek document that would be read or heard by the author of Mark and his audience, but it changes the way that one understands the flow of the psalm. As a Greek text, the psalm is *not* about eschatological vindication of the righteous sufferer who cries out to God and then is saved because of his righteousness, as so many New Testament scholars assume. Instead, David confesses his sin at the outset, cries out to God with vivid descriptions of his suffering, appeals to God's formerly faithful relationship with him, and promises praise if God answers him, a praise that will be so effective that all nations and future generations will come to worship God. Because David is a king, he can make promises of praise that would have nationwide consequences and perhaps even worldwide consequences, although this might be a stretch even for him. One of the more interesting things is that by the end of the psalm, however gloriously envisaged David's promised praise might be, David does not receive God's answer to his attempts at persuasion. The psalm leaves the issue of God's response to David's suffering unresolved.

IV. Reading Mark 15:22-39 in Light of Psalm 21

The propensity of New Testament scholars to read Psalm 21 as a psalm of the Righteous Sufferer that ends with the salvation and vindication of the righteous sufferer clearly affects the way these scholars interpret Mark's Gospel.[35] In such an interpretation of the psalm, Jesus' resurrection in Mark is his vindication because he suffers innocently. Based on the foregoing analysis and interpretation of Psalm 21, the interpretation of Jesus' suffering and death as vindicated in his resurrection in the image of the Suffering Righteous One from the psalm must be reconsidered and modified.

The scene of Jesus' crucifixion and death is punctuated by evocations of Psalm 21 at three moments: Jesus' crucifixion, Jesus' mocking by the bystanders while he hangs from the cross, and Jesus' loud cry just before he dies. I will take each of these moments in turn.

1. Jesus is Crucified

Mark's narration of Jesus' crucifixion is actually very sparse in detail in comparison to the descriptions of his physical maltreatment that follows each of his condemnations (14:65 and 15:17-20). However, at the point at which Jesus is crucified, Mark highlights the evocation of Ps 21:19

[35] Lothar Ruppert is most famous for his study of the motif of the Righteous Sufferer in the Hebrew Bible and Intertestamental Judaism (*Der leidende Gerechte. Eine motivgeschichtliche Untersuchung zum Alten Testament und zwischentestamentlichen Judentum* [Forschung zur Bibel 5; Würzburg, 1972]). In his second monograph on the topic, he summarizes his findings and concludes that by the final stage of the development of this motif (the apocalyptic stage, which is manifest in Dan 11:33-35; 12:1-3; Wis 2:12-20; 5:1-7 and 4 Macc 18:6b-19, among other texts), the idea of the Righteous Sufferer had become a "dogma" (*Jesus als der leidende Gerechte? Der Weg Jesu im Lichte eines alt- und zwischentestamentlichen Motivs* [Stuttgart: KBW Verlag, 1972], 28). Unfortunately, New Testament scholars have accepted Ruppert's conclusions most of the time without question. Although the motif is certainly present in a great deal of literature of the time, it is not omnipresent. The literature that Ruppert uses to trace the motif and construct these developmental lines for the motif are spread over close to a thousand years. He pays no attention to the genre of each of these writings or to the social setting of their construction or reception. By collapsing these gaps in time, culture, and genre, Ruppert ignores discontinuity and thus creates a simplistic picture of the relationship between these texts and the communities that read and heard them. He takes disparate works that may or may not be related to each other literarily, abstracts an idealized figure from these texts, and then claims that the necessity of the suffering of the Righteous One has risen to the level of dogma during this time period. Any use of Ruppert's conclusions to interpret the way New Testament writers narrate Jesus' death should proceed with a large dose of skepticism.

(indicated by the italics) by putting it in the middle of a short chiasm (in bold). Verses 24-25 read, "**And they crucified him**, and *they divided his garments, casting lots for them* [to determine] who would take what. It was the third hour **and they crucified him**."[36] Even though the form of σταυρόω in the beginning of the sentence is in the historical present and the one at the end is not, the sentence clearly frames the reference to Ps 21:9. Mark highlights it to incorporate Psalm 21 into the story of Jesus' crucifixion and to encourage the reader to center his or her efforts on Psalm 21 in order to understand the crucifixion.[37]

Verse 19 of the psalm is what Mark evokes in 15:24, and it is located at the end of a series of descriptions of David's suffering, the last of which describes his extreme persecution and defeat. The imagery evoked by Mark is that of David who is taken for dead after his enemies have mistreated and persecuted him. Psalm 21:13-14 describes David's enemies as "young bulls" and "bulls" (μόσχοι and ταῦροι) surrounding and encircling him and as a "lion" (λέων) ravishing and roaring, ready to pounce. Verses 15-16 continue this metaphorical language, but the imagery communicates David's perception that his situation is life threatening. He is "poured out like water," his "bones are scattered,"

[36] **καὶ σταυροῦσιν αὐτὸν** καὶ *διαμερίζονται τὰ ἱμάτια αὐτοῦ βάλλοντες κλῆρον ἐπ' αὐτὰ* τίς τί ἄρῃ. ἦν δὲ ὥρα τρίτη **καὶ ἐσταύρωσαν αὐτόν**. All translations of the Greek New Testament and the Psalms are mine.

[37] Against Taylor who says, "That they should have divided [the garments] by casting lots, using the dice by which they whiled away the time, is natural, and need not be regarded as a detail suggested by Ps. xxi. (xxii.) 19." However, he goes on to say that Mark's language shows that he has the passage in mind and says, "the question arises how far events have recalled OT passages, and to what extent these have coloured the accounts." He never addresses the question in this case. See Taylor, *The Gospel According to St. Mark,* 589 and Moloney, *The Gospel of Mark*, 320. Along the same lines, Robert H. Gundry says, "We should resist the temptation to think that Mark means to show the fulfillment of OT prophecy by borrowing phraseology from Ps 22:19 (18) when he describes the division of Jesus' garments." (*Mark: A Commentary on His Apology for the Cross* [Grand Rapids: Eerdmans, 1993], 945). Eugene LaVerdiere raises questions about Mark's intention to refer to all of Psalm 22 by questioning why he did not refer to parts of the psalms more illustrative of Jesus' situation. See *The Beginning of the Gospel: Introducing the Gospel of Mark*, vol. 2 (Collegeville, Minn.: Liturgical Press, 1999), 292. Brown says, "The psalm parallels are to secondary details that fill in the story (mostly to incidents involving what other people do to Jesus)." (*The Death of the Messiah*, 2:1452). But the evocations of Psalm 22 (LXX 21) are more than secondary details. I agree with Donald Juel who says, "It is difficult to conceive the passion narratives without allusions to Psalm 22. It is as difficult to explain the allusions to the psalm as secondary." (*Messianic Exegesis: Christological Interpretation of the Old Testament in Early Christianity* [Philadelphia: Fortress, 1988], 116). Moloney repeatedly says that Psalm 22 dominates the passion account in Mark, and thus correctly gives it pride of place in his discussion of the death of Jesus (*The Gospel of Mark*, 317-331).

his "heart has become like wax melting" within him, his "strength has dried up like earthenware," and his "tongue has become stuck" to his throat. In the last line of verse 16, David directs the description to "you" (i.e., to God) and says, "and you sent me down into the dust of death."[38] This implicates God directly in David's suffering. Verse 17 continues the description of David being surrounded by his enemies, and verses 18 and 19 implicate the enemies directly in the actions that cause David to express his nearness to death: "I counted all my bones, but they [his enemies] gazed and looked upon me. They divided my clothes among themselves, and for my clothing they cast lots."[39] These two verses express the perception that David's enemies took him for dead, ready to take the spoils of the victim (his clothes).

Following the expression of God's will for Jesus' suffering found in Gethsemane, the overtones of God's involvement in David's situation of suffering and persecution in Ps 21:17 serve to reinforce God's role in Jesus' crucifixion. If we read Ps 21:13-19 alongside the account of Jesus' crucifixion, it is difficult to look upon God's will for Jesus' suffering as a positive thing.[40] Either that, or one must rethink what it means for Jesus to be crucified according to God's will, as is indicated in the Gethsemane scene.

In verses 13-19, there are three characters that are interwoven in the description of the suffering: David, his enemies and God. From David's point of view, it is clear that he is the victim and his enemies are the ones who inflict his suffering, but God's role is questionable, based on David's implication of God in his life-threatening situation described in verse 16c. Up to this point in the psalm, David continually attempts to elicit God's response by depicting the dissonance between God's past interaction with Israel and David, on the one hand, and God's current inaction in the face of his suffering, on the other hand. God's inaction and abandonment of David is certainly a cause for concern, but in verse 16c, God actively sends him "into the dust of death." The language is hyperbolic, but it points to David's perspective that God approves and causes David's persecution at the hands of his enemies. Furthermore, David, as chosen royal figure, does not see this as acceptable, and this

[38] καὶ εἰς χοῦν θανάτου κατήγαγές με.

[39] ἐξηρίθμησα πάντα τὰ ὀστᾶ μου, αὐτοὶ δὲ κατενόησαν καὶ ἐπεῖδόν με. διεμερίσαντο τὰ ἱμάτιά μου ἑαυτοῖς καὶ ἐπὶ τὸν ἱματισμόν μου ἔλαβον κλῆρον.

[40] Against Moloney who says, "The only ray of light comes from the allusion to Ps 22:19, and the first indication that this took place 'at the third hour.' These hints promise the reader that, in a mysterious way, God's design is being worked out in this brutal murder (cf. 10:45; 14:36)." (*The Gospel of Mark*, 321).

section of the psalm is followed by a four-fold cry for deliverance from suffering. When woven into Jesus' story in Mark, David's challenge to God becomes Jesus' as well.

2. Jesus is Mocked

As we move through Mark's crucifixion scene, the focus of the story begins to shift to those who observe Jesus hanging on the cross. First, Mark overtly reminds the reader of Jesus' kingship by describing the ironic charge written above his head on the cross, "The King of the Jews" (ὁ βασιλεὺς τῶν Ἰουδαίων, 15:26). The actions of the Roman authorities seem to be mocking Jesus as much as the onlookers beginning in the next verse, which is another evocation of Psalm 21, this time of verse 8. Mark 15:29-30 reads, "And the passers-by reviled him, shaking their heads and saying, 'Ha, the one who tears down the Temple and builds it up in three days; save yourself by coming down from the cross.'"[41] Similarly in Ps 21:8 David describes those who look at him (οἱ θεωροῦντές με) mocking him with bodily gestures (speaking with their mouths and shaking their heads). As we move to Mark 15:31-32, Mark tells of a similar mocking by the chief priests and the scribes: "Likewise, the chief priests mocked him among themselves with the scribes and said, 'He saved others, [yet] he cannot save himself; let the Christ, the King of Israel come down now from the cross so that we may see and believe.' Even those crucified with him insulted him."[42]

Much like the evocation of Ps 21:19 in Mark 15:24, 15:29-32 refers to a part of the psalm that is at the heart of a description about the suffering of David. In this case, the mocking comes after Ps 21:4-6, where he appeals to God's past saving actions with Israel, and before vv.10-11, where he appeals to the intimate relationship that he has shared with God from the beginning of his life. The mocking in verses 7-9 is the second wave of descriptions of David's suffering and reads, "But I am a worm and not a person, a disgrace of a man and a reproach of a people.

[41] καὶ οἱ παραπορευόμενοι ἐβλασφήμουν αὐτὸν κινοῦντες τὰς κεφαλὰς αὐτῶν καὶ λέγοντες; οὐὰ ὁ καταλύων τὸν ναὸν καὶ οἰκοδομῶν ἐν τρισὶν ἡμέραις, σῶσον σεαυτὸν καταβὰς ἀπὸ τοῦ σταυροῦ. "Revile"translates βλασφημέω here in agreement with the argument of Adela Yarbro Collins in "The Charge of Blasphemy in Mark 14:64," *JSNT* 26 (4, 2004): 379-401.

[42] ὁμοίως καὶ οἱ ἀρχιερεῖς ἐμπαίζοντες πρὸς ἀλλήλους μετὰ τῶν γραμματέων ἔλεγον· ἄλλους ἔσωσεν, ἑαυτὸν οὐ δύναται σῶσαι· ὁ χριστός ὁ βασιλεὺς Ἰσραὴλ καταβάτω νῦν ἀπὸ τοῦ σταυροῦ, ἵνα ἴδωμεν καὶ πιστεύσωμεν. καὶ οἱ συνεσταυρωμένοι σὺν αὐτῷ ὠνείδιζον αὐτόν.

All who look at me mock me, they speak with their lips, they shake their head[s], 'He hoped in the Lord, let him deliver him, let him save him for he wants him.'"[43] The similarities between Jesus' and David's mocking go beyond Ps 21:8.[44] Jesus has already been mocked and abused by those at his Sanhedrin trial (14:65), and by the soldiers serving Pilate after his trial with Pilate (15:16-20), and is now clearly insulted by all those who are present at his crucifixion, even by the rebels who are crucified with him. Everyone from the most powerful (chief priests and scribes) to the lowliest (those crucified with him), from Roman to Jew, has joined in the mocking. This resonates with the hyperbolic language of Ps 21:7 where David calls himself the insult of humanity and the contempt of a people.

The content of the mocking in Mark 15:29b-30 provides another point of comparison with the mocking in Ps 21:7-9.[45] The passers-by taunt Jesus by referring to his claim to be able to tear down the Temple and rebuild it in three days. Then in verses 31-32, the chief priests and scribes continue the derision by calling on Jesus to act on his status as the Messiah, King of Israel, and to come down so that they may see and believe. If he were the hoped-for Messiah, the King of Israel, then he would be the powerful agent of God, who carries out God's will to deliver Israel. The mockers challenge Jesus to prove this by miraculously coming down from the cross as a demonstration of his power to overcome the authority of Roman justice. A similar mocking occurs in Ps 21:9: "He hoped in the Lord, let him deliver him, let him save him, for he wants him." They mock by saying that if David really were a delight to God, then God would deliver him from his desperate situation. In a sense, his mockers test God, or at least David's relationship with God, which can only be vindicated if God saves him. Similarly, in Mark 15:29-32, Jesus is the beloved Son in whom God is well pleased (ὁ υἱός μου ὁ ἀγαπητός, ἐν σοὶ εὐδόκησα, 1:11), and the onlookers challenge him to save himself. By implication, they challenge his relationship with

[43] ἐγὼ δέ εἰμι σκώληξ καὶ οὐκ ἄνθρωπος, ὄνειδος ἀνθρώπου καὶ ἐξουδένημα λαοῦ. πάντες οἱ θεωροῦντές με ἐξεμυκτήρισάν με, ἐλάλησαν ἐν χείλεσιν, ἐκίνησαν κεφαλήν. Ἤλπισεν ἐπὶ κύριον, ῥυσάσθω αὐτόν· σωσάτω αὐτόν, ὅτι θέλει αὐτόν.

[44] Schweizer raises this possibility, but he does not explore it beyond the sentence that raises the possibility. See *The Good News According to Mark*, 349.

[45] Moloney points this out, but goes in a slightly different direction based on his understanding of Psalm 22 in ways similar to traditional scholarship, which in turn results in his characterization of Jesus on the cross as the innocent righteous sufferer. See *The Gospel of Mark*, 322-23.

God as well. In other words, if Jesus really is God's chosen Messiah, the King of Israel, then why is God not giving him the ability to save himself?[46]

The relationship between God and Jesus finds an analog in the relationship between God and David as expressed in Psalm 21. Not only is the entire story of the chosen, royal David assumed by the ancient hearer of the psalm, but also in verses 4-6 and 10-11 of Psalm 21, David expresses his understanding of the favored relationship between himself and God. In verses 4-6 David reflects back on his heritage and God's interaction with his ancestors. He reminds God that God dwells "among holy ones" (ἐν ἁγίοις) and is "the praise of Israel" (ὁ ἔπαινος Ισραηλ). One of the reasons for this, David goes on, is that when his ancestors hoped in God, God delivered them, and they were not put to shame: "to you they cried out and they were saved" (πρὸς σὲ ἐκέκραξαν καὶ ἐσώθησαν). By his repeated use of "hope" (ἤλπισαν), David expresses the fidelity that God had shown to his ancestors, and in addition, he reflects on his place in this heritage as the chosen leader of God's people. As his ancestors did, he has hoped in God, but he has not received the deliverance that his ancestors received.

In verses 10-11, David's reconsideration of his relationship with God becomes more personal. He reminds God of the nearness and intimacy that they shared, even from birth. David essentially calls God his midwife in 10a and 11a: "For you are the one who drew me forth from the womb" (ὅτι σὺ εἶ ὁ ἐκσπάσας με ἐκ γαστρός) and "Upon you I was cast from the womb" (ἐπὶ σὲ ἐπερρίφην ἐκ μήτρας). And in 10b and 11b, he calls God his hope and his God, even from the point of his birth. The repeated use of womb imagery (γαστήρ, μήτρα, κοιλία) shows the foundational relationship that he has with God. David's rumination on his relationship with God not only reminds God of what they share, but it heightens the abhorrence of what David is experiencing in his suffering.

[46] In contrast, Taylor argues that only the Matthean account of Jesus' mocking uses Ps 21:9 as its model, and he states that in Mark, "ἑαυτόν . . . σῶσαι is the only point of contact with the Psalm and is a reminiscence at most." (*The Gospel According to St. Mark*, 592). Brown argues that the use of Psalm 22 would have caused early Christians "to dramatize the mocking hostility shown to Jesus by those around the cross, challenging his claim to have God's help." (*Death of the Messiah*, 2:1462). I agree to a certain extent with Brown, but I think Mark's use of Psalm 21 goes much deeper than simply using the details of the psalm to dramatize Jesus' death. This is only recognizable if all three of the evocations to the psalm in the Passion Narrative are examined for their role in the overall narrative of Jesus' death.

Although Mark does not express Jesus' relationship with God in ways exactly parallel to Psalm 21, Mark describes Jesus' relationship with God in loving, filial terms, similar in some ways to the intimate relationship with God that David describes in Psalm 21. God speaks only twice in Mark, both times to call Jesus, "my beloved Son" (ὁ υἱός μου ὁ ἀγαπητός in 1:11 and 9:7). Jesus defines his community as a family that does the will of God, who presumably is the head of the family (3:31-35). There is an assumption here that Jesus is close enough to God to know the will of God and discern when people are acting on it. Furthermore, in the parable of the wicked tenants (Mark 12:1-12), Jesus indirectly presents himself as God's Son. He also calls upon God in Gethsemane as "Abba" (14:36), certainly a term of endearment and closeness, and then he admits to being the "Son of the Blessed One" at his trial before the Sanhedrin (ὁ υἱὸς τοῦ εὐλογητοῦ, 14:61-62). Mark expresses an understanding from both God's side and Jesus' side that Jesus is God's chosen and beloved Son. David's relationship with God as described in Psalm 21 heightens the vivid depiction of his suffering and causes the reader to question this relationship, even as David does. So also does Jesus' relationship with God as beloved Son strongly contrast with his treatment that is described in the Passion Narrative. David as chosen, royal figure, as representative of Israel who shared in Israel's covenantal relationship with God, David, who has had a lifelong adherence to this same God, questions God's apparent abandonment, which allows this suffering, and he even accuses God of active involvement in it (Ps 21:16). Perhaps Mark is doing the same by referring to this psalm in his depiction of Jesus' death.

3. *Jesus Cries Out*

After Jesus' mocking by the passers-by and the chief priests and scribes, Mark skips ahead to the sixth hour (approximately noon) and tells us that darkness has fallen "upon the whole land" (ἐφ' ὅλην τὴν γῆν) until the ninth hour (Mark 15:33-34). This cosmic sign continues the apocalyptic depiction of Jesus' advent begun with the appearance of John the Baptist in the initial verses of the Gospel. It is often interpreted as a sign of God's judgment falling upon the earth.[47] But one could also

[47] Ben Witherington, *The Gospel of Mark: A Socio-Rhetorical Commentary* (Grand Rapids: Eerdmans, 2001), 397; Ched Myers, *Binding the Strong Man: A Political Reading of Mark's Story of Jesus* (Maryknoll: Orbis, 1988), 389; Schweizer, *The Good News According to Mark*, 353. Brown points to the link between daytime darkness and the Day of the Lord in Zeph 1:15, Joel 2:2; 3:4 and Amos 8:9-10, and then

view God as finally beginning to act after being silent in the narrative ever since the transfiguration in 9:2-8.[48] Ben Witherington points out that there are three moments in Mark that clearly "reveal the identity of Jesus at the beginning, middle and end of the story," at the baptism, the transfiguration and the crucifixion. He correctly points out, however, that at the third moment, "there is no voice from heaven speaking to Jesus," as one would expect on the basis of the baptism and the transfiguration.[49] This heightens the sense of the absence of God in the midst of Jesus' suffering, and calls into question the relationship between God and Jesus in Mark. There is a larger apocalyptic scenario happening that the audience, and maybe even Jesus as a character in Mark, might not fully appreciate. As supernatural signs swirl around, Jesus hangs on the cross approaching death. If darkness at high noon is possible, then surely saving the life of the beloved Son is possible as well, is it not? But Mark portrays God as distant from Jesus, and this causes the reader to question whether or not Mark fully accepts an apocalyptic scenario where the Messiah must die.[50] The cries of Jesus that follow seem to emphasize this assessment.

At the ninth hour, Jesus makes his now famous cry to God in the voice of David from Ps 21:2: "My God My God, why did you abandon me?" (ὁ θεός μου ὁ θεός μου, εἰς τί ἐγκατέλιπές με; Mark 15:34). Mark does not quote directly from the psalm; instead he transliterates Jesus' cry in David's words from Aramaic to Greek and then translates it into the saying that we have in verse 34. In the previous evocations of the PssLam in the Passion Narrative – namely, in Mark 14:18 and 14:34 – Jesus used the words from Psalms 40 and 41-42, respectively, but only in his cry from the cross does Mark quote Jesus in his native tongue when referring to this PsLam. This does not affect the pattern of evocations to the

he goes on to say, "Against this background one can interpret Mark to mean that while the mockers demanded of Jesus on the cross a sign…God is giving them a sign as part of a judgment on the world." (*Death of the Messiah*, 2:1035). For an alternative view, see Shiner, "The Ambiguous Pronouncement of the Centurion," 10. Shiner points to similar portents in the stories of Romulus (Plutarch, *Romulus* 27.6–28.6), Julius Caesar (Virgil, *Georgics* 1.463-68), Carneades (Diogenes Laertius 4.64), and Pelopidas (Plutarch, *Pelopidas* 295A). Evans makes a similar point (*Mark 8:27–16:20*, 506).

48 Brown, *Death of the Messiah*, 2:1036.

49 Witherington, *The Gospel of Mark*, 398.

50 Against Gundry who says, "The supernatural character of the darkness… magnifies Mark's apologetic point: now that Jesus' prediction of mockery has reached complete fulfillment, God hides his Son from the blasphemers' leering." (*Mark*, 947). In response to Gundry's assessment, Evans says, "In view of the cry of abandonment in v 34, perhaps it is better to think that God has hidden his face from his Son." (*Mark 8:27–16:20*, 506).

LXX PssLam that has been consistent throughout the Passion Narrative because, from a literary perspective, the Aramaic literarily sets up the misunderstanding that ensues right after the cry, presupposing "that the whole scene is constructed in Greek, as the confusion involved in the play upon ελωι and Ἠλία would hardly take place in a Semitic context."[51] What follows the transliterated Aramaic is very close to a word for word quotation from Ps 21:2a.[52] Clearly, Mark assumes that the Greek speaking audience will be more familiar with the LXX than with the MT or the Aramaic, but the literary device of using the Aramaic has the purpose of continuing Mark's major theme of misunderstanding of Jesus.

The scholarly debate about Jesus' cry usually revolves around two interrelated issues: (1) Was Jesus' cry one of despair, hope or something else?[53] and (2) Did he mean to refer to the first verse of the psalm

[51] Moloney, *The Gospel of Mark*, 326, n. 264. See also Brown, *Death of the Messiah*, 2:1061-63; Adela Yarbro Collins concurs: "It is given in Aramaic to prepare for the misunderstanding of some of the bystanders who conclude that Jesus is calling Elijah. Their misunderstanding appears to be deliberate, since the similarity between the two relevant words is not close. Thus, the reaction is presented as additional mockery" ("From Noble Death to Crucified Messiah," *NTS* 40 [1994]: 499).

[52] Ps 22:2a reads, "Ὁ θεὸς ὁ θεός μου, πρόσχες μοι· ἵνα τί ἐγκατέλιπές με" and Mark 15:34b reads, "Ὁ θεός μου ὁ θεός μου, εἰς τί ἐγκατέλιπές με."

[53] Here are some excerpts from the debate as I understand it: For hope or trust in God, see Matera, *The Kingship of Jesus*, 132. Jack Dean Kingsbury says: "Jesus' cry is to God... and it expresses continuing trust in God ('my God') in spite of abandonment into death. On balance, therefore, the scene of 15:33-36 is analogous to that of 15:29-32. In it, Jesus is pictured as going to his death as one who places his total trust in God." (*The Christology of Mark's Gospel*, [Philadelphia: Fortress, 1983], 130). Taylor argues that reading the cry of Jesus as a cry of faith "is a reaction from the traditional view which fails to take the saying seriously. The depths of the saying are too deep to be plumbed, but the least inadequate interpretations are those which find in it a sense of desolation in which Jesus felt the horror of sin so deeply that for a time the closeness of His communion with the Father was obscured." (*The Gospel According to St. Mark*, 594). After pointing out that Luke changes Jesus' last words to an allusion to Ps 31:5 ("Father, into your hands I commit my spirit;" Luke 23:46) in order to portray Jesus' death as noble, Juel says, "It seems almost comical to argue that Jesus chose the opening line from Psalm 22 as his last cry to express his confidence in the God who vindicates the sufferer at the end of the psalm. Other texts would have been far more suitable for such purposes." (*Messianic Exegesis: Christological Interpretation of the Old Testament in Early Christianity* [Philadelphia: Fortress, 1988], 114). Schweizer insightfully holds in tension the abandonment expressed with Jesus' cry with the theological issue of his faith in God in the midst of his suffering: "The cry of Jesus summarizes in an extraordinarily meaningful way both aspects of what is happening here: it is a radical expression of the loneliness of Jesus' suffering. He has to bear not only the experience of being abandoned by men, but also of being forsaken by God. At the same time, however, it is a radical expression of a devotion to God which endures in every adverse experience – a devotion which continues to claim God as 'my God' and

or the entire psalm?[54] As I have been arguing all throughout this study, appeal to the entire psalm is appropriate. If this is done, then Jesus does not cry out in despair; rather he joins Israel's long line of those who cried out to God in the midst of suffering. The scholars who think that Ps 21:2 is not a cry of despair usually read the whole of the psalm and its supposed ending of eschatological vindication as the key to understanding Jesus' cry. We have seen the problems with this understanding of the psalm, so if the cry is not one of despair, and if Psalm 21 is not thought of as ending with the eschatological vindication of the suffering righteous one, then this opens up another possibility. Instead of despair

will not let him go although he can be experienced only as the absent One who has forsaken the petitioner." (*The Good News According to Mark*, 353). Brown argues for taking the cry as literally expressing the "pessimistic pathos" of Jesus and that Jesus is not questioning the existence of God or the power of God to do something, but he is questioning the silence of God (*Death of the Messiah*, 2:1046, 1047). Moloney argues that the sense of abandonment expressed by Jesus in his cry should not be softened but maintained "to capture fully the Markan presentation of the crucified Christ." (*The Gospel of Mark*, 326). Gundry says that the narrative context points to the seriousness of Jesus' cry and concludes, "given these circumstances, not even a Jewish audience – much less Mark's Gentile audience—would hear the cry as pointing to a later salvific passage.... It does not interpret that cry in the light of later verses in Psalm 22, for then phraseology would have been drawn from them." (*Mark*, 967). See Moloney, *The Gospel of Mark*, 326 and Brown, *Death of the Messiah*, 2:1047-51 for two excellent discussions of the scholarship around this issue.

[54] Matera thinks the whole psalm is referred to (*The Kingship of Jesus*, 133). But many others think it is only the first line: C.E.B. Cranfield, *The Gospel According to Saint Mark* (Cambridge: Cambridge University Press, 1966), 458; Juel, *Messianic Exegesis*, 114; Taylor, *The Gospel According to St. Mark*, 594. Donahue and Harrington say, "A literary and theological investigation of Mark's account would rightly place more emphasis on Psalm 22 taken as a whole as the prayer of a suffering righteous person and an important element in Mark's christology" (*The Gospel of Mark*, 451). After briefly considering the function of the psalm in Mark, Daniel Guichard concludes, among other things, that when considered as a whole, the confession of the centurion in Mark 15:39 corresponds with the theme of universality at the end of Psalm 22. See "La reprise du psaume 22 dans le récit de la mort de Jésus (Marc 15,21-41)," *Foi et Vie* 88 (1988): 64. I agree with the impulse to consider the whole of Psalm 21 (LXX), but I do not agree with the characterization of the psalm by Donahue and Harrington and Guichard. Vernon K. Robbins says that those who consider the psalm as a whole, as he does, usually impose the rhetoric of the psalm onto the rhetoric of Markan discourse without considering how Mark's rhetoric differs from the psalm's rhetoric. Of the commentators I have read, Robbins best combines a careful analysis of Psalm 21 with close attention to Mark's use of it. His basic insight is that, because Mark uses the psalm in reverse order, he reverses the rhetoric of confidence, trust and hope that is present in the psalm. See "The Reversed Contextualization of Psalm 22 in the Markan Crucifixion: A Socio-Rhetorical Analysis," in *The Four Gospels: Festschrift for Frans Neirynck* (ed. F. van Segbroeck; 3 vols.; Leuven: Leuven University Press, 1992), especially 2:1175-83. I disagree with Robbins' assessment of the rhetoric of the psalm as having an ending that indicates the vindication of the psalmist, so I disagree with his conclusions about how Mark uses it.

or eschatological vindication, Jesus' cry can be viewed as expressing the outrage, abandonment and/or incomprehension of a chosen royal figure, just as the psalm does. And it could be seen as the final attempt of Jesus to convince God to save him from his suffering.

As with the other two allusions, verse 2 of the psalm comes from a description of David's suffering, this time from the first description. This is the first verse of the body of the psalm, encapsulating the mood of the entire psalm – not despair, but outrage, anger, accusation, questioning and pain at the thought that God has abandoned him in his time of greatest need. As we have seen, the sense of incomprehension and outrage is developed throughout the lament section of the psalm as David reflects on his relationship with God and describes his suffering in increasingly graphic and troubling terms. The psalm ends with a ten-verse promise of praise that is David's last attempt to elicit God's response. The whole psalm is a cry out to God for help and understanding, a challenge to God's inaction and a reminder to God of the deep persecution and suffering that is happening to God's chosen king. Mark's Jesus, God's chosen and beloved Son, a royal figure sent to his death for admitting to being Son of the Blessed One, can be understood as doing something similar as he cries out to God in David's words.

Right after Jesus dies in 15:37, the curtain of the temple tears in two and the centurion makes his now famous declaration, "Truly this was a son of God." These are both powerful statements that the narrative makes, and there has been much debate about their precise meaning and function within Mark's narrative, the discussion of which goes beyond the scope of this paper. These two literary features along with the darkened skies at noon gives the picture of God's beloved Son located at the center of something cosmic and earth-changing. When the dynamics of Psalm 21 are included in the picture, Jesus takes on the character of the suffering, chosen, royal figure of David, crying out to God for deliverance and not receiving an answer. The juxtaposition of the cosmic events with the lamenting king resists simplistic understandings of this event, such as part of a detailed divine plan that is consummated at the resurrection or as the means to apocalyptic end where the Messiah warrior-king conquers by suffering.[55] Somehow, the seriousness of human

[55] Moloney says, "There is an inevitability about the oncoming suffering, death, and ultimate vindication of the Son of Man. It is a necessary, although paradoxical, part of God's design, the fulfillment of what was written of the Son of Man (v. 21a)." (*The Gospel of Mark*, 284; cf. 298). Also see John Painter, *Mark's Gospel: Worlds in Conflict* (London: Routledge: 1997), 185. Evans says, "His death on the cross is not defeat

suffering, something that Mark seems to think is very important, must be integrated into any interpretation of the meaning of Jesus' suffering and death on the cross.

V. Some Implications for Understanding Jesus' Death in Mark

Without the category of the vindication of the suffering righteous or innocent one in the forefront, one begins to notice some features of Mark's narrative that are usually passed over. First, like David in the psalm, Jesus is not innocent. He does not admit his sin, as David does at the beginning of the psalm, but Jesus dies for that which he is accused, namely, being the Son of the Blessed One. In his trial before the high priest, the chief priests, the elders and the scribes, Jesus is silent before his false accusers in Mark 15:55-61a. But then the high priest asks him, "Are you the Messiah, the Son of the Blessed One?" Jesus answers, "I am," and then he quotes Ps 110:1 and Dan 7:13: "And you will see the Son of Man seated at the right hand of the power and coming with the clouds of heaven." These are not the words of an innocent man before his accusers.[56] The innocence of Jesus does not seem to be the issue in

(as Jews and Romans alike would assume) but a prerequisite for accomplishment of mission and attainment of office." (*Mark 8:27-16:20*, 20).
Donahue and Harrington say that the δεῖ in Mark 8:31 "carries an overtone of apocalyptic determinism and will become increasingly prominent as the gospel proceeds" (*The Gospel of Mark*, 261). See also Evans, *Mark 8:27-16:20*, 57 and Marcus, *Mark 1-8* (AB 27; New York: Doubleday, 2000), 72-73. Marcus argues that Mark sets the stage for the entire Gospel by referring to Isa 40:3 at the outset, which refers to God's triumphal return to Jerusalem. "Since... Mark seems to be aware of the larger Isaian context, and since *euangelion* itself implies military victory... Mark may understand 'the good news about Jesus' to be a fulfillment of Isaiah's vision of saving holy war.... In Mark, however, the fulfillment of this well-known Isaian expectation of holy war victory will take place in a paradoxical way. 'The way of the Lord'... is Jesus' 'way' (1:2-3), and the latter will become the leitmotiv of the Gospel's central section.... Mark may thus wish to imply... that it is not the revolutionary struggle against the Romans but Jesus' way up to suffering and death in Jerusalem that truly represents the triumphant return of Yahweh to Zion prophesied by Isaiah." (148-49). This is a summary of Marcus' basic argument in *The Way of the Lord.*

56 This is against Moloney: "Jesus' response [at his arrest in Gethsemane] initiates another themes that will recur across the passion story: his innocence." He goes on to argue that "the readers and listeners to the story know that Judas and his colleagues are the guilty characters in this encounter.... The general background of the suffering of the righteous one is sufficient for Jesus' indications that his violent arrest is the fulfillment of Scripture." (*The Gospel of Mark*, 298). Mark's presentation of Jesus' lack of innocence is different than the other Gospels. In the Gospel of Matthew, Jesus gives the more ambiguous answer, "You said" (σὺ εἶπας) (26:64), and he does not defend

Mark's Passion Narrative. Instead, Jesus dies for being the Son of the Blessed One, something that indicates his success in living God's will fully. If Jesus were innocent, then his punishment would be random and somewhat meaningless for Mark. Because Jesus died for being the Son of the Blessed One, Mark makes a strong statement about the powers of evil that hold sway in the society of his time and the need to confront them at every turn.

This takes us back to the three predictions of Jesus' suffering, death and resurrection in 8:31, 9:31 and 10:33. All three predictions talk about Jesus' impending arrest, mistreatment, death and resurrection. Only the prediction in 8:31 says that these things must happen (δεῖ), but it seems to be assumed in the other two. The fact that all this must happen is oftentimes interpreted as indicating divine design or plan.[57] Also implied in this interpretation is the idea that this all must happen so that Jesus may be vindicated at the resurrection. But there is nothing in these three predictions to necessitate a vindicatory relationship between Jesus's suffering and death, on the one hand, and Jesus' resurrection, on the other hand. In other words, without the overtone of vindication in Psalm 21, nor the idea of Jesus' death as the death of an innocent person, then the predictions could be thought of as having some other kind of logic than that of prediction of wrongful suffering and vindicating resurrection. They could just describe the reasonable course of Jesus' life based upon Mark's presentation of him as God's agent who carries out the will of God in the face of the evil that he confronts.

In 14:21 and 14:49, Mark has Jesus talk about his death as "going as it is written of him," and "in order that Scripture may be fulfilled." These two qualifications of Jesus' death are not directly preceded or followed by specific references to Scripture, and so they do not function as formulaic quotations as they would in the Gospel of Matthew. They are general statements regarding how one is to understand Jesus' death, namely, as according to Scripture, and they are most frequently

himself at the chief priests' accusations before Pilate. However, his lack of defense can be taken as acceptance of the charges, or at least an acceptance of his inevitable death as a result of his actions against the religious authorities. The Gospel of Luke clearly portrays Jesus as innocent, but Jesus does not cry out in the words of Psalm 21 in the Gospel. The Gospel of John also portrays Jesus as innocent, but he is fairly indifferent to the whole matter. Again, Jesus does not cry out in the words of Psalm 21 in this Gospel either. So, the portrayal of Jesus as an innocent victim is more determined by the narrative of each individual Gospel than it is by the evocation of Psalm 21.

[57] Moloney, *The Gospel of Mark*, 173; Donahue and Harrington, *The Gospel of Mark*, 261.

understood as describing Jesus' death as divinely planned, foretold by Scripture, or predetermined in some similar way.[58] Psalm 21 is one of the many Scripture passages evoked in the Passion Narrative of Mark to which the reader/hearer is directed. By reading Psalm 21 as described above, with David's variegated attempts at persuading God to act, including protest, outrage, anger, description of suffering and conditional praise, the general appeal to Scripture in Mark should be read to include an element of faithful challenge to God's perceived inaction in the face of suffering. So, instead of understanding the qualifications of Jesus' death as predicting it in some divinely predetermined way, Psalm 21 makes the situation more complex by adding an element of challenge to God's perceived inaction in course of Jesus' suffering.[59] In Mark, it could be said that Jesus "goes as it is written of him," challenging his suffering and God's perceived part in it, thus encouraging the reader to challenge understandings of God that allow for divine plans of suffering and shameful death, no matter what lies at the other end of them.

The characterization of Jesus in relation to God, and ultimately the Christology and theology of Mark, could also be affected by this reading of Psalm 21. If the story of Jesus' suffering and death is read or heard with the whole of Psalm 21 in mind, then the characterization of Jesus as the Suffering Righteous One might just have to give way to a Jesus who cries out for God to take notice of his suffering and answer his pleas. Instead of a Jesus who goes to his death willingly without a word, Psalm 21 brings up the possibility of a Jesus who goes to his death challenging God to answer his cries from the cross.

[58] Moloney, *The Gospel of Mark*, 284. Donahue and Harrington say that in 14:21, "the divine necessity of suffering is stressed as in the Passion predictions." (*The Gospel of Mark*, 394). Taylor says that 14:21 suggest that the death of Jesus is "in accordance with the divine purpose." (*The Gospel According to St. Mark*, 541). Adela Yarbro Collins argues, "The fated nature of Jesus' death is expressed most clearly in the references to the Scriptures, which foretell or determine it, but also in the way in which God has receded as a character in the narrative.... The personal God recedes and the impersonal force of Scripture controls the events." ("From Noble Death to Crucified Messiah," 485).

[59] Sjef van Tilborg makes a similar observation about Matthew's use of Psalm 22: "The more intensive use of Psalm 22 in Matthew's text causes an intensification of the factual suffering. In a sense we can say that it has become even more absurd and repellent. The narrative is now about a 'Son of God' who hangs on the cross in a burial place and who has been stripped by pagan dogs and is being ogled by them. The more extensive use of the Psalm makes it even more difficult to 'explain' the suffering of the Messiah. If the use of Psalm 22 is intended as proof by prophecy, the least we can say is that the narrator of Matthew's gospel has not been very successful." ("Language, Meaning, Sense and Reference: Matthew's Passion Narrative and Psalm 22," *Hervormde Teologiese Studies* 44 (1998): 906).

I would not want to claim that the entire meaning of Jesus' death in Mark revolves around the proper understanding of Psalm 21. There are certainly elements in the story that support the vindication of Jesus at the resurrection and the idea that Jesus voluntarily dies according to God's will. But reading Psalm 21 as I have argued makes these issues a bit more complex, perhaps injecting a cautionary note to triumphalistic readings of the resurrection in Mark.[60] Instead, the reader is nudged to consider Jesus' death as resulting from his reluctance to compromise his attempts to embody God's will authentically, in contrast to an understanding of Jesus' suffering and death as something that God willed as part of a pre-ordained plan that cannot be changed. The question of Jesus' relationship with God is never fully resolved in Mark, even in the resurrection at the end of the story. Yes, Jesus is raised by God, but there are some curious elements to the scene that prevent me from fully accepting an understanding of the resurrection that claims that Jesus was vindicated by God in the end. The scope of this essay prevents me from treating the problem in the detail it requires, but I will make a few points as a way of anticipating further research.

According to The Oxford English Dictionary, the idea of vindication presumes some sense of unjust condemnation that must be rectified or some sense that something went wrong that now has to be proven otherwise. An overtone of vengeance or triumph could also be implied. But the eight verses in chapter 16 that narrate the resurrection are far from triumphalistic, with a spare description of the resurrection, a lack of resurrection appearances, the fear of the women as the last word of the narrative, and the fact that even though Jesus has been raised he is still "the crucified one." This last epithet is most telling for me because the Greek term used is ἐσταυρωμένον, a perfect passive participle, giving the nuance that Jesus' shameful death happened in the past but has ongoing effects, or even a stative quality, in the present. According to Mark, the resurrection does not undo the suffering and death that Jesus underwent, and his suffering and death have an enduring quality in and effect on the

[60] "Functional avoidance of Good Friday among many Christians is a heresy of long standing. Its tacit justification seems to be that Easter Sunday signals a victory so complete that God effectively annihilated Golgotha. Such confusion makes for a theology that is not merely bad, but heartless and even dangerous. In place of the Christian gospel of God's triumph, it substitutes the bad news of human triumphalism." (C. Clifton Black, "The Persistence of the Wounds," in *Lament: Reclaiming Practices in Pulpit, Pew, and Public Square* [ed. Sally A. Brown and Patrick D. Miller; Louisville: Westminster John Knox, 2005], 56).

present.[61] The relationship between the crucifixion and resurrection of Jesus seems not to be one where the resurrection vindicates Jesus' crucifixion in the sense that it undoes it or proves that Jesus was really innocent of the crimes for which he was crucified. Instead, there seems to be a symbiotic relationship, where the crucifixion conditions the meaning of the resurrection as much as the resurrection conditions the crucifixion. Suffering and resurrection seem equally and inseparably important to Mark; therefore we cannot think of the resurrection as the last word or even the solution to suffering in Mark. The last word will come only in the last days when "you will see Son of Man sitting at the right hand of the Power and coming with the clouds of heaven."

The cross is what makes the story of Jesus so compelling in Mark. Anything that sidesteps the horror or glorifies the suffering distorts Mark's presentation of Jesus' death. Mark's appeal to Scripture was one way that he tried to make sense of Jesus' suffering – a common practice in early Christianity. But as we have seen, the use of Psalm 21, as well as the other PssLam evoked in the Passion Narrative, does not explain away or sidestep the horror by claiming that it is okay because God willed it or by making it the first episode in a divine plan of eschatological vindication of the righteous sufferer. But inclusion of these psalms in the story of Jesus' suffering weaves into the story an ancient tradition of endurance, crying out to God in the midst of suffering, and faithful dissent. It seems to me that Mark's attempt at understanding Jesus' suffering and death is just as much about Mark's appreciation of the horror of human suffering as it is about the hope that belief in Jesus' resurrection can generate for Mark's readers.

[61] Jack Dean Kingsbury notices the detail of the perfect tense, and claims something similar regarding the idea that the resurrection does not "undo" the cross. But he interprets the perfect tense as pointing to the cross as the "decisive event in Jesus' ministry" (*The Christology of Mark's Gospel*, 134).

THE CHARGE OF BLASPHEMY IN MARK 14:64

Adela Yarbro Collins

A great deal of the scholarship on the trial of Jesus before the high priest and the council of Judea in Mark has focused on the question of the historical reliability of the account.[1] One of the issues involved in such studies is the question of responsibility for the death of Jesus, a sensitive issue for Jewish–Christian relations, especially since the Nazis' attempt to exterminate the Jews and the subsequent examination by Christians of their tradition, in which the Christian roots of anti-Semitism have been analyzed. A major problem in the study of the trial of Mk 14 is the discrepancy between the procedures followed there and the procedures mandated by the tractate *Sanhedrin* in the Mishnah for capital cases (*m. Sanh.* 4:1–5:5). If the regulations described in the Mishnah were in force during the time of Jesus, then the trial before the council was illegal, even a gross miscarriage of justice. Herbert Danby has argued persuasively that those regulations were not in force in Jesus' time.[2] Israel Abrahams has noted that the relevant portion of the Mishnah reads like a polemic against the Gospels.[3] Although a detailed analysis is beyond the scope of this article, I am attracted to the hypothesis that Abrahams hinted at only to reject, namely, that the Mishnah passage was composed, at least in part, in order to demonstrate that the high priest and council would not have conducted a trial in such a manner. The rabbis wanted to make the case that the accounts of Mark and Matthew are libelous fabrications. In any case, the regulations regarding trials involving capital punishment in the Mishnah should not be used in historical studies of the trial of Jesus.

* Reprint of *JSNT* 26 (2004): 379-401.

[1] See the review of scholarship in Darrell L. Bock, *Blasphemy and Exaltation in Judaism and the Final Examination of Jesus: A Philological-Historical Study of the Key Jewish Themes Impacting Mark 14:61-64* (WUNT, 2.106; Tübingen: Mohr Siebeck, 1998), 5-29; the concerns of Bock's study are also primarily historical.

[2] Herbert Danby, 'The Bearing of the Rabbinical Criminal Code on the Jewish Trial Narratives in the Gospels', *JTS* 21 (1919–20), 51-76.

[3] Israel Abrahams, 'The Tannaitic Tradition and the Trial Narratives', in *Studies in Pharisaism and the Gospels* (New York: Ktav, 1917–24), II, 129-37; the reference is to 137.

The point about the relevance of the Mishnaic tractate *Sanhedrin* is the only aspect of the question of what actually happened to be addressed by this article. I will focus rather on the cultural presuppositions and rhetorical force of the text of Mk 14:53-64. With regard to the presentation of the event, even when one puts the Mishnah aside, it is clear that the text of Mark portrays the high priest and the other members of the council as proceeding in an unjust manner. Such is implied by the statement that 'the chief priests and the whole council were seeking testimony against Jesus in order to put him to death, and yet they could not find any'.[4] This statement strongly implies a lack of impartiality on the part of the members of the council who were functioning at the time as judges. The next part of the narrator's report, which concerns the false witnesses, implies that the members of the council had sought and found persons willing to appear and bring false testimony against Jesus.[5] The problem was that their testimony did not agree. There was bias against Jesus, but the conspiracy was not sufficiently well planned. Whatever actually happened, it is clear that Mark wishes to make the point that the leaders of the people were trying to frame Jesus and thus condemn him unjustly.

The narrative flow of the passage implies that the purpose of the false testimony was to convict Jesus of blasphemy against the temple and thus against God. This reading is supported by the remarks of the high priest, 'Why do we need witnesses any longer? You heard the blasphemy' (Mk 14:63-64). Witnesses are no longer needed to convict Jesus of blasphemy because he himself has blasphemed in the hearing of the judges. These remarks make clear that the high priest is interpreting the statement of Jesus in 14:62 as blasphemous.

Here again there is tension between Mark and the Mishnah. According to *m. Sanh.* 7.5, the blasphemer is not culpable unless he pronounces the Name itself. Such is clearly not the case in Mark, since Jesus uses the circumlocution 'the Power' rather than the divine name (Mk 14:62). As will be demonstrated below, this limited understanding of blasphemy is attested in the period roughly contemporary with Mark. But this does not mean that this understanding was the official one that the council of Judea would have applied in the case of Jesus. The understanding of blasphemy likely to have been characteristic of

[4] Mk 14:55; all translations of Mark are my own.

[5] Mk 14:56-59. The γάρ of v. 56 links the false testimony with the activity of the members of the council reported in v. 55. Compare Acts 6:13 where the procurance of false witnesses is explicit.

the Sadducees, chief priests and perhaps other leaders as well was a broader one, as will be shown below.

Although Mark portrays the members of the council as biased and unjust, the charge of blasphemy in the trial of Jesus has verisimilitude in the cultural context of the Gospel. Mark did not wish to deny that Jesus blasphemed from the perspective of the high priest and the council. The problem lay, in his view, with their perspective, which failed to acknowledge Jesus as the authoritative agent of God. The narrative of the trial is ironic in the sense that what is blasphemy for the members of the council is true from the perspective of those who accept Jesus as the agent of God. Indeed, in the view of the audiences of Mark, Jesus had already been enthroned as the heavenly Messiah. This conviction intensifies the ironic effect.

Blasphemy in the Cultural Context of Mark

The whole question about blasphemy in the Jewish scriptures and Second Temple Jewish texts needs to be clarified first of all linguistically.[6] Many texts are quite inappropriately interpreted as 'blasphemy'. The first step toward greater clarity is to recognize a significant linguistic difference between Mark, Jews of the Second Temple period, and ordinary Greek speakers of the same period, on the one hand, and modern exegetes on the other. That difference may be illustrated by the fact that contemporary speakers of English use the word-group related to the term 'blasphemy' only with God as the object. We never speak about 'blaspheming' another human being. In ordinary ancient Greek, however, the verb βλασφημεῖν is used with either gods or human beings as the object. This ordinary usage is reflected in the New Testament. In Col 3:8, βλασφημία refers to slander against other human beings; in Eph 4:31, the same noun is equivalent to λοιδορία, which means abusive speech.[7]

[6] For brief introductions to the topic of blasphemy, see Hermann Wolfgang Beyer, 'βλασφημέω, βλασφημία, βλάσφημος', *TDNT* 1 (1964), 622-23; Otfried Hofius, 'βλασφημία, βλασφημέω, βλάσφημος', in H. Baltz and G. Schneider (eds.), *Exegetical Dictionary of the New Testament* (Grand Rapids: Eerdmans, 1990), 219-21; Herbert Chanan Brichto *et al.*, 'Blasphemy', *Encyclopaedia Judaica* [computer file] (CD-ROM edition; Version 1.0; Shaker Heights, OH: Judaica Multimedia, 1997).

[7] Jeremy Foreman Hultin, 'Watch your Mouth: The Ethics of Obscene Speech in Early Christianity and its Environment' (PhD dissertation, Yale University, 2003).

'Blasphemy' in the Hebrew Bible

The situation is quite the same in the Hebrew Bible. There is no specific term in that collection of texts that means 'to blaspheme'.[8] Those who claim that the concept of blasphemy appears in the Hebrew Bible connect it with one or more of the following terms: חרף ('reproach, taunt, despise, scorn'), נאץ ('contemn, spurn, scorn, despise'), גדף ('revile, affront') and the piel of קלל ('curse'). All of these words are used in the Hebrew Bible with both human and divine objects, just as βλασφημεῖν is used in ordinary Greek. Not counting doublets, the term חרף is used 18 times with a human object, 10 times with God as the object and 3 times with a human object closely associated with God. An example with a human object is Ps 119:42, 'Then shall I have an answer for those who taunt (חרף) me, for I trust in thy word.'[9] An often cited set of examples with a divine object is the story of the Rabshakeh, the envoy of King Sennacherib of Assyria, and Hezekiah in 2 Kgs 18–19 and the parallel in Isa. 36–37. In 2 Kgs 19:4, the speech of the Rabshakeh is described as taunting (חרף) the living God. It seems clear that the issue is not 'blasphemy' in the later sense. The Rabshakeh states, 'Has any of the gods of the nations ever delivered its land out of the hand of the king of Assyria?' (2 Kgs 18:33). The envoy taunts the God of Israel just as he would a human opponent, attributing weakness to him. In this text, God is not portrayed as an utterly transcendent being to be treated with awe-filled respect, but a character who engages in conflict and who can be insulted by enemies and defended by adherents.

The term גדף ('revile, affront') is used with a human object in association with חרף ('reproach, taunt, despise, scorn') in Ps 44:16-17 (44:15-16 in the English versions): 'All day long my disgrace is before me, and shame has covered my face at the words of the taunters (חרף) and revilers (גדף), at the sight of the enemy and the avenger.' The latter term also occurs in the story of 2 Kgs 18–19 and Isa 36–37. In 2 Kgs 19:6 = Isa 37:6, the Lord says to Hezekiah through Isaiah, 'Do not be afraid because of the words that you have heard, with which the servants of the king of Assyria have reviled (גדף) me.' Both terms occur in 2 Kgs 19:22 = Isa 37:23: 'Whom have you taunted (חרף) and reviled (גדף)? Against whom have you raised your voice and haughtily lifted your eyes? Against the Holy One of Israel!' In both of these passages, the God of Israel asserts his dignity and power over against the threats and taunts

[8] Bock, *Blasphemy and Exaltation*, 30.

[9] All translations of the MT are from the NRSV unless otherwise noted.

issued by the king of Assyria. The term נאץ ('contemn, spurn, scorn, despise') is used four times with an abstract object, such as 'reproof' or 'counsel'. It is used five times with a human object, eight times with a divine object, and six times with an object closely associated with God, such as God's word or name. An example with a human object is Isa 60:14, 'and all who despised (נאץ) you [Jerusalem] shall bow down at your feet'. Two examples will give an impression of the usage of the term with a divine object. In Isa 1:4 the people are accused of having despised (נאץ) the Holy One of Israel. The context makes clear that it is their unjust deeds that constitute this act of despising God, their failure to 'rescue the oppressed, defend the orphan, plead for the widow' (1:17). In Deut 31:20, the Lord predicts that, when the people 'have eaten their fill and grown fat, they will turn to other gods and serve them, despising (נאץ)' God and breaking the covenant. Here the issue is clearly idolatry. In all these cases, the term has connotations of disrespect. In some cases, it has the connotation of rebellion as well. It is not primarily a verbal offense.

The piel of קלל ('curse') is used with a human object 27 times in the Hebrew Bible. In a further case, the human receiver of the curse is closely associated with God: 'Abishai...answered, "Shall not Shimei be put to death for this, because he cursed (קלל) the Lord's anointed?"'[10] The term is used with an inanimate object three times. God is the object in Exod 22:27 (22:28 in the English versions), 'You shall not curse (קלל) God, nor curse (ארר) a ruler of your people.'[11] Here cursing God or God's anointed is a serious offense, worthy of death. But it is an activity that can apply to ordinary human beings as well. It is not an act that is uniquely related to God's status as God.

The term קלל also occurs in a passage that became a classic text for the later understanding of a transgression or crime roughly equivalent to 'blasphemy'. In Lev 24:10-23, a man who was the son of an Israelite woman, but whose father was an Egyptian, got into a fight with an Israelite man. In the context of this fight, 'the son of the Israelite woman expressly mentioned (נקב) the Name and he cursed (קלל) and they brought him to Moses'.[12] The interpretation of this text is difficult, but

[10] 2 Sam 19:22 (NRSV 19.21).

[11] My translation.

[12] Lev 24:11; my translation. The root נקב usually means 'to curse' in the qal and 'to name, mention, or designate' in the niphal. The qal form, however, in Isa 62:2 clearly means 'to designate', and a similar meaning is likely here also. See Jacob Milgrom, *Leviticus 23–27* (AB, 3B; New York: Doubleday, 2001), 2107-108.

the context suggests that the son of the Israelite woman cursed the other man in the name of Yahweh. In other words, he called upon Yahweh to bring some evil upon the other man. The judgment of the Lord through Moses is that the man should be stoned. Then two legal principles are given in vv. 15-16: 'Whoever curses (קלל) his God shall bear his sin, and the one who expressly mentions the name of Yahweh shall be put to death...'[13] Here we have something distinctive. Cursing God is wicked, but speaking the name of Yahweh is worse. This text seems to be the basis for the later idea of 'blasphemy'.

This story and its legal principles stand in strong tension with a story about Elisha:

> [Elisha] went up from there to Bethel; and while he was going up on the way, some small boys came out of the city and jeered at him, saying 'Go away, baldhead! Go away, baldhead!' When he turned around and saw them, he cursed them in the name of the Lord (ויקללם בשם יהוה). Then two she-bears came out of the woods and mauled forty-two of the boys (2 Kgs 2:23-24).

Here Elisha, a man of God, is portrayed, not only as cursing, but also as expressly mentioning the name of Yahweh. This story is a folk-tale and represents the kind of thing people would say. Leviticus 24:10-23 represents a later, or different, perspective: the view that such cursing is morally reprehensible, indeed worthy of death. The latter perspective seems also to reflect a growing reverence for the divine name.

'Blasphemy' in the Septuagint

The usage of the Septuagint (LXX) is analogous to that of the Hebrew Bible and similar to that of ordinary Greek. The verb βλασφημεῖν, for example, is used, but not as a technical term. This verb is used to translate both גדף and נאץ, but not consistently.[14] The former verb is also translated with ὀνειδίζειν ('mock') and παροργίζειν ('to provoke to anger').[15] נאץ is also translated with παροργίζειν ('to provoke to anger'),[16] μυκτηρίζειν ('to sneer at'),[17] and παροξύνειν ('to provoke').[18] In Dan 3:96 OG (3:29 MT), βλασφημεῖν translates the Aramaic אמר שלה. The word

[13] My translation.
[14] 4 Kgdms 19:6 and Isa 52:5, respectively.
[15] Isa 37:6 and Ezek 20:27, respectively.
[16] Ps 107:11 (106.11 LXX).
[17] Prov 1:30; 15:5.
[18] Deut 32:19; Lam 2:6; 2 Kgdms 12:14.

שלה is related to the Akkadian *šillatu*, which means 'insolence'. The Aramaic phrase and the corresponding term βλασφημήσῃ are thus best translated 'speaks insolently'.[19] In Isa 66:3 LXX, the adjective βλάσφημος replaces 'one who blesses an idol' in the Hebrew. Here, the worship of other gods is interpreted as equivalent to speaking abusively or slanderously to or about God. In all these cases, the word-group βλασφημεῖν is used non-technically, in a sense that could apply equally well to human beings or to God.

In texts composed in Greek, or surviving only in Greek, the usage of the word-group βλασφημεῖν is similar to that of ordinary Greek. In 2 Maccabees, for example, there is a scene in which Judas Maccabaeus and his men are besieging a fort where Timothy and some of his men had taken refuge after a victory of Maccabaeus's army. In this context, the narrator makes the following remark: 'Now the men within, confident in the security of the place, were speaking in an exceedingly insolent manner and sending forth improper words.'[20] The NRSV translates ἐβλασφήμουν here with 'kept blaspheming', but the usual taunting of the foe in a battle is the more likely interpretation. Similarly, αἱ βλασφημίαι in v. 35 should be translated 'the insults', rather than 'the blasphemies', and οἱ βλάσφημοι in v. 36 'the slanderers' rather than 'the blasphemers'.[21]

1 Maccabees 2:6 is an interesting passage in which the noun βλασφημία probably refers to deeds as well as to words: 'And [Mattathias] saw the outrages (βλασφημίαι) that were taking place in Judah and Jerusalem.'[22] This statement follows an account describing the forbidding of burnt offerings in the sanctuary; the command to profane sabbaths and festivals, to defile the sanctuary and the priests, and to build altars and sacred precincts and shrines for idols. It also describes the command to the towns of Judah to offer sacrifice (to other gods) town by town. Finally, it describes the desolating sacrilege, the building of altars in the surrounding towns and so forth.[23]

[19] On the Aramaic phrase and its relation to Akkadian, see Shalom M. Paul, 'A Case Study of "Neglected" Blasphemy', *JNES* 42 (1985), 291-94. Paul himself concludes that 'Such improper speech when directed against God is blasphemy and when uttered against a human being is slander, insolence, impudence, effrontery' (292), but such a distinction is not required by the evidence he cites.

[20] 2 Macc 10:34; my translation.

[21] Similarly, in 2 Macc 12:14, βλασφημούντες should be translated 'speaking profanely' rather than 'blaspheming'.

[22] My translation.

[23] 1 Macc 1:41-61. The noun βλασφημίαι is used in a similar way in 2 Macc 8:4 and should be translated 'outrages' or 'insults' rather than 'blasphemies'.

In Wis 1:6, it is said that wisdom will not hold a βλάσφημος guiltless [of the words] from his lips. The context suggests that the Greek term should be translated 'one who speaks evil' rather than 'blasphemer'. Further comment on this 'evil speaking' comes in v. 8, where there is mention of uttering unrighteous things (ἄδικα); in v. 10, which mentions grumbling (γογγυσμοί); and in v. 11, where grumbling, slander (καταλαλιά) and a lying mouth (στόμα καταψευδόμενον) are advised against.

In the cases discussed so far, the usage of the word-group βλασφημεῖν is not technical. For the cases in which a technical sense seems to be emerging, see the discussions of Philo and Josephus below.

The Evidence of Philo

Philo and Josephus are important witnesses to the understandings of blasphemy in the cultural context of Mark. In one passage of the *Legatio ad Gaium*, Philo uses the verb βλασφημεῖν in one of its classic Greek usages. He describes Helicon, an Egyptian slave, who was educated by his master so that he would be a worthy gift to the emperor Tiberius. Tiberius paid him no attention because he hated Helicon's 'juvenile pleasantries'. But Helicon gained Gaius's attention when he succeeded to the sovereignty because the slave could mock (σκώπτειν) and be witty or jest (χαριεντίζεσθαι) more than other people. Helicon says to himself (in Philo's literary construction) that Gaius's ears 'are wide open and pricked up to listen to those who have studied to combine abuse (τὸ βλασφημεῖν) with sycophancy (τὸ συκοφαντεῖν)'. Helicon also tells himself that he need not look far for material, since he has been reared on the slanders (διαβολαί) against the Jews.[24]

In another passage of the same work, the term is used in a more distinctively Jewish way. Beginning in *Leg Gai* 44 (§349), Philo describes the audience that the embassy from the Jews of Alexandria had with Gaius. Philo begins by making the point that the emperor proceeded unjustly, more as an accuser than an impartial judge. The first direct speech of Gaius reported is 'Are you the god-haters who do not believe me to be a god, a god acknowledged among all the other nations but not

[24] Philo, *Leg. Gai.* 26 §§166-70; text and translation from F.H. Colson (ed.), *Philo* (10 vols.; LCL; Cambridge, MA: Harvard University Press; London: Heinemann, 1962), X, 84-87. Other passages in which Philo uses the word-group related to βλασφημεῖν for the verbal abuse of other human beings include *Migr. Abr.* 20 §§115, 117; *Spec. Leg.* 4.38 §197; *Jos.* 14 §74; *Flacc.* 5 §33.

to be named by you?'[25] When the Alexandrian opponents of the Jewish delegation accuse them of refusing to offer sacrifices of thanksgiving for the preservation of the emperor, the Jews reply that, on the contrary, they have offered sacrifice three times already: at the accession of Gaius to the sovereignty, at his recovery from severe sickness and as a prayer for his victory in Germany. '"All right", he replied, "that is true, you have sacrificed, but to another, even if it was for me; what good is it then? For you have not sacrificed to me".'[26] His concluding remark was 'They seem to me to be people unfortunate rather than wicked and to be foolish in refusing to believe that I have got the nature of a god.'[27] In his reflection on the experience, Philo portrays it as 'torture, the racking of the whole soul through the blasphemies (βλασφημίαι) against God and the menaces launched upon us by this mighty despot'.[28] Philo portrays Gaius as insulting the God of Israel more or less directly by asking what benefit it was if the Jews sacrifice to another on his behalf. This statement ignores the power of God to confer blessings and to control events. The apparently more serious insult was the claim of Gaius to be a god himself and the expectation that the Jews worship him as such. This claim is indirectly but powerfully insulting because it compromises the Jewish affirmation that only the God of Israel is divine, or at least that the people of Israel must avoid worshipping any deity other than their own.

An analogous passage to the one about Gaius concerns an unknown governor of the Roman province of Egypt. Philo tells how this official attempted to do away with the observance of the Sabbath by the Jews so that they could serve him on that day as well. He tried to persuade the Jews by saying that they would surely break the Sabbath if there were a sudden attack by an enemy, a flood, a major fire, a thunderbolt, famine, 'plague or earthquake, or any other trouble either of human or divine agency'.[29] Then he went on,

> I who stand before you am all the things I have named. I am the whirlwind, the war, the deluge, the lightning, the plague of famine or disease, the earthquake which shakes and confounds what was firm and stable; I am constraining destiny, not its name but its power, visible to your eyes and standing at your side.[30]

[25] Philo, *Leg. Gai.* 44 §353; Colson, *Philo*, X, 176-77.
[26] Philo, *Leg. Gai.* 45 §357; Colson, *Philo*, X, 178-79.
[27] Philo, *Leg. Gai.* 45 §367; Colson, *Philo*, X, 182-83.
[28] Philo, *Leg. Gai.* 46 §368; Colson, *Philo*, X, 182-83.
[29] Philo, *Somn.* 2.18 §125; translation from F.H. Colson and G.H. Whitaker (eds.), *Philo* (10 vols.; LCL; London: Heinemann; Cambridge, MA: Harvard University Press, 1934), V, 499.
[30] Philo, *Somn.* 2.18 §129; Colson and Whitaker, *Philo*, V, 499, 501.

Philo's reaction to this remembered or constructed statement by the governor is:

> What shall we say of one who says or even merely thinks these things? Shall we not call him an evil thing hitherto unknown: a creature of a strange land or rather one from beyond the ocean and the universe – he who dared to liken to the All-blessed his all-miserable self? Would he delay to utter blasphemies (βλασφημεῖν) against the sun, moon and the other stars, if what he hoped for at each season of the year did not happen at all or only grudgingly, if the summer visited him with scorching heat or the winter with a terrible frost, if the spring failed in its fruit-bearing or the autumn shewed fertility in breeding diseases? Nay, he will loose every reef of his unbridled mouth and scurrilous (κακήγορος) tongue and accuse (αἰτιάομαι) the stars of not paying their regular tribute, and scarce refrain from demanding that honour and homage be paid by the things of heaven to the things of earth, and to himself more abundantly inasmuch as being a man he conceives himself to have been made superior to other living creatures.[31]

Here the term βλασφημεῖν is used for a human being who claims a greater degree of authority and power than he has a right to do.

Philo's treatment of the texts that later became normative for 'blasphemy' should also be noted. The LXX version of Exod 22:27 (Exod 22:28) reads:

> θεοὺς οὐ κακολογήσεις καὶ ἄρχοντας τοῦ λαοῦ σου οὐ κακῶς ἐρεῖς ('You shall not speak ill of gods, and you shall not revile rulers of your people').[32]

The translator apparently took אלהים as a plural and made the 'ruler' plural also for consistency of style. In Philo's discussion of proselytes in *De specialibus legibus*, he says that Moses counsels them not to presume on the equal privilege and rank that God grants them 'because they have denounced the vain imaginings of their fathers and ancestors' and thus be inclined to 'deal in idle talk or revile (βλασφημεῖν) with an unbridled tongue the gods whom others acknowledge, lest they on their part be moved to utter profane words (ἃ μὴ θέμις) against Him Who truly is'.[33] Philo most likely alludes here to the passage from the LXX cited above.

[31] Philo, *Somn.* 2.18 §§130-32; Colson and Whitaker, *Philo*, V, 500-501. Bock interprets *Dec.* 13 §§61-69 also as dealing with rulers who claim or receive divine honors (*Blasphemy and Exaltation*, 65). This reading is dubious, however, since the 'satraps' (§61) may be the four elements or the sun, moon and stars mentioned earlier in the text; cf. also §66.

[32] My translation.

[33] Philo, *Spec. Leg.* 1.9 §53; text and translation from F.H. Colson (ed.), *Philo* (10 vols.; LCL; Cambridge, MA: Harvard University Press; London, Heinemann, 1937), VII, 128-29.

Philo treats Lev 24:10-23 in the *De vita Mosis* in the context of a discussion of Moses as prophet. He begins with the kind of prophecy in which the prophet asks questions of God and receives responses and gives this passage as his first example. The LXX version of Lev 24:11 reads:

> καὶ ἐπονομάσας ὁ υἱὸς τῆς γυναικὸς τῆς Ισραηλίτιδος τὸ ὄνομα κατηράσατο, καὶ ἤγαγον αὐτὸν πρὸς Μωυσῆν ('And the son of the Israelite woman uttered the Name and cursed, and they took him to Moses').[34]

Philo interprets this text to mean that the man cursed (καταράομαι) God (*Vit Mos* 2.37 §196). This reading is probably based on the word order, in which the object τὸ ὄνομα ('the Name') is placed immediately before the verb κατηράσατο ('cursed') and is separated from the participle ἐπονομάσας ('uttered') by the subject of the sentence. He also emphasizes the man's Egyptian origin on his father's side, assuming that he followed Egyptian religious practices rather than those of his mother. Philo also speaks of the man's offense as κακηγορεῖν ('speaking ill' or 'abusing' or 'slandering' God), but notes that cursing is worse than such speech (*Vit Mos* 2.37 §198). In reflecting upon the case, Philo says:

> O man! Does anyone curse God? What other god can he invoke to ratify and confirm the curse? Is it not plain that he must invoke God to give effect to his curses against himself? Away with such profane and impious ideas![35]

Philo concludes that this incident made the promulgation of a law necessary, alluding to Lev 24:15-16. The LXX text reads:

> καὶ τοῖς υἱοῖς Ισραηλ λάλησον καὶ ἐρεῖς πρὸς αὐτούς Ἄνθρωπος, ὃς ἐὰν καταράσηται θεόν, ἁμαρτίαν λήμψεται· ὀνομάζων δὲ τὸ ὄνομα κυρίου θανάτῳ θανατούσθω ('And speak to the sons of Israel and you shall say to them, "If a man curses God, he will take hold of his sin; but if he utters the name of the Lord [in his curse], let him die"').[36]

Philo interprets the cursing to refer not to the God of Israel, but to the gods of other peoples. Presumably Israelites, unlike the son of the Egyptian father, would not need a law forbidding the cursing of God. He may also have been influenced by the LXX version of Exod 22:27 (22:28), which reads 'gods' instead of 'God'. In any case, he goes on to say:

[34] My translation.
[35] Philo, *Vit. Mos.* 2.37 §199; translation from Bock, *Blasphemy and Exaltation*, 63.
[36] My translation.

> For the world as we know it is full of idols of wood and stone, and suchlike images. We must refrain from speaking insultingly of these (βλασφημία), lest any of Moses' disciples get into the habit of treating lightly the name 'god' in general, for it is a title worthy of the highest respect and love. But if anyone, I will not say insults (βλασφημεῖν) the Lord of gods and men, but even ventures to utter His Name unseasonably, let him suffer the penalty of death... After this, can we still think worthy of pardon those, who, with a reckless tongue, make unseasonable use of the most holy name of the Deity and treat it as a mere expletive (ἀναπλήρωμα)?[37]

The evidence suggests that Philo did not have a concept of blasphemy in the sense that he used the word-group related to βλασφημεῖν exclusively for offenses against God. But, perhaps because of his transcendent understanding of the deity and his high conception of the respect and honor due to that Being, he did use the word-group in a special way when discussing such offenses. The two passages regarding Gaius and the unknown governor of Egypt show that an important part of that new usage involved human beings arrogating to themselves a degree of power and authority that was not fitting to them as finite creatures.

The Evidence of Josephus

Like Philo, Josephus also used the word-group related to βλασφημεῖν with regard to ordinary abusive speech among human beings. For example, in describing the dejection and revolt of the Hebrews after hearing the report of those who scouted out the land of Canaan, he states:

> Once more they blamed (αἰτιάομαι) Moses and loaded him with abuse (καταβοάω), him and his brother Aaron, the high-priest. In this sorry condition, then, amid vituperations (βλασφημίαι) upon the two of them, did they pass the night.[38]

Josephus also uses the word-group with God as the object in the sense of ordinary abusive speech. Thus, in the account of David and Goliath, he has David say:

[37] Philo, *Vit. Mos*. 2.38 §§205-206, 208. Text and translation (modified) from Colson, *Philo*, VI, 550-53.

[38] Josephus, *Ant*. 3.14.3 §307; text and translation from H.St.J. Thackeray (ed.), *Josephus* (9 vols.; LCL; Cambridge, MA: Harvard University Press; London: Heinemann, 1930), IV, 466-67.

> Let this enemy then be reckoned even as one of those wild beasts [the lion and the bear that David had killed], so long has he mocked (ὀνειδίζειν) our army and insulted (βλασφημεῖν) our God, who will deliver him into my hands.[39]

In the context, Goliath had challenged and taunted the Hebrews because not one of them was brave enough to engage in single combat with him; David had heard 'the Philistine reviling (βλασφημεῖν) and abusing' the Hebrew army.[40]

In several passages, Josephus uses the word-group to express the attitude of some outsiders to the Jewish people. For example, in the *Contra Apionem*, he refutes the argument that the Jewish constitution has a late origin because it is not mentioned by the Greek historians. In the course of his refutation, he states:

> I shall then proceed to cite testimonies to our antiquity from external literature, and finally to show the utter absurdity of the calumnies of the traducers of our race (...καὶ τοὺς βεβλασφημηκότας ἡμῶν τὸ γένος ἀποδείξω λίαν ἀλόγως βλασφημοῦντας).[41]

In several places, Josephus alludes to the biblical passages that later became classical for 'blasphemy'. For example, in the second book of the *Contra Apionem*, he states:

> Gladly would I have avoided an investigation of the institutions of other nations; for it is our traditional custom to observe our own laws and to refrain from criticism (οὐ...κατηγορεῖν) of those of aliens. Our legislator has expressly forbidden us to deride (χλευάζειν) or insult (βλασφημεῖν) the gods recognized by others, out of respect for the very word 'God'. But since our accusers expect to confute us by a comparison of the rival religions, it is impossible to remain silent.[42]

Here Josephus alludes to Exod 22:27 LXX (22:28), which uses the plural θεοί to translate the Hebrew's אלהים, as noted above.[43]

In the *Antiquities*, Josephus describes an assembly at Abile near the Jordan at which Moses exhorts the people before his death and presents

[39] Josephus, *Ant.* 6.9.3 §183; text and translation (modified) from H.St.J. Thackeray and Ralph Marcus (eds.), *Josephus* (9 vols.; LCL; Cambridge, MA: Harvard University Press; London: Heinemann, 1934), V, 256-57.

[40] Josephus, *Ant.* 6.9.2 §§176, 177; Thackeray and Marcus, *Josephus*, V, 254-55.

[41] *Apion* 1.11 §59; Thackeray, *Josephus*, I, 186-87. See also *Apion* 1.25 §223; 1.31 §279. In *Apion* 2.13 §143, he uses the term βλασφημία for Apion's attitude to his own (Egyptian) laws.

[42] *Apion* 2.33 §§237-38; text and translation (modified) from Thackeray, *Josephus*, I, 388-89.

[43] He cites the same passage in *Ant.* 4.8.10 §207.

them with 'these laws and this constitution recorded in a book'.[44] In listing some of these laws, Josephus cites a combination of Lev 24:16 and Deut 21:22-23. The former passage, as noted above, reads as follows in the LXX:

> ὀνομάζων δὲ τὸ ὄνομα κυρίου θανάτῳ θανατούσθω (but if he utters the name of the Lord [in his curse], let him die).

Josephus cites it as follows:

> Let him that blasphemeth God (βλασφημήσας θεόν) be stoned, then hung for a day, and buried ignominiously and in obscurity.[45]

Here Josephus substitutes the phrase βλασφημήσας θεόν for the ὀνομάζων δὲ τὸ ὄνομα κυρίου in the LXX. If the verb βλασφημεῖν here is becoming a technical term, Josephus defines 'blasphemy' as uttering or pronouncing the divine name.

In the *Jewish War*, Josephus makes a noteworthy comment about the penalty for blasphemy among the Essenes:

> They are just and scrupulously careful in their trial of cases, never passing sentence in a court of less than a hundred members; the decision thus reached is irrevocable. After God they hold most in awe the name of the lawgiver, any blasphemer of whom (κἂν βλασφημήσῃ τις εἰς τοῦτον) is punished with death.[46]

The *Damascus Rule* prohibited swearing by the 'Torah of Moses', because it contained the Tetragrammaton and other divine names (CD 15:1-3). Josephus's remark may reflect this prohibition. The *Community Rule* stipulates that one who pronounces the name of the deity is to be expelled from the Community (1QS 6:27–7:2). According to the beliefs of the Community, expulsion was equivalent to the death penalty.[47]

Another interesting and relevant passage is the discussion of the slander (βλασφημία) uttered against Hyrcanus by a certain Eleazar.[48] A Sadducee by the name of Jonathan, who was a friend of Hyrcanus, persuaded

[44] *Ant.* 4.8.3 §194; Thackeray, *Josephus*, IV, 568-69.

[45] *Ant.* 4.8.6 §202; Thackeray, *Josephus*, IV, 572-73. See Moshe Bernstein, 'Ki Qelalat Elohim Taluy (Deut. 21:23): A Study in Early Jewish Exegesis', *JQR* 74.1 (1983), 21-45, who discusses 11QTemple 64.6-13's interpretation of Deut 21:22-23 (hanging as the penalty for a blasphemer) in relation to early Jewish exegesis of that passage.

[46] *War* 2.8.9 §145; text and translation (modified) from Thackeray, *Josephus*, II, 378-79.

[47] Yonder Gillihan, 'The Community of Qumran in the Context of Greco-Roman Associations' (PhD dissertation, University of Chicago, in progress).

[48] *Ant.* 13.10.5-6 §§288-98.

him that the Pharisees approved of what Eleazar had said. In order to test this assertion, Hyrcanus asked the Pharisees what penalty they thought Eleazar deserved. They replied that he deserved a whipping and imprisonment. In this regard, Josephus comments:

> for they did not think it right to sentence a man to death for calumny (λοιδορία), and anyway the Pharisees are naturally lenient in the matter of punishments.[49]

This passage is especially interesting in light of Josephus's discussion of the death of James, the brother of Jesus, if the charge in that case was blasphemy, as Richard Bauckham has conjectured.[50] The younger Ananus, newly appointed to the high priesthood, took advantage of the interim between the procuratorships of Festus and Albinus to convene the judges of the council of Judea and to bring James (and others) before it to be judged. In Josephus's words:

> He accused them of having transgressed the law and delivered them up to be stoned. Those of the inhabitants of the city who were considered the most fair-minded and who were exact (ἀκριβής) in observance of the law were offended at this.[51]

Josephus implicitly contrasts these 'fair-minded people' (probably Pharisees) with the Sadducees, who, he says, 'are indeed more cruel than any of the other Jews, as I have already explained, when they sit in judgment'.[52]

As noted above, Josephus rewrote Lev 24:16 to stipulate that the one who 'blasphemes' God shall be stoned to death and so forth. Bauckham has suggested that both Pharisees and Sadducees agreed that the blasphemer should be put to death, but may have disagreed on the definition of blasphemy, the Sadducees defining it more broadly and the Pharisees more narrowly. The leniency of the Pharisees in this case would be

[49] *Ant.* 13.10.6 §294; text and translation from Ralph Marcus (ed.), *Josephus* (9 vols.; LCL; Cambridge, MA: Harvard University Press; London: Heinemann, 1933), VII, 374-75.

[50] Richard Bauckham, 'For What Offense Was James Put to Death?', in Bruce Chilton and Craig A. Evans (eds.), *James the Just and Christian Origins* (NovTSup, 98; Leiden: E.J. Brill, 1999), 199-232. Bauckham concludes that James was executed either for blasphemy or for leading the people astray.

[51] *Ant.* 20.9.1 §§200-201; translation (modified) from Louis Feldman (ed.), *Josephus* (9 vols.; LCL; Cambridge, MA: Harvard University Press; London: Heinemann, 1965), IX, 496-97.

[52] *Ant.* 20.9.1 §199; translation (modified) from Feldman, *Josephus*, IX, 495. Josephus here apparently alludes to his discussion of the Pharisees as relatively lenient in *Ant.* 13.10.6 §294, quoted above.

expressed in their limiting the range of activities that counted as blasphemy.[53] According to *m. Sanh.* 7.5, '"The blasphemer" is not culpable unless he pronounces the Name itself.'[54] It may be that the rabbis of the Mishnah are the successors of the Pharisees in this regard. If the Sadducees advocated stoning for blasphemy in a broader sense, then the account of Mk 14 would reflect accurately the kind of decision the chief priests were likely to make. The penalty is portrayed as crucifixion, rather than stoning, because only the Roman governor had the authority to execute. Finally, Josephus's interpretation of Lev 24:16, in which blasphemy is defined as pronouncing the divine name, may be influenced by the teaching of the Pharisees.

Summary

The foregoing analysis of the usage of terms related to the notion of 'blasphemy' in the Hebrew Bible, the Septuagint and the writings of Philo and Josephus leads to the following main conclusions:

1. In all these bodies of literature, a variety of terms, including the word-group βλασφημεῖν, is used to mean 'taunt', 'revile', 'insult' or the equivalent. The activities designated may have human beings, gods or God as the object. The only difference between using such terms with God as the object and other usages is that the former usage is considered to be worse by those who are loyal to God. In some cases the activities are not verbal.

2. The piel of קלל ('curse') is used in the Hebrew Bible with both human beings and God as the object. When God is the object, it is the same kind of activity as cursing human beings, only worse because of the loyalty and respect that the texts assume are owed to God. According to the LXX (Lev 24:15-16), cursing God is a crime worthy of death.

3. In the Hebrew version of Lev 24:10-23, cursing another human being by calling upon God (and expressly mentioning the name Yahweh) is defined as an offense worthy of death.

4. In the *Legatio ad Gaium* and the *De somniis*, Philo uses the word-group βλασφημεῖν to mean a specific kind of insult to God, namely, speech that compromises the Jewish affirmation that only the God of Israel is divine. Specifically, this insult involves a human being claiming

[53] Bauckham, 'For What Offense?', 223.

[54] Translation from Herbert Danby (ed.), *The Mishnah* (London: Oxford University Press, 1933), 392.

a greater degree of authority and power than he has a right to do and, directly or indirectly, claiming divine status for himself.

5. The LXX, Philo and Josephus forbid insulting (βλασφημεῖν) the gods of other peoples. Philo explains this as a means of assuring the avoidance of insulting the God of Israel.

6. In his interpretation of Lev 24:16 and Deut 21:22-23, Josephus defines 'blasphemy' as uttering or pronouncing the divine name. This crime is to be punished with death. The *Community Rule* (1QS 6:27–7:2) calls for the expulsion of any member who pronounces the name of the deity; such expulsion was, in principle, equivalent to death.

7. According to Josephus, the Essenes considered the offense of 'reviling' or 'blaspheming' (βλασφημεῖν) Moses a crime punishable by death.

8. The Pharisees and the Sadducees seem to have agreed that 'blasphemy' was punishable by death, but differed on what constituted 'blasphemy'. The Pharisees may have narrowed the definition to pronouncing the divine name, whereas the Sadducees may have defined the offense more broadly.

'Blasphemy' in the Gospel According to Mark

The word-group βλασφημεῖν is used in Mark in a range of ways analogous to the usages attested in the works of Philo and Josephus. The clearest example of the usage of the term for ordinary abusive speech directed against human beings is Mk 15:29. I quote vv. 29-32 to give the context:

> And those who were passing by reviled (βλασφημεῖν) him, shaking their heads and saying, 'Hah! You who are about to throw down the sanctuary and build (another) in three days, save yourself by coming down from the cross!' Similarly, the chief priests also mocked (ἐμπαίζειν) him among themselves along with the experts in the law, saying 'He saved others; himself he cannot save; let the Messiah, the king of Israel, come down now from the cross, in order that we may see and believe'. And those who were crucified with him also insulted (ὀνειδίζειν) him.

The word βλασφημεῖν in v. 29 should not be translated 'blaspheme' because, in the context, it is used synonymously with ἐμπαίζειν ('mock') and ὀνειδίζειν ('insult'). These are among the synonyms of βλασφημεῖν in its usual sense in ordinary Greek usage, the LXX, Philo, and Josephus.[55]

[55] Donald Juel argued that 'the evangelist wishes the term to mean more than "slander" or "deride"' in 15:29 and that the allusion to the testimony of the false witnesses is 'an ironic signal' to the audience that these passers-by are the ones guilty of blasphemy,

A second passage in which the relevant term most likely has its ordinary sense is Mk 7:22. I quote vv. 21-23 to indicate the context:

> For from within, from the hearts of human beings, come evil intentions; acts of unlawful intercourse, stealing, murder, adultery, greediness, and wickedness; deceit, licentiousness, an evil eye, abusive speech (βλασφημία), arrogance, foolishness; all this evil goes out from inside and profanes the human being.

The list of vices here seems consistently to concern the relations among human beings. It is analogous to the passages in Colossians and Ephesians mentioned in the opening part of this article. Thus, the translation 'abusive speech' for βλασφημία is better than the translation 'blasphemy'.[56]

In Mk 3:28-29, the word-group is used first for abusive speech in general and then with the Holy Spirit as object:

> 'The sons of men will be forgiven for all the abusive speech (βλασφημίαι) that they utter (βλασφημεῖν); but whoever insults (βλασφημεῖν) the Holy Spirit does not obtain forgiveness for all eternity, but will be guilty of an eternal sin.' For they said, 'He has an unclean spirit.'

The translations 'blasphemies' and 'blaspheme' for the noun and the verb in v. 28 would inappropriately limit the speech in question to language that offends God directly. If one translated these terms as above, but then translated the verb in v. 29 (with the Holy Spirit as object) with 'blaspheme', the parallelism would be lost. It seems best to conclude that this passage does not concern 'blasphemy' as such.[57]

There are two passages in Mark that concern 'blasphemy' as such: the one that is the subject of this article and 2:7. In the latter context, when Jesus says to the paralytic, 'Child, your sins are forgiven', some of the scribes in the house say to themselves, 'Why does this man speak in such a way? He blasphemes (βλασφημεῖν). Who is able to forgive sins except the one God?' Jesus' use of the passive voice implies that it is

not Jesus; *Messiah and Temple: The Trial of Jesus in the Gospel of Mark* (SBLDS, 31; Missoula, MT: Scholars Press, 1977), 103. This reading may represent a subtle connotation or second level of meaning, made possible by the range of usages of the word βλασφημεῖν.

56 Juel came to a similar conclusion, arguing that the term be translated here 'slander' or 'defamation' (*Messiah and Temple*, 102).

57 Contra Juel, who argues that 3:28-29 implies that remarks like 'He has an unclean spirit' constitute blasphemy because of Jesus' relationship to God through the Spirit (*Messiah and Temple*, 102-103).

God who forgives the man's sins. Underlying the scribes' response, however, may be a concern about *how* God forgives sins. According to the Torah (especially Leviticus), the priest was supposed to make atonement for the sins of the people in the temple. More important is the clue given in the last part of the scribes' statement, εἷς ὁ θεός ('the one God'). The implication is that Jesus is inappropriately acting as God's agent or even arrogating divine power to himself. If such activity were unauthorized, as the scribes assume, it would be highly offensive to God. The scribes' response is analogous to Philo's reactions to Gaius's claims to divinity and to the unnamed governor's equation of his own power with that of destiny.[58] For those Jews who did not accept Jesus as the Messiah, and thus as God's fully authorized agent, his declaration of forgiveness of sins would appear arrogant: an encroachment upon divine prerogatives and a usurpation of a role not appropriate to his status.[59]

As noted in the introduction to this article, the narrative flow of Mark 14:55-64 implies that the purpose of the false witnesses was to convict Jesus of blasphemy. Verse 58 summarizes their testimony: 'We heard him saying "I will destroy this sanctuary, which is made with hands, and after three days I will build another, which is not made with hands".' The intention of destroying the current sanctuary would no doubt have appeared blasphemous to some, especially to the chief priests who administered it. Since it was God's house, the intention of destroying it would be viewed as an attack on Godself. The second part of the saying was also open to the charge of blasphemy. In the Dead Sea Scrolls, the expectation is expressed of an eschatological temple to be created by God that would last forever.[60] According to *Jub* 1.29, 'the temple of the Lord will be created in Jerusalem on Mt Zion' in the new creation.[61] The saying attributed to Jesus seems to reflect such expectations. If, as seems likely, this temple was envisioned as a divine creation, the alleged claim of Jesus to build it himself would sound blasphemous. Jesus would not only be encroaching on divine prerogatives, but also claiming to be able to do something no human being could reasonably be expected to

[58] See point 4 in the summary above and the preceding section 'The Evidence of Philo'.

[59] As Juel has pointed out, this passage is important as the only other place in Mark besides 14:63-64 where Jesus is accused of blasphemy; Juel concluded that the use of the term in 2:7 implies that Jesus' words constitute 'an infringement on the prerogatives of God' (*Messiah and Temple*, 102).

[60] 11QT 29.6-10; 4QFlorilegium 1.1-13. The *Description of the New Jerusalem* probably also describes the eschatological temple.

[61] Translation from James C. VanderKam, *The Book of Jubilees* (2 vols.; CSCO, 510-11; Scriptores Aethiopici, 87-88; Leuven: Peeters, 1989), II, 7.

accomplish. The false testimony, however, came to nothing since the witnesses did not agree.

As noted in the same section above, the context suggests that it is the statement of Jesus in 14:62 that leads to his conviction for blasphemy and the judgment that he deserved the death penalty. Jesus' affirmative response alone to the question of whether he is the Messiah would have been insufficient to convict him of 'blasphemy'. It may well have been sufficient grounds for a conviction of the offense of rebelling against Rome. Similarly, this affirmative response, ἐγώ εἰμι, alone was unlikely to be interpreted as a claim to divinity. It is an ambiguous formulation that can signify a simple positive response, 'Yes, I am he', or be an allusion to Scripture that implies divinity.[62] The charge of blasphemy is related primarily to the saying based on a combination of Ps 110:1 and Dan 7:13.[63]

With regard to the part of the saying based on Ps 110:1, it is clear that at least some Jewish circles in the late Second Temple period had no problem with the idea of a heavenly Messiah, an exalted patriarch or a principal angel sitting or standing at the right hand of God or even sitting on God's throne itself.[64] To envisage Enoch, Moses, an angel or a heavenly Messiah sitting on God's throne, however, is a very different thing from confronting a living human being who predicts that he himself will be so enthroned.[65] Such a prediction might seem close to Gaius's claim to be a god or the governor of Egypt's claim to be 'constraining destiny', claims that so offended Philo. The rabbis, perhaps in response to claims about Jesus, but plausibly in response to claims about Enoch, Moses or the Messiah, rejected the idea of 'two powers in heaven'.[66]

With regard to the part of the saying based on Dan 7:13, it is clear that the Markan Jesus identifies himself with the 'one like a son of man' of Dan 7. This identification is equivalent to a messianic claim.[67] It has

[62] Raymond E. Brown, 'Appendix IV: Egō Eimi – "I am"', in idem, *The Gospel according to John i–xii* (AB, 29; Garden City, NY: Doubleday, 1966), 533-38.

[63] With Bock, *Blasphemy and Exaltation*, 28-29, and contra Juel, *Messiah and Temple*, 104-106.

[64] Bock, *Blasphemy and Exaltation*, 113-83; Larry W. Hurtado, *One God, One Lord* (Philadelphia: Fortress Press, 1988), 17-92.

[65] Cf. Bock, *Blasphemy and Exaltation*, 236.

[66] Alan F. Segal, *Two Powers in Heaven: Early Rabbinic Reports about Christianity and Gnosticism* (SJLA, 25; Leiden: E.J. Brill, 1977).

[67] Compare the messianic figure in the Similitudes of Enoch (*1 En.* 37–71) and the messiah in 2 Esd 13, both of which figures are based on the one like a son of man of Dan 7:13; cf. also the interpretation attributed to Rabbi Akiba of Dan 7:9 (*b.Ḥag.* 14a).

been argued that the 'coming on the clouds' refers to Jesus' return to vindicate the elect and to judge those who have judged Jesus.[68] At least the second part of this argument, regarding judgment, is dubious. It is not well founded in the text of Dan 7, for one thing. The ancient of days exercises judgment, and then the human-like figure is given dominion. For another, in Mk 13, divine judgment is expected to descend upon Jerusalem before the appearance of the Son of Man. When the Son of Man comes, the only activity mentioned is his sending out the angels to gather the elect. Although it is too much to say that, according to Mark, the allusion to Dan 7:13 in Mk 14:62 implies judgment, it is appropriate to infer that it implies the vindication of Jesus. When he appears on the clouds 'with great power and glory' (13:26), then his messianic claim will be verified before the eyes of his accusers.

The judgment that Jesus had committed 'blasphemy' is based on the saying that alludes both to Ps 110:1 and Dan 7:13 because in that saying Jesus predicts that he will be enthroned beside God and will return or be manifest with divine glory. This prediction is analogous to Gaius's claim to divinity and the governor of Egypt's claim to be 'constraining destiny'. Philo defined these claims as 'blasphemy'. Josephus and the Pharisees defined the kind of 'blasphemy' punishable by death as pronouncing the divine name. It is likely that the Sadducees, a group to which the chief priests probably belonged, defined 'blasphemy' more broadly, like Philo, and would have considered Jesus' saying to be blasphemous. Since the Sadducees had a reputation for being harsh with regard to punishments, the portrayal of the chief priests condemning Jesus to death for this broader kind of 'blasphemy' would make sense to first-century audiences.[69]

Conclusion

In the Markan trial of Jesus, the high priest and council do not follow the regulations described in the Mishnaic tractate *Sanhedrin* because those regulations were most likely not in effect in the first century.[70] According to *m. Sanh.* 7.5, culpable 'blasphemy' consists in pronouncing the divine name. Josephus and the *Community Rule* take similar positions.[71] In Mk 14:62 Jesus is condemned to death for blasphemy, even though

[68] Bock, *Blasphemy and Exaltation*, 202-203, 206-207.

[69] See the section 'The Evidence of Josephus' above.

[70] See the introduction to this article above.

[71] See point 6 in the summary above and the preceding section 'The Evidence of Josephus'.

he uses the circumlocution ‘Power’ (δύναμις) and does not pronounce the divine name. But this definition of blasphemy was probably neither universal nor official in the first century. The chief priests, as Sadducees, apparently defined ‘blasphemy’ in a broader manner and probably had no compunction about executing offenders.

As argued in the opening part of this article, the Gospel according to Mark portrays the judges of Jesus in the trial of ch. 14 as biased and unjust. It does not, however, imply that the charge of blasphemy was entirely without foundation. Philo’s *Legatio ad Gaium* and *De somniis* show that he at least, and probably other Jews, considered it ‘blasphemy’ to claim to be a god or to have divine power. Jesus’ saying in 14:62 fits this definition. In that saying, the Markan Jesus claims to be a messiah of the heavenly type, who will be exalted to the right hand of God (Ps 110:1). Being seated at the right hand of God implies being equal to God, at least in terms of authority and power. The allusion to Dan 7:13 reinforces the heavenly messianic claim. The ‘coming on the clouds’ has a dual role. On the one hand, this motif, typical of divine beings, signifies the universal power that Jesus as Messiah will have. On the other, the statement that the members of the council ‘will see’ him applies especially to his ‘coming on the clouds’ in a public manifestation of his messianic power and glory.

The condemnation of Jesus for blasphemy has a powerful ironic effect on the implied audience of Mark. For them, the first part of 14:62 has already been fulfilled in the resurrection and exaltation of Jesus to the right hand of God. The Gospel advocates the acceptance of the second part as soon to be fulfilled (Mk 9:1; 13:30). For the high priest and the members of the council as characters in the narrative, however, these claims of Jesus were audacious impositions upon the majesty and power of God. By making them, Jesus ignored the limits that applied to all who feared the Lord.

THE FUNCTION OF THE CHARGE OF BLASPHEMY IN MARK 14:64[1]

Jeffrey B. Gibson

I

At Mark 14:64, at the conclusion of Jesus' "trial" before the Sanhedrin, Mark has Jesus' chief interrogator and judge, the (here unnamed) high priest, proclaim that Jesus has committed the crime of βλασφημία ("blasphemy"), the willful and arrogant derision of the power and majesty of the God of Israel.[2] The judgment, which secures a death sentence for Jesus from the rest of the Sanhedrin, is issued after and in direct response to Jesus' announcement in Mark 14:62 that he is indeed "the Christ, the Son of the Blessed" whom his interrogator and all the Sanhedrin will eventually "see" being exalted by the God of Israel to this God's "right hand" and (if καὶ ἐρχόμενον μετὰ τῶν νεφελῶν τοῦ οὐρανοῦ ["and coming with the clouds of heaven"] is a separate claim – see below, note 6) also as one invested and acting with the authority to judge Israel and the world.[3]

Of the many questions that surround the interpretation of this passage, the one that I wish to deal with here is one that has not only long intrigued interpreters, but which (if I judge things aright) has recently

[1] The following is a slightly revised version of a paper originally published in *Proceedings of the Midwest Society of Biblical Literature* 24 (2004): 125-139.

[2] On the nature of the crime of βλασφημία, "blasphemy," see H.W. Beyer, "βλασφημεω, βλασφημία, βλασφημος," *TDNT* 1:621-625; Raymond A. Brown, *The Death of the Messiah* (ABRL, 2 vol.; New York: Doubleday, 1994), 1:520-523; E.P. Sanders, *Jewish Law From Jesus to the Mishnah* (London: SCM/Philadelphia: Trinity Press International, 1990), 67-80; Craig A. Evans, *Mark 8:27–16:20* (WBC 34B; Thomas Nelson & Sons: Nashville, 2001), 453-455.

[3] The judgment – ἠκούσατε τῆς βλασφημίας· τί ὑμῖν φαίνεται; οἱ δὲ πάντες κατέκριναν αὐτὸν ἔνοχον εἶναι θανάτου. "'You have heard the blasphemy. What is manifest to you?' And they all condemned him to be worthy of death." Mark 14:63 – Ἐγώ εἰμι, καὶ ὄψεσθε τὸν υἱὸν τοῦ ἀνθρώπου ἐκ δεξιῶν καθήμενον τῆς δυνάμεως καὶ ἐρχόμενον μετὰ τῶν νεφελῶν τοῦ οὐρανοῦ. "I am, and you will see the Son of Man sitting at the right hand of Power and coming with the cloulds of heaven." This is given in reply to the high priest's question Σὺ εἶ ὁ Χριστὸς ὁ υἱὸς τοῦ εὐλογητοῦ; "Are you the Christ, the Son of the Blessed?"

received renewed attention due to the publication in 2000 of Darrell Bock's *Blasphemy and Exaltation in Judaism*.[4] Why is it that Mark presents the high priest and the Sanhedrin as responding in the way they do to Jesus' declaration? What, according to Mark, is the reason the high priest and those gathered with him pronounce Jesus a blasphemer and worthy of death?

One answer that has long been given (and which Bock's work on blasphemy and exaltation in Judaism ultimately attempts to show, if not to prove, is a real possibility) is, of course, that *historically this is exactly what the high priest did*. Jesus was actually pronounced guilty of the crime of blasphemy during a "trial" before the Sanhedrin and Mark is here simply passing on historical tradition.[5]

But critical scholarship has tended to reject this answer for a variety of reasons, among which (and for our purposes, perhaps the most crucial) is the observation, grounded in both narrow and wide studies of the idea of "blasphemy" in first century Judaism, that nothing that Mark reports Jesus as saying at Mark 14:62 would or could have been characterized as Mark says it was. As Raymond Brown and others have argued, the claim to be Christ/Messiah (or Son of God – if a separate title here) was never considered blasphemous.[6] And given that (as Bock himself has demonstrated) Judaism recognized that certain human figures, including the Messiah and the one designated by Daniel and Enoch as "(the) Son of Man," had been or could be divinely called "to sit" at

[4] Darrell L. Bock, *Blasphemy and Exaltation in Judaism and the Final Examination of Jesus: A Philological–Historical Study of the Key Jewish Themes Impacting Mark:14:61-64* (Grand Rapids: Baker, 2000).

[5] Cf. Bock, *Blasphemy and Exaltation*, 3, 209-233. Bock's recent book is not the only place where he has set out to explore and attempt to defend the historicity of this charge. See his earlier studies "The Son of Man Seated at God's Right Hand and the Debate of Jesus' 'Blasphemy'" in *Jesus of Nazareth Lord and Christ: Essays on the Historical Jesus and New Testament Christology* (ed. Joel B. Green and M. Turner; Grand Rapids: Eerdmans/Carlisle: Paternoster, 1994), 182-191; and especially "Key Texts on Blasphemy and Exaltation in the Jewish Examination of Jesus," *SBL Seminar Papers 1997* (SBLSP 34; Atlanta: Scholars Press, 1997), 115-160. It was within the 1997 SBL Session devoted to discussing this second essay, and in a private conversation with Darrell immediately afterwards, that the thesis of this present essay was germinated.

[6] On "the Son of the Blessed (God)" as a separate title in Mark 14:61, see David Catchpole, *The Trial of Jesus: A Study in the Gospels and Jewish Historiography from 1770 to the Present Day* (Leiden: E.J. Brill, 1971), 143-148, 200. On the claim to being Messiah not being blasphemous see Brown, *The Death of the Messiah*, 1:534-536; Sanders, *Jewish Law*, 67-80; Pace J.C. O'Neill, *Who Did Jesus Think He Was* (London: E.J. Brill, 1995) who argues that Jewish Law stipulated that it was forbidden for the Messiah to announce himself.

God's right hand and to exercise judgment over Israel and the nations, neither was a claim such as we find Jesus apparently making about his right to heavenly enthronement.[7]

Given this, it would seem that if we are to answer the question I wish to deal with here, we must move away from historical investigation about what was and was not considered blasphemous in Judaism in the first century and how this does or does not square with what Mark says is the occasion and cause of the charge leveled against Jesus, and adopt some other approach.

The one that I will explore here involves following the lead given us when we take into consideration what Ernst Lohmeyer, Vincent Taylor, and other scholars have noted is indicated by the fact that the question from the high priest which begins the portion of Jesus' interrogation that culminates in the blasphemy charge (i.e., εἶ ὁ Χριστὸς ὁ υἱὸς τοῦ εὐλογητου "Are you the Christ, the Son of the Blessed?") is fronted with an unnecessary σὺ ("you"). According to Lohmeyer and Taylor, this σὺ is "emphatic and contemptuous," and since εἶ by itself in this interrogative context would mean "are you," the sense of the question Mark has the high priest ask is not "*Are* you the Christ, the Son of the Blessed," but "Are *you* of all people [God forbid!] the Christ...?"[8] If so, then, for Mark, what lies at the heart of the blasphemy charge – that is to say, what offends the high priest's and the Sanhedrin's sensibilities and makes them feel that the God of Israel has been denigrated and insulted – is not *what* Jesus claims about himself. Rather, it is the fact that it is *Jesus* who is making messianic claims.

[7] Brown, *The Death of the Messiah*, 536-538. See also Donald Juel, *Messiah and Temple: The Trial of Jesus in the Gospel of Mark* (SBLDS, 31; Missoula: Scholars Press, 1977), 97-102. I say "apparently" here because there is some reason to believe that in Mark's eyes, καὶ ὄψεσθε τὸν υἱὸν τοῦ ἀνθρώπου ἐκ δεξιῶν καθήμενον τῆς δυνάμεως κτλ. is not actually a claim but only a declaration on Jesus' part of his certainty that he will be vindicated by God as "the Christ, the Son of the Blessed." As Juel notes (*Messiah and Temple*, 104-105), "From the remainder of the passion story it is clear that for Mark, the titles 'the Christ, the Son of the Blessed'[and not 'the Son of Man'] are decisive. Jesus is tried, rejected, mocked, and executed as 'the King of the Jews,' 'the Christ, the King of Israel' [not as 'the Son of Man']." And if the centrality of the *messianic* imagery in the passion story indicates that this is where the evangelist intends to place the emphasis in 14:61-62, "it is reasonable to infer not only that the charge [of blasphemy] is to be related to the messianic claim," but that the Son of Man saying does not function "as an independent source of information or a separate claim."

[8] Ernst Lohmeyer, *Das Evangelium des Markus* (Göttingen: Vandenhoeck & Ruprecht, 1963), 328; Vincent Taylor, *The Gospel According to Mark* (London: MacMillan, 1952), 567. See also Evans, *Mark*, 448; Robert Gundry, *Mark: A Commentary on His Apology for the Cross* (Grand Rapids: Eerdmans, 1993), 886.

But why, according to Mark, would the high priest and the Sanhedrin feel so strongly not only that Jesus of all people is not someone whom God would ever ordain as his Messiah (or make judge of Israel and the nations), but that the claim on the part of Jesus to the contrary convicts Jesus of blasphemy? The answer lies, I think, in establishing six things.

1. Who, according to Mark, God was in the eyes of the high priest and the Sanhedrin. The high priest's and the Sanhedrin's judgment that Jesus is a blasphemer means, after all, that Jesus has offended their conception of who God is.
2. What, according to Mark, the temple – the edifice whose destruction the Markan Jesus, claiming divine warrant, symbolically enacted in Mark 11:15-17 before astonished and enraged Sanhedrinists – represented to the high priest and the Sanhedrin.[9]
3. What, if anything, the Christology of the high priest and the Sanhedrin was – that is to say, who, in Mark's eyes, the temple aristocracy believed the Messiah was, in kind and character, to be, what it was that the God of Israel has called him to do, and what the means were that this God had ordained as fitting for the accomplishment of the task(s) assigned to him.
4. Who it is, according to the high priest and the Sanhedrin, who gets to do what Jesus apparently claims is his right to do, namely, to sit at God's right hand.
5. What, if anything, the Markan Sanhedrinists thought to be the case with respect to the question of what period in Israel's remembered and anticipated national history they and the rest of Israel now stood.
6. Who or what, at the point of Jesus' "trial," the Markan Sandedrinists know Jesus to be.

1. God in the Eyes of the Sanhedrin

There seems little reason to doubt that with respect to their vision of God, Mark intends us to see that those who condemn Jesus as a blasphemer accept and profess what is asserted both in the most famous of all Jewish prayers, the Shema:

> Hear O Israel, Yahweh our God, Yahweh is one (Deut 6:4)

[9] Cf. Mark 11:18. On Mark's portrayal of Jesus' action in Mark 11:15-17 as an action symbolizing the destruction by God of the temple, see Morna D. Hooker, *The Gospel According to Saint Mark* (London: A & C Black, 1991), 266; Rikki E. Watts, *Isaiah's New Exodus in Mark* (Grand Rapids: Baker, 2000), 318-332.

as well as in the Psalms that are derived from or grounded in it, such as Ps 96, which note that

> … great is the LORD, and greatly to be praised;
> he is to be revered above all gods
> For all the gods of the peoples are idols,
> but the LORD made the heavens…
> Say among the nations "The LORD is King!" (NRSV)

That is to say, the Markan Sanhedrinists believe that the God of Israel, the creator God, was alone Lord of the universe and that he had entered into covenant with Israel, electing her to be his people for the express purpose of making his name known among the nations who were in rebellion against him.[10]

There is also little doubt that Mark intends us to see that for the Sanhedrinists, Yahweh was one who had not only chosen to dwell among his people on the mount named Zion where the temple in which they worshiped their God now stood and that he would defend this hill against all attackers and usurpers; he also was irrevocably committed to defending and vindicating his people when they were rendered desolate by the nations who refused to accept his sovereignty.[11]

But most important of all was their belief that Yahweh had called Israel to announce and sustain her identity as his people through obedience to a code of "purity" – or, as Marcus Borg has labeled it, a "politics of holiness" – that stressed two things: (a) "separation" from both "the pollutions of the nations" and then from those Jews who had rendered themselves as "sinners" by going over to the ways of the nations, and (b) the necessity of strict adherence to, observation of, and zeal for certain practices and institutions which marked off

[10] That Mark presents the Sanhedrinists as accepting and professing what is said about the God of Israel in the Shema is clear from the fact that Mark has members of the Sanhedrin not only allude to the Shema at Mark 2:5, but ground their initial critique of Jesus's claim to be able to forgive sins within the theology about God that the Shema expresses. On this, see Robert Guelich, *Mark 1–8:26* (WBC 34A; Dallas: Word, 1988), 87; Joel Marcus, *Mark 1–8* (AB 27; New York: Doubleday, 2000), 222. It is also clear in Mark's story of the question on the greatest commandment (Mark 12:28-34).

[11] This, I would argue, is implied in Mark's story of the Sanhedrin's questioning of Jesus's authority for his temple action (Mark 11:27) and Jesus' parable of the wicked vineyard tenants (Mark 12:1-12), both of which are set in the temple and occur after Jesus, claiming divine warrant, has engaged in an action the target of which is the truth of this belief. On Mark's view of the significance of Jesus' temple action, see below.

Jew from Gentile, especially temple, Sabbath, fasts, food laws, and "cleanliness."[12]

2. *The Temple in the Eyes of the Sanhedrin*

Our main source for understanding what, according to Mark, the temple represented to the members of the body which condemns Jesus as a blasphemer is the statement that Mark has Jesus utter immediately following, and as the justification of, what has traditionally but wrongly (at least for Mark) been called the "cleansing of the temple." As is well known the statement is a composite quotation the elements of which are taken from Isaiah 56:7 and Jeremiah 7:11. Jesus charges the temple aristocracy with turning the temple into a "den of thieves." They have altered its divinely intended and final purpose of being a "house" where the outcasts of Israel and all the nations will join together in prayer and worship with those whom the God of Israel has already gathered to be joyful in his presence.[13]

Contrary to a long standing view that is still frequently mooted, for Mark the target of the statement is not some real or imagined economic exploitation on the part of the temple aristocracy of those who bought sacrificial animals from the temple stock or who traded foreign currency for the coinage acceptable for the payment of temple taxes, let alone the temple's commercialization.[14] Rather, the target, in Mark's presentation of things, is the fact that, as in Jeremiah's day, the temple had been made over by those responsible for insuring that it would fulfill the purpose for which God had intended it to bring blessings to the nations – into a focal point of the hope of national liberation *from* those nations and was now being put forward as a symbol both of a divine guarantee of secu-

[12] This, I maintain, is evident from the fact that it is over perceived violations of their definitions of purity and their (or their retainers') strictures on fasting, Sabbath observance, eating with sinners, food laws, and the sanctity and fate of the temple that Mark has the members of the Sanhedrin speak out. See further Jerome H. Neyrey, "The Idea of Purity in Mark's Gospel," *Semeia* 35 (1986): 91-128.

[13] Cf. Isa 56:6-8.

[14] For the longstanding view see, e.g. James R. Edwards, *The Gospel according to Mark* (Grand Rapids: Eerdmans/Leicester: Apollos Press, 2002), 343. As Marcus Borg has shown *(Conflict, Holiness, and Politics in the Teachings of Jesus* [Harrisburgh: Trinity Press International, 1998], 186-187), this view is excluded both by the language of the statement as well as by the fact that there is little evidence for economic trickery or the fleecing of temple pilgrims in exactly this period. See, too, Nicholas Thomas Wright, *Jesus and the Victory of God* (Minneapolis: Fortress, 1996), 419-421; Watts, *Isaiah's New Exodus*, 326-330.

rity against Israel's enemies when Israel was beset by them and of God's ultimate subjugation of the nations to Israel.[15] It is the ground of the claim that, according to Jesus (Mark 13:6, 21-22), will be made by false christs and false prophets about how *flight from Jerusalem and the temple is not necessary* even when the "abomination of desolation" appears and Jerusalem is on the verge of being laid waste.

For the Sanhedrin, then, the temple represents a warrant for pursuing a path of religious exclusivism and revolutionary zeal.

3. *The Christ and his work according to the Sanhedrin.*

There are at least three places in Mark's Gospel where Sanhedrinist Christology is revealed: (a) in the notice of the chief priests mocking Jesus on the cross at Mark 15:24-32; (b) in the story of Peter's "confession" at Caesarea Philippi (Mark 8:27-31) where, according to Mark, Peter gives voice to the Christological views of "men"; and (c) in Jesus' question about the Son of David at Mark 12:35-37.

a. *Chief Priests' Mockery*

Within the larger story of Jesus' crucifixion – a story linked inextricably with Mark's accounts of Jesus' Sanhedrin "trial" through the repetition there of this "trial's" major motifs of temple charge, mockery, Jesus as Messiah, and blasphemy – Mark presents members of the Sanhedrin as moved, when seeing Jesus upon a Roman cross where he is openly proclaimed as Israel's King, to exchange among themselves a particular jibe against him.[16] This jibe both takes up and follows on from the public recrimination derisive passers-by have just hurled at Jesus after noting that he was one who supposedly claimed the ability to destroy and rebuild the temple.[17] It also extends that recrimination to include both a taunt over the fact that "this Christ, this King of Israel... saved others... but he can't save himself!" and a call to Jesus to provide for them a display of power which would both reverse and repudiate as unfitting for him the fortune he is suffering at the hands of the enemies of Israel and show him to be God's Christ. "Let this Christ, this King of Israel, come down now from the cross, that we may see

[15] On this, see Borg, *Conflict*, 186; Wright, *Jesus and the Victory of God*, 420-421.

[16] On this, see Richard T. France, *The Gospel according to Mark* (Grand Rapids: Eerdmans, 2002), 648.

[17] The Sanhedrinists are described as mocking Jesus "in like manner" (ὁμοίως).

and believe."[18] It is unlikely, as is sometimes thought, that what is expressed in all of this, especially in the adversative contrast between "he saved others" and "he cannot save himself," is a sense on the part of the Sanhedrinists of how ironic it is that one who has been able to heal others and restore their physical well being cannot preserve his own life. For Mark not only casts the wording of the taunt in terms of themes found in his story of Jesus' "trial" and in scenes paralleling the cross mockery (Jesus as Messiah and as judge of the nations, Jesus as King); he likens the taunt's origin and character to the vindictive and sarcastic remarks of the passers-by, the substance of which is rooted in and calls to mind the temple charge of Mark 14:58.[19] By this he makes clear that the claims that the Sanhedrinists here focus on, react to, and are intent to skewer and deride, are those made by or about Jesus during his Sanhedrin "trial." Notably, neither Jesus' healings nor his role as a miracle worker were ever taken up or mentioned as an issue in that "trial" (or even in the mockery which followed it), let alone seized upon as things which laid the ground for any charge or insult made against him.[20] Rather, what we have here is an inverse expression of a fundamental belief of the Sanhedrinists – that a God-sent "deliverer" who cannot or will not secure his own survival, and even more importantly, who allows himself to be subjected to humiliation and defeat by the nations, and who will not rule over them, cannot be God's Χριστός.[21]

This is noteworthy. For its implication is that what Markan Sanhedrinists do believe about God's Christ is that he is one who will reveal himself in might and that he will be both divinely enjoined to resist those who stand

[18] Ἄλλους ἔσωσεν, ἑαυτὸν οὐ δύναται σῶσαι· ὁ Χριστὸς ὁ βασιλεὺς Ἰσραὴλ καταβάτω νῦν ἀπὸ τοῦ σταυροῦ, ἵνα ἴδωμεν καὶ πιστεύσωμεν ("He saved others, he cannot save himself. Let the Christ, the King of Israel, now come down from the cross, in order that we may see and believe."). On this jibe as something rooted in and developed out of the derision heaped on Jesus by the passers-by, see Taylor, *Mark*, 592.

[19] For the link to the words of the passers-by cf. Mark 15:31. ὁμοίως καὶ οἱ ἀρχιερεῖς ἐμπαίζοντες πρὸς ἀλλήλους μετὰ τῶν γραμματέων ἔλεγον ("likewise also the high priests were mocking towards one another with the scribes saying,"). The link to the temple charge is easily seen when we compare the words of the taunt – Οὐὰ ὁ καταλύων τὸν ναὸν καὶ οἰκοδομῶν ἐν τρισὶν ἡμέραις σῶσον σεαυτὸν καταβὰς ἀπὸ τοῦ σταυροῦ. ("Woe the one who destroys the temple and builds it in three days! Save yourself by coming down from the cross!") – with the words of the temple charge in Mark 14:58 – Ἡμεῖς ἠκούσαμεν αὐτοῦ λέγοντος ὅτι Ἐγὼ καταλύσω τὸν ναὸν τοῦτον τὸν χειροποίητον καὶ διὰ τριῶν ἡμερῶν ἄλλον ἀχειροποίητον οἰκοδομήσω. ("We heard him saying, 'I will destroy this handmade temple and during three days build another not made with hands.'").

[20] Cf. France, *Mark*, 648.

[21] Ibid.

against him and God's elect and divinely empowered to rule as a king who defeats the nations when they attempt to subjugate him to their power.

b. *The "confession" at Caesarea Philippi*

In his story of Peter's "confession" at Caesarea Philippi, Mark presents Jesus and Peter as engaged in a heated dispute over the question of the means by which Jesus as Messiah is to achieve the fulfillment of his messianic vocation.[22] In Mark 8:31 Jesus declares in the first of three passion predictions, or, to use the phraseology of C. Myers, "death portents," that in accordance with his understanding of the will of God in this regard, the messianic task (which is portrayed by Mark as the decisive victory of God's sovereignty over the world) is to be accomplished only through suffering and a willingness to be subjected to death (πολλὰ παθεῖν καὶ ἀποδοκιμασθῆναι) at the hands of enemies.[23] But at Mark 8:32 Peter disdains this declaration. In his demeanor towards Jesus and in his reaction to Jesus' announcement, he [Peter] not only vociferously asserts that, on the contrary, suffering and death are *not* God's plans for his Messiah, he also implicitly proposes that Jesus *as Messiah* should deny what he has just said and adopt some other means to execute his divine commission – which, as I have argued elsewhere, Mark goes on in Mark 8:34–9:1 and in Mark 9:30-37 and Mark 10:32-45 to explicate as involving the Messiah acting as a triumphalistic warrior king who saves Israel and brings it to its destiny by waging wars of deliverance.[24]

22 See James L. Mays, "An Exposition of Mark 8:27–9:1," *Interpretation* 30 (1976): 174.

23 On "death portents" cf. Ched Myers, *Binding the Strong Man* (Maryknoll: Orbis, 1988), 238. The two other passion predictions/death portents appear at Mark 9:31 and Mark 10:33-34. On God's victory over the world see William Lane, *The Gospel according to Mark* (Grand Rapids: Eerdmans, 1974), 304; T.A. Burkill, *Mysterious Revelation* (Ithaca: Cornell University Press, 1963), 154. That the Markan Jesus' perception of the path he is to follow in accomplishing the messianic task is rooted in his understanding of God's will on this matter is apparent from his description at Mark 8:31a of that path as something he *must* do (Καὶ ἤρξατο διδάσκειν αὐτοὺς ὅτι δεῖ "and he began to teach them that it is necessary"). For, as Wilbert J. Bennett Jr. has noted ("The Son of Man Must...," *NovTest* 17 [1975]: 113-29, esp. p. 128), δεῖ here corresponds to, but in meaning is more pregnant than, γέγραπται ("it is written") and refers to a perception of particular compulsion or constraint, behind which stands the will of God. See, too, Hugh Anderson, *The Gospel of Mark* (London: Oliphants, 1976), 217.

24 Peter takes Jesus aside (προσλαβόμενος) and rebukes him (ἐπιτιμᾶν). The gesture described by προσλαβόμενος implies a presumptuous and patronizing sense of superiority on the part of Peter, and his employment of the strong vocabulary, used througout the Gospel in connection with the silencing of demons, expresses the heightened degree of his opposition to Jesus' declaration. See Jeffrey B. Gibson, *The Temptations of Jesus in Early Christianity* (Sheffield: Sheffield University Press, 1995), 220-237.

Then, as is well known, Mark has Jesus declare that the Christology that Peter shows himself believing in and holding to, the Christology out of which his rebuke of Jesus arises, is specifically that "of men" '(τῶν ἀνθρώπων, Mark 8:33). In doing this, Mark not only labels Peter's Christology as false and misguided and in opposition to God's own decree, *he, through Jesus, identifies it with the Christology held and espoused by the Sanhedrin.* For, as Mark's use of the expression τῶν ἀνθρώπων in Mark 7:1-15 shows, Mark has alerted his readers to the fact that, when used as it is here as an antonym for "of God" and in a context of debate about God's will, the phrase stands as a cipher for positions held by the Jewish religious authorities who stand in opposition to Jesus.[25]

Here then the Christology of the Markan Sanhedrin is revealed as one grounded in a triumphalist vision of the Messiah and the messianic task.

c. *The Question about the Son of David*

Mark reports that at the end of a series of debates with the temple aristocracy and their retainers that arises out of Jesus' explicit challenge to their Zion ideology, Jesus asks a question that notes not only that the Sanhedrin has a Christology, but that this Christology is explicit. The Messiah is υἱὸς Δαυίδ, the Son of David.

Now, as Lohse and others have demonstrated, in Mark's time Son of David Christology was rooted in a set of messianic expectations that finds its preeminent expression in such texts as Psalms of Solomon 17 and 4 Ezra 12 in which the work that the υἱὸς Δαυίδ, the "Lord's anointed," would do on the commission of the God of Israel is centered in three things:

- gathering a people from among ethnic Israel and leading them in the ways of righteousness;
- insuring that there was among them none of the "arrogance" displayed by the children of the covenant who, when persecuted by one

[25] Cf. Mark 8:33. On this concept "of men" see Ulrich W. Mauser, *Christ in the Wilderness* (Naperville: Alec R. Allenson, Inc., 1963), 131, n. 1. That Mark sees Peter's Christology and that of the Sanhedrin as one and the same is also indicated in the fact that Mark frames and sets up Peter's rejection of Jesus' views on the nature of messiahship and the messianic task with a notice from Jesus of how he as Messiah will be rejected by the "elders and chief priests and scribes" (i.e., the Sanhedrin in Mark), and thus intimates not only that there is a formal similarity between the two rejections, but that the occasion and cause of the one is the same as the occasion and cause of the other.

who "did in Jerusalem all the things the Gentiles do for their god in their cities" for obedience to the practices which kept Israel distinct from the nations and ensured deliverance from oppression, went over to the Gentiles and adopted their ways; and

- "shattering unrighteous rulers," "purging Jerusalem from nations that trample (her) down to destruction" by "destroying them with a rod of iron."[26]

Accordingly, what Jesus' declaration that the Sanhedrin believes the Messiah to be David's Son shows us regarding Mark's presentation of Sanhedrinist Christology is that it is one that is grounded in the view that the Messiah is to be a warrior king of Israel who is to be raised up and elected by God for a particular dual purpose: (1) to maintain and reinforce the traditional ethnic and ultimately national boundaries between Israel and the nations by enforcing, ruthlessly if necessary, obedience on the part of Jews to the practices and institutions by which her God-ordained separateness had historically been announced and sustained, and (2) to purge the land of Israel, and especially Jerusalem and the temple, of Gentiles through holy war.

4. The Sanhedrinist View of Who Gets to "Sit at God's Right Hand" ?

At first glance, given the data available to us, it appears that the only answer that we can give to the question of who the Markan Sanhedrinists believe gets to "sit" in God's presence is a negative one: *not Jesus*. But is this really all that can be said? Before we come to any conclusion on the matter, let us first take note of the answer to our present question that, as Bock has shown, was given in the Judaism of Mark's day. Besides certain angelic figures, those who were perceived as having the right and authority to "sit at the right hand of God" were first and foremost the major luminaries of Israel's history (Abraham, Moses, David, Elijah, and Ezra) who were remembered either as those who had been instrumental in bringing Israel into existence or who had helped to maintain Israel as faithful people by calling it to be obedient to the Law and to uphold its distinctiveness among the nations. But this group also included notably the Maccabean martyrs who "consecrated themselves for the sake of God" in order to bring about punishment of the enemies of Israel and the purification of the land from the pollution of the nations, the Enochian Son of Man who comes to the rescue of the righteous, and the Davidic

[26] See Eduard Lohse, "υἱὸς Δαυίδ" *TDNT* 8: 480-82.

deliverer who is dedicated to giving to the Sons of Light "rest from all the sons of Belial who will seek to cause them to stumble that they may destroy them and swallow them up" [4Q174. 7-8].[27] Is this catalogue something the Markan Sanhedrin would endorse? Are these figures the ones who, in their eyes, would be enthroned with God? To a large extent, the final answer to these questions depends on whether or not these figures are in any way the antitheses of who, according to Mark, the Sanhedrin knows Jesus to be. But since, as we have seen, Mark presents the Sanhedrin as believing that the Messiah was to be one of the figures which Judaism perceived as ultimately having the right and authority to "sit" in the presence of Israel's God, then we may state preliminarily that the answer is yes.

5. Where Israel Was according to the Sanhedrin

Notably it is Mark's presentation of the Christological beliefs of the Markan Sanhedrin which allows us to pinpoint where, according to Mark, the Sanhedrin viewed Israel within the scheme of its remembered and anticipated history. Since no one hopes, as the Markan Sanhedrin obviously does, for deliverance from national oppression unless one is under it, or for a king who will free his nation from Gentile domination unless it is subjected to it, or for a ruler who leads his people into a land purged of the pollution of profane enemies unless they are deprived of it, the Markan Sanhedrin believes, as apparently many Jews of Mark's period actually did, that (to use Tom Wright's summation of things) the nation was (still) "in exile."[28] But it is not only here that Mark shows us this. That the Markan Sanhedrinists hold to this belief is also what Mark indicates, if not underscores, in his notice at 1:5 that "all the people from the region of Judea, *including all the inhabitants of Jerusalem*," traveled out to and accepted, "while confessing their sins," the "the baptism of repentance" being administered by one whom Mark specifically portrays as announcing the end of Israel's exile and the beginning of a new exodus.

We should not miss the import of this last point. For it signals that, according to Mark, the Sanhedrinists believed that the God of Israel was now setting things in motion to liberate his people from their present bondage.

[27] See Bock, *Blasphemy and Exaltation*, 113-162.

[28] See Nicholas Thomas Wright, *The New Testament and the People of God* (Minneapolis: Fortress, 1992), 268-272.

6. Jesus according to the Sanhedrin

Who is Jesus in the view of the Markan Sanhedrinists? He is – and this Mark shows the Sanhedrinists knew *before* Jesus' open declaration of his identity at his "trial" – one who has claimed to be authorized and empowered by the God of Israel to act and speak on his behalf specifically with respect to the question of the divine plan for the liberation of Israel from its exile. More importantly, he is, according to Mark, one whose claim to act on God's behalf and speak in his name they were initially convinced was true. We see this in Mark's notice at Mark 2:12 that constituent and representative members of the Markan Sanhedrin, give "glory to God" after Jesus proves through a "sign" that he does not, as they first think, engage in blasphemy when he claims the right and ability to forgive sins, but is, as he claims, God's agent, appointed and empowered to heal and restore.

But, as is shown in their (and their retainers') expressions of concern over what Jesus says and does subsequent to their initial acceptance of him as God's agent, he is also one *who does not go on to do what they think one so appointed and empowered should do.* Rather than enforce the boundary markers by which Israel's distinctiveness is maintained, he breaks them down. Rather than maintain the practices by which Israel announces its determination to remain separate (food laws, not eating with the "unclean," purity) and shields itself from becoming polluted by the nations, he abandons them and goes so far as to proclaim that they are no longer in force (Mark 7). Rather than support the temple and the Zion ideology behind it, he declares that the temple is now superfluous and that reliance on it as surety against Israel's destruction is the very thing that will bring its destruction about. Rather than proclaim that the Gentiles are doomed, he declares that they are the object of God's favor. Rather than call Israel to engage in holy war, he calls it to the cross. And most notable of all, he does all of this in the name of Israel's God.

The Reason for the Charge

With all of this before us, we are now in a position to answer the question of why it was, according to Mark, that the high priest and the Sanhedrin accuse Jesus of the crime of blasphemy. It is because in stating that *he* is Messiah, the Son of the Blessed, *Jesus deprives God of his righteousness*. By affirming that *he* has been elected to sit at God's right hand, Jesus claims that God has no intention, as the Sahedrinists believe God has, of fulfilling his covenant promises to Israel to restore her fortunes, to bring her home, and to make her renowned and praised among all the peoples of the earth by "turning away her enemies," repaying them in kind for their oppressions against his people, and establishing her as ruler and judge over them. For by their lights, the path that Jesus advocates as divinely mandated for Israel is not only one that God does not endorse, it is one that, if followed, will bring his elect to ruin and make God's name a mockery among the Gentiles.

II

But why does Mark tell us this? It is, I contend, because Mark wished to present those who brought Jesus to his death as fellow travelers with, if not actually members, of the faction within Judaism which fermented and fostered the Jewish rebellion against Rome.

Several considerations favor this contention. First, the views on God, the election of Israel, on how God would demonstrate his covenant faithfulness to Israel, and on the nature and work of the Messiah that, in Mark's eyes, were held by the Sanhedrin are those of the Zealots. Second, the temple ideology that Mark identifies as that of the Sanhedrin is that which was propounded by the Zealots.[29] Third, those whom the Sanhedrin regard as worthy of sitting at God's right hand are figures who for the Zealots were the embodiment of their ideal of zeal.[30] Fourth, the display of disdain and hostility that the Markan Sanhedrin shows towards those who hold the view that God does not wish the triumph of his people was something for which the Zealots were known and which they placarded as a badge of their zeal.[31]

But what most strongly indicates Mark's intent to identify those who condemn Jesus to death with the Zealots is the fact that at an astounding number of points, Mark's narrative of the trial of Jesus recalls an event that occurred at the beginning of the War, and notably, shortly after the victory over Cestius Gallus, whose defeat was interpreted not only by the Zealots, but also by many who until then had stood against the war, as a sign that God fully endorsed the Zealot cause and sanctioned the

[29] On this, see Martin Hengel, *The Zealots* (Edinburgh: T. & T. Clark, 1989), 206-224.
[30] Ibid., 149-171.
[31] See Josephus, *B.J.* 2.274-76; 2.406-07; 2.418; 2.562; 4.138-46; 4.208-333; 4.334-44 (on which, more below); 7.263-266; *Vita* 17-22.

newly begun holy war. This was the trial of Zacharias, the son of Baris, by a Zealot Sanhedrin. According to the report of Josephus,

> ... the Zealots set up sham courts and faked trials. They had decided to liquidate one of the most distinguished citizens, Zachariah, son of Baruch, as they were annoyed by his burning hatred of wrong and love of freedom, and his wealth made them hope not only to plunder his property but also to get rid of a man capable of destroying them. They therefore issued a categorical order, summoning seventy men in public positions to the temple, where they turned them into a stage jury with no authority. Then they charged Zachariah with trying to betray their country to Rome and sending an offer of treason to Vespasian. There was no proof of the charges, no evidence at all, but they said that they themselves were quite convinced of his guilt and claimed that that should satisfy anyone. Zachariah realized that his fate was sealed: he had been treacherously summoned to a prison, not a court. But certain death was not going to deprive him of free speech – he stood up, scoffed at the incredibility of the charges, and in a few words disposed of the whole indictment. Then, turning the tables on his accusers, he methodically detailed all their illegalities and mercilessly exposed their mismanagement of affairs. The Zealots howled with rage and could hardly keep their hands off their swords, determined as they were to play out this farce, this sham trial to the end, and eager also, to find out whether the jurors would risk their own lives in the cause of justice. But the seventy brought in a unanimous verdict of Not Guilty, choosing to die with the defendant rather than bear the responsibility for his destruction. The Zealots greeted his acquittal with shouts of indignation, and were all enraged with the jury for not realizing that the authority bestowed on them was a mere sham. Two of the most unscrupulous fell upon Zachariah, murdered him in the middle of the temple, and jested over his dead body: 'Now you have got our verdict too, and your trials are over.' With that they threw him out of the temple and into the valley beneath. Then they showed their contempt for the jurors by belabouring them with the backs of their swords and driving them from the precincts. For one purpose only they refrained from murdering them – that they might go into every part of the City and let all the citizens know that they were slaves. (*B.J.* 4.334-344)[32]

Here, as in Mark 14:54-63, we have a capital trial before a hastily summoned Sanhedrin. Here, as in Mark 14:54-63, the trial occurs in the temple precincts and in an atmosphere not only of crisis but of eschatological expectation centering in the God of Israel's imminent deliverance

[32] Translation is that of G.A Williamson, *The Jewish War* (Hamondsworth: Penguin, 1970), 261-262.

of his people from oppression and the destruction of Israel's enemies. Here, as in Mark 14:54-63, those who convene the trial believe in holy war. Here, as in Mark, we have the appearance of false witnesses and the sounding of the theme of a predetermined verdict. Here, as in Mark, the one brought into court is a figure who is known and identified as standing in opposition to the ideology of those who have convened his trial. Here, as in Mark, the accused speaks out forcefully against the ideology of those who would condemn him. Here, as in Mark, the remarks of the accused evoke from his accusers both physical and verbal expressions of rage and indignation. Here, as in Mark, we find an outworking of a theme that standing on the side of the accused creates risks for those who might do so. And here, as in Mark, the one accused is handed over to mockery and an ignominious death.

In the light of these parallels, it seems difficult to escape the conclusion that Mark has cast his story of Jesus' Sanhedrin "trial" and condemnation so as to call to mind the Zealot trial and condemnation of Zacharias. If so, then another conclusion follows: Mark wishes to identify those who tried and condemned Jesus with those who tried and condemned Zacharias.

III

But why would Mark wish to make such an identification? One answer seems obvious: to account for the rejection of Jesus by the representatives of his own people by laying bare the ideology that was that rejection's ground and motivation. But I think there is more to it than this. As I have argued elsewhere – assuming with Joel Marcus and others that the *Sitz im Leben* of Mark's Gospel was the Jewish War, and working from clues given in Mark 13 in Jesus' warnings about being led astray by false christs and false prophets who, on the basis of Dan 9:26-27 and 11:31-35 (with their notices that those who are loyal to God shall not flee but stand firm and take action when a pagan ruler begins to set up in the temple the abomination that makes desolate), proclaim that divine deliverance of Jerusalem from its enemies was imminent – there is a very strong case for seeing that the occasion for the Gospel of Mark was Mark's perception that those for whom he writes were being seduced into thinking that God authorized his faithful to disdain as foolishness the way of the cross that Jesus had demanded of them and to join with the Zealot cause, embracing as "of God" the ideology and the praxis of holy war.[33] If this is so, then Mark's identification of the Sanhedrin with the Zealots and his portrayal of why it was that the Sanhedrin viewed as blasphemous Jesus' claim to be the one whom God would vindicate as his true Christ, was to make plain something that the author of the Epistle to the Hebrews says his readers would become guilty of should they deny their original confession – "crucifying the Son of God for themselves all over again and holding him up to contempt."

[33] See my unpublished paper entitled "Mark 14:38 as a Key to the Markan Audience" presented at the Annual Meeting of the Mark Group of the Society of Biblical Literature Toronto, Ontario, Canada, November 2002. Cf. Juel Marcus, "The Jewish War and the *Sitz im Leben* of Mark," *JBL* 111 (1992): 441-462. See also Adela Y. Collins, *The Beginning of the Gospel: Probings of Mark in Context* (Philadelphia: Fortress, 1992), 73-91; Gerd Theissen, *The Gospels in Context: Social and Political History in the Synoptic Tradition* (Minneapolis: Fortress Press, 1991), 264-284.

THE "TRIAL SCENE" CHRONOTOPE IN MARK AND THE JEWISH NOVEL[1]

Michael E. Vines

The account of Jesus' examination before a hastily convened session of Jewish priests, elders, and scribes in Mark chapter fourteen has a good claim to being the narrative climax of Mark's story of Jesus.[2] Although the plot of the Gospel shifts from rising action to falling action at chapter eight with Peter's recognition that Jesus is "the Christ" and Jesus' subsequent prediction of his passion, the trial scene is the dramatic climax of a central tension that has been building since at least the third chapter. In Mark 3:6 we read that the Pharisees and Herodians began to conspire together to orchestrate Jesus' destruction. In chapters fourteen and fifteen, they achieve their goal.

In Jesus' final confrontation with the Jewish religious leaders, the most dramatic moment is the High Priest's question and Jesus' defiant reply. Although Jesus has been reticent to speak plainly of his messianic identity elsewhere in the Gospel, preferring instead to speak in vague terms about "the Son of Man," here he openly affirms that he is indeed "the Christ, the Son of the Blessed" and adds to this claim an ominous prediction of his future vindication and enthronement in heaven. This declaration comes as little surprise to the reader of the Gospel, who has known the truth of Jesus' identity since the opening verses of the Gospel (1:1, 11), but it is a shocking declaration to the Jewish leaders who have gathered to pass judgment upon him. The High Priest is outraged and charges Jesus with blasphemy for his impertinent claim to divine power, and Jesus is subsequently denounced to Pilate, apparently as a political revolutionary.

As one might reasonably expect, the scholarly investigation of Mark 14:55-65 has been vigorous. The scene raises a number of crucial

[1] Research for this paper was made possible in part by a grant from the Wabash Center for Teaching and Learning in Theology and Religion.

[2] So identified by, for example, R. T. France, *The Gospel of Mark* (NICGNT; Grand Rapids: Eerdmans, 2002), 598; and Marinus de Jonge, *Christology in Context: The Earliest Christian Response to Jesus* (Philadelphia: Westminster Press, 1988), 61.

historical-critical questions, not the least of which are: whether Jesus' reply actually constituted blasphemy under Jewish law; whether this specially called meeting was in any sense a "legal trial"; and whether or not the details of the account can be regarded as historically reliable given the private nature of the meeting. The literature on these matters is extensive and cannot be rehearsed or summarized here.[3] The scene has also been the subject of literary-critical examinations that have explored the redactional activity of Mark within the trial scene and the narrative role of the trial within Mark's Gospel.[4] Although the early form critics believed that Mark incorporated a pre-existing passion narrative with little modification, redaction critical investigations have revealed more extensive activity within the passion narrative on the part of the evangelist.[5] My purpose in examining the Markan trial scene is neither to explore its historical-critical problems nor to elucidate its function within the Gospel narrative. Instead, I intend to probe the authorial contribution to the passion narrative by comparing the Markan trial scene with scenes of martyrdom found in second temple Jewish literature.

Elsewhere, I have proposed that Mark's Gospel is related to the genre of Jewish novelistic literature produced in the second temple period.[6] My thesis was not necessarily that the Gospel of Mark is a Jewish novel pure and simple, but that the composition of the Gospel was influenced in subtle ways by Jewish novelistic literature. This level of influence is most notable in the temporal and spatial qualities of Mark's narrative, or what Mikhail Bakhtin calls chronotope, and may be detected as well in Mark's extensive use of dialogue and irony.[7] The Gospel of Mark also

[3] For a detailed examination of questions such as these see Darrell L. Bock, *Blasphemy and Exaltation in Judaism. The Charge Against Jesus in Mark 14:53-65* (Biblical Studies Library; Grand Rapids: Baker, 2000).

[4] Donald Juel, *Messiah and Temple: The Trial of Jesus in the Gospel of Mark* (SBLDS 31; Missoula, Mont.: Scholars Press for the Society of Biblical Literature, 1977); and John R. Donahue, *Are You the Christ? The Trial Narrative in the Gospel of Mark* (SBLDS 10; [Missoula, Mont.]: Society of Biblical Literature, 1973).

[5] For form critical assessments of the Markan evangelist's editorial activity see: Karl Ludwig Schmidt, *The Place of the Gospels in the General History of Literature* (trans. Byron R. McCane; Columbia: University of South Carolina Press, 2002), 30; Rudolf Karl Bultmann, *The History of the Synoptic Tradition* (rev. ed.; Oxford: B. Blackwell, 1972), 275; and Martin Dibelius, *From Tradition to Gospel* (trans. Bertram Lee Woolf; Library of Theological Translations; Cambridge: J. Clarke, 1971), 180. For a redaction critical assessment see Donahue, *Are You the Christ?*

[6] *The Problem of Markan Genre: The Gospel of Mark and the Jewish Novel*, (Academia Biblical 3; Atlanta: Scholars Press, 2002).

[7] For a more detailed discussion of Bakhtin's literary theory, especially as it relates to matters of genre and literary comparison, see *The Problem of Markan Genre*, 33-67.

shares an important theme with Jewish novelistic literature, namely the violent persecution of the righteous servant of God. Within the world of the Jewish novel, violent persecution serves to test the faithfulness of God's servant and to set the stage for his or her vindication. The vindication of God's servant in turn functions to discredit his or her persecutors. The purpose of the present paper is to examine martyr accounts in Second Temple Jewish texts to see what light they might shed on the narrative structure and theological purpose of Jesus' trial before the Sanhedrin in Mark 14:53-65.

In a recent article on Jewish tales of martyrdom, Jan van Henten examined Jewish stories of martyrdom in Dan 3, 6; 2 Macc. 6:18-31, 7; 4 Macc.; *b. Ber.* 61b; *b. 'Abod. Zar.* 17b-18a.[8] In examining these accounts, Van Henten identified five common features, which in summary form are as follows:

1. Authorities issue an enactment carrying the death penalty;
2. The content of the enactment jeopardizes Jewish faithfulness to God;
3. When faced with this dilemma, the hero chooses to remain faithful to God and forfeit his or her life;
4. An examination, generally involving dialogue between tormentor and victim, frequently involving the use of torture;
5. A description of the execution.

These five features provide a useful beginning point for our investigation.

1) In the martyrdom accounts, hostility directed at specific Jewish individuals or at the Jewish people as a whole, is codified in legislation guaranteed to bring the hero into conflict with the authorities. While in the Jewish novels more generally these edicts sometimes authorize the wholesale extermination of the Jews, as in Esther (3:9-15), most often in the Jewish tales of martyrdom they outlaw specific practices mandated by Torah. The penalty for violating the edict is death, generally by torture. Clearly, there is no such edict in Mark. Nevertheless, very early in the Gospel, Jesus' words and actions bring him into such sharp conflict with the Jewish religious leaders that they conspire to have him killed (3:6). Jesus' conflict with the religious leaders is over his authority

[8] Jan W. van Henten, "The Martyrs as Heroes of the Christian People: Some Remarks on the Continuity Between Jewish and Christian Martyrology, with Pagan Analogies," in *Martyrium in Multidisciplinary Perspective: Memorial Louis Reekmans* (ed. M. Lamberigts and P. van Deun; BETL 117; Leuven: Leuven University Press, 1995), see esp. pp. 306-7.

to interpret Torah in a manner that deviates from "the tradition of the elders" (2:16, 18, 24; 3:2-4; 7:1-13). So, although there is no official edict in Mark that outlaws Jewish practices, the Gospel shares a similar concern for loyalty to God and God's laws, and the punishment for deviating too far from accepted Jewish practice is death.[9]

2) The practices outlawed in the tales of Jewish martyrdom range from specific practices, such as strict monotheism in the case of the three young men in Daniel (Dan 3:10-12) and daily prayer (Dan 6:6–9), to the complete prohibition of all Jewish practices under Antiochus Epiphanes in 2 Maccabees and 4 Maccabees (2 Macc 6:1; 4 Macc 4:23). In each case, the Jewish hero is singled out for his or her devotion to God as expressed through acts of piety and adherence to Torah. In terms of its function within the plot of these stories, the goal is clearly to create a dilemma for the hero with only two possible alternatives: either loyalty to God which results in death, or apostasy which results in life. Since there is no edict in Mark outlawing specific Jewish practices, the challenge facing Jesus is also more subtle: What precisely is the proper way for one to demonstrate faithfulness to God? Jesus and the Jewish leaders are engaged in a deadly struggle over precisely this issue. The Jewish leaders believe that devotion to God is best expressed through careful adherence to the dictates of Torah, especially as filtered through the teachings of the elders. This is precisely the view of devotion championed by the Jewish martyrs (Dan 1:8; 2 Macc 6:11, 19-20, 7:2; 4 Macc 5:16-21).

For Jesus, the path of devotion is one of love (Mark 12:31), sacrifice (Mark 9:35, 10:43-45), and compassion (Mark 6:34, 8:3), especially as these are expressed toward those who have been marginalized by official Judaism (1:40; 5:25; 7:26; 9:36-37, etc.). Jesus is prepared to ignore the conventional interpretation of the law in order to address these more fundamental issues of justice (2:27-28; 3:4-6). By repeatedly challenging Jesus (3:2; 8:11; 10:2; 12:13), the Jewish leaders try to deflect Jesus from remaining true to his understanding of God's will.

Though the Gospel of Mark lacks an edict outlawing Jewish practices, we see that the challenge facing Jesus is similar to that of the Jewish martyrs: Will Jesus remain true to his mission to declare the radical nature of the coming Kingdom of God, or will he collapse under pressure and

[9] Whether or not Jesus' words and actions were properly considered a capital offense in the first century is rather immaterial for the purposes of this investigation. What matters is that Mark portrays Jesus' determination to act in accordance with what he perceives to be the will of God as a matter of "life and death."

adopt a more conventional mode of piety? However, we also see that Mark has subtly subverted the normal pattern of the Jewish martyr stories by challenging their defense of traditional standards of piety centered on Torah observance, supplanting it with an alternative understanding of piety more resonant of the Hebrew prophets (Amos 5:15, 21-24; Hos 6:6, 12:6; Mic 6:8).

3) The various edicts in the Jewish martyr stories sanctioning Jewish practices inevitably create a dilemma for the Jews: should they succumb to the edict and betray their religious principles, or should they remain faithful to Torah and suffer torture and death. The path of secrecy and compromise is excluded. In several instances the hero either considers, or is offered, an easy way to avoid persecution and death (Esth 4:13-14, 2 Macc 6:21-22 and 4 Macc 5:6-13). In each case this offer is refused. To remain loyal to God, the hero must publicly display loyalty to Torah, even if it results in death. If we look more broadly at Jewish novelistic literature, we see that the willingness to sacrifice one's life for the sake of God, God's law, and God's people is an almost universal theme. Both Esther and Judith boldly risk their lives to save the Jewish people from slaughter. Tobit also risks his life to remain faithful to his Jewish way of life (Tob 1:19; 2:8). What sets the stories of martyrdom apart from these Jewish novels is the trial and execution of the hero, a feature absent in Esther, Judith, and Tobit. In the martyrdom stories, the hero is confronted by the authorities, who demand compliance with the official edict and back up those demands with threats of torture and death.

Jesus faces similar pressures in the Gospel of Mark. Very early in the Gospel we learn that the Jewish religious leaders have decided to plot Jesus' death (3:6). While in chapter three it might be possible to conclude that Jesus is unaware of these hostile machinations, by the time we reach the passion predictions in chapters eight, nine, and ten this conclusion is no longer possible. Jesus is fully aware that his actions and teaching have placed him at risk of violent persecution and death (8:31; 9:31; 10:33-34). At the same time, it is also important to note that within the story world of Mark's Gospel, Jesus' actions and teaching are fully affirmed as conforming to the will of God, as revealed on two important occasions by the voice from heaven (1:11; 9:7). Therefore, Mark's depiction of Jesus shows that he believed his words and actions conformed to the will of God, nevertheless, this is precisely what places Jesus' life in jeopardy. The scene in the Garden of Gethsemane suggests that Jesus may have briefly wrestled with the possibility of secretly slipping away or compromising with the religious authorities (14:35-36), but he rejects this option. Throughout the Gospel, Jesus remains unwavering in his devotion to his understanding of God's will, advocating his message in public and defending it against criticism, even though he knows that it will inevitably result in his trial, torture, and execution.

4) The central focus of the Jewish tales of martyrdom is the trial scene itself. Each account builds up to the direct examination of the hero, who is generally asked to violate Torah and conform to the edict. The reply of the hero to this charge is the scene's climactic moment. It is worth noting that these events are reported dialogically. That is, the narrator allows the characters to speak for themselves rather than simply reporting their speech from a more remote narrative vantage point. This allows for a greater sense of verisimilitude in the story and heightens the dramatic effect of the moment. In this moment of dialogic exchange, the martyr is able to directly confront the hubris of his or her persecutor. The martyr reminds the tormentor that they both stand in the presence of a superior authority who will judge them both, and while it may seem important to conform to the king's command under the threat of torture and death, it is more important to be obedient to God.

Like the martyrs in Daniel, 2 Maccabees and 4 Maccabees, Jesus is also examined before his persecutors. The focus is somewhat different. Jesus is not asked to recant or conform to the wishes of the investigative body and torture is used as punishment rather than as means of persuasion.[10] The condemnation of Jesus is a foregone conclusion. The Jewish leaders are only looking for the evidence necessary to condemn Jesus, and yet their plans are frustrated by disagreements among the witnesses. The examination is therefore somewhat of a sham. Nevertheless, the climactic moment is the dialogic examination of Jesus, wherein the High Priest directly questions Jesus about his own sense of mission: "Are you the Christ, the Son of the Blessed One?" However, this is an occasion for Jesus to do more than simply affirm or deny the High Priest's question. His full reply exhibits the hallmarks of those given by the Jewish martyrs. He is indeed the Messiah, but the affirmation that follows is a statement of confidence in apocalyptic vindication and an implicit claim of future judgment against those who oppose God's Messiah.

5) The final component of the martyr stories is a detailed, and often gruesome, account of the torture and execution of the victim. Often in

[10] An intriguing possibility is that, under the influence of this feature of the martyrdom accounts, Mark shifts the theme of recanting under pressure to Peter by intercalating the trial scene with that of Peter's denial.

horrific detail, the narrator reports the fate of the hero. This frequently involves an account of how those who are present are led to greater confidence in God's provision. In those accounts where the victims are spared (Dan 3, 6) the focus is on the ironic punishment meted out against their accusers (3:22, 6:24) and the king's acknowledgment of God's power and authority (3:28-29). In the case of the Maccabean martyrs, these reports serve to illustrate the heroic resolve of the martyr and to undermine the authority of the king by showing that his methods of persuasion are powerless and ineffective.

The account of Jesus' execution in Mark is comparable (14:65; 15:16-20, 24). It reports in detail the cruel treatment of Jesus at the hands of the Jewish leaders and the Roman centurions. The mistreatment of Jesus has no effect on his resolve and, like the martyr stories, this underscores the powerlessness of the Jewish leaders and their Roman accomplices. Mark also reports the effect these events had on the faithful. Oddly, the martyr stories serve to reinforce the determination of others, but in the case of Jesus, everyone else falls away, leaving Jesus completely isolated, both literally and figuratively. Although he puts it to a somewhat different use, Mark also makes good use of irony in his account. Jesus' persecutors do not meet the fate they intend for their victim, as they might have in a typical Jewish novel, but they are guilty of betraying God's purposes at the very point when they think they are serving God by purging the land of a false teacher.

This somewhat formalistic comparison of Mark with the Jewish tales of martyrdom, using the five elements of the Jewish martyr story as identified by Van Henten, indicates that Mark's account of Jesus' trial is comparable, but certainly not identical. This tension is typical of formalistic literary analysis and below I will offer a chronotopic comparison at a higher level of abstraction.[11] Nevertheless, at this point, there seems to be enough of a pattern to invite further investigation.

Other features beyond those identified by van Henten also support a comparison of Mark's trial narrative with the martyr stories. While some of the Jewish martyrs are confident of deliverance from the evil intentions of their attackers in the present (Dan 3, 6), the Maccabean martyrs are notable for their hope in a future vindication beyond death (2 Macc 7:9, 14; 4 Macc 9:7-8, 10:15; 13:16; 15:3; 16:25; 17:12). This hope

[11] On the inherent problems of formalism, see P. N. Medvedev and M. M. Bakhtin, *The Formal Method in Literary Scholarship: A Critical Introduction to Sociological Poetics* (trans. Albert J. Wehrle; Cambridge: Harvard University Press, 1985).

fuels their resistance, since they are confident that death is not the end. The martyrs anticipate fully restored bodies (2 Macc 7:11) and eternal life as a reward for their faithfulness to God.[12] Belief in eternal life helps explain their casual disregard for the threats of their persecutors. However, their hope extends beyond their own hoped for vindication, they are also confident that their persecutor, Antiochus Epiphanes, will be appropriately punished for murdering the righteous (2 Macc 7:17, 19, 31-36; 4 Macc 9:9, 32; 10:11, 15, 21; 11:3, 23; 12: 12, 14, 18; 18:5).

In response to the high priest's question, Jesus likewise appeals to a future vindication by God. Since Jesus has already anticipated that his arrest will end in his death at the hands of the Jewish leaders (8:31; 9:31; 10:33–34; 12:7), his only hope is that God will reward him for his faithfulness. Yet Jesus' words go well beyond the hopes expressed by the Maccabean martyrs. The seven brothers hope only to "be with God" (4 Macc 9:8) in the presence of Abraham, Isaac, and Jacob (4 Macc 16:25). Jesus hopes not only to be with God, but to be "seated at the right hand of Power."[13] The comparison with the Maccabean martyrs suggests that Jesus' statement is an implicit claim that torture and death will not change his resolve to follow his own sense of loyalty to God. God will be his judge, and Jesus anticipates his full vindication, and even exaltation, by God.

Furthermore, Jesus' words take on an apocalyptic tone that is not present in 4 Maccabees. In language borrowed from Daniel 7, Jesus alludes to his role as the representative man who will possess "dominion, glory, and kingdom" (cf. Mark 14:62, Dan 7:13-14). Commentators continue to debate whether Jesus' statement in 14:62 refers to exaltation or judgment at the *parousia*.[14] The general trend now seems to emphasize exaltation. However, even if Jesus' statement refers only to his exaltation, this is still a rather thinly veiled threat aimed at the Jewish leaders. Prosecuting, torturing, and executing the future Son of Man, who will be exalted by God to the right hand of power, bodes ill indeed for the Jewish leaders. It therefore seems likely that Mark's intention was for the reader to hear a pronouncement of future judgment against those who condemned Jesus.

[12] M. de Jonge, "Jesus' Death for Others and the Death of the Maccabean Martyrs," in *Text and Testimony: Essays on New Testament and Apocryphal Literature in Honor of A. F. J. Klijn* (ed. Tjitze Baarda; Kampen: J. H. Kok, 1988), 149.

[13] Although an objection might be raised at this point, since the statement is made only of the "Son of Man," by this point in the narrative the reader has little choice but to see this phrase as a reference to Jesus (14:41).

[14] See France, *Gospel of Mark*, 502-3, 611-12 and the literature cited there.

In that case, the connection with the accounts of the Maccabean martyrs grows even stronger, since the martyrs regularly remind Antiochus that he will be judged by God for his actions. Jesus' statement in 14:62 thus takes on a more pronounced tone of defiance. The religious leaders, who presume to judge God's final envoy, will themselves receive a more lasting judgment.[15] In a sense then, just as in the tales of the martyrs, the deep irony of the trial scene is that it is not Jesus who is on trial, but his persecutors. From the standpoint of the Markan evangelist, Jesus' faithfulness to God is unimpeachable; it is the religious leaders who are in danger of betraying God by tormenting and murdering God's "beloved Son" (1:11; 9:7; 12:6). According to the Markan evangelist, attributing the actions of God's spirit to Satan is blasphemy and places one outside the sphere of God's mercy (3:29-30). Jesus was filled with God's spirit at the time of his baptism (1:10), and he ministered to those in need through the power of God's spirit.[16] The failure of the Jewish leaders to recognize the power of God at work in Jesus and their decision to put him to death constitutes a fatal insensitivity to the workings of God. The implication of Mark's Gospel is that the religious leaders have lost their ability to rightly discern the power of God and therefore they wrongly oppose the actions of Jesus. Therefore, according to the standards of blasphemy established in the Markan text, it is ironically not Jesus who is guilty of blasphemy, as the high priest claims, but the Sanhedrin.

Another intriguing point of contact between Mark and 4 Maccabees is their similar notions of what Sam Williams has termed "effective death."[17] In his book, Williams offers a very careful and thorough defense of the thesis that New Testament notions of Jesus' effective death for others, an idea that he claims has its origins in Greco-Roman literature, was most likely transmitted to the authors of the New Testament through 4 Maccabees.[18] In developing his argument for the probable influence of 4 Maccabees on the New Testament, Williams notes that the traditions of the Maccabean martyrs were centered in Syrian Antioch, the onetime capital of Antiochus Epiphanes.[19] Since commen-

[15] De Jonge, "Jesus' Death for Others," 143; and idem, *Christology in Context*, 175.

[16] De Jonge, *Christology in Context*, 56.

[17] Sam K. Williams, *Jesus' Death as Saving Event: The Background and Origin of a Concept* (HDR; Missoula, Mont.: Scholars Press, 1975), 179. See also Christian Grappe, "De l'intérêt de 4 Maccabées 17.18-22 (et 16.20-1) pour la Christologie du Nouveau Testament," *NTS* 46, no. 3 (2000): 342-57.

[18] Williams, *Jesus' Death as Saving Event*, 233-34.

[19] Ibid., 248-53.

tators often identify Antioch as a possible provenance for the Gospel of Mark, this raises the intriguing possibility that Mark also came directly under the influence of this tradition.[20] According to Williams, it is only in 4 Maccabees (17:21-22) that we find a parallel to Paul's use of the term ἱλαστηρίον ("expiation," or "propitiation," Rom 3:25). In addition to this parallel use of terminology, it is clear that 4 Maccabees interprets the death of the Jewish martyrs as in some sense efficacious of the salvation of the Jewish nation (4 Macc 1:11; 6:28).[21] Although in 4 Maccabees, the salvation purchased by the blood of the Jewish martyrs is limited to deliverance from the tyranny of Antiochus Ephiphanes, readers in the first century may indeed have found this a useful model for understanding the tragic death of God's Messiah.

While the terminology is different, Jesus' claim in Mark 10:45 that "the Son of Man also came not to be served but to serve, and to give his life (ψυχὴν) as a ransom (λύτρον) for many" is the clearest statement in the Gospel of this notion of effective death.[22] This idea is buttressed as well by the words of Jesus in Mark 14:24 where Jesus declares that the cup of wine represents "my blood of the covenant, which is poured out for many."[23] In 4 Maccabees we find similar expressions:

Be merciful to your people, and let our punishment suffice for them. Make my blood their purification, and take my life in exchange for theirs (καὶ ἀντίψυχον αὐτῶν λαβὲ τὴν ἐμὴν ψυχήν). (4 Macc 6:28-29)

The tyrant was punished, and the homeland purified – they having become, as it were, a ransom (ἀντίψυχον) for the sin of our nation. And through the blood of those devout ones and their death as an expiation (ἱλαστηρίου), divine Providence preserved Israel that previously had been afflicted. (4 Macc 17:21-22)

At the earliest stage of the Jesus tradition, Marinus de Jonge notes, no positive significance was attached to the death of Jesus. The emphasis rested instead upon Jesus' vindication by God, his death being only a

[20] Paul Feine, Johannes Behm, and Werner Georg Kümmel, *Introduction to the New Testament* (trans. Jr. A. J. Mattill; 14th rev. ed.; Nashville: Abingdon, 1966), 70; Joel Marcus, *Mark 1-8: A New Translation with Introduction and Commentary* (AB 27; New York: Doubleday, 2000), 1:36-37; and Helmut Koester, *Introduction to the New Testament: History and Literature of Early Christianity* (Hermeneia: Foundations & Facets; Philadelphia: Fortress Press, 1982), 2:166-67.

[21] A similar idea is also expressed in 2 Macc 7:37.

[22] That Mark preferred λύτρον over ἀντίψυχον of 4 Macc 6:29 and 17:21, which both mean "ransom," is probably due to the relative obscurity of the later term in the LXX and the greater frequency of the former, although Mark prefers the singular to the more common plural.

[23] De Jonge, *Christology in Context*, 179-82; idem., "Jesus' Death for Others," 148.

necessary precursor.[24] De Jonge connects the work of Lothar Ruppert and others on Jesus as God's suffering servant with passages in the Hebrew Bible that describe God's faithfulness in interceding for those who trust God implicitly in the face of great danger, alluding specifically to figures like Daniel and his three companions. This theme of physical, real-time deliverance of the faithful is expanded in the apocalyptic portions of Daniel into an eschatological deliverance that includes a resurrection and vindication of the dead who faithfully served God.[25] The resurrection and vindication of Jesus is different, as de Jonge points out, since Jesus' resurrection was not part of a general resurrection of the faithful. His resurrection shows that God is on his side, but it only foreshadows a future vindication of all of God's faithful servants.[26] Nevertheless, de Jonge notes, by "meditating on texts and traditions about the suffering, death and vindication of servants of God and righteous persons in the past," the early Christians arrived at a deeper understanding of Jesus death, "always, of course, linking Jesus' death implicitly or explicitly with his victory over death, his resurrection and exaltation."[27]

The early church came to believe that Jesus was God's final emissary to a wayward people.[28] In the Gospel of Mark, this notion achieves its clearest expression in the parable of the wicked tenants (12:1-12). As God's beloved Son (12:6), Jesus is wrongly persecuted and killed by the Jewish leaders because he faithfully announces the coming kingdom of God (1:14-15). The similar accounts of the wrongful torture and death of the Maccabean martyrs would have provided a helpful model for understanding how Jesus' death could be something other than a tragic failure. Like the Maccabean martyrs, Jesus did not deserve death, yet just as the martyrs hoped that their death would alleviate the wrath of God and bring the day of deliverance; the early church came to believe that Jesus' death could atone for sins and inaugurate the "last days." Furthermore, just as the martyrs hoped to live with God forever as a reward for their heroic obedience, Jesus, since he was God's final envoy and "beloved Son," was all the more likely to dwell with God after death and even to reign with God at "the right hand of power."

[24] De Jonge, "Jesus' Death for Others," 143.

[25] In addition to Daniel 12:1–3, de Jonge also cites *1 Enoch* 102-104, and *2 Baruch* 48:48–50; 52:6–7 (de Jonge, "Jesus' Death for Others," 144).

[26] De Jonge, "Jesus' Death for Others," 144.

[27] Ibid., 142.

[28] Ibid., 143.

As a way of summarizing the results of this investigation we are now in a position to offer some preliminary observations about the chronotope of the Jewish martyr stories and how this might compare to the Gospel of Mark. The narrative space of the Jewish martyr story is clearly a hostile and confined space. The martyr is confined in a room with his or her tormentor. Although the characters are allowed to interact dialogically, true dialogue which might involve persuasion and compromise is out of the question. Both parties are entrenched in their position, and the time for compromise, if there ever was such a time, is past. A collision between the ideas espoused by the martyr and the demands of the tormentor is inevitable. The hostile nature of the space is emphasized by the presence of implements of torture, and the narrative description of brutality.

The Jewish martyrs are able to bear up under these horrific conditions because they are convinced that God will vindicate their claims and reward their loyalty. The space of the martyr story, which is confined horizontally, is nevertheless open vertically. God, who is not otherwise present as a character in the narrative, is watching from a superior vantage point, and will reward those who remain loyal and avenge their death by punishing those who torment them. The chronotope shows signs of development at this point, from the early stories of Daniel where deliverance is immediate, to the stories of the Maccabean martyrs, who can only hope for a future, heavenly vindication.

The temporal quality of the martyr stories is characterized primarily as a time of testing. The hero's fidelity to Torah, as expressed by observing *kashruth* and other outward acts of piety, is subjected to intense scrutiny. The hero's values must survive the most demanding test imaginable. Under threat of death, and more to the point, intense pain and suffering, the martyr must persist in his or her defiance of the tormentor's demands. The tormentor observes no boundaries in the attempt to enforce compliance with his demands. Pain and suffering offset by unwavering fidelity on the part of the hero are the hallmarks of this chronotope.

The hero's confidence in vindication is bolstered by a sense that death will somehow be efficacious for God's people, who are to one degree or another, guilty of apostasy. The time of the martyr story is therefore characterized as a time of sacrifice for others. The hero dies to assuage the wrath of God and bring the time of deliverance ever nearer. As the focal point of God's wrath, expressed through the physical abuse of the tyrant, the martyrs believe that their heroic persistence will make up for the apostasy of their nation and will provide an example of loyalty to their nation. The temporal quality of the martyr stories is therefore supercharged with significance. The fate of a people hangs on the heroic determination of the martyr to resist the violent assault of the king.

How does the Gospel of Mark compare to this chronotope of Jewish martyrdom? The temporal and spatial qualities of Mark's account of Jesus' trial before the Sanhedrin show a number of striking similarities to those of Jewish tales of martyrdom. Like the martyr accounts Jesus' trial takes place in a private space. After his arrest, Jesus is led from the public space of the garden of Gethsemane, into the private space of the High Priest's house. Jesus, who was before his arrest always accompanied by his disciples, is now alone with his accusers. This space is unmistakably hostile. The Jewish leaders are actively seeking testimony so that they can condemn Jesus, and the reader knows from the preceding narrative that their intention is not simply to charge Jesus with a minor infraction, but to have him put to death. The hostility of the Jewish leaders, which Mark has carefully cultivated up to this point in the narrative, is now concentrated in a confined space and focused on an isolated individual.

Although the physical space of the trial scene is private and confined, its metaphysical space is open. God is present in the background of the narrative without breeching the boundary separating divine and human space. Instead, Jesus acknowledges the vertical openness of this space by calling attention to future time of heavenly enthronement and divine judgment. Of course, what is distinctive about Jesus' statement is that it is Jesus himself who will be "seated at the right hand of power" to act as judge and therefore God is never named directly. The point of Jesus' declaration would seem to be, in part, that in spite of the Jewish leader's attempt to conduct a secret meeting far removed from the crowds whom they fear (12:12; 14:2), there is (or will be in the future!) a heavenly judge who sees all and will ultimately judge fairly and impartially.

The narrative function of the Markan trial scene is to provide a final test of the hero and the hero's commitment to the values he has espoused. Jesus, who Mark has depicted as being steadfast in his commitment to God and the values of God's kingdom, must now stand firm in a final, climactic challenge of his fidelity to God. The forces arrayed against Jesus are not implements of torture, as in the accounts of the Maccabean martyrs, but the hostile schemes of the religious leaders. Jesus' antagonists are actively seeking, not the truth, but witnesses who will provide the grounds necessary for a negative verdict against Jesus. That these witnesses fail to agree in their testimony only underscores the hostile nature of their intent. The question the high priest puts to Jesus, "Are you the Christ the Son of God?" presents Jesus with an ultimate decision. He can either deny his own self-understanding – namely that he is God's beloved Son (1:11; 9:7; 12:6) and Messiah (1:1; 8:29), or he can affirm the high priest's designation and lay claim to his divinely bestowed identity. Denial would presumably result in acquittal, although that possibility is never seriously entertained within the Markan narrative, while affirmation results in condemnation, torture, and ultimately death.

In the narrative build up to the trial scene, we see that in a number of ways Mark has charged the trial scene with tremendous importance. The reader of Mark's Gospel knows that the intentionally vague figure of the Son of Man is the one who will "give his life as a ransom for many" (10:45), and that Jesus intends to offer up his body and blood on behalf of "many" (14:24). The parable of the wicked tenants indicates, indirectly through the use of the phrase "a beloved son," that Jesus is God's Son, who is sent by God in a final effort to lay claim to God's own vineyard, but who is nevertheless killed by God's unscrupulous tenants in a vain attempt to rob God of his property (12:7-8). Thus, the trial scene is not simply about the life and death of a single man, rather the fortunes of "the many" are at risk in the dramatic showdown between Jesus and his accusers. The final words of the parable of the wicked tenants underscore the dramatic importance of the trial. After the son is killed, the owner of the vineyard will have no other choice but to "destroy the tenants and give the vineyard to others."[29] Therefore, according to Mark, the trial of Jesus represents the single most important moment in God's relationship with Israel.

Conclusion

At the somewhat abstract level of chronotope, Mark's account of Jesus' trial bears a striking resemblance to the accounts of the Jewish martyrs, especially those in 4 Maccabees. Certain details do not fit – there is no formal edict condemning Jesus, he is never directly asked to recant or renounce his position, etc. – but the temporal and spatial qualities of the

[29] Once again we see that the "coming of the Son of Man on the clouds of heaven" in Mark 14:62 may not be as benign as some commentators seem to think. When God, or his divinely appointed agent, comes next it will be to judge and destroy.

scene are similar. The chronotopic similarities extend beyond the mere narrative requirements of a trial scene and touch deeper theological concerns of the Markan author, namely the concern to portray Jesus' suffering and death as having a profound significance for others. That the details are somewhat different should not detract from the importance of the comparison. Mark may well have been constrained by the facts surrounding Jesus' passion, or influenced by other sources beyond those of the Jewish martyr tales, to tell the story in this particular way. Nevertheless, it seems that these martyr stories have influenced Mark's reworking of the tradition.

If that is so, it is interesting to note how Mark has creatively adapted the martyr stories by subverting one of their core values. In Mark, it is not *kashruth* that is being tested, as in the martyr stories, but more fundamental values of love, compassion, and justice. In this fashion, Mark uses stories that originally supported the values advocated by the Jewish religious leaders and bends them to a new purpose. Jesus dies a sacrificial death on behalf of others like the Maccabean martyrs, but the kingdom values he champions are very different. Moreover, for Mark, Jesus is not just another in a long line of Jewish martyrs.[30] Jesus is God's final envoy, and while the Maccabean martyrs died in a heroic attempt to resist the oppressive policies of Antiochus Epiphanes, Jesus dies to ransom "the many" (10:45; 14:24) in preparation for God's coming kingdom (1:15). Therefore, while Mark has been influenced by the martyr stories, he has not followed them slavishly. Instead he has creatively adapted existing literary models, often subverting their core values in the process, in order to use them as the vehicle for a radically new message.

[30] De Jonge, "Jesus Death for Others," 151.

INNOCENCE AND GUILT: APOLOGETIC, MARTYR STORIES, AND ALLUSION IN THE MARKAN TRIAL NARRATIVES

Kelli S. O'Brien

Jesus' condemnation by the Romans with the involvement of the high priests was the virtual equivalent of "a trial at the Old Bailey in which the Archbishops of Canterbury and York were the chief witnesses for the prosecution," wrote D. E. Nineham. Mark had "to show that, contrary to appearances, Jesus had been entirely innocent of the charges brought against him."[1] This provocative statement has a number of implications for the nature of the Markan Passion Narrative and of Mark's audience. In Nineham's view, Mark's audience would have agreed with Jesus' condemnation and had to be convinced otherwise, and the Markan Passion Narrative is apologetic.

Yet one wonders whether condemnation did in fact imply guilt to Mark's audience. It is not entirely certain that the leadership of Jerusalem, in full collaboration with Rome, enjoyed absolute respectability. The people of Qumran can hardly be accused of excessive dependence on their opinions. Josephus rails against arbitrary displays of power by the high priest Ananus II (*Ant.* 20.9.1). In addition, passages such as 1 Kings 22:24-28, Jeremiah 26, and 2 Chronicles 24:20-22 show prophets suffering at the hands of the Jewish leadership, both secular and cultic. Second Temple literature adds to these texts with stories of suffering prophets, such as *The Martyrdom of Isaiah* (5.1-14) and *The Lives of the Prophets* (2.1; 3.2, 18-19; 6.2; 7.2). These accounts of undeserved suffering by the prophets at the hands of Jewish leaders, along with stories such as Daniel 3 and 6 and 2 Maccabees 6-7, belonged to a large body of literature in the late Second Temple period which recognized that righteous people suffer and that leaders are not always what they should be.

While apologetic considerations are more often attached to the Gospel of Luke than to Mark, Nineham is not alone in seeing apologetic interests

[1] D. E. Nineham, *The Gospel of St. Mark* (Middlesex: Penguin, 1963), 366.

there. Others conclude that there is a consistent effort in the Markan trials to demonstrate that Jesus is innocent or that in the Gospel as a whole there is a similar effort to clear Jesus from various accusations.[2] In what follows, however, I will argue that the Jewish trial in Mark functions much less like apologetic than a martyr story. The trial presents Jesus as guilty as charged, but Jesus' guilt serves ironically to underscore his faithfulness and his true relationship with God. While the explicit narrative of the trial is brief and less than crystal clear, allusions to Scripture provide valuable evidence on this question and point clearly in this direction. One of the main obstacles to resolving the issue is a lack of scholarly consensus on the literary questions – what is meant by apologetic and how apologetic differs in function from a martyr story. Thus the discussion will begin by establishing the nature and limits of apologetic and martyr stories. It will then proceed to examine the Markan Jewish trial, including what its allusions to Scripture have to contribute to its meaning and tenor.

What is Apologetic?

Few would argue that Mark belongs to the literary genre of apology, in the sense of Plato's *Apology*. More difficult to determine is whether Mark has apologetic functions. That is, does Mark, whatever its genre might be, use "apologetic means" to accomplish an "apologetic end"?

The answer depends a great deal on how the term *apologetic* is defined. Modern scholars use it in several ways and with increasing breadth. In the narrowest senses, Mark is by definition *not* apologetic; in the broadest sense, it clearly *is*. In the *via media*, we are presented with a valid question on the topic. Therefore arriving at a reasonable definition is essential. Early definitions are lacking, since apology appears not to have been a formal genre in the Roman period.[3] Since modern scholars use the term apologetic in several senses and there is little explicit discussion on the topic, it will be necessary here to lay out the possibilities and evaluate them.

Scholarly uses of the term can be imagined as a series of concentric circles. The center circle contains the literal meaning of the term: a

[2] See, e.g., Edwin K. Broadhead, *Prophet, Son, Messiah: Narrative Form and Function in Mark 14-16* (JSNT Supplement Series 97; Sheffield: JSOT Press, 1994), 163-70; Otto Piper, "God's Good News: The Passion Story According to Mark," *Interpretation* 9 (1955): 180; Arthur Droge, "Apologetics, New Testament," *ABD* 1:303; Barnabas Lindars, *New Testament Apologetics* (Philadelphia: Westminster, 1961), 49, 184.

[3] Mark Edwards, et al., ed., *Apologetics in the Roman Empire* (Oxford: Oxford University Press, 1999), 2.

defense speech in a trial setting. It applies equally well to a literary or fictive speech in such a setting, such as Plato's *Apology*. In the second and larger circle, the term is applied to literature written to defend people who face persecution, for example, Philo's *Embassy to Gaius* or Justin's apologies. An appeal is made to a reasonable and just third party to stop the serious mistreatment of Jews or Christians. In the third circle, the term is applied to literature written to defend a way of life to outsiders who criticize it. While in theory this circle is larger than the last, in practice it contains very few members – Josephus' *Contra Apionem* being one of the few surviving examples – because few ancient works were written to outsiders.[4] As Victor Tcherikover pointed out, access to and interest in an author's work comes mainly from members of the author's own social world, and most authors appear to write in ways that appeal to insiders.[5] Apologetic of this nature may have occurred more often in personal contacts between members of competing social groups.

Up to this point, there is little controversy. Most would accept all three of these definitions as valid uses of the term apologetic. It is also reasonably clear that Mark does not fit them. The fourth circle is the point at which consensus on the extent of the term apologetic breaks down. Here the term is applied to works which are directed to insiders, members of the author's social group. These works are written to strengthen the identity of the group and to justify the group's way of life within a larger social system. This definition requires consideration, and we will return to it.

The fifth and broadest circle understands apologetic to include religious propaganda or literature written to persuade others to accept a position or to adopt a certain way of life.[6] This definition is used by a large number of authors. Droge, for example, defines apologetic as "the art of persuasion" and "missionary propaganda."[7] Robert Gundry entitles his commentary, *Mark: A Commentary on His Apology for the Cross*, stating that the Gospel puts forward the Markan understanding of the cross in an attempt to convert non-believers.[8] Under this definition, the Gospel of Mark would indeed have an apologetic function.

[4] Martin Goodman ("Josephus' Treatise *Against Apion*," in *Apologetics in the Roman Empire* [ed. Mark Edwards, et al.; Oxford: Oxford University Press, 1999], 50-51) argues that *Contra Apionem* was directed to Gentiles.

[5] Victor Tcherikover, "Jewish Apologetic Literature Reconsidered," *Eos* 48 (1956): 171-79.

[6] Cf. Helmut Koester, *Introduction to the New Testament* (Philadelphia: Fortress, 1982), 2:338-40.

[7] Droge, *ABD*, 1:302.

[8] Robert Gundry, *Mark: A Commentary on His Apology for the Cross* (Grand Rapids: Eerdmans, 1983), 1026. This definition is also used by some who argue that Acts is an apology for Paul.

The problem with this definition is that it can be applied to virtually *any* persuasive work. David Aune warns that the term apologetic is "used so comprehensively that it is effectively drained of any generic significance. 'Apologetic literature' must be distinguished from 'missionary propaganda', even though these terms only describe general types of literature, not literary genres."[9] Loveday Alexander concurs: "Part of the problem here is the wide range and fuzzy definition of the term 'apologetic' itself, which threatens to undermine its descriptive usefulness altogether."[10] Applying the term apologetic to any piece of literature which attempts to move others to the author's position is unhelpful. According to such a definition, this essay is apologetic, along with most of what scholars write and say.

This definition, though problematic, perhaps arose out of a valid and important observation. As Elizabeth Schüssler Fiorenza put it, apologetic and missionary propaganda can function "like two sides of the same coin."[11] Apologetic often does contain propaganda. It does not follow however that all propaganda is therefore apologetic. This slip is rather easily made, sometimes even by those who would wish to avoid it. Loveday Alexander makes the necessary distinction when she rejects a particular Pauline speech in Acts as apologetic, because while the scene contains accusations and polemic, it presents no defense. She writes, "Mud has a disturbing tendency to stick, and it is a dangerous strategy for an apologetic writer to bring accusations to the reader's attention without taking the trouble to refute them."[12] If charges are made and not rebutted, the material is not apologetic. While apologetic material may function as propaganda, not all propaganda is apologetic.

[9] David E. Aune, "Romans as a Logos Protreptikos in the Context of Ancient Religious and Philosophical Propaganda," in *Paulus und das antike Judentum* (ed. Martin Hengel and Ulrich Hecked; Tübingen-Durham-Symposium im Gedanken an den 50. Todestag Adolf Schlatters; WUNT 58; Tübingen: J. C. B. Mohr [Paul Siebeck], 1991), 111.

[10] Loveday Alexander, "The Acts of the Apostles as an Apologetic Text," in *Apologetics in the Roman Empire*, 16.

[11] Elizabeth Schüssler Fiorenza, "Miracles, Mission and Apologetics: An Introduction," in *Aspects of Religious Propaganda in Judaism and Early Christianity* (ed. Elizabeth S. Fiorenza; Notre Dame: University of Notre Dame Press, 1976), 2-3.

[12] Alexander, "Acts of the Apostles," 34. Unfortunately, Alexander herself forgets the distinction she makes here, when she discusses the convergence between apologetic and missionary propaganda in the New Testament (e.g., 1 Peter 3:15, cf. 2:12; 3:1) and second century apologists. She goes on to say that this "feature of apologetic," i.e., that apologetic can function as propaganda, is also found in older Jewish martyrology, such as the speeches of the martyrs in 2 Macc 6:18-7:42. At the same time, she admits that in these stories it is "not always easy to tell what the precise charge is or how (if at all) it is rebutted" (pp. 39-40).

Similarly apologetic contains polemic; in fact polemic is an important part of ancient apology. Martin Goodman writes, "It was characteristic of ancient trials that the parties attempted to discredit the personality of their opponents."[13] Nevertheless not all polemic is apologetic. In an ancient law court the prosecutor's speech will certainly contain polemic, but it is equally certainly not an apology.

Metaphorical uses of terminology are helpful and appropriate, but when terms are stretched beyond their breaking point, they become useless. The central meaning of the term *apology* is the notion of defense against an accusation. That accusation may be literal and legal or metaphorical, addressing important criticisms with social rather than legal ramifications.[14] If accusation or defense is missing, however, the essence of apologetic is gone, and the term is best not applied. So, material with persuasive or polemical functions should be considered apologetic only if it also contains a defense against a charge.

With this in mind, we can return to the fourth circle: apologetic material includes literature written to insiders in order to strengthen the group's self-identity within a larger and competing culture. This category contains a large number of Jewish and Christian works. Gregory Sterling applies this category, for example, to Josephus' *Antiquities of the Jews* and to Luke-Acts.[15] Many of Philo's works would qualify. This sort of literature encourages insiders to maintain their way of life and to have pride in it, even though that way of life is challenged by that of the surrounding culture. Here we have the *via media* and a definition which presents us with a valid question regarding nature of Mark's Gospel. Whether Mark was written to strengthen insiders against challenges from without is genuinely subject to debate.

Tcherikover rejects this category of literature as apologetic. While he does not give a strict definition of the term, his argument implies that apologetic requires not only that a charge be defended against, but that the defense must be directed toward the people who bring the charge.[16] This may be too restrictive. As Tcherikover himself argued, it would

[13] Goodman, "Josephus' Treatise *Against Apion*," 54.

[14] For the social ramifications of Josephus' critics, see Goodman, "Josephus' Treatise *Against Apion*," 55-58.

[15] Gregory E. Sterling, "Luke-Acts and Apologetic Historiography," *SBLSP* 28 (1989): 326-342; *Historiography and Self-Definition: Josephos, Luke-Acts and Apologetic Historiography* (Leiden: Brill, 1992) passim, esp. 17, 223-25. See also Harold W. Attridge, "Jewish Historiography," in *Early Judaism and Its Modern Interpreters* (ed. Robert Kraft and George W. E. Nickelsburg; Atlanta: Scholars Press, 1986), 312.

[16] Tcherikover, "Jewish Apologetic Literature Reconsidered," 169-183.

have been difficult for most members of a marginalized group to get the attention of the larger culture. Furthermore, a group's self-defense would often not resonate with the larger group, since the two groups had differing value systems and authoritative literature. Yet the group may well be affected by those charges. Its members may have doubts and need clarification. Thus authors write concerning those charges to their own members, to assuage their doubts and to encourage them.[17]

Material which addresses criticisms made by outsiders but is directed to insiders does contain the characteristics essential to apologetic: a charge and a defense against that charge. Such a definition is not too broad, since it applies to a distinct body of literature and has not lost its metaphorical connection to its basic meaning as a defense against an accusation at trial. To qualify, works must "wrestle with doubts and uncertainties felt by members."[18] Material which simply educates or encourages members to maintain a way of life in face of ordinary troubles falls outside the category. Also outside the category are works which reflect charges against or criticisms of a group but do not defend against them. A great deal of material about the suffering of the righteous fits into this category, including martyr stories to which we now turn.

Martyr Stories

George Nicklesburg compared the Markan Passion Narrative to other stories of "persecution and vindication" in Jewish literature. He lists a number of elements the latter texts have in common, such as a provocation, a conspiracy, trial and condemnation, and an ordeal. He concludes that the Markan Passion Narrative shares most of these elements.[19]

Nicklesburg is sometimes taken to task for bringing too many stories into the circle of martyr texts. Robert Doran notes dryly, "one finds a little understated his comment, when comparing the narrative of 2 Maccabees 7 to those of Daniel 3 and 6: 'Different from the heroes in Daniel, the brothers actually die.'"[20] Jan Willem van Henten identifies a

[17] See Sterling, *Historiography and Self-Definition*, 224-25.

[18] Mark Edwards, et al., "Introduction," in *Apologetics in the Roman Empire*, 5.

[19] George W. E. Nickelsburg, "The Genre and Function of the Markan Passion Narrative," *HTR* 73 (1980): 153-84, esp. pp. 155-65.

[20] Robert Doran, "The Martyr: A Synoptic View of the Mother and Her Seven Sons," in *Ideal Figures in Ancient Judaism: Profiles and Paradigms* (ed. John J. Collins and George W. E. Nickelsburg; SBLSCS 12; Chico: Scholars Press, 1980), 189. He is quoting Nickelsburg, *Resurrection, Immortality, and Eternal Life in Intertestamental Judaism* (HTS 26; Cambridge: Harvard University Press, 1972), 94.

number of martyr texts and sketches their common narrative pattern: the enactment of a decree with the death penalty in conflict with what faithfulness to God requires; a person chooses to die rather than obey the authorities; this is declared in an examination; and that person is executed. Because Daniel and his friends do not die, these stories cannot be classified as martyr texts.[21]

However van Henten notes that Daniel 3 and 6 share a number of elements with martyr texts, indeed all of them except for the death of the heroes.[22] The fact that Daniel and his friends do not die may not be as great a consideration as it would appear at first. As Kenneth Grayston notes, while Jewish Scripture calls Jews to bear witness to their God, "nowhere is it said that faithful, devout Jews bear witness to God and his commandments by suffering, even dying."[23] That is, the primary function of the "martyr," to bear witness, does not in the Jewish mindset *require* one to die. Daniel and his friends bear exemplary witness; whether the outcome is their death or rescue does not depend on them. The same point could be made for the story of the Jews who put their lives at risk to prevent the statue of Gaius from being erected in the temple (Josephus, *J.W.* 2.184-203; in an alternate version, Agrippa risks his life, *Ant.* 18.289-309). Their lives are spared, but they set them at risk in witness to God and the Law.

Van Henten notes that his classification of the narrative elements should not be considered as describing a genre; the Jewish martyr texts he is describing belong to several different genres.[24] Instead his martyr texts simply contain a number of common narrative elements. It is reasonable to conclude that just as there is apologetic material and the distinct genre of apology (like the common distinction between apocalyptic and apocalypse), there is also material which shares motifs and worldviews of martyr literature and the distinct genre of martyrology itself. Van Henten notes quite a few types of texts which he considers related to martyr texts because they share many of the same motifs.[25]

[21] Jan Willem van Henten, *The Maccabean Martyrs as Saviours of the Jewish People: A Study of 2 and 4 Maccabees* (Supplements to the Journal for the Study of Judaism 57; Leiden: Brill, 1997), 8.

[22] Van Henten, *The Maccabean Matryrs*, 8-9.

[23] Kenneth Grayston, "Atonement and Martyrdom," in *Early Christian Thought in Its Jewish Context* (ed. John Barclay and John Sweet; Cambridge: Cambridge University Press, 1996), 250.

[24] Van Henten, *The Maccabean Matryrs*, 7.

[25] Van Henten, "Matryrion and Martyrdom: Some Remarks about Noble Death in Josephus," in *Internationales Josephus-Kolloquium, Brüssel 1998.* (Münsteraner judaistische Studien 4; Münster: Lit, 1999), 130-33.

By making his criteria slightly less strict, what van Henten calls "martyr texts" can be combined with what he calls "related literature," because they all share martyr motifs and worldviews, even though they do not necessarily include all of the elements of what van Henten calls a "martyr text." For the lack of a catchy adjective (corresponding to "apologetic" or "apocalyptic"), I am afraid I will simply call this larger group of texts "martyr stories."

Martyr Stories and Apologetic

As will be discussed below, the Markan Jewish trial is closer to a martyr story than apologetic. Literary apologies proclaim the innocence of a party. Socrates did not corrupt the youth and was not an atheist. In *Contra Apionem*, Josephus argues that the Jews are truly an ancient people, that they are not hostile to foreigners, etc. In martyr stories, the emphasis is quite the reverse: the party is guilty as charged. Daniel knows the king's law, but he prays to Israel's God three times a day, windows wide open (Dan 6:10). The violation is intentional and never denied. Daniel's friends treat the king with open contempt in their refusal to obey him (Dan 3:16-18). They say, "we have no need to present a defense to you."[26] Their defense will be their God. The seven sons ardently refuse to obey Antiochus' law, the last son in particular declaring, "I will not obey the king's command" (2 Macc 7:1-42, esp. v. 30). Eleazar refuses even the appearance of keeping that law, saying such a thing would be a disgrace (2 Macc 6:24-28). In the *Martyrdom of Isaiah*, Isaiah's opponents accuse him of saying things "against Jerusalem and against the cities of Judah that they will be laid waste," etc., things which he did indeed say, and he makes no defense (3.6-10). In all these cases, the story emphasizes that the martyr does indeed do what he is accused of doing. In van Henten's words: "when Jews are forced – for instance after their arrest – to decide between complying with the decree or remaining faithful to their religion and Jewish practice, they choose to die rather than obey the authorities."[27] That the hero disobeys the authorities is essential to the nature of a martyr story: the hero is guilty as charged.

These stories rely on a kind of irony. In the *Martyrdom of Isaiah*, the narrator does not point out that Isaiah has said the things he is accused

[26] All quotations NRSV, unless otherwise noted.
[27] Van Henten, *The Maccabean Martyrs*, 8.

of saying or why he said them, but the reader is expected to make those connections: Isaiah spoke in obedience to God. In 2 Maccabees, Eleazar and the seven brothers are killed for not obeying Antiochus' laws, but they do so to obey God's laws. The spokesman for the seven sons says, "We are ready to die rather than transgress the laws of our ancestors" (2 Macc 7:2). This is so also in Daniel, where Daniel and his friends keep God's laws at all costs. For these stories to work, "guilt," not innocence, is necessary. The reader must recognize however that although the martyr is guilty according to the human standard applied, such guilt actually demonstrates the martyr's glorious faithfulness.

There is another important distinction between a martyr story and apologetic. In an apology the author appeals to disinterested and reasonable third parties for justice, if merely in a fictive sense. In martyr stories, there is no appeal. Indeed, in 2 Maccabees, the suffering is expressly God's will (2 Macc 6:12-16; 7:18). Any attempt to stop it, to avoid it, would demonstrate lack of faith. Eleazar "went up to the rack of his own accord" (2 Macc 6:19). In 4 Maccabees, both the seventh son and the mother throw themselves into the fire (4 Macc 12:19; 17:1). In later Christian martyr stories, the martyrs sometimes urge the judge to put them to death.[28] There is no attempt to stop the punishment, because justice is not the point. Rather, the focus is on the martyr's steadfast acceptance of the will of God, even in the deepest suffering.

As a consequence, the martyr will be vindicated. In Daniel 3 and 6, Daniel and his friends are vindicated by being miraculously rescued. Nebuchadnezzar and Darius themselves attest to that vindication (Dan 3:28-30; 6:25-27). Several of the seven sons declare that they will be rewarded: "the King of the universe will raise us up to an everlasting renewal of life, because we have died for his laws" (2 Macc 7:9).

Yet while the martyr will be vindicated, the unjust official is sometimes, though not always, condemned for enforcing an unjust law and is threatened with divine retribution. This is a focus in the story of the seven sons, where several have sharp words for Antiochus and one declares, "Do not think that you will go unpunished for having tried to fight against God!" (2 Macc 7:19; cf. 7:34-36). "Tyrant" is an epithet found frequently in the material.

[28] For example, *Mart. of Polycarp* 11; *Mart. of Pionius* 8, 17-18; *Mart. of Maximilian* 5; *Mart. of Julius the Veteran* 3, in Herbert Musurillo, *The Acts of the Christian Martyrs* (Oxford: Clarendon, 1972).

Apologetic and martyr stories are fundamentally different. Like apology, martyr stories can function as propaganda. They can bolster the community and help it define itself with respect to a hostile environment. Yet at their core, martyr stories and apologetic are opposites. While apologetic presents a defense against a charge and an appeal for justice, in a martyr story the hero is guilty as charged and there is no attempt to avoid even torture and death.

Use of Scripture in the Jewish Trial

We must therefore ask whether the Jewish trial in Mark contains a defense against a charge and an appeal for justice in Jesus' case, or, in contrast, emphasizes Jesus' "guilt" in order to demonstrate his true faithfulness while it simultaneously condemns those who condemn him. Unfortunately, a strong case cannot be made from straightforward reading of the explicit narrative. While several charges are made against Jesus, it is difficult to tell whether they are meant to be taken as true or not. The meaning of Jesus' only statement at the trial is not fully clear. When the high priest asks him if he is the Christ, the son of the Blessed, he answers, "I am." But what does one make of the remainder of his statement, "and you will see the Son of Man seated at the right hand of the Power and coming with the clouds of heaven" (Mark 14:61-62)?

Mark resists an easy reading; the author does not draw out connections for the reader, as do Matthew and Luke. Still the author communicates meaning in distinct, though more subtle, ways. For example, it is well known that Mark interprets material by juxtaposing or combining separate stories, such as sandwiching pericopes about the disciples' spiritual blindness between two pericopes about healing the blind (Mark 8:22-10:52). Setting functions in a similar fashion. Another important but neglected device is allusion to Scripture. Very often the author uses allusion to Scripture to indicate the underlying meaning.

An example will perhaps help to illustrate the point. While the Gospels of Matthew and Luke both tell the reader explicitly that John the Baptist is Elijah, Mark does not.[29] Instead, Mark uses allusions to Scripture to convey this idea. The Gospel begins with two Scripture

[29] Matt 17:13, in an addition to the Transfiguration story; Luke 1:17 in Gabriel's speech to Zechariah.

quotations, the second being Isa 40:3: "the voice of one crying out in the wilderness, 'Prepare the way of the Lord, make his paths straight.'" Next John the Baptist appears in the wilderness, preaching and baptizing, that is, crying out and preparing the way of the Lord. Mark 1:2 quotes Mal 3:1: "See, I am sending My messenger before your face to prepare your way." Mal 3:23 (or 4:5), at least in one reading, identifies that messenger as Elijah. Allusions to Scripture signal to the reader: John the Baptist is Elijah.

Locating the Allusions

Allusions will prove particularly helpful in determining whether the author had apologetic concerns in the Jewish trial. Yet with allusion again we run into the obstacle of a literary term with such a "wide range and fuzzy definition" that scholarly discussion suffers. The problem is illustrated by the large number of Scripture passages which have been suggested as references in the Markan Passion Narrative. The Jewish trial is a particular hot spot. For the thirteen verses of the Markan Jewish trial, Mark 14:53-65, scholars have suggested over fifty different references. Which of these are allusions?[30]

Unlike an intertextual parallel (a juxtaposition of two texts made by the reader without considering historical context, etc.), *allusion* is grounded in the text and tied to the intention of the author, at least insofar as the intention of the author can be determined from the text. To qualify as an allusion, there must be verbal correspondence between the passages, correspondence sufficient to point to a specific text, not merely to a group of texts or to a motif. Obviously an exact quotation is sufficient; even a single very distinctive word may be enough. A single *common* word is not. "Supercalifragilisticexpialidocious" is unmistakable; "atrocious" alone does not have the same effect. A string of common words sometimes points to a specific text, as "that's the way it is" points to Walter Cronkite.

While there are other criteria essential to establishing the presence of an allusion, sufficient verbal correspondence is where the majority of suggested allusions fail. In my survey, seventeen of the allusions suggested for the Jewish trial scene have no significant words in com-

[30] See Kelli S. O'Brien, "The Use of Scripture in the Markan Passion Narrative" (Ph.D. diss., The University of Notre Dame, 2001), 39-83.

mon (that is, nothing more distinct than "and," "at," "he," etc.). Another seventeen share only one significant word, and that word is extremely common (such as, υἵος, "son", or ζητέω, "to seek"). These 34 suggestions may be eliminated. All three suggested allusions to Isaiah 53 fall in these two categories. The most common suggestion is that Jesus' silence reflects the silence of the servant in Isa 53:7, but the texts share only the single common word *silence* (Mark from σιωπάω, MT from אלם, both meaning "to be silent"; LXX, ἄφωνος, "silent"), which is not enough verbal correspondence to indicate an allusion.

The following passages met all of the criteria for an allusion:[31]

- Mark 14:55 and Ps 37:32
- Mark 14:56-57 and Exod 20:16//Deut 5:20
- Mark 14:61 and Isa 36:21
- Mark 14:62 and Dan 7:13 and Ps 110:1
- Mark 14:65 and Isa 50:6

A brief summary of why these allusions were accepted will be helpful. Mark 14:55 is linked to Ps 37:32 by common words, ζητέω and τὸ θανατῶσαι αὐτόν, "to put him to death," and common themes. The allusion to Exod 20:16 or Deut 5:20 is fairly secure, with the rare word ψευδομαρτυρέω, "to bear false witness," in common, and a quotation of the Decalogue earlier in Mark 10:19. The allusions in 14:62 are undisputed. The correspondence of Mark 14:65 and Isa 50:6 is secured by the correspondence of three words – πρόσωπον (face), ἐμπτύω (spit) and ῥάπισμα (strike), the latter two words rare in both the LXX and the New Testament. The allusion to Isa 36:21 in Mark 14:61 is more problematic. The words in common are σιωπάω καὶ οὐκ/οὐδεὶς ἀποκρίνομαι (silent and did not answer/no one answered). The words occur consecutively, and only the form of the words is changed. This parallel does not appear to have been seen by Matthew or Luke or, to my knowledge, by any other author since. Thus the parallel must be considered with extra suspicion. The verbal correspondence may be coincidence. Yet this episode in Isaiah is used often in Second Temple literature and shares a number of themes with the Jewish trial in Mark.[32] The total evidence indicates that Mark 14:61 may be treated as a possible allusion to Isa 36:21.

[31] See Ibid., 84-134, 250-76.
[32] See Ibid., 179-83.

Analyzing the Meaning of the Allusions

As noted above, the function of allusion in Mark is more than ornamentation. It communicates the meaning of the narrative to the reader. The allusions in the Jewish trial have a good deal to tell us about whether the author of Mark had apologetic or other purposes in the narrative. Of course, the allusions have more to communicate than on this particular issue alone, but it is on this issue that the following discussion will focus.

False Testimony: Mark 14:56-57 and Exod 20:16//Deut 5:20

The trial begins with false witnesses and a reference to the ninth commandment: you shall not bear false witness against your neighbor (Mark 14:56-57/Exod 20:16//Deut 5:20). While the implication of *false* witness is usually that what the witnesses say is not true, the case in Mark is more complex. The witness is false, because the witnesses do not agree, and the charge is not pursued (14:59). Yet the statement, "I will destroy this temple that is made with hands, and in three days I will build another, not made with hands" (Mark 14:58), is very similar to a saying in John 2:19, "Destroy this temple, and in three days I will raise it up." This saying was probably part of the Jesus tradition, and the reader may have been expected to recognize it. In any case in Mark 13:2, Jesus speaks against the temple. Of course, literally the witness is false: in neither Mark nor John does Jesus state that *he* would destroy the temple. Yet we should not miss the fact that the author chose as his particular example of false witness something so close to the tradition and with such telling words, "in three days I will build another, not made with hands." In the Johannine tradition, the temple that will be rebuilt in three days is the temple of Jesus' body (John 2:21). Mark may intend that here or may mean to say that in three days Jesus will build up a community for God.[33] In either case, the passage is ironic, and the reader is expected to understand that even though the witnesses do not agree, the charge is in some sense true and refers to the meaning of the passion.

Rather than emphasizing Jesus' innocence, the passage emphasizes the guilt of those who testify against him with its allusion to bearing

[33] See Donald Juel, *Messiah and Temple* (SBLDS 31; Missoula: Scholars Press, 1977), 159-209.

false witness. The story of the rich man also alludes to this commandment, and the rich man, who seems unable to let go of his possessions to follow Jesus, *is* able to avoid this sin (Mark 10:17-22). The use of the Decalogue in Mark and in early Jewish texts demonstrate that these commandments are considered fundamental, basic. Philo writes of false witness that "...this kind of crafty wickedness outstrips all other offences in its impiety" (*Decal.* 138-41).

Seeking to Put Him to Death: Mark 14:55 and Ps 37:32

It is not only those who give false witness who are condemned in this account. The judges themselves are decidedly unjust. Their intention is to kill Jesus, and to that end they plot to arrest him by stealth (14:1) and seek testimony against him:

> Now the chief priests and the whole Council were *seeking* (ἐζήτουν) testimony against Jesus *to put Him to death* (τὸ θανατῶσαι αὐτόν). (Mark 14:55)

Mark 14:55 alludes to Ps 37:32, which in context reads:

> 32 The wicked watch for the righteous, and *seek to put him to death.* (ζητεῖ τοῦ θανατῶσαι αὐτόν)
> 33 The Lord will not abandon him into his hand, or let him be condemned when he is brought to trial.
> 34 Wait for the Lord, and keep to His way, And He will exalt you to inherit the land; You will look on the destruction of the wicked.

Notice the appropriateness of the imagery, including condemnation and trial.

The Commentary on Psalms, 4Q171, interprets Psalm 37. It understands the person described as "the righteous one" to be the Teacher of Righteousness, who will not be overcome by the wicked one, that is the Wicked Priest, who seeks to do him harm. In contrast, the commentary tells us, the Wicked Priest will be handed to the "violent of the nations" in judgment.[34] Ps 37:33 points to the vindication of the Teacher of Righteousness; the Wicked Priest will be judged because of Ps 37:34.

There are a number of connections between the Qumran interpretation of this psalm and its possible interpretation in Mark, but here the most obvious and salient must do: God will protect the righteous one and not abandon him, and God will destroy the wicked.

[34] Translation by Geza Vermes, *The Complete Dead Sea Scrolls in English* (New York: Penguin Books, 1997, rev. ed. 2004).

In the case of Mark, that claim is difficult to make. Jesus is condemned at trial, and while he is being executed he cries out that God has abandoned him. Yet the claim may nevertheless hold in a spiritualized sense. The end result of Jesus' ordeal is his vindication, rather his exaltation. By suffering as he does, Jesus is "seated at the right hand of the Power," where he will reign until he comes to judge the wicked and restore the chosen. The Righteous is condemned only to be vindicated at the resurrection and abandoned only to be received into the heavenly court. Ironically, loss and abandonment actually mean glorification.

The psalm, and its explicit interpretation in 4Q171, is concerned not only with the protection of the righteous, but also with the punishment of the wicked. Ps 37:34-36, 38 reiterate the judgment the wicked face. Such statements make up almost every other verse of the psalm, which intersperses reassurances for the righteous with certainty that the wicked will be judged. Thus the focus is simultaneously the security of the righteous and coming judgment for those who seek to harm them.

What is not at issue in the psalm is innocence. Righteousness of a certain kind is assumed in the psalm. Yet while the psalm reassures those who trust in the Lord, those reassurances seem to be spoken to people who may be wavering in their trust. "Do not fret," it urges, "commit your way to the Lord" (vv. 1, 5). "Depart from evil, and do good" (v. 27) screams for attention in this context. While it would go too far to conclude that the author of Mark is communicating lack of faith or goodness with the use of this psalm (it has no such connotation in 4Q171), the psalm does not work to prove righteousness. There are a number of psalm texts which are well suited to that task, for example, Ps 7:3-5; 17:1-5; 26:1-12; 35:7-19; etc.; cf. Job 29-31. If Mark had been anxious to prove Jesus' innocence, he might have used one of these. He did not.

As for messianic apologetic, the psalm does little. It does have royal attribution, but otherwise says nothing about God's anointed. It provides assurances that extend to all who commit their way to the Lord. 4Q171 understands the psalm this way, applying its assurances to the Teacher of Righteousness (not a messianic figure) and to the community as a whole.

Blasphemy and Judgment: Mark 14:61 and Isa 36:21

Mark 14:61 may be an allusion to Isa 36:21. Let us see what it would add to the trial narrative, if it were included.

Blasphemy plays an important role in Mark in the relationship between Jesus and the leaders of Jerusalem. Jesus is not convicted on the basis of false witness, but for blasphemy. Yet that charge may ironically point back to the false witness. βλασφημία ("blasphemy") often means "slander" and in that sense is a synonym for ψευδομαρτυρία ("bearing false witness"). The leaders who sought witnesses to slander Jesus now convict him of slander. Again ironically, earlier in the narrative Jesus condemned them of blasphemy against the Holy Spirit and states they are "guilty of an eternal sin" (Mark 3:29-30).

The possible allusion to Isa 36:21 would again emphasize the theme of blasphemy. When the false witnesses speak, Jesus "*is silent and does not answer anything* (ὁ δὲ ἐσιώπα καὶ οὐκ ἀπεκρίνατο οὐδέν.)." Isa 36:21 reads, "*They were silent and no one answered a word* (καὶ ἐσιώπησαν, καὶ οὐδεὶς ἀπεκρίθη αὐτῷ λόγον)."[35] Here, during a siege of Jerusalem, Sennacherib's agent, Rabshekah, blasphemes (ὀνειδίζω) God (Isa 37:4, 6) by saying that Israel's God is no more able to save Jerusalem from Assyrian military might than the gods of the other nations could save them (Isa 36:18-20). The people of Jerusalem respond to this blasphemy with silence: "They were silent and no one answered a word." God however is not silent. After promising that Jerusalem will indeed be saved, the angel of the Lord kills 185,000 of the Assyrian troops (Isa 37:36).

Isaiah 36 is almost ignored in Christian literature, but it receives a good deal of attention in Jewish literature of the Second Temple period.[36] A notable parallel occurs in 1 Macc 7:34-43, where the story of Nicanor and the Maccabeans is clearly written to parallel this story in Isaiah. The narrative in 1 Maccabees takes up the theme of blaspheming God, as well as mockery and threats to Jerusalem, in this case specifically to the temple, and emphasizes the punishment the offenders receive, as does every other use of the story in Jewish literature.

Similarly, the Jewish trial in Mark, indeed the whole Passion Narrative, takes up the themes of blasphemy and mockery, threats to the temple, and the assurance that those who depend on God will be saved. The thematic correspondence with Isaiah 36-37 strengthens the case for the allusion. If an allusion is meant, Jesus' silence at the false witness, blasphemy, brought against him parallels the people's silence at the blasphemy Rabshekah brings against God. Instead of acting like Hezekiah

[35] Author's translations.

[36] See Sir 48:17-25; Jud 6:2-3; 1 Macc 7:41; 2 Macc 8:19; 15:22-24; *T. Adam* 4.6; Josephus, *Ant.* 10.1.2-4.

who prays to God for help, the Jerusalem leaders act like the Assyrians in that they slander God's agent and later even imply that God is unable to save as they mock Jesus on the cross (Mark 15:31-32). Use of the passage would be a strong condemnation of the Jerusalem leaders. As Jewish literature alluding to the passage emphasizes the Assyrians' punishment, Mark would be emphasizing the future punishment of the Jerusalem leaders. Since that punishment leads to the vindication and deliverance of Jerusalem, use of the passage would again point to God's future vindication and deliverance of Jesus.

Jesus Exalted: Mark 14:62 and Dan 7:13; Ps 110:1

Jesus' answer to the high priest in Mark 14:62 is a strong allusion to Dan 7:13 and Ps 110:1. This passage is rich in interpretive possibilities and hints at the redemptive meaning of the passion in Mark. We must confine ourselves, however, to the question of whether these passages function as apologetic.

First note that these passages show little concern to prove Jesus' innocence. Words concerning innocence and righteousness do not appear at all in these passages (though "holy ones" appears in Dan 7:22, 25, 27). Instead, they are concerned with power. Daniel 7 speaks of thrones and implies that the Son of Man will sit on one with the Ancient of Days.[37] This coincides with Ps 110:1, where the LORD requests that "my lord" sit at God's right hand. In Daniel 7:10-11, the Son of Man appears immediately after the court sits in judgment and does away with the king-beasts. Ps 110:5-6 declares that God will crush the kingdoms and judge the nations. Both passages speak of a kingdom of surpassing power, as well as of this new state lasting for eternity (Dan 7:14; Ps 110:4, 5-6).

Thus one primary focus of these allusions is Jesus' vindication, which goes well beyond anything expressed in the allusions treated so far. Jesus will not merely be protected. He will be exalted. He will be given an eternal kingdom.

That kingdom will not appear as a relief to his enemies. Psalm 110 is particularly threatening. The line alluded to runs, "The Lord said to my lord, 'Sit at my right hand until I make your enemies your footstool.'" Verses 5-6 speak of their total destruction. Daniel 7 is also concerned

[37] John J. Collins, *Daniel: A Commentary on the Book of Daniel* (Hermeneia; Minneapolis: Fortress Press, 1993), 301.

with judgment. The fourth beast is utterly destroyed (Dan 7:11, 26). The other beasts have their kingdoms taken away and given to the holy ones of God (Dan 7:12, 27).

In Mark 14:62, the allusions to Dan 7:13 and Ps 110:1 paint a consistent picture. Jesus is about to be exalted as a heavenly king and his reign will be everlasting. That reign will mean the judgment and subjugation of his enemies.

Vindication: Mark 14:65 and Isa 50:6

Mark 14:65 reads as follows:

> Some began to *spit* (ἐμπτύειν) on him, to cover his *face* (τὸ πρόσωπον), and to beat him, saying to him, "Prophesy!" The guards also took him over and *struck* (ῥαπίσμασιν) him.[38]

This alludes to Isa 50:6, which emphasizes obedience to God, even in difficult circumstances:

> The Lord GOD has opened my ear, and I was not rebellious, I did not turn backward. I gave my back to blows, and my cheeks to *strikes* (ῥαπίσματα); I did not turn my *face* (πρόσωπόν) from the insult of *spitting* (ἐμπτυσμάτων). (Isa 50:5-6)[39]

The reason for this steadfastness is the expectation that God will ultimately vindicate him:

> The Lord GOD helps me; therefore I have not been disgraced; therefore I have set my face like flint, and I know that I shall not be put to shame; he who vindicates me is near. (Isa 50:7-8a)

Using trial language, the speaker indicates that no one can overcome him, since God is on his side:

> Who will contend with me? Let us stand up together. Who are my adversaries? Let them confront me. It is the Lord GOD who helps me; who will declare me guilty? All of them will wear out like a garment; the moth will eat them up. (Isa 50:8b-9)

Like the speaker of Isa 50:6, Jesus submits to the trial, humiliation, and violence in obedience to God's will.

Here we have a passage which could certainly be understood as an argument for Jesus' innocence. Jesus is not guilty, but endures these punishments out of obedience. Still the focus is not on the speaker's

[38] NRSV modified.
[39] NRSV modified.

innocence but on his vindication by God. While the trial imagery does not include the speaker's self-defense, he will not be put to shame because God will act in his defense. On the other hand, those who condemn him will wear out like a garment eaten by moths. Again the passage condemns Jesus' opponents and contains a threat, though mild.

Summary: Vindication and Judgment

Taking the allusions together, a consistent theme is God's vindication of God's agent, something contained in nearly every passage. Ps 37:32 promises protection to the righteous, though the wicked seem to prosper; Isa 36:21 indicates protection against God's enemies, however powerful; Isa 50:6 speaks of vindication in the midst of trial and humiliation; Dan 7:13 and Ps 110:1 speak of exaltation. Only one passage, Isa 50:6, could be considered an attempt to defend Jesus' innocence, but even here innocence as a theme is subordinated to expectation of God's vindication. This is consistent with the explicit narrative in the Jewish trial, which does not clear Jesus from the charges made against him. The allusions focus on Jesus' vindication and take his righteousness for granted.

Judgment of Jesus' enemies is also a focus in most allusions. Using Exod 20:16 to portray the witnesses as false underscores the heinousness of their behavior and how contrary it is to the behavior necessary to enter the Reign of God. That use is particularly apparent in the emphasis on the subjection of enemies in Ps 110:1. Ps 37:32 points no less to the destruction of the psalmist's enemies, and Isa 36:21 focuses entirely on that subject. It is also a factor in Dan 7:13. The temple leaders face judgment, which Mark knows either to have come already or to be coming imminently, as a conclusion to the First Jewish Revolt. This emphasis on the guilt of the leadership is entirely in line with Mark's emphasis both on the destruction of the temple and the unworthiness of its leaders in chapters 11-13.[40] As with the allusions in the Jewish trial, the temple,

[40] On the "cleansing of the temple," see Juel, *Messiah and Temple*, 130-31; Ed P. Sanders, *Jesus and Judaism* (Philadelphia: Fortress, 1985), 61-76. On the use of temple allusions in the Parable of the Wicked Tenants, see G. J. Brooke, "4Q500 and the Use of Scripture in the Parable of the Vineyard," *Dead Sea Discoveries* 2 (1995): 268-294; Craig Evans, "On the Vineyard Parables of Isaiah 5 and Mark 12," *BZ* 28 (1984): 82-86; Evans, "Jesus and the Dead Sea Scrolls from Qumran Cave 4," in *Eschatology, Messianism, and the Dead Sea Scrolls* (ed. Craig Evans and Peter Flint; Grand Rapids: Eerdmans, 1997), 91-100.

its destruction, and the rejection of its leadership form an important focus of the entire Passion Narrative.

It is perhaps worth noting that all of the suggested allusions, with the exception of the possible allusion to Isa 36:21, have court themes. The allusion to Exod 20:16 highlights the commandment against bearing false witness. Isaiah 50 and Psalm 37 refer to trials. Daniel 7 refers to the heavenly court sitting in judgment. Even Psalm 110, which relies on more warlike imagery, begins with an invitation for "my lord" to sit at the Lord's right hand, ostensibly in a heavenly court. It is possible that the trial imagery is part of what drew early Christian attention to these passages.

The Jewish Trial Fits the Martyr Story Pattern

The Markan Jewish trial fits the pattern exhibited in Jewish martyr stories more closely than that of apologetic. There is no attempt to defend Jesus' innocence against the charges brought against him. Jesus' only response is that he is "guilty": "I am" (Mark 14:62). The council condemns him of blasphemy based on Jesus' own testimony, and Jesus does not protest or attempt to stop the injustice.

Jesus has been condemned for blasphemy, not cleared of it. It is important to remember Alexander's remark that mud tends to stick and that bringing accusations to the reader's attention without refuting them is not the tactic of an apologist. Likewise the false testimony is in some sense true. While Jesus did not say that he would destroy the temple, the reader is meant to compare this to Jesus' statement that the temple would be destroyed and to note the telling phrase about the temple being rebuilt in three days without hands. The passage is ironic, not apologetic.

Instead the focus of the allusions is on Jesus' vindication by God and the guilt and future punishment of Jesus' opponents. This is similar to the pattern of a martyr story. The martyr is indeed guilty as charged, but the martyr is obedient to God. The stories emphasize God's vindication of that obedience and judgment of those who perpetrate such injustice against the faithful.

The judgment passages in the Jewish trial are clearly polemical. If the Isa 36:21 passage is included, the polemic is extreme, and the Jewish leaders are compared to the Assyrians. Polemic is a characteristic of ancient trials. However while polemic can be a part of ancient apologetic, it is not sufficient by itself. It must be accompanied by an effort at defense. A charge with no defense, a trial whose literary purpose is to demonstrate the faithfulness of the one condemned, fits the type of the martyr story, not apologetic.

Wider Apologetic Concerns

While the use of Scripture in the Jewish trial points away from an apology for Jesus' innocence, it would be rash to conclude on just this basis that the Gospel never uses any apologetic of any kind.

One must ask, for example, does Mark employ apologetic in another sense in the Jewish trial? The Gospel, particularly the trial, does function to strengthen the resolve of readers, who are perhaps subject to mistreatment themselves. Jesus' injunctions to stand firm (Mark 8:34-38; 13:9-13) are emphasized in the contrast between Jesus' boldness and Peter's cowardice; this demonstrates to the audience what is necessary for discipleship and encourages the reader to persevere. Yet that is not a defense against a criticism. Encouragement is not apologetic.

Does Mark employ messianic apologetics in the Jewish trial to defend against Jewish criticism of Jesus as Messiah? This cannot be ruled out. Psalm 110 and Daniel 7 present Jesus as Messiah and indicate that after he is crucified, he will be exalted. In the remainder of the allusions, however, messianic apologetic is absent. At the same time, by having Jesus' claim to be the Messiah declared blasphemous by the high priest, to have the council agree to that charge, and most importantly to have that charge go unanswered tells against messianic *apology*. There is a great deal here that clarifies what is meant by *Christ*, but little to counter those who would argue Jesus was not the Christ. Something closer to messianic apologetic occurs in the temple debates in Mark 11:27-12:12 and 12:35-37.

This last observation leads to another: apologetic appears to be present in other sections of Mark. Mark 11-12, at least arguably, presents messianic apologetic. Droge finds apologetic in the first half of the Gospel: "Like other evangelists, Mark is also anxious to respond to Jewish accusations that Jesus was demon-possessed (3:19b-30 par.), that he did not fast (2:18-22 par.), keep the Sabbath (2:23-3:6 par.), or observe laws of ritual purity (7:1-23 par.), and that he associated with sinners and claimed authority to forgive sins (2:1-12 par.)."[41] While the

[41] Droge, *ABD* 1:303.

nature of some of these passages is debatable (some serve to illustrate who Jesus is), some may serve apologetic interests, defending Jesus himself or Christian practice where it is being condemned by other groups.

Moreover, while there is no apparent apologetic in the Jewish trial, the same cannot be said of the Roman trial. Since there are no allusions to Scripture in the Roman trial, analysis is limited to explicit narrative.[42] Here Jesus' conduct is ambiguous. His answer to Pilate's question, "Are you the King of the Jews?," is a non-answer, "You say so" (15:2). He does not deign to answer Pilate's vague, "See how many charges they bring against you" (15:4). In neither case does Jesus make a defense. On the other hand, this exchange looks nothing like a martyr story. It lacks the clarity, even audacity of the martyr faced with an unjust judge.

The presentation of Pilate is clearer. The narrator tells us that Pilate "realized that it was out of jealousy that the chief priests had handed him over" (15:10). He asks the crowd why they want Jesus crucified, saying, "Why, what evil has he done?" (15:14). Pilate clearly does not find Jesus guilty but hands him over to be crucified for political convenience (15:15). Jesus is cleared of the charges but killed. What is one to make of this?

One response is to call this *Roman* apologetic. Pilate and Rome are not guilty of this man's death; the Jewish leaders are. Vernon Robbins observes that the scene acquits "Pilate of any premeditation, or even desire to crucify Jesus." He goes on to say, "Pilate, so the narrative implies, delivered Jesus over for crucifixion only because he got 'caught' [by the chief priests] in the context of a setting of his usual benevolence – releasing a prisoner to the people in Jerusalem each year at their Passover festival."[43] It is certainly true that Pilate is acquitted of premeditation to crucify Jesus; yet Robbins seems on less solid ground concluding that Pilate was "caught." Did Pilate's "generosity" in releasing a prisoner somehow also *require* him to crucify innocent people who were brought to trial before him at the same time? As brutal as the Romans could be, one wonders whether a prefect was authorized to sentence to death a man he knew was innocent. One also wonders whether such a defense of Rome would have held much water with those readers who had suffered under their brutality. Whether Mark was

[42] See O'Brien, "Use of Scripture," 283-97.

[43] Vernon K. Robbins, *Exploring the Texture of Texts: A Guide to Socio-Rhetorical Interpretation* (Valley Forge: Trinity Press International, 1996), 25.

writing to Christians in Rome who had endured the persecutions of Nero or to Christians in or near Palestine who had endured the Roman response to the Jewish Revolt, that would be equally problematic. Since Pilate *did* sentence Jesus to death, emphasizing that Pilate believed Jesus was innocent merely emphasizes that Pilate was unjust. The behavior of the Roman soldiers, who mock and beat Jesus in the next scene, does little to exculpate the Romans either. If there is a defense of the Romans in Mark, it is rather weak.

Another possibility for Pilate's declaration of Jesus' innocence is that Mark's readers would have taken the Roman charge much more seriously than the high priest's charge. Mark's readers might have been either more scandalized by such a charge or more threatened by it. Since Jesus treats Pilate with some contempt, it seems less likely that they would have been more scandalized by it. If readers were allied with Roman interests, the Roman trial as a whole might have raised more problems than it resolved. On the other hand, it is reasonably likely that Mark's readers were threatened by the Roman charges. In the context of the Jewish Revolt, with recent persecutions of Christians in Rome, Mark's audience may well have been eager to avoid any further conflicts and anxious about a charge that they were dangerous to the state.

Another likely possibility is that the author wants the reader to understand clearly the meaning of the term "Christ" or "King." Illustrating who the Messiah is and what that means has been one of the primary tasks of the Gospel, especially in the Passion Narrative. While Jesus is King of the Jews, it is not true that Jesus was attempting to become a political king. That is not the nature of the Messiah. Jesus' power will come when he is "seated at the right hand of the Power" (Mark 14:62), not from anything that could be stopped by Roman soldiers or Roman crosses. If this is the case, then the author's primary concern is less to defend Jesus than to define him.

There does not appear to be enough evidence in this pericope to decide firmly between these possibilities. More of the Gospel needs to be taken into account. Whether and how the author of Mark employs apologetic in the remainder of the Gospel requires further examination. How much of what is apparent apologetic is simply an attempt to explain Jesus? How much is actual apologetic, reflecting charges made by others in the society? Answers to these questions could be used, with other evidence in the Gospel, to reconstruct Mark and his implied audience. Anxiety to refute Jewish criticisms of daily life would demonstrate that the audience considered itself Jewish in some sense. Anxiety to refute Roman criticisms would demonstrate either a delicate relationship with Rome or alliance with it. A careful and judicious examination of the Gospel, to see where apologetic genuinely lies, would tell us a great deal about whose opinions mattered to the group and what accusations needed to be countered.

Conclusion

While other Markan pericopes may have apologetic function, the Jewish trial does not. The overt narrative of the Jewish trial, like a martyr story, demonstrates Jesus' "guilt," not innocence. Allusions to Scripture are similar. They show Jesus as righteous and obedient to God. They assume innocence rather than argue for it. The allusions in the Jewish trial, again like the martyr stories, focus on Jesus' vindication and his adversaries' future punishment. Mark's audience appears to be unmoved by accusations from the Jerusalem leadership that Jesus was not the Messiah, that he was guilty of a true crime, and that he should be rejected. Like the people at the Dead Sea, the Christian community to which Mark writes seems to have little regard for the opinions of the Jewish leadership in Jerusalem and great regard for the worth of the man whose death founded their community.

THE IRONY OF POWER IN THE TRIAL OF JESUS AND THE DENIAL BY PETER – MARK 14:53-72

Tom SHEPHERD

In Markan studies of the trial of Jesus and the denial by Peter two questions of interpretation have drawn much attention – the charge of blasphemy and the broader question of the relationship of the disciples to Jesus, fallible followers or rejected leaders.[1] Many studies address these issues directly through literary, historical, redactional, social science, or other methods. In this study I propose an indirect approach. I will look at a related topic and then trace the implications it suggests for these contested issues. The advantage of this tactic is that the related topic does not have as its focus or goal to prove or disprove what the charge of blasphemy or the role of the disciples might be. As a topic somewhat more neutral to the debate, it may carry more weight in its outcomes in relation to the contested issues. These outcomes can stand as a verification or check of other research, bringing another line of evidence to bear on the issues.

The related topic I wish to address in this paper is power. Specifically, I wish to answer the question, What power transactions take place within the trial of Jesus and the denial by Peter?[2] To place this question in context I will review how Mark depicts the use of power throughout the

[1] See for instance Darrell Bock, *Blasphemy and Exaltation in Judaism and the Final Examination of Jesus: A Philological-Historical Study of the Key Jewish Themes Impacting Mark 14:61-64* (Tübingen: Mohr Siebeck, 1998) with its summary of many others' work, Werner Kelber, *The Oral and the Written Gospel* (Philadelphia: Fortress Press, 1983), Ernest Best, *Disciples and Discipleship: Studies in the Gospel According to Mark* (Edinburgh: T&T Clark, 1986), Clifton C. Black, *The Disciples according to Mark: Markan Redaction in Current Debate* (JSNT Supplement Series 27; Sheffield: JSOT Press, 1989), and Elizabeth Struthers Malbon, "Disciples/Crowds/Whoever: Markan Characters and Readers," *Novum Testamentum* 28 (1986): 104-130, and Malbon, "Texts and Contexts: Interpreting the Disciples in Mark," *Semeia* 62 (1993): 81-102 and Malbon, *In the Company of Jesus: Characters in Mark's Gospel* (Louisville: Westminster John Knox, 2000).

[2] By "power transactions" I mean the use of abilities or language to change physical, social, or spiritual status. An example is Jesus healing the leper in Mark 1, or forgiving the paralytic in Mark 2.

Gospel, especially the power of Jesus, and also note reactions to his power. Since the trial of Jesus and the denial by Peter are in the form of an intercalation in Mark, I will review the function of this story telling device. This will be followed by an analysis of Mark 14:53-72 for power transactions. Lastly, I will note the implications that this topic has for the charge of blasphemy and the relationship of the disciples to Jesus in Mark.

Power in Mark

It will be our purpose here to illustrate how the evangelist envisages and categorizes power in order to have a pattern of meaning within which to place the power transactions taking place within the trial and denial scenes. In one sense, it is possible to say that every scene of the Gospel contains an expression or transaction of power between individuals. While this is true, the breadth of analysis required to illustrate such transactions extends far beyond the available space for this study. Instead, we will focus on key words that express power and also make general statements about power relationships found throughout the Gospel.

The common words for power in Mark come from three roots, δύναμις / δύναμαι / δυνατός, ἰσχυρός / ἰσχυρότερος / ἰσχύς / ἰσχύω, and ἐξουσία. The first two roots focus on the ability to do some activity, while ἐξουσία centers on a status of power that enables one to make decisions or do mighty deeds.[3]

Δύναμις / δύναμαι / δυνατός are the most common terms for power in Mark, appearing together a total of 49 times (δύναμις 10 times, δύναμαι 33 times, δυνατός 5 times, and we add ἀδύνατος used once as a contrast to δυνατός in 10:27). Far and away, the interesting feature of the use of these terms in Mark is the negation of power or ability. Of the 49 uses by the evangelist, 21 are linked to a negative such as οὐ, οὐκ, μή, μηκέτι, etc.[4] Another 11 have possible or implied links to a negative (such as the question in 10:26 "Then who can be saved?").[5] Clearly, the negation of power or ability to do something plays a key

[3] See Werner Foerster, "ἔξεστιν, ἐξουσία, κτλ," *TDNT* 2:560-575, note especially p. 562.

[4] 1:27; 2:4, 19; 3:20, 24, 25, 26, 27; 5:3; 6:5 (twice), 19; 7:18, 24; 9:3, 28, 29, 39; 10:27 (ἀδύνατος); 12:24; 15:31.

[5] 1:40; 2:7; 3:23; 7:15; 8:4; 9:22, 23; 10:26, 38; 13:22; 14:5.

role in Mark. And this negation of ability even extends to Jesus in several fascinating passages – 1:45 (Jesus can no longer enter a city publicly; cf. 1:44, the leper does not obey); 3:20 (they cannot eat a meal); 6:5 (Jesus could not do a miracle there, lack of faith the cause); 7:24 (he could not escape notice; cf. 7:36, he commands them not to speak, they tell the more); 15:31 (he saved others, he cannot save himself).[6]

Juxtaposed to this rather intriguing inability of Jesus to do certain things is his obvious power to do amazing miracles – heal lepers, rebuke fevers, cast out demons, calm wind and waves, raise the dead, and his obvious authority in teaching (see below). Indeed, everyone in the Gospel who comes to him for help receives it, and no one bests him in argumentation.[7] We will note below how this rather interesting paradox about Jesus and power (what he can and cannot do) reappears in the trial scene.

Ἰσχυρός / ἰσχυρότερος / ἰσχύς / ἰσχύω in comparison with δύναμις / δύναμαι / δυνατός are used much less often in Mark, only 9 times.[8] This word group has as its subject such diverse groups as Jesus, the strong who do not need a physician, Satan, a demoniac, the disciples, any person, and Peter. Although such diversity of subjects for the terms is present, yet there actually is a recurring theme – Jesus is powerful. In 1:7 John the Baptist says Jesus is stronger than he. In 2:17 the sick need a physician, clearly Jesus, who is "authorized" as a "physician" to help sinners. In 3:27 the strong man, Satan, will be bound, it is implied, by Jesus. In 5:4 while no one can subdue the demoniac, Jesus does. In 9:18 where the disciples fail in exorcising a mute spirit, Jesus succeeds. In 14:37 where Peter fails to stay awake and pray, Jesus pours his heart out to God in prayer. Consistently, the message concerning this word group is that Jesus is able to do what others cannot.

It is worthwhile to place the concept of ability and inability discussed above within the context of Elizabeth Struthers Malbon's interesting perspective on the Markan characters in their relationship to Jesus.[9] Malbon

[6] One can also add Jesus' prayer in 14:35-36 which receives a rather obvious "no" answer. On the relationship between Jesus' suffering and the question of power cf. Sharyn Dowd, *Prayer, Power, and the Problem of Suffering: Mark 11:22-25 in the Context of Markan Theology* (Atlanta: Scholars Press, 1988), 157-158, 161.

[7] There is the interesting exception of the Syrophoenician woman who is desperate to save her daughter and uses Jesus' own reasoning to get what she wants. Is this another illustration of what Jesus cannot do, cannot say "no" to desperation?

[8] 1:7; 2:17; 3:27 (twice); 5:4; 9:18; 12:30, 33; 14:37.

[9] See Elizabeth Struthers Malbon, "'Reflected Christology': An Aspect of Narrative 'Christology' in the Gospel of Mark," *Perspectives in Religious Studies* 26 (1999): 127-145. Note especially the discussion on pp. 130-136 on areas of conflict in Mark, and the diagrams on pp. 144-145.

points to three areas of conflict in Mark – the struggle between God and Satan, the struggle between Jesus and the authorities, and the conflict between Jesus and the disciples. In relation to what Malbon calls the transcendental characters, we note here that Jesus always wins in conflict with the "bad" transcendental characters, Satan, demons, unclean spirits. In relation to the "good" transcendental characters, Jesus receives the Holy Spirit, is ministered to by angels, and submits to God. There is a clear sense of hierarchy and "sidedness." Jesus will always win against the bad side and will receive help from and submit to the good side.[10]

But it is in relation to Malbon's category of the human characters that an interesting fact arises concerning Jesus' ability and inability. All of the instances of Jesus' inability that we have noted above have to do with the human characters, and not on just one side of the controversy. In 1:45 and 7:24 it is issues of publicity that Jesus in unable to keep under wraps. Playing upon the secrecy motif this inability of Jesus suggests that the message about him, this εὐαγγέλιον, has a characteristic nature that not even Jesus himself can stop from spreading.[11]

But the inabilities of Jesus in 6:5 and 15:31 have to do with human characters that do not believe in him.[12] He is unable to do miracles for those without faith (6:5), and, in the mocking words of his enemies, he cannot save himself (15:31). Both ideas revolve around the issue of healing (σῴζω) in either its physical or deeper salvific form.[13] It is instructive that the evangelist posits that such healing or saving requires more than a divine component to take place, especially in light of the fact that Jesus never has any difficulty in overcoming the demonic transcendental characters. Human willingness or belief is requisite for Jesus

[10] Malbon notes the hierarchal concept in her statement, "While the conflict between God and Satan is clearly a mismatch in God's favor,..." Ibid., 133, cf. also p. 131.

[11] The secrecy motif is better described as a secrecy/revelation motif since both ideas are prevalent in the Markan narrative and to analyze only secrecy is to miss the key to the motif's meaning.

[12] The case of 3:20 could be added ("they were not able even to eat bread"). This lack of taking meals leads Jesus' relatives to set out to take charge of him because they feel he is acting insanely. This is a case of "friends" (relatives) who prove to be outsiders (see 3:31-35).

[13] I assume here that the use of σῴζω in 15:31 is pregnant with a meaning beyond Jesus being able to physically save himself from the suffering of the cross. Certainly it does not hold this broader salvific sense for the religious leaders who make the statement, but it does carry much deeper meaning from the narrator's perspective. The irony of the religious leaders' words carries a powerful weight. Before they state that he cannot save himself they say "he saved others," (15:31). At the foot of the cross, the enemies of Jesus declare him to be the Savior.

to heal in 6:5. Its absence makes healing impossible. In 15:31 what the religious leaders mockingly call impossible would be possible if Jesus the man had willed it earlier by running away rather than wrestling with God in prayer in Gethsemane. Again the component of human willingness enters. Transcendental characters can be conquered against their will, "conquering" human characters seems to require their consent.[14]

The use of ἐξουσία in Mark can be conveniently divided into the two halves of the book. In chapters 1-8 the term is used five times.[15] In each case it is connected with miraculous powers used by Jesus or his disciples, either to cast out demons, or to cause a person to walk.[16] There is also a link to the teaching of Jesus in 1:22, 27. The predominant pattern seems to combine a concept of δύναμις with ἐξουσία. However, the usage in 2:10 is especially interesting in that it links the power to cause the paralyzed man to walk with the authority of Jesus to forgive sins. Not surprisingly when Jesus actually tells the man his sins are forgiven in 2:5 this calls forth from the religious leaders the charge of blasphemy (2:6-7). It is instructive then, that this early in the Gospel there is a conjunction of miraculous power, divine authority, and a sharp reaction with the charge of blasphemy. Again we will see the conjunction of these ideas in the trial scene.

In the second half of Mark ἐξουσία (or its cognate κατεξουσιάζω in 10:42) appears six times, but never in conjunction with miraculous powers.[17] In these cases the primary focus is on the status of authority given by a higher authority figure, or used by that higher authority figure (great ones 10:42; an assumed authority higher than Jesus, never named, 11:28-29, 33; and a householder 13:34). The uses in 10:42 and 13:34 particularly relate to Jesus' teaching about authority to his disciples with a sense that they are not to use authority as the world does, but are to be

[14] A rather interesting reversal of our expectations. We expect transcendental characters to conquer without "permission" but hardly expect that humans must give consent.

[15] 1:22, 27; 2:10; 3:15; 6:7.

[16] Anne Dawson maintains that the term ἐξουσία is best translated "freedom to act" in Mark. She places ἐξουσία within the context of the Roman world *Res Gestae* inscription and posits that the influence of this text extended throughout the Mediterranean world. However, in Mark, ἐξουσία is used only in relation to Jesus' healing and teaching ministry and his sharing of ἐξουσία with his disciples for healing and teaching. When he heals or forgives sin or teaches, it hardly seems as though he has been given "freedom to act" in this way. Rather, it seems more appropriate to think of his ἐξουσία as "power" or "authority" to act in a certain way. See Anne Dawson, *Freedom as Liberating Power* (Novum Testamentum et Orbis Antiquus 44; Göttingen: Vandenhoeck & Ruprecht, 2000), 10-11. See also pp. 58-62 and 127-129.

[17] 10:42; 11:28 (twice), 29, 33; 13:34.

faithful to their Master in service to others.[18] The uses in Mark 11 center around the question of Jesus' authorization for his action of clearing the temple. Jesus' repartee against his opponents suggests that he recognizes that to approach such a topic with these leaders is to invite dangerous repercussions. But their inability to answer his question leaves hanging the issue of his authorization to clear the temple. However, the reader needs no further instruction on the topic. He/she already knows that the power of God is the motive force and authority in all of Jesus' actions.

The above noted terms give some idea of the extent of expressions of power and authority within Mark, but do not catch all of the nuances. Besides the above noted key terms related to power, Mark also indicates concepts of power via the use of titles, actions of Jesus, and reactions to him. The titles linked to Jesus are in highest concentration in chapter 1 with a comparison between Jesus and John the Baptist and with the declaration at the baptism, in chapter 8 with the confession of Jesus as Messiah, in chapter 9 at the transfiguration, and in chapters 14 and 15 in the trial scenes and the cross. The titles used for Jesus and positively affirmed by the implied author's standards of judgment are consistently ones of high status – mightier one, holy one of God, Lord, Son of God, Messiah, King of the Jews.[19] Except in the Passion Narrative these are often linked with theophanic displays of the glory or the voice of God.

Not surprisingly, Jesus is at the center of power and power relations in the book. He uses power in both positive and negative ways. His positive use of power involves healing the sick, casting out demons, raising

[18] Tat-Siong Benny Liew, in "Tyranny, Boundary and Might: Colonial Mimicry in Mark's Gospel," *JSNT* 73 (1999): 7-31, makes the point that Mark continues a system of controlling authority in the new kingdom, in this case the authority of Jesus and of God. However, it seems to me that Liew misses several important points concerning Mark's story. First, the uses of ἐξουσία in Mark 1 do not necessarily mean that Jesus' message is his authority (Liew, "Tyranny," 24). In Mark 1:22, the congregation is amazed at his teaching before he does any healing. The evangelist notes that this occurs because he was teaching them as one having authority. The ἐξουσία gives power or credence to his teaching, it is not necessarily equivalent to it. Second, Liew acknowledges Jesus' words of Mark 10:42-45 as Jesus' manner of dealing with his disciples (Liew, "Tyranny," 18), but then Liew goes on to indicate that Jesus treats the disciples like slaves and "gophers" (would not "go-fers" be a better way to put it?). This is to deny that Mark 10:42-45 means anything about the use of authority. Indeed, Liew concludes (Liew, "Tyranny," 27), "... Mark still understands authority as the ability to have one's commands obeyed and followed, or the power to wipe out those who do not." But this viewpoint misses the true irony of the Markan view of power, as will become evident below.

[19] See below for negative valuations of Jesus by the unenlightened or negative characters in the story.

the dead, feeding people, teaching people, instructing his disciples, and foretelling the future.[20] However, some of Jesus' use of power carries a negative connotation, at least for those he "conquers." The demons resist him but are defeated. The Gadarene demoniac's case is instructive in this regard. The man bows before Jesus (προσεκύνησεν αὐτῷ 5:6) but the demons in him resist. They beg not to be sent out of the country and are allowed to enter the pigs (the demons seem to win by not being sent away). But then the pigs all drown (the demons lose). However, the local people are afraid and ask Jesus to leave the region (Jesus seems to lose). But then he sends the healed man back to tell his story (Jesus wins). This incident illustrates the back and forth struggle between spiritual forces in the book, and the "sidedness" of the conflict. It depends on which "side" you are on as to how you see the use of power. For the demons Jesus is an invader ("Have you come to destroy us?" 1:24). But for people he is a deliverer, a savior.

But Jesus is not only resisted by demons. People resist his use of power as well. From the beginning of chapter 2 the religious authorities become opponents of Jesus' use of power. They question his authority to forgive sin (2:7), his association with "sinners" (2:16), and his disciples' Sabbath observance (2:24), and they disagree with his healing on the Sabbath (3:2). They also react to his ministry by claiming he casts out demons by Beelzebub (3:22). They complain about purity issues (7:1-5) and take deep offense at his clearing of the temple (11:28). Their resistance culminates in the trial before the high priest (14:55-65) and the crucifixion (15:29-32). Throughout these passages the religious leaders use negative titles or valuations with reference to Jesus, in sharp contrast to what disciples, God, and even demons say about him.[21] Interestingly, there is a power reversal in the Passion Narrative. Where Jesus had been the conquering healer and savior, he becomes the passive pawn (except for his exalted claim in the trial, see below), arrested, tried, beaten, crucified. It is only in the resurrection that the reversion to power occurs.

In summary, Mark displays power in numerous ways, focused around Jesus and the reaction to him. The display of power is paradoxical. On the one hand, Jesus is the mighty healer, conqueror of demons, feeder of 5000, able to walk on water, addressed with positive, powerful titles. On the other hand, he experiences provocative negations of his power – the inability to silence witnesses and to escape notice (tying into the secrecy/revelation

[20] All illustrations of his positive sense of using power to serve, 10:42-45.

[21] The friendly scribe in 12:28-34 is an intriguing exception.

motif), the limitation on healing because of unbelief, the prayer in Gethsemane that receives a negative answer, the negative titles applied to him by the religious leaders, and finally death on the cross where he cannot save himself. It is truly an intriguingly paradoxical view of power, both in its positive and negative displays. We now turn to the trial of Jesus and the denial by Peter to investigate the display of power in these scenes.

The Trial of Jesus and Denial by Peter

I have argued elsewhere that the trial of Jesus and the denial by Peter in Mark 14:53-72 is a Markan intercalation which fulfills a narrative function of displaying dramatized irony.[22] To briefly reiterate my argumentation in these studies: I began with a list of the passages most commonly designated as intercalations by numerous scholars.[23] I then carried out a narrative analysis of these passages investigating their settings, characters, actions and plot, time relationships, narrator and implied reader, and features of style. What emerged from this research was a set of story telling characteristics which define Markan intercalation (helpful in determining if a proposed passage is an intercalation, and helpful for recognizing just how the story telling technique is displayed). What also emerged was the narrative function which the intercalations have in common – displaying dramatized irony.

Some of the interesting story telling characteristics that define Markan intercalation include:

1. **Settings** – The outer and inner stories are focalized in separate locations, but may end in the same location.[24] The outer story is never completely defocalized when the inner story begins. There is always

[22] See Tom Shepherd, *Markan Sandwich Stories: Narration, Definition, and Function* (Andrews University Doctoral Dissertation Series 18; Berrien Springs, Mich.: Andrews University Press, 1993), and Shepherd, "The Narrative Function of Markan Intercalation," *NTS* 41 (1995): 522-540. Cf. James Edward's perspective on intercalation in James R. Edwards, "Markan Sandwiches: The Significance of Interpolations in Markan Narratives," *Novum Testamentum* 31 (July 1989) 3: 193-216, and Geert van Oyen's critique of my work and others in Geert van Oyen, "Intercalation and Irony in the Gospel of Mark," in *The Four Gospels 1992: Festschrift Frans Neirynck*, (ed. F. van Segbroeck, et. al.; 2 vols.; Leuven: Leuven University Press, 1992), 2:949-974.

[23] Twenty passages at least have been suggested, but the ones I studied (3:20-35; 5:21-43; 6:7-32; 11:12-25; 14:1-11; 14:53-72) were listed in common by more scholars. See Shepherd, *Markan Sandwich Stories*, 388-392.

[24] "Focalization" here refers to the manner in which story participants are brought together at a certain time in a certain place in the story. Defocalizaiton is the reversal of this process where they are dispersed.

some gap for the outer story that is not filled until the rejoining of the outer story.

2. **Characters** – Major characters (with the exception of Jesus and sometimes his disciples) do not pass between the inner and outer stories. It is as though the stories are brought together, but held apart.
3. **Actions and plot** – Parallel actions are done by contrasting characters or contrasting actions are done by parallel characters.

With regards to the narrative function of Markan intercalation I found that the evangelist by his story telling technique brought two stories together not only in the telling, but also in the way the characters of the stories have so many parallels and contrasts to one another. And yet, the evangelist also held the stories apart via lack of character cross over between stories, and via the focalization and defocalization techniques noted above. This bringing of stories together while holding them apart for comparison led to a consideration of irony.

The subject of irony has a rich history. G.G. Sedgewick outlines this in his interesting, *Of Irony: Especially in Drama*.[25] For the ancient Greek rhetoricians irony was to say one thing and mean another.[26] For Socrates it took on another trait, that of understatement. He treated his students as the "wise ones" of whom he asked questions as the εἴρων ("one who says less than he thinks").[27] Using a method of self-discovery, he would lead the students through questions which would illustrate who really was the wise one and who were the ignorant and bring about learning.

This sense of understatement and of someone who does not realize that they are really ignorant was displayed in ancient Greek plays such as those of Aristophanes and Sophocles.[28] An ironic character (εἴρων) was set against a boaster (ἀλαζών) who was ignorant of his real position. The εἴρων would understate his abilities or position and would triumph over the ἀλαζών in the end, to the delight of the audience who were in on the irony.

This concept of irony in dramatic scene, or dramatized irony, is well illustrated by D.C. Muecke's definition of irony in *The Compass of Irony*.[29] Muecke explains that irony has three characteristics:

[25] G. G. Sedgewick, *Of Irony: Especially in Drama* (Toronto: University of Toronto Press, 1967).
[26] Ibid., 5.
[27] Ibid., 10-13.
[28] See Ibid., 34-36 and Stephen Smith, *A Lion with Wings: A Narrative-Critical Approach to Mark's Gospel* (Sheffield: Sheffield Academic Press, 1996), 192-195.
[29] D. C. Muecke, *The Compass of Irony* (London: Methuen & Co., 1969), 19-20.

1. Irony has a two-layered characteristic. There is the lower level, the situation as viewed by the victim of the irony. Then there is the upper level, the situation as it appears to the observer or ironist.
2. There is opposition between the two levels, they stand in contrast to one another.
3. Someone does not see the irony – the ἀλαζών.

Muecke names the three qualities, duality, opposition of terms, and alazony, respectively.

It is exactly these three characteristics which appear in the Markan intercalations. The technique of the evangelist in bringing two stories together, and yet holding them somewhat separate from each other, lends itself to displaying ironic situations. As there are two stories that comment on one another there are two levels of meaning for the reader to consider. The character contrasts – similar characters doing opposite actions or opposite characters doing similar actions – fits the opposition of levels characteristic of irony. And there are always characters in the intercalations who take the role of ἀλαζών. Because the traits of dramatized irony appear consistently in all the intercalations I studied, it seems appropriate to suggest that this was an intentional story telling technique of the evangelist.[30]

In the intercalation of 14:53-72 the central dramatized irony centers around the actions of Peter in contrast to those of Jesus. Put succinctly, the dramatized irony is that as Peter fails in his discipleship by denying Jesus with an oath, he actually proves that Jesus is the Messiah by fulfilling one of Jesus' predictions (14:27-31).[31]

This brings us to the question of how power is displayed in the trial of Jesus and the denial by Peter and how this interacts with the question of irony in the two scenes linked via intercalation. We noted above that Mark presents Jesus as a complex powerful figure. He has amazing abilities: healing, teaching, commanding, walking on water, raising the dead, and he is addressed with powerful positive titles. But he also is

[30] On intended versus unintended irony see Smith, *A Lion with Wings*, 217-218. Note his reference to blasphemy in 2:7 and 14:61-62 in this context, p. 218.

[31] Cf. the close of the trial scene where Jesus is mockingly called on to prophesy, 14:65. In 14:66-72 Peter "answers" their command and proves Jesus right. The mockers are thinking of Jesus' prophecy about sitting at God's right hand in 14:62, as van Oyen rightly points out, van Oyen, "Intercalation and Irony," 971, holding this up for ridicule in comparison with Jesus' inability to respond to their demand for prophecy (traditionally seen as a demand for telling who struck him). But the mockers become one set of alazons since they do not see what the reader does – that Peter fulfills Jesus' prophecy of 14:27-31 to the letter.

limited in what he can do and his display of power calls forth negative titles from the religious leaders.[32]

In the trial scene the display of power changes. Jesus no longer leads in the action, he is the recipient of actions. The religious leaders are in control and, as the summary statement 14:55 states, they seek testimony against Jesus to put him to death.

But the trial does not seem to proceed as planned. As the evangelist succinctly summarizes – "they did not find it" (the testimony they sought, 14:55). There are three unsuccessful attempts to procure damning testimony against Jesus, first by false witnesses who do not agree (14:56), then two false witnesses bring a charge against Jesus that he stated he would destroy the hand made temple and during three days construct another, not made by hand (14:58), and finally the high priest asks Jesus about the charges against him, to which he responds with silence (14:60-61). As Dowd points out, at this point it seems the trial could still lead to acquittal, they have not proved anything.[33]

All of this takes an abrupt turn when the high priest asks Jesus directly if he is the Christ, the Son of the Blessed One. The high priest uses his position of authority to try to force Jesus to condemn himself. Jesus responds in the most affirmative terms. He says, "I am, and you will see the Son of Man seated at the right hand of Power and coming with the clouds of heaven."[34] Jesus' response makes a claim to almost the highest position of authority imaginable. He claims he will sit at God's right hand (interestingly for our discussion, using the term "Power" as a circumlocution for God's name) and, quoting Dan 7:13, that he will come on the clouds, all of this visible to the religious leaders bringing charges against him.

It is this which leads finally to Jesus' condemnation. The high priest tears his robes (likely a sign of horror at Jesus' claim to power and the disrespect to God the high priest interprets this to mean).[35] Then he calls Jesus' words blasphemy, as negative and strong a rejection of Jesus'

[32] For a useful modern classification of power see Dennis H. Wrong, *Power: Its Forms, Bases and Uses* (New York: Harper & Row, 1979) 21-64. There is a useful chart on p. 24.

[33] Dowd, *Prayer, Power, and the Problem of Suffering*, 157.

[34] Note the circumlocution for the divine name by both the high priest and Jesus.

[35] See John R. Donahue and Daniel J. Harrington, *The Gospel of Mark* (Sacra Pagina Series 2; Collegeville, Minn.: Liturgical Press, 2002), 423. Cf. Raymond Brown, *The Death of the Messiah* (ABRL, 2 vol.; New York: Doubleday, 1994), 2:517-519, and Robert H. Gundry, *Mark: A Commentary on His Apology for the Cross* (Grand Rapids: Eerdmans, 1993), 914, 917.

claim as were positive and powerful the words of Jesus.[36] The death sentence follows and then the beginning of the application of physical force to Jesus – spitting on him, blindfolding him, hitting him, mocking his prophetic powers, and more blows.

Turning to the denial by Peter we see parallel and contrasting patterns of power relations. Typical of intercalations in Mark, contrasting characters do similar actions and similar characters do contrasting actions. In contrast to the highest religious authority of the nation who accuses Jesus, it is only a slave girl and by-standers who point the finger at Peter, seeking to link him to Jesus.[37] Peter recognizes this as a threat, and unlike his Master, he immediately responds to save himself. The accusations and denials build to the climax when Peter uses the terms ἀναθεματίζω ("to be under a curse") and ὀμνύω ("to swear an oath"), calling on God as witness and judge of the veracity of his claim to not know "this man of whom you speak."[38] It is then that a rooster crows and Peter suddenly remembers Jesus' prophecy. He breaks down in tears – his own loss of power to a position of weakness, as he recognizes his failure and alazony.

We noted above that the Markan intercalations fulfill a function of illustrating dramatized irony. Does this extend to the issues of power displayed in the trial and denial scenes? I think it does so in the following ways. Jesus' enemies seek the death sentence against him, the ultimate withdrawal of power, but they seem powerless to bring the plan to fruition until Jesus, acknowledging the authority of the high priest, makes a claim to almost the highest position of authority possible. This

[36] Cf. the parallel to 2:5-10 where Jesus forgives sins and the scribes call this blasphemy but which Jesus proves by causing the man to walk.

[37] "*only* a slave girl " in the sense of the standards of judgment of that era.

[38] It is clear that ὀμνύω means "to swear an oath" in this passage. Peter takes a judicial oath. Less certain is the meaning of ἀναθεματίζω. The term and its related noun ἀνάθεμα ("something dedicated to the deity, cursed") are used only ten times in the New Testament (cf. the parallel term καταθεματίζω ["to curse"] in Matt 26:74 and the noun καταθέμα ["accursed thing"] in Rev 22:3, the only uses for these terms in the New Testament). Some argue that Peter is directly cursing Jesus (cf. Brown, *Death of the Messiah*, 1:604-605 and Gundry, *Mark*, 890). Mark's use and the parallel term in Matthew are the only instances where there is no direct object or reflexive object named in the New Testament uses (one may also include Rev 22:3 which simply speaks of there being no more curse). But if Mark wished to make the point that Peter actually cursed Jesus, it seems odd that he does not supply the object. Furthermore, the content of his swearing and oath is expressed in 14:71, "I do not know this man whom you speak of." Could he really name Jesus in a curse if he wished to say he did not know him? Therefore, it seems more likely that Peter curses himself, similar to a present day type of oath, "May God strike me dead with lightning if I am not telling the truth!"

makes it possible for the religious leaders to fulfill their plan – they declare his statement blasphemy and pass the death sentence on him. But in fulfilling their plan they actually make it possible for Jesus to attain the claim he has made. It is through resurrection that he will sit at God's right hand. The irony, therefore, is rather rich. The powerful cannot fulfill their plan until Jesus makes his declaration of power, gives them the power to act, so to speak. But in bringing him to death, removing his power, they actually bring him to power at God's right hand.

In the denial scene the irony is also present, but to understand this it is necessary to consider the denial scene in conjunction with the scene of Jesus' prediction of Peter's denial in 14:27-31. Jesus there predicted his own death, the scattering of his followers, and his resurrection and reunion with them. But Peter counters that he will not forsake Jesus. Then Jesus predicts his denial. But Peter continues to insist, "If it is necessary for me to die with you, I will never deny you!"

Exegetes have noted the way that 14:27-31 illustrates a shift in the disciples – now they are prepared to die with Jesus.[39] Peter's rejection of Jesus' prophecy of his denial lays claim to Jesus' maxim in 8:35b, "But whoever loses his life for my sake and the Gospel's will save it." One might say that Peter counters the power of Jesus' prophetic gift, by a claim to living by Jesus' maxim in 8:35b. It is a claim to power and strength on Peter's part that uses one saying of Jesus (the appeal of 8:35b) against another (the prophecy of 14:27-31). But in Mark 14:72 with the conjunction of his own failure and the remembrance of Jesus' prophecy, Peter comes to a new understanding of himself, and weeps – a demonstration of weakness.

Where is the irony in this? Just this – Peter laid claim to 8:35b in his rejection of Jesus' prophecy in 14:27-31, but in his denial of Jesus he actually fulfills not only the words of Jesus in 14:27-31 but also Jesus' words in 8:35a, and 8:36-38. He seems the perfect fulfillment and illustration of one who seeks to save his life but loses it, who is ashamed of Jesus in this "adulterous and sinful generation." Thus we answer the original question we raised, "what power transactions take place in the trial of Jesus and the denial by Peter?" Jesus gives up power to gain it, and Peter seeks to preserve power but loses it.

[39] See Thomas P. Haverly, "Reversals in Mark's Passion Narrative and the Characterization of Peter," (paper presented at the annual meeting of the Society of Biblical Literature, November 1989), 16-17. See also Thomas Haverly, "Conversion Narratives: Wesley's Journal and Mark's Gospel," *Journal of the Wesleyan Theological Society* 24 (1989): 54-73; William Lane, *The Gospel of Mark* (NICNT; Grand Rapids: Eerdmans, 1974), 512; and Gundry, *Mark*, 851.

It is a repeat of that paradoxical concept of power which we saw illustrated in the expression of Jesus' amazing abilities brought into conjunction with his inability to do certain things, and in his teaching that power must be used to serve others, not to be served by them, 10:42-45. But in the trial this concept of power is displayed within the context of irony – things are not as they seem on the surface. The intercalation brings before the reader the characters who should be alike, but are not; the trial that is failing to convict, but finds its great opening when the accused makes a claim to almost the highest authority possible. The conviction of Jesus will lead to his death – and his resurrection, and thus his ascension to the power he claimed. The denial by Peter actually turns out to prove that Jesus is Messiah and brings Peter where he has not been before – weakness.[40] The ironic vision of power in Mark is that the path to power is through weakness. A man must lose his life to save it.

Implications of the Irony of Power

The concept of the irony of power in the trial of Jesus and the denial by Peter has implications for the two questions we raised at the beginning of this study – the charge of blasphemy and the question of discipleship.

The charge of blasphemy has been an area of intense research, revolving around the question of just what the blasphemy would consist of and whether the scene as depicted in Mark can lay a claim to historical veracity. In considering this issue sometimes the narrative setting of the charge is overlooked or underestimated. This may be based in the distinction between history as a diachronic phenomenon and narrative as a synchronic depiction. However, Petri Merenlahti, following Kari Syreeni, has recently illustrated how there are actually three levels that interplay, the concrete world of history, the symbolic world of ideology, and the text world of story.[41] Much of the debate over the charge of blasphemy addresses the concrete world of history. Attempts are made to comb the text world for historically verifiable data that help us to reconstruct what actually happened. However, following Syreeni's lead, we can utilize the text's expression of story and ideology to at least give a clearer window on the concrete world of history, if not to even narrow the possible options for what actually occurred.

[40] Below we will see what implication this has for the question of discipleship in Mark.
[41] See Petri Merenlahti, *Poetics for the Gospels? Rethinking Narrative Criticism*, (London: T & T Clark, 2002), 119-124.

It is obvious from what we have said above that the narrative of Mark depicts a decidedly Christian ideology on the events of the life of Jesus.[42] He is the hero of the story, the Son of God proclaimed as such from the beginning. Power is displayed throughout the Gospel as the interplay between opposing groups, those for or against Jesus, and Jesus himself as the central player. The concept of "blasphemy" carries strong ideological weight. From the perspective of a speaker in the narrative, the one whose actions or words receive this epithet is wrong, bad, cut off from God. Since this term in both its verbal and nominal forms is found on the lips of Jesus' opponents in chapters 2, 14, and 15, in each case applied to Jesus, it is clear that the evangelist's own ideology stands in contrast to the ideology of these leaders as depicted in the story.[43]

In Mark 14 the charge of blasphemy by the high priest is made in response to Jesus' claim to sit at God's right hand in the future. As depicted by the evangelist, what did this charge mean? Since we are working at the level of narrative, it is possible to use the characteristics of the intercalation story-telling device to narrow the semantic domain of the terminology for blasphemy. Because in Markan intercalations contrasting characters often perform similar actions (or vice versa), the inner story's use of the term "blasphemy" likely has parallel terminology in the outer story that can serve as an interpretive key to the evangelist's ideological meaning in utilizing the term in the inner story. This in turn can inform concrete historical investigation of the charge against Jesus at his trial.

The powerful charge of blasphemy (βλασφημία) by the high priest in the inner story finds its echo in the outer story in Peter's use of words of

[42] I find the term "ideology" somewhat inadequate for describing the interaction of the implied author with the implied reader in the text of Mark. Ideology suggests a viewpoint or set of values that guide a person in expressing their perspective on reality. This is true as far as it goes. However, it seems to me that in dealing with a religious ideology that posits belief in a Supreme Being who reveals truth to humanity, there is a vertical aspect of the value system which goes beyond the mere horizontal perspective of people with differing opinions, values, and world views interacting with one another. The belief in this Supreme Being and the consequent revelation held in common by the author and the reader creates a sense of sacred text which defines a community with a broader world view and experience than the term "ideology" implies. Theology might well be a better term to use, though it is usually seen as the encapsulation of beliefs about the divine and other common theological categories. These do not often encompass the broad type of values and valuation which are inherent within the term ideology. So, while protesting the semantic domain of "ideology" as inadequate, I will use the term.

[43] Jesus himself uses the nominal and verbal forms in chapter 3 and the nominal form in chapter 7. He applies the term to rejection of his ministry and in a general sense of affront to God.

power, ἀναθεματίζω and ὀμνύω. We noted above the way in which these two terms call on God as witness to the veracity of Peter's words. The legitimacy of God's authority becomes the grounds for Peter's claim that he does not know Jesus. Because of the interconnections of the intercalation it is likely that the high priest's charge of blasphemy makes a parallel link to God's authority. The legitimacy of God's authority becomes the grounds for the high priest's charge that Jesus' words are blasphemy. That is to say, the high priest charges that Jesus' words are absolutely in contrast with the authority and position of God and out of step with the high priest's ideology. Where Peter called on God as his witness that he was telling the truth (which he was not), the high priest utilized his sense of God's position and honor to call down an imprecation on Jesus' claim (in the Markan story also incorrect). It thus seems likely that the charge of blasphemy has more to do with these issues than with the pronunciation of the Tetragrammaton.[44]

This finding seconds the work of Darrell Bock on the charge of blasphemy.[45] After careful consideration of blasphemy and of the concept of exalted figures in Judaism, Bock concludes that Jesus' words were considered blasphemous on two levels – as a claim to comprehensive authority, and as an attack on the religious leadership.[46]

On the question of discipleship in Mark there are two main opposing groups – those who see the Gospel of Mark as a rejection of the disciples versus those who see the disciples as "fallible followers" who are not rejected.[47] At first glance, it appears the evidence presented here favors the first group, since there is a rather strong ironic tie between Peter's denial and Jesus words in 8:36-38 concerning saving one's physical life but losing eternal life by being ashamed of Jesus.

But it seems to me that such a stance misses an enduring picture of this intercalation that teaches a deeper lesson and which links to the ironic view of power that appears throughout Mark. At the end of the trial scene there is a rather gruesome picture of Jesus beaten and buffeted by his enemies. They not only mock his words and prophetic power, they attack his person. At the end of the denial scene there is another tragic picture – a

[44] See Gundry, *Mark*, 894 and 915-916 for the position that Jesus pronounced the Tetragrammaton. However, note Gundry's further point about dishonoring God with a curse, pp. 916-917.

[45] Bock, *Blasphemy and Exaltation.*

[46] Ibid., 209.

[47] Cf. Kelber, *Oral and Written Gospel*; Black, *Disciples according to Mark*; Best, *Disciples and Discipleship*; and Malbon, "Disciples/Crowds/Whoever" and "Texts and Contexts" noted above.

grown man, broken down, crying. It is the last physical depiction of one of the twelve disciples in the Gospel of Mark.[48]

What is striking is that both scenes end with such weakness. Certainly Jesus and Peter have followed different paths to this point, Jesus through bold confession, Peter through cowardly denial. But it appears something has actually moved forward for Peter here. First, he claimed to be strong in 14:27-31, countering Jesus' prediction by seeming to affirm the courageous stance of 8:35b, "but whoever loses his life for my sake and the Gospel's will save it." Then he proved to be weak in Gethsemane where he could not stay awake to pray even for an hour, 14:37. And finally he completed his display of weakness in 14:66-72 by the denial. It all ends in tears – he is no longer strong but weak and recognizes it. What this means is that he has been stopped in his resistance to Jesus' words, stopped from fooling himself that he is strong. His experience of weakness places him in the "sick" group for whom the physician came (2:17), someone to be pitied and helped rather than rejected.[49] Thus, at the end of this story, Peter in his deep failure, comes surprisingly and intimately close to Jesus in weakness.[50]

Thus the trial of Jesus and the denial by Peter bring home the same point about the ironic view of power in Mark's Gospel. The path to true power is not through the application of force as the "rulers of the Gentiles" do (10:41-45).[51] Nor is it even through a bold affirmation of one's own ability to go with Jesus to death even if the Master says it will turn out otherwise. Rather it is through an experience of weakness, self discovery, and service to others, a path the world cannot see nor withstand. It joins the concept of weakness and strength in a tension of Christian experience that represents true discipleship.[52]

48 This assumes that the Gospel concludes at 16:8. In 16:7 the message is sent to the disciples and Peter to meet Jesus in Galilee, but they are not personally displayed in the story at the tomb.

49 Notice the tie to service in 10:42-45 this suggests. Jesus will serve even his failing disciples, cf. 16:7.

50 We also must remember the irony that, in denying Jesus, Peter has fulfilled Jesus' prophecy and thus proved him to be the Messiah.

51 Thus Liew, "Tyranny," is mistaken about the imperial sense of power in Mark. While Jesus and God are taken as supreme in rulership, the path to power and its application in the Christian community leads through a valley of weakness. Indeed, Jesus' path to power is through the cross. This is starkly different than the imperial model of the first century, and indeed, than the imperial and even democratic models of the twenty-first century.

52 I am indebted to Jeffrey Gibson and Joanna Dewey for the focus on service as a key concept in power relationships in Mark.

LIST OF CONTRIBUTORS

Sharyn Dowd, PhD in New Testament from Emory University, is Associate Professor of Religion at Baylor University, Waco, Texas, USA.
sharyn_dowd@baylor.edu

Elizabeth Struthers Malbon, PhD in Humanities from Florida State University, is Professor of Religious Studies and Interdisciplinary Studies at Virginia Polytechnic Institute and State University, Blacksburg, Virginia, USA.
malbon@vt.edu

Mark Goodacre, DPhil in Theology from the University of Oxford, is Associate Professor of Religion at Duke University, Durham, North Carolina, USA.
goodacre@duke.edu

Geert Van Oyen, PhD in Theology from Katholieke Universiteit Leuven (Belgium), is Professor of New Testament at Utrecht University, Utrecht, The Netherlands.
gvoyen@theo.uu.nl

Jocelyn McWhirter, PhD in Biblical Studies from Princeton Theological Seminary, is Assistant Professor of Religious Studies at Albion College, Albion, Michigan, USA.
jmcwhirter@albion.edu

William Sanger Campbell, PhD in New Testament from Princeton Theological Seminary, is Assistant Professor of Theology and Religious Studies at The College of St. Scholastica, Duluth, Minnesota, USA.
bcampbel@css.edu

Stephen P. Ahearne-Kroll, PhD in Biblical Studies (NT) from The University of Chicago Divinity School, is Assistant Professor of New Testament at Methodist Theological School in Ohio, Delaware, Ohio, USA.
sahearne-kroll@mtso.edu

Adela Yarbro Collins, PhD in the Study of Religion from Harvard University, is the Buckingham Professor of New Testament Criticism and Interpretation at the Yale University Divinity School, New Haven, Connecticut, USA.
adela.collins@yale.edu

Jeffrey B. Gibson, DPhil in Theology from the University of Oxford, is Lecturer in Humanities at Harry S Truman College and Columbia College, Chicago, Illinois, USA.
jgibson000@comcast.net

Michael E. Vines, PhD in Biblical Studies from Union Theological Seminary and Presbyterian School of Christian Education, is Associate Professor of Religious Studies at Lees-McRae College, Banner Elk, North Carolina, USA.
vines@lmc.edu

Kelli S. O'Brien, PhD in Theology from the University of Notre Dame (Notre Dame, Indiana), is Assistant Professor of Theology at the University of Scranton, Scranton, Pennsylvania, USA.
obrienk4@scranton.edu

Tom Shepherd, PhD in Religion from Andrews University Theological Seminary (Berrien Springs, Michigan), is Professor of Religion at Union College, Lincoln, Nebraska, USA.
toshephe@ucollege.edu

INDEX OF AUTHORS

INDEX OF ANCIENT TEXTS

Old Testament Pseudepigrapha

Qumran Literature

Contributions to Biblical Exegesis and Theology, 45
Edited by Tj. Baarda (Amsterdam), A. van der Kooij (Leiden), P.W. van der Horst (Utrecht), G. Van Oyen (Utrecht), E. Noort (Groningen), and K. De Troyer (Claremont).

1. J.A. Loader, *A Tale of Two Cities, Sodom and Gomorrah in the Old Testament, early Jewish and early Christian Traditions*, Kampen, 1990
2. P.W. Van der Horst, *Ancient Jewish Epitaphs. An Introductory Survey of a Millennium of Jewish Funerary Epigraphy (300 BCB-700 CE)*, Kampen, 1991
3. E. Talstra, *Solomon's Prayer. Synchrony and Diachrony in the Composition of 1 Kings 8, 14-61*, Kampen, 1993
4. R. Stahl, *Von Weltengagement zu Weltüberwindung: Theologische Positionen im Danielbuch*, Kampen, 1994
5. J.N. Bremmer, *Sacred History and Sacred Texts in early Judaism. A Symposium in Honour of A.S. van der Woude*, Kampen, 1992
6. K. Larkin, *The Eschatology of Second Zechariah: A Study of the Formation of a Mantological Wisdom Anthology*, Kampen, 1994
7. B. Aland, *New Testament Textual Criticism, Exegesis and Church History: A Discussion of Methods*, Kampen, 1994
8. P.W. Van der Horst, *Hellenism-Judaism-Christianity: Essays on their Interaction*, Kampen, Second Enlarged Edition, 1998
9. C. Houtman, *Der Pentateuch: die Geschichte seiner Erforschung neben einer Auswertung*, Kampen, 1994
10. J. Van Seters, *The Life of Moses. The Yahwist as Historian in Exodus-Numbers*, Kampen, 1994
11. Tj. Baarda, *Essays on the Diatessaron*, Kampen, 1994
12. Gert J. Steyn, *Septuagint Quotations in the Context of the Petrine and Pauline Speeches of the Acta Apostolorum*, Kampen, 1995
13. D.V. Edelman, *The Triumph of Elohim, From Yahwisms to Judaisms*, Kampen, 1995
14. J.E. Revell, *The Designation of the Individual. Expressive Usage in Biblical Narrative*, Kampen, 1996
15. M. Menken, *Old Testament Quotations in the Fourth Gospel*, Kampen, 1996
16. V. Koperski, *The Knowledge of Christ Jesus my Lord. The High Christology of Philippians 3:7-11*, Kampen, 1996
17. M.C. De Boer, *Johannine Perspectives on the Death of Jesus*, Kampen, 1996
18. R.D. Anderson, *Ancient Rhetorical Theory and Paul*, Revised edition, Leuven, 1998
19. L.C. Jonker, *Exclusivity and Variety, Perspectives on Multi-dimensional Exegesis*, Kampen, 1996
20. L.V. Rutgers, *The Hidden Heritage of Diaspora Judaism*, Leuven, 1998
21. K. van der Toorn (ed.), *The Image and the Book*, Leuven, 1998
22. L.V. Rutgers, P.W. van der Horst (eds.), *The Use of Sacred Books in the Ancient World*, Leuven, 1998
23. E.R. Ekblad Jr., *Isaiah's Servant Poems According to the Septuagint. An Exegetical and Theological Study*, Leuven, 1999
24. R.D. Anderson Jr., *Glossary of Greek Rhetorical Terms*, Leuven, 2000
25. T. Stordalen, *Echoes of Eden*, Leuven, 2000
26. H. Lalleman-de Winkel, *Jeremiah in Prophetic Tradition*, Leuven, 2000
27. J.F.M. Smit, *About the Idol Offerings. Rhetoric, Social Context and Theology of Paul's Discourse in First Corinthians 8:1-11:1*, Leuven, 2000
28. T.J. Horner, *Listening to Trypho. Justin Martyr's Dialogue Reconsidered*, Leuven, 2001
29. D.G. Powers, *Salvation through Participation. An Examination of the Notion of the Believers' Corporate Unity with Christ in Early Christian Soteriology*, Leuven, 2001

30. J.S. Kloppenborg, P. Hoffmann, J.M. Robinson, M.C. Moreland (eds.), *The Sayings Gospel Q in Greek and English with Parallels from the Gospels of Mark and Thomas*, Leuven, 2001
31. M.K. Birge, *The Language of Belonging. A Rhetorical Analysis of Kinship Language in First Corinthians*, Leuven, 2004
32. P.W. van der Horst, *Japheth in the Tents of Shem. Studies on Jewish Hellenism in Antiquity*, Leuven, 2002
33. P.W. van der Horst, M.J.J. Menken, J.F.M. Smit, G. van Oyen, *Persuasion and Dissuasion in Early Christianity, Ancient Judaism, and Hellenism*, Leuven, 2003
34. L.J. Lietaert Peerbolte, *Paul the Missionary*, Leuven, 2003
35. L.M. Teugels, *Bible and Midrash. The Story of 'The Wooing of Rebekah' (Gen. 24)*, Leuven, 2004
36. H.W. Shin, *Textual Criticism and the Synoptic Problem in Historical Jesus Research. The Search for Valid Criteria*, Leuven, 2004
37. A. Volgers, C. Zamagni, *Erotapokriseis. Early Christian Question-and-Answer Literature in Context*, Leuven, 2004
38. L. Galloway, *Freedom in the Gospel. Paul's Exemplum in 1 Cor 9 in Conversation with the Discourses of Epictetus and Philo*, Leuven, 2004
39. C. Houtman, K. Spronk, *Ein Held des Glaubens? Rezeptionsgeschichtliche Studien zu den Simson-Erzählungen*, Leuven, 2004
40. H. Kahana, *Esther. Juxtaposition of the Septuagint Translation with the Hebrew Text*, Leuven, 2005
41. V.A. Pizzuto, *A Cosmic Leap of Faith. An Authorial, Structural, and Theological Investigation of the Cosmic Christology in Col 1:15-20*, Leuven, 2006
42. B.J. Koet, *Dreams and Scripture in Luke-Acts. Collected Essays*, Leuven, 2006
43. P.C Beentjes. *"Happy the One who Meditates on Wisdom" (SIR. 14,20). Collected Essays on the Book of Ben Sira,* Leuven, 2006
44. R. Roukema, L.J. Lietaert Peerbolte, K. Spronk, J.W. Wesselius, *The Interpretation of Exodus. Studies in Honour of Cornelis Houtman*, Leuven, 2006

PRINTED ON PERMANENT PAPER • IMPRIME SUR PAPIER PERMANENT • GEDRUKT OP DUURZAAM PAPIER - ISO 9706

N.V. PEETERS S.A., WAROTSTRAAT 50, B-3020 HERENT